The Culture & Civilization of China

中國文化与文明

Yale University Press
New Haven and London
New World Press
Beijing

Fu Xinian
Guo Daiheng
Liu Xujie
Pan Guxi
Qiao Yun
Sun Dazhang

Chinese
Architecture

*English text edited
and expanded by*

Nancy S. Steinhardt

Calligraphy for series title by Qi Gong, president of
the China National Calligraphers' Association.

Frontispiece: Wangshi Garden, Suzhou, Jiangsu province

Designed by Bessas & Ackerman, Guilford, Connecticut

based on original series design by Richard Hendel

Set in Monotype Garamond

Type by dix!

Color separations and prepress by Redstone, Inc., New York

Printed and bound in China by C & C Offset Printing Co., Ltd.

Library of Congress Cataloging-in-Publication Data

Chinese architecture / English text edited and expanded by

Nancy S. Steinhardt.

    —(The culture and civilization of China)

Includes bibliographical references and index.

    ISBN 0-300-09559-7

    1. Architecture—China—History. I. Steinhardt, Nancy Shatzman.

II. Series.

    NA1540. H574 2002

    720'.951—dc21   2001007638

A catalogue record for this book is available from the British Library.

The paper in this book meets the guidelines for permanence and

durability of the Committee on Production Guidelines for Book

Longevity of the Council on Library Resources.

10 9 8 7 6 5 4 3 2 1

Publication of this book

was made possible by the generous support of

R U T H   A N D   B R U C E   D A Y T O N

Yale University Press gratefully acknowledges

the financial support given to

The Culture & Civilization of China by:

The Henry Luce Foundation, Inc.

Patricia Mellon

John and Cynthia Reed

The Rosenkranz Foundation

The Starr Foundation

THE CULTURE & CIVILIZATION OF CHINA

Each book in this series is the fruit of cooperation between Chinese and Western scholars and publishers. Our goals are to illustrate the cultural riches of China, to explain China to both interested general readers and specialists, to present the best recent scholarship, and to make original and previously inaccessible resources available for the first time. The books will all be published in both English and Chinese.

The partners in this unprecedented joint undertaking are the China International Publishing Group (CIPG) and Yale University Press, which together conceived the project under the auspices of the U.S.-China Book Publication Project. James Peck is director of the U.S.-China Book Publication Project and executive director of The Culture & Civilization of China series.

CONTENTS

CHRONOLOGY

ca. 2070–1600 B.C.E.	XIA DYNASTY
ca. 1600–1046 B.C.E.	SHANG DYNASTY
1046–221 B.C.E.	ZHOU DYNASTY

        Western Zhou 1046–770 B.C.E.
        Eastern Zhou 770–221 B.C.E.
            Spring and Autumn Period 770–476 B.C.E.
            Warring States Period 475–221 B.C.E.

221–207 B.C.E.	QIN DYNASTY
206 B.C.E.–220 C.E.	HAN DYNASTY

        Western Han Dynasty 206 B.C.E.–9 C.E.
        Xin Dynasty (Wang Mang Interregnum) 9–23
        Eastern Han Dynasty 25–220

220–280	THREE KINGDOMS

        Wei 220–265
        Shu 221–263
        Wu 222–280

281–420	JIN DYNASTY*

        Western Jin 281–316
        Eastern Jin 317–420
        Sixteen States 304–439

420–589	SOUTHERN DYNASTIES*

        Liu Song 420–479
        Southern Qi 479–502
        Liang 502–557
        Chen 557–589

386–581	NORTHERN DYNASTIES

        Northern Wei 386–534
        Eastern Wei 534–550
        Western Wei 535–557
        Northern Qi 550–577
        Northern Zhou 557–581

581–618	SUI DYNASTY
618–907	TANG DYNASTY
907–979	FIVE DYNASTIES (in the north)

        Later Liang 907–923
        Later Tang 923–936
        Later Jin 936–947
        Later Han 947–950
        Later Zhou 951–960

902–979	TEN KINGDOMS (in the south)

        Shu 907–925
        Later Shu 935–965
        Nanping or Jingnan 907–924
        Chu 927–951
        Wu 902–937
        Southern Tang 937–978
        Wu-Yue 907–978
        Min 907–946
        Southern Han 907–971
        Northern Han 951–979

947–1125	LIAO DYNASTY
960–1279	SONG DYNASTY

        Northern Song 960–1127
        Southern Song 1127–1279

1038–1227	XI XIA (WESTERN XIA) DYNASTY
1115–1234	JIN DYNASTY
1271–1368	YUAN DYNASTY
1368–1644	MING DYNASTY
1644–1911	QING DYNASTY

*The Western and Eastern Jin dynasties together with the Southern dynasties are frequently referred to as the Six Dynasties.

Introduction

PART I *Nancy S. Steinhardt*

Chinese architecture has been studied less than the architecture of almost any other great civilization on the globe. In Asia as well as the West, the architecture of China is often defined by a single image, the Forbidden City. Even the best-known features of Chinese construction — ceramic tile roof, pagoda profile, or garden pavilion — have not been brought together in a common vocabulary to illuminate distinctive Chinese forms and styles.

The scale of Chinese architecture — in influence, grandeur, and history — is nevertheless without parallel. The history of architecture in China can be traced through nearly ten millennia. Chinese-style tombs, palaces, monasteries, gardens, and other architectural features add their distinctive forms to more than five thousand kilometers of landscape in Asia, from Kyoto to Kashgar.

One frequent comment about Chinese architecture — that it all looks alike — is both supported and dispelled by the artwork in this book. How the many generations of builders documented their work, thereby teaching their skills to subsequent generations, led to a unique system of construction that over time resulted in magnificent technological accomplishments.

First and foremost among these achievements is the interlocking network of wooden supports. Known as the timber frame, it is literally as well as figuratively the skeleton of a Chinese wooden building and, moreover, China's major technological contribution to architecture

worldwide. A wooden frame has supported buildings on Chinese soil for as many as seven millennia, long before the notions of empire or even China were forged. Two other features of Chinese architecture that have been used in combination with the timber frame for many thousands of years are the foundation platform and the decorative roof. These three remain the core of any Chinese structure that uses wood. In more developed buildings, they are known as the foundation, pillar network, and roof-frame network. In still more developed wooden buildings, a fourth fundamental wooden component is added, the bracket set. This component first appeared in the late centuries B.C.E., then developed into a network of pieces that joined pillars to the roof frame.

The importance of joinery cannot be overstated. Since the earliest use of wood as a building material, Chinese pillars, beams, struts, brackets, and roof frames have been cut to interlock perfectly, without the use of fasteners or adhesives. It is unclear whether Chinese builders knew from the start that this kind of joinery allowed for expansion in humid weather, contraction in the cold, and strong resistance to earthquakes. But time has proved that Chinese timber-frame buildings can withstand almost any climate and earthquakes as powerful as 7 or 8 on the Richter scale. Such structures were susceptible only to fire and to natural rotting, which was counteracted by replacing parts as needed.

Detail from *Palace City in Beijing,* Ming dynasty,
Museum of Chinese History

The ease with which builders can replace pieces of structures is perhaps the most ingenious of the many attractive features of Chinese wooden construction. It has allowed not only economical repair but also tremendous potential for modifying a structure, or even transforming it completely. When a Buddha hall was desired, an imperial residence could be made into one by merely changing the interior design: a throne was removed and an altar for images put in its place. When new rituals entered the Buddhist faith, often the changes needed were as minor as moving or reducing the number of pillars to make a larger worship space or extending the front aisle for devotees. When a family grew or became more wealthy, the core structure of its residence could stand unaltered while side rooms were added by new rows of columns, bracketing above them, and a roof. For these reasons, there was little incentive to tear down and replace an entire structure. It was more likely for a building to be carefully dismantled and either rebuilt elsewhere or reused as parts in other architecture.

Although wood, brick, stone, mud-earth, ceramic tile, and even metal are used in Chinese construction, Chinese builders achieved such unparalleled flexibility, adaptability, and versatility in wood that most masonry construction, both freestanding and in funerary architecture underground, imitated the details of wooden architecture. That kind of imitation, as well as the ease of adaptability from secular to religious or small to large, was made possible by another extraordinary feature of the Chinese building system: modularity. The Chinese module and submodule were implemented very early, long before the first text, from the twelfth century, that explains their system.

The system itself, intended for court-sponsored building projects — is elaborate. It prescribes eight ranks, each based on the cross section of one component of the Chinese bracket set. Ideally, the fundamental pieces of the building — every other bracket-set piece, the heights of columns, lengths of beams, and distances between these vertical and horizontal structural features — were determined by a proportion, which was in turn decided by the specific rank of a building. Although exceptions were made for practical reasons specific to a structure, such a system was generally followed and meant that pieces of wood for columns, posts, and small and large supports were pre-sized and could be pre-cut. Thus it was possible for a building in southeastern China to closely resemble one in the northwest; a Buddhist hall in the Yellow River valley could look very much like one along the Yangzi, and a hall on the Central Plain could be a near clone of one on the slope of an isolated mountain. As long as two buildings were of the same rank, the parts of their timber frames were generated by the same module.

Two other fundamental features of Chinese construction are inherent in the system just described. The modular and easily amendable wooden support system does not require a great architect to guarantee its success. Historically, Chinese architecture has been largely the art of craftsmen, not just the men who cut and joined wooden members, but bricklayers, stone carvers, decorative painters, and those who specialized in what the Chinese call minor carpentry, which included the carving of door, cabinet, or window designs.

Indeed, China's early architects remain mostly unknown. Those whose names have been documented were court employees with official rank. Some are discussed in this book. The role of these "architects" was primarily to supervise construction and less often to design large-scale building projects, even entire cities. They were usually known in Chinese as builders, master craftsmen, or by their official position in, most often, the Board of Works. In Chinese, the words for both architecture and architect, *jianzhu* and *jianzhushi* or *jianzhuzhe,* are primarily twentieth-century terms, as modern as the concept.

The clearly defined, prescribed, easily implemented system that could be adapted for religious and secular purposes, and on a grand or humble scale, has had a far-reaching and profound influence on the architecture of other Asian cultures. Because Chinese architecture could be built almost as easily outside China as within the walls of its palace cities, Chinese buildings and Chinese building forms have been sought and cultivated both by invaders who strove to establish themselves on Chinese soil and by non-Chinese leaders of strong empires beyond China's borders. The golden and azure roof tiles that projected above the low walls of a Chinese palace, military commandery, prefectural capital, or commercial town were the most potent of symbols: they proclaimed entry into the Chinese sphere and all that was associated with it. Beneath those roofs and behind those walls a Japanese courtier could protest his allegiance to his emperor through ritual death and a grandson of Chinggis Khan could drink mare's milk in a felt tent, but to the one who approached the architectural spaces from outside, the message was that a power as great as China must be reckoned with.

The walls of Chinese buildings serve a different purpose than do the pillars, beams, and brackets: they represent the Chinese concept of space. The Chinese have built enclosures and have related buildings to one another within defined or implied enclosures for almost as long as they have put structures on the soil. In fact, the origin of the Chinese concept of urbanism is traced to pounded-earth walls that have been excavated at Neolithic settlements since the third millennium B.C.E. When the Chinese provided a word for these enclosures, *cheng,* it was the same word they used for city. In other words, nearly four millennia ago, the Chinese drew no distinction between a city and a wall. A city did not exist in China without a wall, and the presence of a wall meant that a city was inside.

On a smaller scale, spaces soon came to be walled by enclosing arcades, and inside those arcades were court-yards on which buildings faced. In some cases the arcades directly connected buildings; in others, more than one building stood inside the courtyard or an adjoining wall helped define the interrelation between buildings and building groups. Indeed, the concept of architecture in China rarely includes just one building; it signifies a group.

Perhaps it is this expansive definition of architecture as an interrelated group of structures in a defined space that has led to the broad (at least by Western standards) understanding of what architecture is. In China today, architecture is cities, palaces, temples, tombs, gardens, and decorative carpentry. Given the importance of en-closure in Chinese space, the inclusion of cities in the Chinese definition of architecture is not surprising. The inclusion of gardens, too, or landscape architecture, is understandable when one enters a Chinese garden, for it is as much a repository of buildings as of nature.

Traditional writings on Chinese architecture also stretch the bounds of definition — they touch on topics of history and culture that tell us far more than how buildings and building groups were planned and created. Such writings also often feature historical research, prose, poetry, and Chinese literary genres that combine prose and poetry — aspects that have been studied at least as rigorously as the buildings themselves. For many thousands of years, architecture was not a specialty, but instead was a part of the overall religious and imperial culture of China. Not until the beginning of the twentieth century did the Chinese become interested in construc-tion as a design-inspired pursuit of architects. In the 1920s and 1930s Chinese students went abroad to Japan and the United States to learn how to be architects. They returned to China, a core group of no more than twenty, to establish China's first architecture schools and to com-mence the historical investigation of old buildings. Before war broke out across China in the 1930s, these scholars were able to contribute what are today some of the most valuable studies of China's premodern buildings. Many of the buildings first described in those writings were lost during the war, and after the conflict most of the scholars became teachers and architects.

The Chinese authors of this book were students of that first group of Chinese men and women who went abroad to learn the profession of architecture. They are thus a di-rect link both to the beginnings of architectural history in China and to the vision of their teachers. Their under-standing of Chinese architecture represents that vision, and their line drawings reproduced in this book, along with some drawn by their first-generation teachers, show the training of China's very first architects.

From the inception of this book at meetings in Beijing in 1992, it has been a goal of mine to present Chinese-style architectural history to the Western reader. This is only partly because, like the Chinese authors, I had been intro-duced to the field by a student of the first generation of Chinese architects and architectural historians (in my case in Taiwan). It was equally because the study of Chinese architecture is still relatively new. As we worked on the book, we were aware of new ideas and theories about Chinese architecture, all of which are based on the build-ings themselves. And we were also aware that the ideas and approaches that may eventually lead to a synthetic study of Chinese architecture would have to be balanced and verified by new archaeological discoveries. Impor-tantly, too, we agreed that, so far, Western theoretical approaches to Chinese architecture have been most eluci-dating for single buildings or subsets of Chinese architec-ture, such as buildings of a certain type from one time period or place. The reader will thus find no dearth of new ideas about Chinese architecture in this book. But we have limited our interpretation, refraining from suggesting how Western ideas about architecture and architectural history might be applied to the study of Chinese buildings.

Many Chinese architects and architectural histori-ans believe that a clear separation exists between pre-twentieth-century and twentieth-century buildings. This book is concerned exclusively with the first group, what we might call traditional Chinese architecture. In addition to well-known sites, however, the most important of the newly discovered early wooden buildings are here, in description if not in pictures. A few of the most recently uncovered tombs and villages are discussed as well, even though ongoing excavations may dramatically improve or change our understanding of the architecture of any time period or geographic region.

The book is organized chronologically by dynasty, in large part to dispel once and for all the myth that Chinese architecture has not evolved over time. We also decided to maintain the traditional Chinese presentation of the topic, the one used in the Chinese version of this book and in many of the books by China's first architectural historians. This means that, to the extent material is available, each chapter includes sections on cities, palatial architecture, religious architecture, tombs, and gardens, and in some cases discussions of bridges, walls, fortifications, academies, or architectural writings.

One who reads both the Chinese and English versions of this book will notice differences. From the beginning, the English book has been viewed as a serious and probing introduction to the field for an educated reader, but not one who has necessarily spent enough time in China to see many of its buildings. To achieve this goal, the book is longer than its Chinese counterpart. The additions include historical and cultural background and explanations of Chinese religions that were not necessary for the Chinese edition, but these changes, approved by all of the book's editors, Chinese and American, were not intended to alter the basic meaning of the Chinese text.

Introduction

PART II *Qiao Yun*

Classical Chinese architecture has had a long and creative history. The earliest buildings and building sites can be dated back some seven thousand years, and important examples of classical architecture run into the thousands. Such features as a structural system based on gracefully wrought timber, meticulous and comprehensive city planning, a rich and resplendent use of color and ornamentation on buildings, the poetic style of garden design in the fashion of natural landscapes, and the arrangement and axial layout of buildings in conjunction with courtyards begin to suggest the distinctive characteristics of the remarkable architectural legacy this book explores. Written by some of China's greatest architectural historians, some practicing architects as well, this book recounts for international readers the story of China's architectural achievements, the forms they took, and some of the factors that shaped them.

From earliest times, the Chinese have lived, worked, and shaped their unique civilization on varied and often challenging terrain. The 9.6 million square kilometers of China, the largest country in Asia, stretch from the Zengmu Reef in the Nansha Archipelago in the south to the Heilongjiang River near Mohe in the north, and from the Pamirs in the west to the confluence of the Heilongjiang and the Wusuli River in the east. Most of the settled areas are in the northern temperate zone or the subtropics in the East Asian monsoon zone.

Those who lived in China in ancient eras adapted their architecture to their particular environments with a wide array of styles and forms. Those living in the middle reaches of the Yellow River, for example, a loess plateau with thick layers of loose soil and dense forests, created dwellings made to resist cold, wind, and rain: the simple wooden structures had earthen walls, with roofs made of mud and grass or thatch, and faced south to get more light in the winter and resist the north wind. In south China, by contrast, houses mainly faced south or southeast in order to get the southeast wind from the sea. In some places, stilted houses were built so that air might move freely underneath and help avoid dampness. Construction materials included bamboo and reeds that were abundant in the south, in addition to mud and wood. In mountainous areas, stone was widely used for house construction because it was so readily available.

Chinese architecture has also been shaped by some fifty-six distinct ethnic groups. The Han people are the most numerous and constitute 94 percent of the total population, but other groups, living elsewhere near sometimes different local building materials, modified the traditions according to their own needs and customs, giving rise to innovations that could be copied. In the loess plateau in north China and the Yellow River valley, the Han people dug cave dwellings or built houses with walls made of rammed earth. Later people learned to make bricks with yellow earth, and thus more durable dwellings. In south China, where the weather is damp and rainy, people built houses with bamboo and timber on stilts; on the Qinghai-Tibetan plateau, where there is little precipitation and the climate is dry and the temperature varies greatly between day and night, most houses have thick walls and flat roofs. In Mongol areas, by contrast, a nomadic life fit with easily movable yurts. In northeast China, houses with pointed arch roofs are common. The shaping of architecture by the natural environment is evident, and such differences contributed greatly to China's rich architectural history.

For more than four thousand years China's imperial cities have shared certain architectural characteristics regardless of where they were built. Early patterns were clearly taking shape no later than the Shang dynasty (ca. 1600–1046 B.C.E.), ones that brought together economic, military, and political needs with those of rank and principles of classification. The form of the city itself was designed to be a testament to imperial power and served to legitimize the ruler. The location of palaces, government buildings, bell and drum towers, and other public buildings in the center created a central axis, which became a defining characteristic of Chinese imperial cities. By the Warring States period (475–221 B.C.E.) much of this was written in such works as the "Record of Trades." Key aspects of Chinese architecture developed over the millennium within this imperial system of city planning.

Chinese architecture was deeply influenced as well by the great belief systems so long interwoven with the history of Chinese civilization. Among them none was more important than Confucianism, which began its rise to prominence in the fifth century B.C.E., during the Zhou dynasty. After Emperor Wudi (141–86 B.C.E.) of the Western Han dynasty advocated "revering the teachings of Confucius alone and banning all other schools," Confucianism became the predominant ideology for more than two thousand years. Although Daoism spread in the late Han dynasty and Buddhism was introduced then and flourished long thereafter, these two belief systems never proved quite so influential. By the time they became prominent, many Chinese architectural forms had already been established within a largely indigenous civilization, gradually emerging from the ongoing cultural exchanges and synthesis within its own territory and among its own ethnic groups.

By the time of the early Shang and Zhou dynasties, even before the emergence of Confucianism, the wooden frame and the courtyard style — later so central in Chinese architecture — had already emerged. During the Qin and Han dynasties, a distinctive system of architecture, from single structures to complexes of buildings to plans for cities, had become closely meshed with the political, economic, and cultural contexts so decisive for the later evolution of architectural forms. When Buddhism and its ideas and architectural innovations entered China, they were gradually assimilated, greatly enriching and yet not supplanting the earlier and deeply persistent concepts and patterns of building.

Nevertheless, Confucianism proved most influential to China's architecture in the earliest periods in numerous ways. Confucianism regarded rites as central to successful state administration and standards of personal behavior, and this produced and reinforced various styles and types of buildings, such as palatial halls, temples, altars, and mausoleums. Its emphasis on the imperial system of power and the centrality of the emperor as the Son of Heaven is evident in the ways the capital city placed the palace at its center, symbolizing the supreme power of the emperor. The square-shaped, symmetrical capital city, with houses located on both sides of a central axis, was designed to reinforce the vision of the imperial center as the correct and moral ordering focus for society and daily life. To worship heaven and earth was a critical imperial responsibility architecturally embodied in a host of buildings — the Temple of Heaven, the Temple of Earth, the Imperial Ancestors' Temple, the Altar for Worshiping the God of Agriculture, and the Altars for Worshiping the Sun and the Moon. Filial obedience also entailed the construction of ancestral temples and tombs, and the correct ordering of senior and junior, superior and inferior, upper and lower, permeates architectural forms even in the smallest details. Hence the width of rooms, style, color, and decorations on the roof all were strictly stipulated according to one's social status, and even if it was sometimes ignored, officially no one was allowed to break the rule.

Still, Chinese architecture was at times greatly influenced by outside ideas and cultures. Exchanges of building techniques and architectural arts between China and other countries become evident especially beginning with the Western Jin dynasty, and from that time on an extensive transfer of ideas took place with both eastern and western neighbors. As early as the third century C.E., Buddhist grotto carving was introduced from India, and up through the Sui and Tang dynasties came a dazzling number of grottoes, from those in Dunhuang to the Northern Wei grottoes at Yungang in Datong, to those at Xiangtangshan near Handan, Hebei province. The stupa was another architectural type introduced from India.

The Nepalese artisan Anige, who served in the Yuan court for more than forty years, designed the pagoda in the Miaoying Temple in Beijing.

Islam proved another influence on China, following its introduction in the seventh century. It came via Persia through Xinjiang to the hinterland of China, or by sea route to Guangzhou, Quanzhou, Yangzhou, and other places on China's southeastern coast. Beginning in the Tang dynasty, many Arabian and Persian merchants settled in China, some for dozens of years, and some for generations. With Islam came Islamic architecture, as the sojourners built religious buildings, such as the Huaisheng Mosque in Guangzhou and the Shengyou Mosque in Quanzhou. During the Song, Yuan, Ming, and Qing dynasties, Muslims constructed many mosques in western China and coastal areas; during the Yuan dynasty there were thirty-five mosques in the capital alone. All these buildings introduced Arabian and west Asian architectural styles and practices to China. Over time, mosques and religious buildings with Chinese styles appeared, but the layout, roof style, and outer and inner decorations retained Arabian characteristics and flavor, greatly enriching the content of Chinese ancient architecture.

Much has been written in this book and elsewhere about the strength of the timber frame and the significant technical achievement of the modular system. But the size and majesty of Chinese structures and building groups can obscure the details that speak to the importance of artistry in the many cultures that contributed to the Chinese architectural tradition. Chinese architecture developed its overall approach and major characteristics from how these various aspects came together, such as the structural frame, the building groups, ornamentation and attention to detail, and gardens and their distinct views. Each of these features deserves a few words here.

The Wooden Structural Frame

The structural system using wooden beams and columns was first used extensively in the Spring and Autumn period (770–476 B.C.E.), and it became well developed during the Han dynasty (206 B.C.E.–220 C.E.). Wooden structural frames can be roughly divided into three types: *tailiang* (column, beam, and strut), *chuandou* (column and tiebeam), and *jinggan* ("log cabin"). In a tailiang structure — the most popular type — columns, or pillars, are erected on bases along the length and depth of the house. Beams, or lintels, placed on top of the columns span the spaces between them horizontally; lintels also connect two parallel sets of

frames. Above the beams, further sets of posts may be erected to make a second story, and so on. To form the roof, purlins run the length of the building, resting on the tops of the uppermost columns, as does a ridge pole at the peak of the roof. Rafters are laid on top of the purlins, sloping down from the ridge to the eaves. In the interior of the building, the space defined by four columns constitutes a bay, or "room." A house might consist of one, two, three bays, or more, and a large ceremonial hall could have as many as fifteen or more bays.

Dougong refers to the unique system of brackets placed on top of columns to provide further support to beams or overhanging eaves. Each bracket set is formed by a large wooden block, called *dou,* which rests on the column and provides a firm base for the pieces called *gong,* bow-shaped arms that in turn support the beam (or other dou) above them. The bracket components resting on any one column and supporting any one beam may be multiplied almost endlessly, allowing the column to support ever greater weight; at the same time they perform an integral function in holding the entire building structure together. Dougong evolved from a simple bed for supporting a beam into intricate grids of complex bracket sets, reaching the peak of development during the Tang-Song period. During the Yuan, Ming, and Qing dynasties, bracket sets became smaller and lost some of their structural function. By this time, dougong were used, largely as decoration and to reflect social status, sometimes more than for support of a roof.

The merits of the wooden structural frame were many. One of them was cost efficiency, because the dense forests in the middle reaches of the Yellow River in ancient China provided abundant timber resources, making wood cheaper and more accessible than stone or bricks. Another was that, because the weight of the building was borne by the wooden frame, the walls were not load-bearing, so all they had to do was enclose and divide up the space. The result was great flexibility in making doors and windows and in selecting materials for the walls. This design feature fit with various climatic conditions: the height of the house, the thickness and materials of the walls, and the location and size of doors and windows all could be made in accordance with the local climate. Such structures had an added advantage: they tended to diminish the damage from earthquakes. The resilient quality of timber and the flexibility of the mortise and tenon joinery made these structures quite elastic; even the walls might collapse, but the wooden frame would usually survive.

The wooden structural frame also allowed for a great flexibility in the form of houses as well as their construction. There were solid walls, grille walls, walls with windows, walls made of removable screens, or no walls at all, just exposed columns (such as in pavilions). Some houses were surrounded by a veranda, or there might be vestibules and exposed columns in front and back. Doors, windows, columns, and walls were often decorated in different styles according to different locations and available materials. Roofs were rich and varied: gable, hip, mansard, flat, and pointed roofs, as well as compound-eave roofs, appeared as early as the Han dynasty. Combination hip-and-gable roofs, single-sloped and cross-sloped roofs, gilded roofs, arch roofs, and domes appeared later. Large overhanging eaves were often adopted to protect the wooden structures from rain while also allowing unobstructed lighting. Upbent roofs, folded-up roofs, and raised roof corners later offered buildings a light and graceful image.

Ancient Chinese buildings have three parts: the base, the body, and the roof. Important buildings were always built on a base, usually of one layer, though large halls, such as the Hall of Supreme Harmony (the largest wooden building in China) in the Forbidden City of the Ming and Qing dynasties in Beijing, merited a three-layer base. Buildings could be rectangular, square, hexagonal, octagonal, or circular in plan.

Building Groups

Traditional Chinese architecture, whether imperial palace or common residential house, usually means a group composed of many separate buildings. The buildings were always laid out according to a certain orientation, usually along a north–south axis with the main building facing south; only a few architectural complexes, owing to specific limits of topography, religious beliefs, or geomancy were otherwise. This layout, largely originating in the middle reaches of the Yellow River, allows buildings to face the sun and helps shelter them from the cold north wind, and was seen as compatible with the patriarchal system and ethical code of Chinese society as reflected in Confucian ideology. The main building was located on the central axis, and secondary buildings were situated in front of it to form a square or rectangular courtyard, providing the place with a sense of security.

When one courtyard was not enough, more might be built in front of the main building, behind it, or symmetrically on both sides of it. The Temple to Confucius at Qufu in Shandong province, for instance, had ten courtyards located on the main axis, and many more on both sides. The layout of the Forbidden City in Beijing had an even more magnificent display of courtyards. Temples, mausoleums, and other buildings for ceremonial use were regulated more strictly, although these layouts were neither dull nor rigid, and the space in multicourt complexes was quite adaptable. A house in Beijing might have a set of four varied courtyards: the first a long court traversing the main axis, the second an oblong enclosed on three sides, the third a square, and the fourth a long arcaded court on the axis. The four courtyards might not only have different plans but could be surrounded by buildings of different elevations, with flowers and trees, rockery, and landscaping designed to create a quiet and refreshing environment.

Ornamentation

Every part of a traditional Chinese building was decorated, using a large variety of colors and different materials. Terraces and steps at the base of a building were engraved, and decorative railings often surrounded both. Roof outlines provided the greatest opportunity for ornamental features. One of the most impressive roofs in China, at the Hall of Supreme Harmony in the Forbidden City, has multiple eaves, five ridges, and four valleys. Each end of the main ridge is decorated with a large dragon, its tail stretching upward and its mouth opened as if to swallow the ridge. Adding to the exquisite detail, nine zoomorphic ornaments of colored glass mark each corner of the eaves of the other four ridges.

Walls, doors, windows, and partitions were decorated too. Partitions, curio stands, and bookshelves adorned as well as divided interior spaces. Ceilings also served ornamental purposes. In an ordinary residence the ceiling might be made simply of wooden strips or sorghum stalks nailed to the joists, then covered with paper pasted to this backing. In the lattice ceiling, used for important buildings, wooden studs formed a trellis network between beams, and the open spaces between studs were then filled with color paintings on wooden boards. The most complicated treatment, the coffered ceiling, was more decorative than the lattice ceiling and was usually reserved for the upper part of a palatial hall or a Buddhist altar. In it, wooden framework, usually in three layers, forms sunken panels in the ceiling, with each panel square at the bottom and circular at the top. Each panel resembles a well in shape, and often the central panel is painted with water-flower patterns: hence the name *zao-jing* (*zao* meaning algae, and *jing* a well).

Color paintings on buildings are another distinguishing feature of Chinese construction, evolving from the use of paint to protect beams, columns, doors, windows, and other wooden components against pests and decay. Strict regulations governed such painting of buildings. Common people were forbidden to paint color pictures on their houses. In royal palaces, different motifs were used for different buildings; the highest and most prestigious motif was the dragon, magnificent and sumptuous, placed on important palace halls. On secondary buildings various color patterns, simple but elegant, were painted. Pavilions, kiosks, and towers in the gardens were often decorated with color paintings of mostly mountains and water, grass and insects, flowers and plants, which are known as Suzhou style after the city where they are frequently found.

Gardens

Like classical Chinese poetry, painting, and music, gardens were imbued with an artistic purpose. Mountains, water, rock and stone, flowers and plants, together with their associated buildings, expressed the vision of an artistic creation. Gardens were designed in such a way that the beauty of nature was elevated to the beauty of art, expressing the creator's ideas through refinement, utilization of the best aspects of the materials, and observation. The viewer, inspired by the scene, could enhance the artistic vision as well, and by so doing attain an experience filled with spiritual enjoyment.

Three broad categories capture the artistic concerns of classic Chinese gardens: the natural realm, administering world affairs, and immortality. The natural vision is common in the private gardens of scholars, especially those of southeastern China. Such gardens have long been associated with the famous ancient Chinese philosophers Laozi and Zhuangzi, who stressed freedom from affectation and indifference to fame or worldly gain. Confucianism, with its stress on practical results and the great importance attached to a sense of social duty and human relations, fit well with an ethos of gardens as a vision of managing world affairs. Imperial gardens capture this dimension well, as evident in half of the forty scenic spots in Beijing's Yuanming imperial garden. Buddhists and Daoists, with their stress on nirvana and immortality, built gardens to deities, such as royal gardens and gardens in temples in every region of China.

The creativity of classical Chinese architecture is evident in its legacy of rich and varied forms, colors, and ornamentation, and its ordering of space. Beauty emerged out of the exquisite integration of artistry and function, materials and structure. Raised terraces guard against dampness, large eave overhangs protect against rain, lattices on windows and doors facilitate the mounting of paper to admit light, and decorated tiles are an integral component of roofing materials. Even the painted frieze, so decorative in spirit, developed from a need to preserve timber by the application of paint. Buildings from small residences to temples and immense palaces, with their gardens and courtyards and innumerable doors and gates, sought a harmonious and unified layout in their architectural composition, one in which contrasting attributes of space, high and low, near and far, wide and narrow, spare and dense, yield a rich texture of varied visual effects. The scholars writing this book explore this remarkable architectural legacy and how such accomplished skill and artistry developed over thousands of years. In so doing they offer both a history of China's extraordinary architectural tradition and an understanding and appreciation of its most distinctive contributions.

CHAPTER I

The Origins of Chinese Architecture

LIU XUJIE

The soil of China holds myriad treasures. Beautiful pottery and jade, buried foundations, remnants of wooden beams and stilts — all tell a tale of the early beginnings of Chinese architecture, a story that enriches our understanding of Chinese culture itself. Though the varied climates and geography of China have led to a diversity of architectural forms, a highly distinctive and magnificent world of architectural design has emerged over millennia of innovation and synthesis. As archaeologists brush aside layers of sediment from the Yellow River valley to Hangzhou Bay to the Inner Mongolian plain, they reveal evidence of pillar foundations, timber frames, and even a Goddess Temple, adding to our knowledge about the origins of one of the world's most enduring and continuous architectural visions. Out of a dynamic narrative that spans the development of farming, social groups, and traditions of worship and war come foreshadowings of architectural forms and characteristics that were to mark the rest of Chinese history.

We know from discoveries of coarse stone utensils and simple fireplaces that starting almost a million years ago, during the Middle Pleistocene period, early peoples throughout China lived in caves and cavelike dwellings. In time, clans and tribes in the middle reaches of the Yellow River valley came to build semisubterranean shelters with wood frames, grass, and mud,

Details, figure 1.10 *(opposite)* and figure 1.2 *(above)*

Figure 1.1. Remains of a house from the Middle Neolithic period, found in Dahe village, Zhengzhou, Henan province

and with loess for walls. Vertical pit cave houses, for example, were dug into the ground and opened into a single round room; the one at Tangquangou in Henan province is about two meters deep and two meters across.

Stilts were a feature of early dwellings along the Yangzi River. According to two great Chinese classics, the *Han Feizi* and the *Mozi,* the early Chinese "built nests on high and dens in the ground"—that is, some peoples lived in caves during the winter and in stilted residences when the weather turned warm and wet. Vestiges of both architectural forms are still seen in the twenty-first century: semisubterranean homes are used in parts of Henan, Shaanxi, and Shanxi provinces, and houses raised on stilts dot the marshes and swampland of south China.

The Neolithic period (6000–2000 B.C.E.) marks the true emergence of the wooden frames so characteristic of Chinese architecture. As early as seven thousand years ago, Neolithic peoples knew how to use mortise and tenon—a method of joinery that employs notches and inserts—to build wood-beamed houses. (The world's oldest examples are at the Hemudu site in Zhejiang.) By the end of the era these techniques were well developed, and such homes were made in circular, square, or oblong shapes, depending on their function.

More than a thousand Neolithic sites have been discovered so far, offering both a trove of examples of early architecture and insights into the transition from hunting, fishing, and gathering to farming and trade specialization. Pottery and woven objects appeared during this era, suggesting the division of labor. Communal dwellings grew to shelter populations that may have been in part kinship-related but also had ties through more complex clan structures. And the residents of these clan communities operated kilns, kept livestock in sheds, built walls and moats for defense, worshiped at altars and in temples, and were buried in groups of graves.

Understanding the multiplicity of these Neolithic cultures and peoples, and the different areas in which they flourished, is no easy task, and it remains the subject of ongoing, intensive archaeological excavations. What these myriad sites so far reveal architecturally is a considerable diversity of styles and structural forms that were influenced by various materials and climates. Dwellings ranged from horizontally dug cave houses, vertical pit caves, and semisubterranean cave dwellings to aboveground dwellings of various shapes, houses elevated on stilts, and "big houses" located centrally in some of the Neolithic villages. Such regional variations, and the differing times that they first appeared, offer early glimpses of China's architectural beginnings.

Early Neolithic sites on China's North Central Plain along the Yellow River, for example, were relatively small, generally about ten to twenty square kilometers, with graves located nearby. During the Middle Neolithic period, represented by the Yangshao culture (5000–3000 B.C.E.), we find semisubterranean dwellings with circular and rectangular forms with floors at or above ground level. The well-preserved remains of a house in Dahe village suggest that it had several spaces of different shapes and sizes—an elaboration of the single-room style (fig. 1.1). By this time, wooden pillars and beams were prevalent, and a tradition had begun of using rammed earth and unbaked mud bricks. Roofs, supported by wooden posts or made from earth, were probably covered with thatch. During the later part of the Yangshao culture, some early homebuilders made horizontal cave houses by digging into the sides of dirt cliffs, such as those found at Caiyuan village, in the Ningxia Hui autonomous region. Some of the Caiyuan homes are elaborate, with an outdoor courtyard, entryway, and hallway into the cave in addition to the cave chamber. Entries were on the east—foreshadowing what was to become a fascination with cardinal directions in Chinese architecture—and a hearth was located in the middle of the chamber, beneath a vaulted ceiling.

The Longshan culture (2900–1600 B.C.E.), a continuation of the Yangshao, was a time of considerable architectural advances: the expansion of clan settlements into towns, and the construction of many houses entirely aboveground. Examples of this culture are found in Shandong, Henan, southern Shaanxi, and southwestern Shanxi province, and suggest that the later periods of Yangshao and Longshan spawned the most highly developed

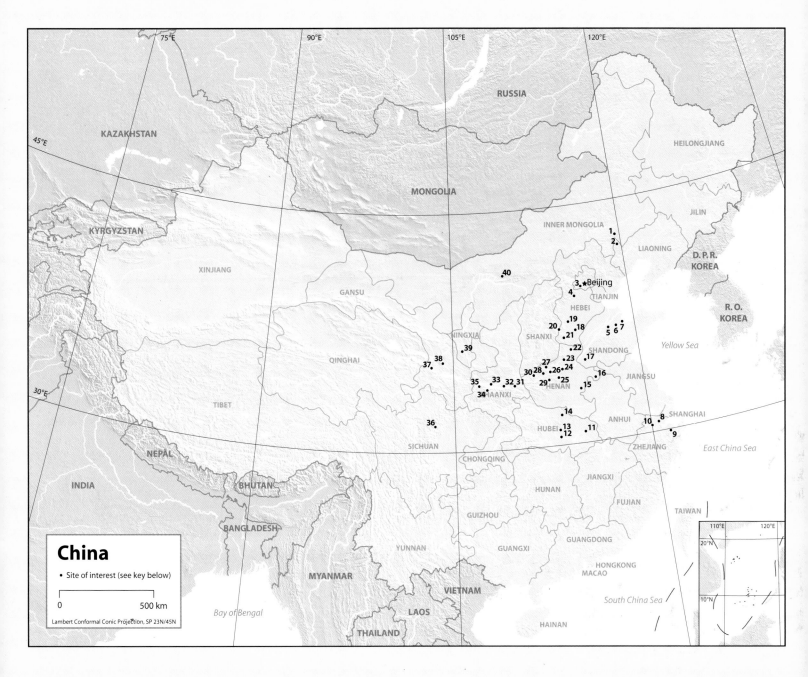

Map 1.
Sites of Early Chinese Architecture

Figure 1.2. Timber building members, circa 5000 B.C.E., unearthed at Hemudu, Zhejiang province

civilization in the Yellow River valley at the time. Houses in this area were painted with white lime, in anticipation of a much later style of whitewashed walls. In addition, a few examples of rammed-earth foundations have been found, as well as evidence of a rammed-earth city wall, one of the oldest in China.

The middle reaches of the Yangzi River show variations from those in the Yellow River area. At Qujialing and Shijiahe, both in Hubei, houses were four-sided and large, with as many as thirty bays in a row. Their walls, framed by wooden posts and lintels, were shaped from a mixture of straw and mud. These large-scale clan communities were densely settled: several towns occupied an area of just one square kilometer. Most Qujialing and Shijiahe sites were enclosed by rammed-earth walls and moats and had water gates for drainage.

In the lower reaches of the Yangzi River area in Zhejiang province, by contrast, residents of the towns of Majiayao in Jiaxing county, Liangzhu in Yuhang county, and especially Hemudu in Yuyao county lifted their homes onto stilts to avoid the snakes and mosquitoes that went along with the hot, humid climate. Hemudu dwellings had multiple rooms, and excavated wooden pieces suggest that mortise and tenon joinery was used to build them (fig. 1.2). The flourish of latticework on a covered arcade testifies to the artistry then emerging. A sacrificial altar made of rammed earth from this time has been uncovered at Yaoshan, Yuhang county. The altar was square, with each side measuring twenty meters, and two meters high. The surface consisted of a red clay platform, a gray soil ditch, and pebbles.

Other regions offer additional examples of the diversity from which Chinese architectural patterns were to emerge. In Inner Mongolia and northeast China, the Neolithic cul-

ture of Hongshan emerged and spread across northern Hebei, southeastern Inner Mongolia, western Liaoning, and northwestern Jilin. An extensive use of stone seems to have been unique to villages there. At Ashan, for example (discussed more fully later), piled stone was a dominant architectural style. The outer walls of multiclan houses, and the walls that separated the clans, were made of heaped rocks, as was a large altar on a stone foundation.

Banpo, the largest known Neolithic village site, offers a particularly rewarding study of life during this period and contains some of the oldest semisubterranean dwellings of their kind (fig. 1.3). By the mid-1900s about 3.5 square kilometers (of an estimated 60 kilometers) had been excavated. Surrounding the large village is a ditch five to six meters deep and wide, believed to have been built for both drainage and defense. Most of the individual homes were square or circular and had a fire-pit hearth at the center. To create them, builders dug a shallow foundation, perhaps one meter deep, then bound together two or four poles with cord to support a roof frame made of branches, straw, and perhaps mud on top (fig. 1.4). Entrances were sloped walkways with thatch overhangs. Neighborhoods of dwellings were separated by ditches about two meters both wide and deep.

As communities developed, more kinds of buildings were needed. At Jiangzhai, for example, which was composed of some 100 to 180 homes surrounded by a moat, groups of about ten dwellings surrounded one of five or so "big houses," which in turn enclosed a large open plaza. These big houses, which were built in various shapes at other sites as well, were the largest of all structures and seem to have been created either for clan chieftains or for public events.

Though we still know little of such early develop-

Figure 1.3. Excavation site of a Neolithic village at Banpo, Shaanxi province, circa 3000 B.C.E.

Figure 1.4. Reconstruction drawing of a house from Banpo site

ments, one possible indication of the emergence of private ownership is the presence of storage holes — burrows dug in the ground, either inside or outside a Neolithic house, to hold personal items. Some are believed to have been abandoned cave dwellings; others may have been used for storing refuse.

In addition to villages, towns grew, often in strikingly symmetrical shapes. Shijiahe, nearly a perfect square, was the largest uncovered by the end of the twentieth century — a kilometer on each side. Other towns shaped like ovals, rectangles, and trapezoids also have been discovered. Although during the Neolithic period topography and other natural conditions still determined the location of towns, the presence of these developments signals that people were beginning to work together at increasing levels of sophistication, discovering new materials and methods for building.

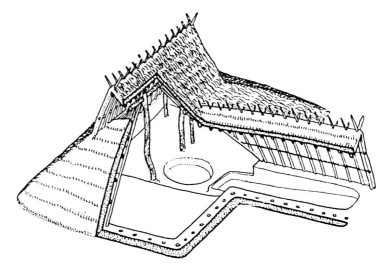

Ancient Burials, Sacrifices, and Ritual Architecture

The beliefs of these Neolithic peoples are not known, but religious practices and methods of burying the dead are richly evident in archaeological excavations. In Paleolithic times, corpses were traditionally concealed in the back of natural cave dwellings. Such a collection of human remains was found at Shanding cave at Zhoukoudian, the site associated with Peking Man. At other sites, for example those of some matrilineal clan societies, deceased adults were taken to a burial ground outside the village. Their remains were placed in a simple rectangular pit, accompanied by no furnishings and only a few decorative items and objects of daily life. Discoveries at Banpo confirm that during the Yangshao culture the remains of children were put in pottery urns and buried near their homes.

In 1987, extraordinary remains found in a tomb in Puyang, Zhejiang province, suggested that symbolism was associated with burial practices. Inside were a middle-aged man and three children, framed by piles of shells resembling the shape of a dragon and a tiger. The mosaics were upside down and faced away from the man's body (fig. 1.5). It is not known just how this relates to the belief in the Han dynasty that the dragon has a special relationship with the eastern quadrant of the earth, and the tiger with the western, though some speculate about the possibility of a linkage. In a shallow grave near this find was another group of shells, arranged like a dragon, a tiger, a deer, and a spider.

Altars of raised-earth platforms, precisely placed stone piles, and rock walls suggest that religious life in general was of considerable significance during the late Neolithic era. One altar from the Liangzhu culture (3300–2000 B.C.E.), at Yaoshan in Zhejiang, illustrates the elaborate style of religious structures made then. Of its three levels, the innermost and highest was a platform of rammed red earth, about seven by six meters (fig. 1.6). A ditch made from grayish earth surrounded it, and to the west, north, and south were three platforms of yellowish earth paved with cobblestones. Along the north and west are remains of a stone wall. Twelve graves, arranged in two rows on the altar, are believed to belong to those who performed the ceremonies.

A Neolithic altar was also found in Ashan, Baotou city. There, eighteen groups of stones piled in circles extended along a 51-meter north–south line. The southern pile was the largest, 8.8 meters in diameter; 2.1 meters

Figure 1.5. Grave with shells in the shape of a dragon and a tiger, Puyang, Zhejiang province

Figure 1.6. Site of a sacrificial altar from the Liangzhu culture,
Yaoshan, Yuhang county, Zhejiang province

Figure 1.7. Remains of Goddess Temple at Niuheliang, Liaoning
province

Figure 1.8. Hand of a goddess unearthed at Niuheliang

Figure 1.9. Face of goddess, Niuheliang

of its height remain today. Northernmost was the smallest pile, 1.1 meters in diameter, of which 0.2 meter of height can still be seen. The other sixteen piles of stone have diameters between 1.4 and 1.6 meters and heights that range from 0.35 to 0.55 meter. The piles are 0.8 to 1 meter apart. Excavation suggests that three stone walls surrounded the entire ritual complex. Of these, the inner wall seems to have been U-shaped; all that is known of the other two is that sections remain beyond the loop of the inner U at the south.

The Yaoshan altar, as well as all other Neolithic religious structures found to date, is surpassed in scale and complexity by the Hongshan culture's Goddess Temple at Niuheliang in Liaoning. There the remains are spread over a fifty-kilometer area and include those of what archaeologists labeled a "goddess temple" and two large stone tombs, one on the summit of a hill (fig. 1.7). What remains of the sacrificial altar is a large base constructed with polished stone slabs. The sacrificial area, which is about sixty by forty meters, extends about one meter into the ground and is composed of a center, front, back, and two wings made of polished blocks of sandstone. The smaller temple, twenty-two meters by eight meters, seems to have had two parts, one with many rooms and the other, on the northern end, with a single room. Excavations of the single room have unearthed clay body parts, including a head, torso, and arms probably belonging to the goddess who gave the site its name; many of these are painted in alternating patterns of brown crosses, yellow and white triangular patterns, and cross-hatched designs. Excavation elsewehere at the site has found hands of the goddess, as well as statues that range from life-size to three times human size (figs. 1.8 and 1.9).

Technical and Artistic Achievements in Neolithic Architecture

Chinese architecture as we know it was born in the Neolithic period. Although the early Neolithic peoples had primitive tools and little knowledge of production techniques, they managed to create homes, villages, pottery kilns, and altars. Indeed, three forms of dwelling constructed throughout Chinese history trace their origins to Neolithic times: horizontal cave houses, homes supported by timber frames, and houses raised on stilts.

Of these, the timber-frame house was to have the most profound effect on Chinese construction. Even at a site as old as Hemudu we see mortise and tenon joinery, and by the end of Neolithic times, this technique had replaced binding with ropes as the primary means of building support.

It is also clear that care was given to where individual structures and villages were constructed. Before launching a new project, considerable thought evidently was given to the proximity to drinking water, the direction of the sun's rays, the potential for drought or flood, and the ease of defense. By this time, too, distinctions were being made between living quarters, areas for handicraft manufacture, and graveyards. All would be further distinguished in later Chinese construction.

Neolithic peoples of China invented new techniques for building and used them well. For example, *hangtu,* the pounding or ramming of layers of earth, was used to make walls, altars, and house foundations. Like the timber frame, hangtu was to become ubiquitous in Chinese construction. Other construction elements that remained features of Chinese architecture for the next several millennia were sundried mud bricks, mud walls built above a wooden frame, earthen floors that were hardened through heating, whitewashed surfaces, and aprons (for drainage) along the exterior of a building. Indeed, this period marks the emergence of an architectural aesthetic in China, with the introduction of whitewashed walls and the appearance on buildings of crosshatching and triangular patterns reminiscent of designs painted on Neolithic pottery. Finally, the importance of "centrality" develops, as seen by the enclosure of buildings as well as the symmetry in homes, altars, and the layout of villages.

The Three Dynasties Period: Innovation, Planning, and the First Glint of Bronze

The Three Dynasties (Sandai) period marks the end of Neolithic clan society. The era was critical in shaping many customs and institutions found throughout the rest of Chinese history. The actual nature, development, and scope of the relationship among the three dynasties — the Xia, the Shang, and the Zhou — remain subjects of continued research and debate. So is their relationship to the many other states developing in these years. As now understood, the Xia, Shang, and Zhou were three originally distinguishable cultural groups that developed in different areas. Although chronologies of the period are still being revised and debated, many scholars believe that the Xia culture, the first to emerge, developed around 2070 B.C.E. In general, Xia culture was centered in southwestern Shanxi, Henan, Shandong, and southern Hebei.

The Shang dynasty, which followed the Xia, flowered during 1600–1046 B.C.E. and was the first glorious period of bronze technology in China. The borders of Shang included Xia and extended beyond to Shaanxi in the west, Hubei in the south, and all of Hebei as well as Shandong.

The dates are more certain for Zhou, the last of the three dynasties: the Western Zhou (1046–770 B.C.E.) lasted until the Zhou capital was moved from Chang'an (Xi'an) eastward to Luoyang in Henan province; and the Eastern Zhou, the period when Luoyang was the capital, lasted from 770 to 221 B.C.E. Eastern Zhou is itself divided into two periods, the Spring and Autumn period from 770 to 476, and the period of Warring States from 475 to 221. Zhou territory spread from Gansu in the west, across Inner Mongolia to the Yellow Sea in the east, and to northern Guangdong in the south.

Several significant social changes signaled the end of China's Neolithic clan society. Larger-scale agriculture developed. Water conservation and more ambitious irrigation projects spread. In Shang society, kingship and divine power became integrated. The kings of the Shang dynasty completely monopolized the sacrificial powers and religious authority on which political power was based. With the Western Zhou the worship and offering of sacrifices to ancestral deities became the spiritual support for the hierarchical lineage system. This integration of political power and religious authority was one of the basic characteristics of the Three Dynasties. Culturally and philosophically, the Eastern Zhou became famous as the period of the "hundred schools of thought" and the age of China's great sages and philosophers, Confucius, Mencius, Laozi, and Zhuangzi.

During the Three Dynasties period, village-centered clans were transformed into states with true urban centers. Excavations of possible Xia sites have not yet yielded a comprehensive and self-contained human urban unit like Banpo. But the sites of several Shang capitals have been discovered in Henan province and confirm the profound changes that occurred. Yin, the site of the last Shang capital, in Anyang county, Henan, has been studied

Figure 1.10. Ruins of Yin, last capital of the Shang dynasty, on the west bank of the Huan River, Anyang county, Henan province

since the late 1920s, and various palatial foundations, sacrificial structures, dwellings, and cemeteries have been identified (figs. 1.10 and 1.11). Sacrificial burial of humans and animals is evident at all the Shang royal cities, as are more, and more varied, grave goods, including horse carts. By the Shang period, too, residential architecture was primarily aboveground, and there is good evidence that ceremonial structures were built above tombs. Multi-chamber construction was apparently used not just in big houses but also in individual dwellings, gardens probably were built, and the Neolithic planning principles of four-sided rectangular enclosure and axial symmetry are present in all known Shang sites.

By Zhou times, cities existed in every part of China. The capitals Feng and Hao near Xi'an, and Luoyi near Luoyang, are well documented in literature of the time. And excavation has yielded a lot of new information about the hundreds of state capitals, such as those of the states of Qi, Lu, Yan, Chu, or Zhao. Although these capitals were built in a wide range of sizes and scales, all had inner walled cities within outer walls. This makes sense, given that the

rapid rise in Zhou urbanism is directly linked to the frequency of wars between the states. Walls were both a symbol of a ruler's strength and a means of defense against an attacking neighbor. Walls also were erected at the northern borders of states, including Qin, Yan, Chu, and Qi, to protect residents from invaders from the north. (Some of these barriers were later joined to form the Great Wall.) Remains of the Qi wall, for example, show a base nearly seven meters wide in places, and a top that varied in height (fig. 1.12). Large stones were usually piled as a foundation, then earth was rammed above it layer upon layer. Traces of wood, possibly the remains of round posts used to hold the wall in place, have also been discovered there.

Zhou rulers built larger and more elaborate palaces than did their Shang predecessors, as well as palaces separate from the main palace area that could be used either as places of pleasure or as a place to stay on their travels throughout their realm. Chinese construction technology had not yet made it possible to build multistory buildings made from wood and stone. The solution: high foundation platforms.

The inability to build tall structures also influenced tombs for the afterlife. During the Zhou dynasty, most graves for nobility were placed in elaborate underground palaces. By the Warring States period, however, technological advances had encouraged the building of mounds and sacrificial structures above such tombs. These advances also led to significant progress in the use of pottery tiles for roofs, bricks for paving floors, and even bronze in a few building parts.

Cities of the Three Dynasties

Cities changed greatly during the Three Dynasties period, but this history has been difficult to trace with any certainty for the earliest years because Xia sites have been so hard to find or fully confirm. According to literary records, for example, Xia moved its capital many times during its approximately four-hundred-year history, but the locations of these ancient capitals remain in dispute. Some believe that two rammed-earth walls found at Wangchenggang, Dengfeng county, Henan, were part of Yangcheng, capital of the first emperor, Yu, of the Xia dynasty. Carbon-14 dating of coffins, pottery pieces, and fragments of bronze objects found at several pit graves there support this view.

Remains of a second Three Dynasties town in Henan were discovered in 1979 in Pingliangtai, Huaiyang county. Scientific tests determined those remains to be about 4,130 years old, slightly older than the ruins at Wangchenggang. The four rammed-earth walls of the square village Pingliangtai were each about 185 meters long, 3.5 meters high, and 13 meters wide. More than ten building foundations were excavated, some that had been raised on earthen platforms and others that had been built on ground level. Residential walls were made of sun-dried mud bricks that were rectangular, square, and even triangular. Straw mixed with mud was smeared on the wall

Figure 1.11. Reconstructed palace of the Shang capital at Yin

Figure 1.12. Remains of the Qi wall from the Warring States period, Shandong province

surfaces; also excavated were pieces of pottery tubes (probably used for drainage) and copper dregs.

These examples show great development in architectural techniques and styles: rammed earth became commonly used for foundations and walls, adobe brick and white lime began to be set in floors, and wainscot and wall decorations appeared. Buildings of all kinds — pit houses, semisubterranean homes, and ground-level dwellings with single or multiple rooms — were constructed more solidly and uniformly. In addition, there appeared raised platform structures, horizontally dug cavelike dwellings, and courtyards surrounded by houses or walls. But certainly one of the most important changes was the rise of city walls, built to protect inhabitants and to promote their political power. This political might was reinforced with architectural plans that put the leader in the very middle. The plans of the city discovered in Pingliangtai and the one in Wangchenggang, for example, both show ornate and nearly identical buildings perfectly arranged to face a common central square.

We know much more about the Shang capitals. Bronze inscriptions tell us that Shang kings ruled from seven cities: Xibo, Ao, Xiang, Geng, Xing, Yan, and Yin. An excavation of a Shang site at the city of Zhengzhou, Henan province, is believed to be the second Shang capital, Ao, where the tenth Shang ruler, Zhong Ding, may have moved. Like Shixianggou, another Shang site in Henan, the Zhengzhou settlement was enclosed by a wall of pounded earthen layers that was nearly straight on three sides and irregular on the fourth. The Zhengzhou wall was even longer than the one at Shixianggou, almost seven kilometers in perimeter, and the city was oriented nearly due north–south. Pounded-earth palatial or residential foundations have been uncovered at Zhengzhou, as have bronze foundries and evidence of workshops and tomb areas outside the city wall. The Zhengzhou site was also larger than an earlier Shang walled settlement at Yanshi, believed by some to have functioned more in a military role. In the southern part of the Yanshi city were smaller "cities," each with its own palace city enclosed by a rammed-earth wall. Within the palace city was a large palace foundation, tens of meters long and wide. On either side of it were foundations of other palaces. The foundations for Palace 4 include a main hall, a courtyard, corridors in the east, west, and south, a south gate, and a west-side door (fig. 1.13). Traces of a drainage system have been found nearby (fig. 1.14).

Remnants of the last Shang capital, Yin, established by Pan Geng, are believed to have been discovered in northwestern Anyang county, Henan. The capital is believed to have been about six by four kilometers. Yin was a composite of sites, one of which was primarily residential and the other primarily funerary. Excavations at the largely residential sector, Xiaotun, have led to reconstructions of a great house and smaller residences. The multichamber great house is believed to have been elevated on a platform and approached by several stairways from the front. The smaller dwellings also had more than one room, but their foundations and approaches were on a smaller scale. Like the thatched roofs, walls were framed in wood, but they also were plastered and probably whitewashed. Some residences oriented north–south and others oriented east–west have been found.

Since the discovery in the 1930s of royal graves at Xibeigang, the tomb architecture of Anyang has made the city famous. Thirteen large tombs, believed to include buried Shang kings, have been excavated, along with fourteen hundred sacrificial burial pits. The excavations confirm that the spatial principles present in the

Figure 1.13. Site of Palace 4 in the Shang city of Erlitou (Yanshi), near Luoyang, Henan province

Figure 1.14. Traces of the drainage system in Yanshi

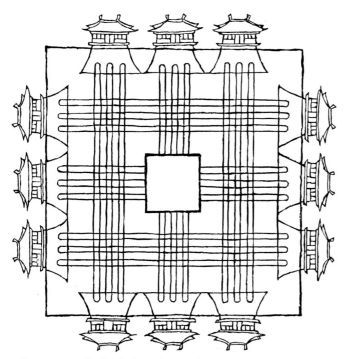

Figure 1.15. Idealized plan of Wangcheng

residential architecture of China before 2000 B.C.E.—orientation according to the four cardinal directions and the placement of important structures in a central place with stairs leading up to them—were employed in these large tombs roughly five hundred years later. These principles characterized residential and funerary architecture for the rest of Chinese imperial history.

Finally, the archaeological record has led scholars to believe that Panlongcheng in Hubei may have been a town of Shang nobility. The site, dated mid-Shang and surrounded by a city wall 1.1 kilometers in perimeter, is rhomboid-shaped and located on high ground bordering Panlong Lake. Residences, handicraft workshops, and cemeteries have been found outside the ancient town.

Literary records and bronze inscriptions both tell us that in the early years of Western Zhou, King Wen built a capital at Feng and King Wu built a capital at Hao. Both sites were destroyed in the last years of the Western Zhou by Quan Rong invaders. Feng and Hao are believed to have been on the west and east sides, respectively, of a tributary of the Wei River, northwest of the modern city Xi'an, but little is known about their dimensions, shapes, or structures.

When King Ping, first ruler of the Eastern Zhou, ascended the throne, he moved the capital eastward to the site of King Wu's former capital Hao. Ping's new city, Luoyi, was abandoned in Zhou times, but later, in the Western Han dynasty, the site became a prefectural capi-

tal. A second Eastern Zhou capital, on a larger site in the vicinity of Luoyang, has yielded even better evidence of Eastern Zhou urbanism. A rammed-earth foundation has been discovered in the southern part of the city that some believe to be the remains of the palaces and ancestral temple of the Zhou kings. In the northern section, kilns and bone and stone workshops have been found. Two of the main wall sections believed to date from Zhou times have been excavated; neither yielded proof of a four-sided city wall but both were oriented roughly north–south.

Archaeologists have so far been unable to determine if there is any close link between such a site and one of the earliest and most important written descriptions of a city in Chinese, that of Wangcheng ("ruler's city"), which survives in the "Record of Trades" section of the *Rituals of Zhou*. Although the *Rituals* is believed to date from Zhou times, the "Record of Trades" is considered a first-millennium B.C.E. replacement for a lost section of the original text. One passage in it reads:

> The master craftsman constructs the state capital. He makes a square nine li on each side; each side has three gates. Within the capital are nine north–south and nine east–west streets. The north–south streets are nine carriage tracks in width.

Illustrations of this passage from the last Chinese dynasty, the Qing, show the ideal Chinese capital: a perfect square with north–south and east–west streets that extend the entire length and width of the city, gates positioned at the place where those streets join the outer city wall, and palaces located in the exact center. Although it might be argued that all later Chinese imperial urbanism strove to realize this form, in fact no city actually achieved this goal. Nonetheless, the plan symbolizes Chinese imperial power—in particular, the beliefs that the Chinese emperor should be viewed as the center of the world, facing south, and that the number nine is associated with him and is supreme (fig. 1.15).

Of excavated cities, the Zhou city at Qufu, the capital of the state of Lu, is one of the few that follows this prescription for Wangcheng in the *Rituals* passage, at least for the relation between palaces and walls. Qufu's urban history extended more than eight hundred years, from the eleventh to the third centuries B.C.E. Its rectangular outer wall enclosed an area of ten square kilometers and had eleven gates, through which passed major streets spanning the entire width or breadth of the city. (On either side of some of the gates are foundations of battlements, perhaps forerunners of more sophisticated protection attached to Chinese walls in later times.) The main street led from the east gate of the south wall to the palaces of Qufu, located just northeast of the center of the city.

Linzi, capital of the state of Qi, is another example of a major Zhou city. Built in 894 B.C.E. during the first year of the reign of King Yi of the Western Zhou, it is composed of a small rectangular inner city in the southwest corner of a larger, roughly rectangular outer city with an area of about seventeen square kilometers. Seven city gates and seven major roads have been excavated, as have workshops for handicrafts and residences. The smaller city, with an area of three square kilometers, has five wall gates. In the northwest part of the city a large pounded-earth foundation is believed to have been the palace of the duke of Qi. A remarkably well-designed system of paved stone drainage pipes passed beneath both cities: the longest was thirty meters wide and twenty-eight hundred meters long.

Palaces

Most palaces, gardens, altars, and temples of the Three Dynasties were created within cities and towns. Except for certain altars and temples, those that seem today to be isolated are almost certainly part of a more complex architectural setting. In China during the last two millennia B.C.E., it would have been almost impossible for a palace to be sustained away from a support system of workers.

Palaces — the architectural symbols of royal power — offer fascinating details about early Chinese architecture. Some of the earliest foundations of palace remains have been excavated at Erlitou (Yanshi), adjacent to the city of Luoyang. Each palace had a main building that was enclosed by a covered arcade and oriented almost exactly north–south. Walls raised on pounded-earth foundations and supported by wooden columns and beams are believed to have been smeared with mud, and it seems that roofs were thatched. One of the palaces was eight bays across the front, the center six of which appear to have been open to the outside. The entire building was enclosed by a covered arcade made of wood with a tile roof, a prototype of the covered corridors that would connect almost every Chinese building complex in later times. Possibly the even number of bays across the front of the main hall (defined by the pillar holes) was symbolically important in Three Dynasties society.

Other palatial structures have been discovered at the last Shang capital, Yin, near today's Anyang. Excavations on the east side of a southward bend in the Huan River have yielded tremendous results, including evidence of moats and waterways. No palace wall has been found there, but many more structures than are known or suspected at Erlitou have been uncovered. The individual structures may have opened onto courtyards, and the great house is thought to have been an "auditorium." In addition to rectangular and square plans, L-shaped and U-shaped foundations exist there.

Although greatly damaged by water, buildings in the southeast of Xiaotun reveal tantalizing clues about palace construction. Seventeen or so foundations or parts of foundations were probably part of a symmetrically laid out building complex, perhaps a ceremonial sector created later than the structures to the north. Sacrificed human remains have been uncovered beneath the foundations on the west side of this area, and beneath the foundations on the east are sacrificial animal burials.

From the overall layout, it seems that the Xiaotun palaces and temples were located in the center of the capital. But when surrounding residential areas are included in the scheme, the palaces and temples are slightly to the north, close to the river. This off-center location gave convenient access to water, yet with the advantage of being higher than the surroundings and thus safe from flooding. A drainage system ran throughout the palace and temple area, where fifty-three large-scale rammed-earth foundations have been discovered, many facing courtyards.

Three gates also have been found in this central area of Xiaotun. Beneath each gate lay five or six sacrificial burials of a man holding a spear and a shield. The location of these burials, near the great hall, further suggests that the royal court of Shang lived in that area — no burials like these have been found in the approximately fifteen building foundations in the northern part of the site.

The plans of palatial architecture changed little from the Xia to late Shang periods, but wooden-frame construction improved. Wooden pillars were implanted more deeply into the earth, some irregularly shaped stone pillar bases were used, and in some cases bronze pieces were placed between the foot of the pillars and the stone pilasters, probably to help keep the pillars straight and protect the wood from weather.

So far, no Western or Eastern Zhou palaces that can be associated with specific rulers have been found. We have hints of their architectural plans from the "Record of Trades," the same section of the *Rituals of Zhou* that offers the description of Wangcheng: "On the left (as one faces south, or, to the east) is the Ancestral Temple, and to the right (west) are the Altars of Soil and Grain. In the front is the Hall of Audience and behind are the markets." Conceivably, the symmetrically arranged building complex in the southern sector of Xiaotun was designed to follow this plan. Other textual references to palaces of the Zhou mention "three courts and five gates," similar to the wall-enclosed palace at Fengchu, Qishan county, Shaanxi province (discussed below, at fig. 1.16). Scholars have disagreed for centuries about the purposes and locations of these courts and gates as described in the text. Perhaps the only consensus is that each of the three court buildings would have looked different from the others, according to the importance of the affairs conducted within.

Palaces built more for pleasure than governance, as well as other unusual buildings, were also constructed during this time, and parks appeared. Ancient literature mentions five building projects of the Xia ruler Jie: Xuanshi (a lathe room), Yaotai (a pottery platform), Changyegong (the palace of the lengthened night), Xianglang (the corridor of images), and Shishi (a stone room). Although it is unclear exactly what these structures were, they certainly seem to be a departure from the palatial architecture so far described. Similarly, there are textual references to Qinggong (a leaning palace), Lutai (a black platform), Qiongshi (a red room), and Shaqiugong (the palace of sand dunes), all built by the last Shang ruler. Even more surprising, in King Zhou's biography in the historical record *Shi ji*, written near the end of the first century B.C.E., we are told that he "gathered rare dogs and horses, and other exotic beasts, filling foot after foot of his palace. . . . He once had a great gathering with dancing and music at Shaqiu where wine flowed in pools and meat hung on trees. Naked men and women chased one another in the garden. King Zhou drank until the wee hours of the night." The *Bamboo Annals* (Zhushu jinian), believed to have been written during the period of the Warring States, seems to refer to this same place, using the term *ligong*, literally "detached palace." "At the time of King Zhou," we are told, "the capital Yin was enlarged slightly. A distance away to the south was Zhaoge, in the north were Handan and Shaqiu."

Texts suggest that by the Shang dynasty other detached palaces existed and kept their function throughout much of Chinese history. During the early Zhou period, King Wen is said to have built Lingzhao and Lingtai, both places of natural beauty that contained only a few man-made structures. Ordinary people could enter these state parks for hunting or fishing.

From the last years of the Western Zhou period to the Spring and Autumn period, the lords of each state actively competed for power. Buildings and parks became important symbols of this power. Fuchai, for example, king of the state of Wu (near present-day Suzhou), took three years to build Gusutai, a winding, sprawling pleasure land filled with thousands of singing girls and concubines. In one area, the Palace of the Spring Night, those in attendance would drink through the night. It is interesting that the names of other known detached palaces and buildings in formal palaces — Zhanghuatai and Yuzhangtai of the state of Chu, Zhangtai of Qin, and Langyatai of Qi — end in *tai*, which means platform or terrace. It may refer to a kind of architecture suited to pleasurable activities, or to a structure raised on an especially high platform, perhaps a pavilion.

Sacrificial Structures and Tombs of the Three Dynasties

Many people were sacrificed and buried at the Xia city Yangcheng and the late Shang capital Yin, although not much about the practice of ritual sacrifice is understood. Both human and animal sacrificial burials have also been uncovered in a clan village west of Gaocheng county, Hebei, dated to the mid-Shang period.

The earliest Chinese people almost certainly performed ritual sacrifices related to heaven and earth, and following the ceremonies, in the tradition of *fanyi*, or burned burial, sacrificial animals were consumed by fire and their ashes buried. Many animal remains, as well as broken and burned pieces of gold, bronze, jade, ivory, bone, stone, and pottery, have been found at the late Shang site of Sanxingdui in Sichuan. Also uncovered were large masks and standing figures thought to be of performers of the ritual.

Ceremonial appeals to the ancestors and the soil are believed to have been conducted in the ancestral temple and at the soil altar, respectively. The remains in the southern sector of Xiaotun at Anyang and references to rituals in the "Record of Trades" suggest that in both Shang and Zhou times altars may have been built in front of the palace and on either side. In later times, these locations became standard in Chinese ritual practice. Some believe that the building complex found in Fengchu village, Shaanxi, was used primarily for the performance of rituals (fig. 1.16).

Upon entering the Fengchu complex, one first encountered a screen wall, an early example of a feature that was to become common in Chinese palatial architecture. Be-

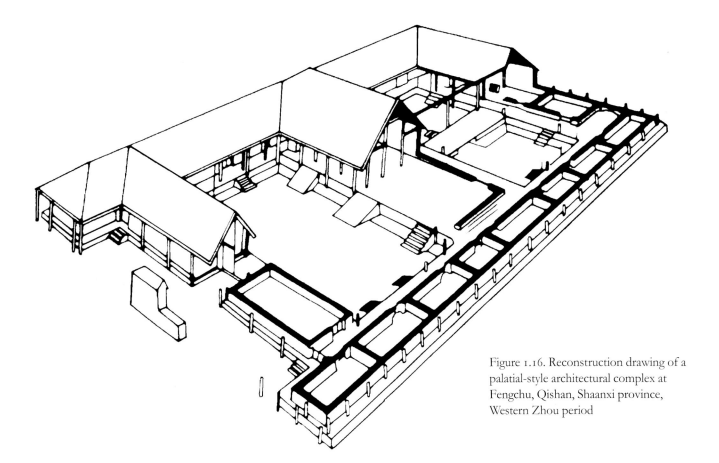

Figure 1.16. Reconstruction drawing of a palatial-style architectural complex at Fengchu, Qishan, Shaanxi province, Western Zhou period

hind this screen was a gate with a passage through its center, then the principal hall, and finally an enclosing covered arcade from which two small rooms projected at the front. There were three courtyards — a large one between the front gate and the principal hall and smaller ones east and west behind the principal hall. Excavation near the main hall suggests that it was supported with pillars and had mud-brick walls and pottery drainage pipes. Not only does the layout of the Fengchu site seem to follow textual descriptions of the "three courts" system mentioned above, digging beneath rooms of the western side corridor uncovered inscribed tortoise shells and oracle bones, suggesting that it was once a ceremonial complex of a king or possibly a feudal lord.

A second excavation site with a possible Zhou ritual complex is Yongcheng, capital of the state of Qin in Shaanxi province; it also may be an example of a three-court, five-gate scheme characteristic of a royal Zhou ancestral temple. Its three principal halls were arranged in an inverted U-shape, apparently with a "great temple" in the back center, a "luminous temple" to the east, and a "solemn temple" to the west. Each building is partitioned, probably in accordance with the different functions of each space. The site was enclosed with a wall, and

bronze structural pieces were certainly used — sixty-four were found, including L-shaped ones that were discovered in three different pits (fig. 1.17). Roofs were covered with both flat and cylindrical tiles, and many carts and sacrificial burials of humans and animals were found beneath the courtyards and pounded-earth platforms.

No tombs of Xia rulers have been discovered, possibly because neither mounds nor branches were used to cover their graves. It is said that when the legendary Emperor Yu died he was buried in a tomb at the side of Mount Huiji, but no further clues exist.

Shang tombs have been easier to find, and the massive graves excavated at the last Shang capital, Yin, exemplify the high point of Shang royal burial. Surrounding a rectangular burial space at Tomb 1001 in Xibeigang was a two-layer platform with a sacrificial dog grave in a pit on the side. The largest tombs were approached by ramps from four sides, whereas the smaller ones had such approaches only at the front and back.

Another important tomb from the Shang capital belonged to Lady Hao, the wife of King Wu Ding. Located in Xiaotun, it was a simple pit tomb with four side platforms but no approach ramps. Traditionally, attendants for the tomb occupant were sacrificially buried on the side

Figure 1.17. An L-shaped bronze structural member unearthed from the remains of Yongcheng, capital of the Qin state in Shaanxi province

platforms of the approach ramps, and beyond the tomb were pits for sacrificial burials of slaves, horses, and carts. Because the tomb of Lady Hao had no such ramp, however, a sacrificial hall—not a mound—was built on top for sacrifices. It is believed that similar structures were built above other tombs of Shang royalty in their cemetery at Yin.

The tombs of Zhou royalty were probably similar to those of the Shang. Some Zhou feudal lords had tombs with approach ramps from four sides. But mounds do appear on top of graves beginning in the Zhou dynasty, probably during the Spring and Autumn period. Among the most important tombs of the era is that of the Marquis Yi of Zeng, of the Eastern Zhou, uncovered at Leigudun in Hubei in 1978. The tomb attracted international attention because of the extraordinary bronze objects found there, including a set of sixty-five bells weighing a total of 2,500 kilograms. Yet the tomb is equally significant in the history of Chinese funerary architecture. Dug in about 433 B.C.E., the tomb of Marquis Yi is an irregularly shaped vertical pit tomb, thirteen meters deep and more than two hundred square meters in area. It was divided by wooden planks into four chambers. The principal chamber, on the east, contained the marquis' corpse. It was placed in multiple coffins, and the space between the outer coffin and the chamber walls was filled in with charcoal, clay, and earth to seal it as completely as possible. Also in the eastern chamber were the coffins of eight women who had been sacrificially buried, as well as the coffin of a sacrificial dog. Thirteen coffins that contained sacrificial females were arranged in the western chamber. The other two chambers were filled with exquisite objects of bronze, gold, copper, lacquer, wood, jade, and other materials.

Another important mausoleum from Eastern Zhou times belonged to a ruler of the Zhongshan kingdom who was buried at the end of the fourth century B.C.E. in Pingshan county of Hebei province. The ruler planned to be buried in a line together with his wife and concubines (fig. 1.18). Although only his tomb and that of one female exist, we are certain of his intent because beneath his tomb an extraordinary artifact was unearthed: a bronze plate known as *zhaoyu tu,* or picture of the omen area (fig. 1.19). Engraved on the ninety-six by forty-eight-centimeter plate is a bird's-eye view of his planned necropolis, with south shown at the top as is customary in early Chinese maps. The names of the intended occupants of the five halls are given, as are dimensions of (and distances between) each hall, the two enclosing walls, the front gates, and the small back halls. Equally impressive, an inscription decrees that a copy of this plate was to be kept in the palace so that future generations would know how to replicate their ancestral plan. Although other maps are known from the Eastern Zhou period, the bronze plate from the Zhongshan necropolis is the earliest Chinese site plan drawn to scale. Furthermore, excavation has confirmed that the funerary temples plotted on the face of the bronze plate were indeed constructed above the graves.

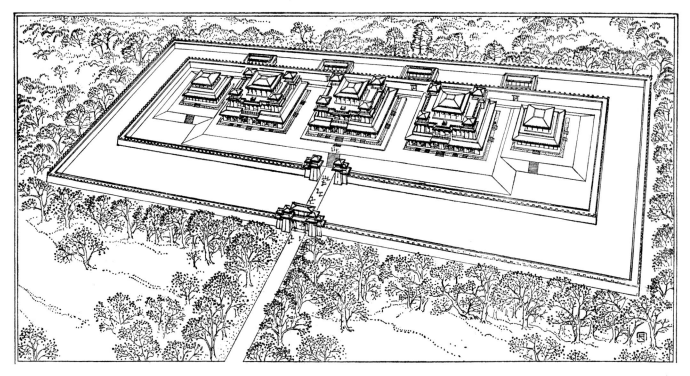

Figure 1.18. Reconstruction drawing of the king of Zhongshan's tomb complex aboveground in Pingshan county, Hebei province. The tombs were built in the last decades of the fourth century B.C.E.

Figure 1.19. Bronze plate showing the Zhongshan necropolis

Figure 1.20. Decorative patterns of the Warring States period

Clearly there was some variation in the burial practices of Zhou rulers and aristocrats. Even some of the most fundamental shapes and designs vary: for example, although there are mounds at the Pingshan site, there is no evidence of them at Spring and Autumn period tombs excavated in Fengxiang, Shaanxi, where instead a ditch surrounds the burial area. But there is one commonality among almost all Zhou graves found in the Central Plain area. During that time, the dead were usually entombed in wooden coffins and placed underground in earthen pits, which sometimes were lined with wooden planks.

In other regions, burial practices and tomb structures followed local customs. In the Jiangnan region in Jiangsu province, for instance, the deceased were placed on a paved stone surface or in small stone chambers, then earthen mounds were built above them (perhaps to avoid damage from the high water table). In the mountainous regions of Fujian, Jiangxi, Hunan, and Guizhou, wooden coffins were put in caves in high cliffs. And in Yunnan, coffins were made of stone slabs. None of these funerary practices were prevalent or even common elsewhere in China.

In the Zhou dynasty, the social status of a tomb's occupant was extremely important. The status of an individual determined not only whether ramps would be used in constructing the tomb, but also the number of coffins in which he or she could be buried. Sumptuary laws allowed for seven layers of coffins for the royalty, five for feudal lords, three for officials, and a double coffin for lower-ranking officials. Similar rules governed burial goods. Royalty and ministers of the state were allowed to be buried with nine bronze tripods, high-ranking officials with seven, officials with five, and officials of the lowest ranks with three or only one. Excavations of tombs, however, show that these regulations were not strictly enforced. Apparently some officials received special privileges and sometimes the burial traditions were simply ignored.

Architectural Achievements of the Three Dynasties

During the period of the Three Dynasties, architectural planning made more elaborate building projects possible. Site surveys were almost certainly made and plans drawn before major building got under way, although evidence for this is much better for the Zhou dynasty than for earlier times. When King Wu of Zhou decided to build his capital at Luoyi, for example, he sent his highest-ranking official, the duke of Zhou, to survey the site. The event is so famous that it is recorded in illustrated versions of early Chinese histories. But plans were made not only for cities; they were also probably part of the preconstruction process for the palaces and altars of Yongcheng and for the royal tombs at Xibeigang. Surviving plans include that for the Zhongshan necropolis, discussed earlier, and a site design drawn in quartz and mica discovered inside the walls of one of the residential sectors of the Shang site in Hebei.

Although scholars have not been able to determine the purpose of every Three Dynasties structure based on foundation remains, we do know that different buildings served different purposes. Kiln sites and remnants of ancient bronze foundries are easily recognizable, and there is good evidence that certain individual structures were offices, prisons, residences, or altars.

In these years the Chinese refined their use of wood and earth, which had long been primary construction materials. By the beginning of the Shang dynasty, the Chinese were using the timber frame, a support system composed of vertical columns and horizontal beams. And in an improvement of the mortise and tenon system, interlocking pieces known as *dou* (blocks) and *gong* (arms) were used to support roofs. Evidence of these wooden pieces as well as doors and windows comes from engraved bronze vessels and from the joining system used in wooden coffins. Earth was used to make city walls and building foundations. Most often, thin layers of earth were rammed together with pieces of wood and rubble in them. There is some evidence that certain buildings, perhaps for the ruling elite, were elevated on extremely high foundation platforms.

During the Three Dynasties period, pottery or brick tiles were used for flooring, roof decoration, drainage pipes, and as the railings around wells. Bronze fittings were also added to buildings. These additions improved the structural quality and helped buildings last. Charcoal and clay, used as sealants during the Zhou dynasty, thwarted water damage and tomb robbers.

The various degrees of social rank of the nobility are evident in palaces and official buildings. In the Shang dynasty, ramps led up to the tombs of kings but only simple pit tombs were dug for other members of high society. By the Zhou dynasty, the architecture of the aristocracy and rulers was very much a system of silent visual symbols, so that if the textual specifications were followed (and tomb excavation shows that this was not always the case), the rank of the highest-ranking resident was apparent from the exterior of a town or building complex. Regulations about color, for example, specified

that cinnabar symbolized the ruler; black, high-ranking officials; blue, officials; and yellow, lesser officials.

Units of measurement appear in Zhou writings, and it is possible that standardized sizes of building parts emerged at this time. If so, this practice would have been a predecessor of the comprehensive standardization of imperial building that occurred in medieval China. In the Zhou dynasty, *gui,* a carriage track, was the unit for measuring the width of a road. The heights and widths of city walls were measured in terms of *ren, zhi,* and *xun*—which, unlike gui, had no relation to actual objects. Individual buildings were measured in *zhang, chi,* and *cun,* all still in use. And the area of a room was measured in *yan,* or mats.

As technical advances made it possible to build taller structures, their exteriors changed. Reconstructions of buildings illustrated in this chapter reflect the opinion among Chinese archaeologists and architectural historians that three roof types were built during the Three Dynasties: roofs with four slopes, and thus four roof ridges emanating from the central or main roof ridge (a predecessor of a later roof style called *si'a);* roofs with two slopes and two flat building sides; and pointed roofs. Besides some pillars that were color-coded to the rank of the occupant, only two colors were typically used in Chinese architecture of the earliest dynasties: white, for whitewashed walls, and black for the floors.

Decoration flourished during the Three Dynasties, and the patterns are distinctive (fig. 1.20). Bricks in the shape of the Chinese character *shan* (mountain) and drain pipes with tiger-head patterns have been excavated at the Eastern Zhou capital of Yan. Concentric circles, spirals, mythical and ferocious beasts, mountains floating in clouds, and multiple rings are among the patterns preserved in ceramic tiles and hollow brick tiles. Triangles, rippling waves, and swirls appear on bronzes and lacquerware.

By the close of the Three Dynasties period, the rudiments of construction to satisfy fundamental human needs and aspirations had developed into a coherent, although in some ways still limited, structural system. The great capitals with palaces at their centers testify to considerable architectural accomplishments: the development of techniques for ramming earth, the building of complex wooden structures, the manufacture and utilization of new building materials, the design of buildings and layout of cities, and the use of color and decoration. Upon the unification of China under the First Emperor, Qin Shi Huangdi, Chinese architecture was able to develop rapidly because of the stable groundwork that had emerged during these early years.

CHAPTER 2

The Qin and Han Dynasties

LIU XUJIE

If Chinese architecture took root during the Three Dynasties, it first flowered when China was unified under the dynasties of Qin and Han. Qin Shi Huangdi, the first emperor of a unified China, built enormous palaces and mausoleums, including his famed underground world populated with terra-cotta warriors, horses, and chariots. He connected the defensive barriers along the northern border to make the Great Wall, built the Lingqu canal, and created roads that made transit across China possible. Qin's grand projects were matched architecturally by those of the far more long-lived Han dynasty. The Han capital cities of Chang'an and Luoyang were filled with many palaces (some used for governance and others for more pleasurable pursuits), gardens, and parks. To the north, the Han expanded and improved the Great Wall.

Through it all, the wooden structures that had slowly evolved over previous eras grew far more complex, sophisticated, and strong. The more stable timber frames made it possible to build high wooden towers, which gradually replaced the high-platform buildings long associated with the Three Dynasties period. Complementing these breakthroughs were advances in brick making, masonry construction, and arches of various kinds, as well as the first use of iron parts on a significant scale.

Details, figure 2.4 *(opposite)* and figure 2.15 *(above)*

The Qin

Though Qin was originally a small vassal state on the western edge of Zhou territory, by late in the Warring States period (475–221 B.C.E.) a series of reforms had dramatically increased its importance. In particular, Shang Yang, a Qin official, espoused Legalism (one of the "hundred schools of thought" that stressed the role and power of the state), and Gongsun Long, a later leader associated with "the Chinese Sophists," proposed sweeping changes that propelled the Qin's rapid rise to power. After almost a century of warfare, the Qin emerged victorious over their archrivals, the Qi, in 221 B.C.E. Qin Shi Huangdi, as he became known, ruled an empire significantly larger than that of the Zhou dynasty.

The First Emperor, fearful of uprisings among the conquered former states, centralized power and suppressed both the slightest deviation from his severe laws and any schools of thought that might contend with his vision of Legalism. As part of this effort, he unified China's systems for law and bureaucracy, weights and measures, and writing, and he standardized currency, measurements, and conveyances. But his excesses and severe policies eventually cost the Qin their empire: when he died, rebellion spread throughout China and led to the fall of the Qin in 206 B.C.E.

What we know about Qin city planning comes from the remains at Xianyang, which was the Qin capital from 350 B.C.E. to the end of the empire. Situated on the north bank of the Wei River, the city measured 6 kilometers east to west by 7.5 kilometers north to south. Because the city was destroyed in wars at the end of the Qin empire, and because the course of the Wei River has shifted four kilometers northward, little of the Qin capital survives and not much excavation has occurred there. But pieces of the north, west, and south walls enclosing the Qin palace area, the "palace city," have been found and indicate that this area was in the northern part of the larger walled capital. The palace area is believed to have been about 900 meters east to west and 580 meters north to south. The foundations of eight palatial buildings have been located; so have five workshops west of the main palace area and one to its east. Pottery workshops believed to have been used by the local population were found about 4 kilometers west of the palace, as were more than one hundred wells. An additional palace, accessible via a long bridge across the Wei River, was built to its south.

The Han

Xianyang was destroyed at the end of the Qin dynasty. A new capital for the Han, Chang'an, was created nearby, by the leader Liu Bang, known as Han emperor Gaozu after he became the first emperor of the new dynasty. The Han city was roughly rectangular, with a 22.7-kilometer outer wall that enclosed an area of 35 square kilometers (fig. 2.1). Each wall had three gates. The major thoroughfares in the city passed through two of these gates, one northward through Heng Gate to the Wei River and the other eastward through Xuanping Gate in the direction of Luoyang. After passing through the Heng Gate one could follow its street, which was a remarkable 50 meters wide, for 5.5 kilometers, almost the entire north–south span of the city. In all there were eight main roads running north–south and nine east–west, interconnecting a city that grew to some 240,000 residents by the end of the Western Han.

Most of the space inside the Han capital was taken up by five palace complexes: Changlegong, Weiyanggong, Guigong, Beigong, and Mingguanggong (in this context, the transliteration *gong* means "palace" or "palace complex"). There were also government offices, arsenals, and two markets. Commoners usually lived outside the city walls, in simple dwellings to the north or east. The ancestral temple and the soil altar were near the ritual complex

Figure 2.1. Plan of Chang'an, Western Han capital

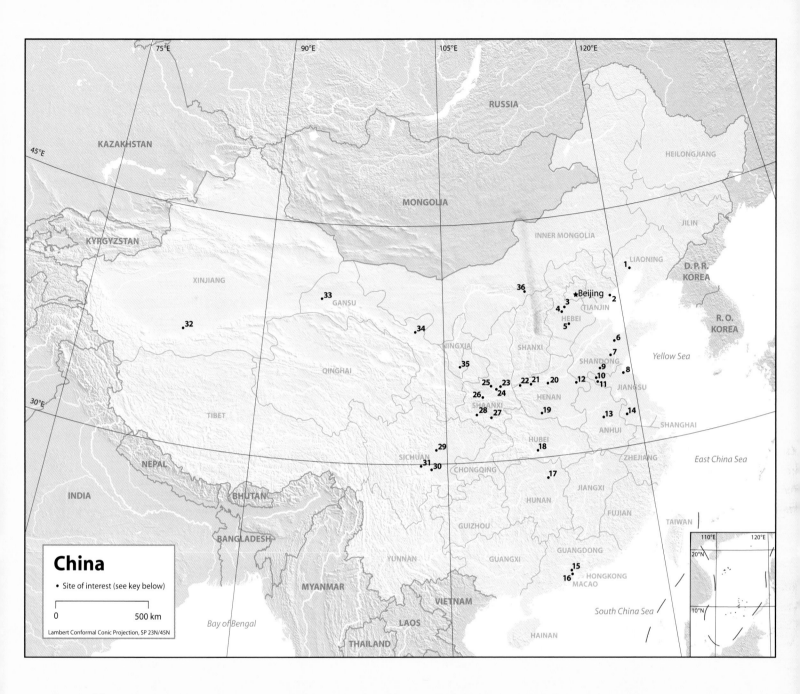

Map 2.
Qin and Han Sites

Beigong
(North Palace)

Nangong
(South Palace)

Luo River

Figure 2.2. Plan of Luoyang, Eastern Han capital, redrawn from
Wang Zhongshu, *Han Civilization* (New Haven: Yale University
Press, 1982)

south of the city. During the long reign of Emperor Wudi
of Han (140–87 B.C.E.), Zhang Palace, Jianzhang Palace,
and Shanglin Park were built to the west.

The plan of Han Chang'an did not follow the prescription of the *Rituals of Zhou*: that is, there was no symmetrical scheme with a palace area in the center and
regularly laid-out streets. One reason for this departure
is that the new palaces, Weiyang and Changle, were built
before the completion of the southern wall (Changle
stood on the ruins of a Qin palace). Geography also
played a role — the northwestern wall followed the bank
of the Wei River. But although palaces may not have
been at the geographic center of Han Chang'an, they
were a vital part of the city. No later Chinese capital
would have so many palaces, with such a large percentage of the walled part of the city devoted to them.
Unfortunately, this spectacular city is not well preserved.
During the last years of the Han dynasty, war broke out
in the capital, which led to almost total destruction of
the city and abandonment of the site.

After the death of the powerful Han Wudi, corruption
was rampant. At the beginning of the first century C.E.,
power was usurped by Wang Mang, a family member of
an empress, who began a ruling dynasty that called itself
Xin. The era of Xin ascendancy (9–23 C.E.) is thus often
called the Wang Mang interregnum.

The new ruler did not last. Neither the Chinese peas-
antry nor the former Han nobility accepted Wang Mang,
and in 23 C.E., the Han court was restored. The new
ruler, Emperor Guangwu (r. 25–57 C.E.), moved his capital eastward to Luoyang. The period from 23 C.E. to the
true collapse of Han, in 220, is thus known as the Eastern
Han, or Later Han, dynasty.

To move the capital eastward was to follow in the foot-
steps of Zhou rulers from the first millennium B.C.E. Indeed, Chang'an and Luoyang were to be among the most
popular locations for imperial city construction through
the rest of China's history. Yet like Han Chang'an, the
second Han capital was not built on the Zhou site; rather,
palaces that had existed from Qin times were rebuilt or
reused. Building had also occurred at Luoyang during the
first half of the Han dynasty, when it had been a capital
city, but not the main one.

Luoyang was smaller than Chang'an during the Han —
only about thirteen kilometers around at its outer wall —
and it had two significant features not present in the first
Han capital. First, the shape of the outer wall was a
quadrilateral, almost rectangular (fig. 2.2). Although like
so many earlier Chinese cities natural features helped
define its boundaries (in this case, the Luo River in the
south and the Mang Mountains in the north), the end
result was a city with three much straighter walls than
those at the earlier Han imperial city. Second, Luoyang
had two palace areas, north and south. Each emperor
chose one as his primary official and residential complex,
but the two were joined by a covered walkway so that he
could pass secretly between them.

Eastern Han Luoyang had ten major thoroughfares,
five east–west and five north–south. As in Chang'an,
main streets passed through the twelve city gates — four
at the south (whose ruins are now beneath the Luo
River), two at the north, and three each on the east and
west sides. The southern gates on the east and west sides
of the city were joined by a boulevard 2.8 kilometers
long. Twenty-four streets are named in texts about Han
Luoyang, and excavation has shown them to have been
between twenty and forty meters wide.

In response to the unprecedented economic development during the Western and Eastern Han dynasties, many

cities and towns sprang up away from the national capitals. Some Han cities rose at sites that had urban histories from the period of the Warring States, such as Linzi and Handan. Other Han cities with histories that dated to the first millennium B.C.E. or even earlier —Wan, Jiangling, Nanjing, Hefei, Panyu, and Chengdu —remain cities today. Little is known about the plans of most of these in Han times. One exception is a Han city in Nanyang county, inside the area associated with Wangcheng of the Zhou dynasty. The city in Nanyang county was nearly square, about 1.4 kilometers on each side, surrounded by a wall six meters wide at its base. Excavation of administrative structures, storage buildings, residences, and wells has shown that ceramic tile was used on walls, floors, and well platforms, and in the drainage system.

The scattering of towns and cities during the Han dynasty meant that each was encouraged to develop its own defense system. Enter *wubao,* also known as *wubi:* fortified structures where many people lived in the manner of clan communities in earlier times. From the outside, wubao resembled castle towns, with high walls, deep moats, and high turrets at the corners of the walls and in the center. Wubao are believed to be represented in a mural from an Eastern Han tomb found in Lujiazhuang, Anping county, Hebei, and in elaborate pottery models for tombs unearthed at Mayinggang in Guangzhou, Suiyang East Village in Henan, and Leitai in Wuwei county, Gansu (fig. 2.3). The larger wubao were as large as villages, and the smaller ones were more on the scale of courtyard-style residences. Some had adjoining farmland, pens for domesticated animals, and ponds. Most wubao were entered by a gate at the center of the south wall and had a courtyard behind the entrance. Inside the courtyard were the main halls as well as subsidiary buildings, such as kitchens, lavatories, and pigsties. The back gate was not directly across from the front one; rather, it was in the north corner of the east wall.

The Great Wall

While cities were being transformed, the tremendous effort to build the Great Wall began. During the Warring States period, the states of Qin, Yan, and Zhao had erected walls along their northern borders to help defend against potential invaders, such as the Xiongnu. The First Emperor of China improved this system by connecting the pieces of wall and adding beacon towers. Remains of the wall are evident in Guyuan today (fig. 2.4). During the reign of Han

Figure 2.3. Pottery model of architecture excavated in Wuwei county, Gansu province

Figure 2.4. Remains of the Qin Great Wall in Ningxia
Hui autonomous region

emperor Wudi, wars were launched against the Xiongnu, and the Great Wall was extended to the region of Dunhuang in Gansu on the west and northward beyond the Tianshan mountain range. At this time, parts of the wall were actually doubled in thickness, and the cities, towns, defensive passes, and beacon towers were all fortified to create a large and comprehensive system of defense.

The border defense system had five basic architectural components. First were the border towns, the equivalents of county-level administrative posts. Of varying shapes, most of them had moats, walls, gates, wall towers, corner towers, streets, administrative offices, shops, residences, and storehouses. Some had additional wall fortifications and beacon towers. The border towns were the administrative and military centers, and garrisons, of their regions.

Second, checkpoints were usually situated on major roads at dangerous places of strategic importance. Most were built as part of walls, gates, or other defensive structures. Relief sculpture from the Han dynasty includes numerous examples of two-story and three-story towers. Third were the fortifications, wall-enclosed entities similar to border towns but administratively one rank lower. Square or rectangular in plan and ranging from about 50 to 150 kilometers square, the outer walls were made of pounded earth or stone. Often the additional wall fortification was placed at the entrance gate. Deep moats and spikes made the perimeter even more impenetrable.

The beacon towers, the fourth component, were high towers on platforms where lookout guards could warn of an enemy attack with smoke signals. The towers were positioned on or inside the Great Wall about 130 meters apart. Circular or square with earth or stone foundations, their diameters range from 5 to 30 meters, and they may have been 10 meters high or more (fig. 2.5). Below the towers were small rooms that served as living quarters for the guards. The fifth and final component was the wall and moats.

Whenever possible, the wall part of the Great Wall backed onto mountains or was positioned to make full use of strategic vantage points at China's northern border. In other words, the Great Wall was a combination of natural topography and man-made construction. Some of the wall was made of pounded earth and paved with stone. Other parts used Chinese tamarisk and reeds, bundled and arranged in a checkerboard pattern on the ground, then filled in with sand and stone. Next, tamarisk and reed were piled on the flat surface to form the wall face. When made wet and allowed to harden, it made an extremely durable wall. Examples can be seen near Dunhuang, where portions about three meters thick and four meters high survive.

Figure 2.5. Han beacon tower

Palaces of the Qin

Information about palatial architecture of the Qin comes from both excavated evidence and literary records. Between 1974 and 1982, three large groups of palatial foundations were discovered in Xianyang. The largest and most magnificent, and a fairly complete one, is Palace 1, a two-level building complex with the upper level raised about six meters higher than the lower one (fig. 2.6). This upper-level, L-shaped complex extended sixty meters east to west and forty-five meters north to south. The principal hall was located roughly in the middle, with a large pillar positioned in its center. This hall could be entered on all but its west side. To its north, the hall joined the covered arcade that surrounded the entire palace complex. A smaller hall to its southeast, with a single southern entry, is thought to have been the emperor's residence. Additional rooms whose purposes are still unknown were located west of the principal hall. All these structures are believed to have been on the upper level.

The lower level joined the upper level on the north and south. To the south, adjoining the enclosing corridor, were five rooms. On the eastern side were bathing chambers, suggesting that the concubines and palace ladies may have lived there. Two large rooms on the northern side of the upper level might have been residences for palace guards. Both levels were enclosed by covered corridors, and there were drainage and sewage systems on the perimeters. Staircases were located on the east and west sides of the palace complex.

The L-shaped plan has led to the theory that a palace complex similar to this one, perhaps even symmetrically placed, was located to its east. Such a structure has not

Figure 2.6. Reconstruction drawing of Palace 1 in the Qin capital Xianyang, near Chang'an, Shaanxi province

yet been found, but another palace complex, number 3, has been unearthed south of Palace 1. Although nearly destroyed, traces of wall paintings have been discovered on what may have been the side walls of the surrounding covered arcade. Delicate renderings of figures, horses and carriages, and trees in red, black, blue, green, yellow, white, and other colors further illustrate the daily life of Chinese royalty at this time.

The Xianyang palaces were not spacious enough for the ambitious First Emperor and the many activities of his court. So in 212 B.C.E., the thirty-fifth year of his reign, he built audience and palatial halls south of the Wei River in what had until that time been Shanglin Park. The halls must have been breathtaking. The First Emperor's biography in *Shi ji* (Records of the Historian) describes one palace compound alone measuring 675 meters east to west by 112 meters north to south. Ten thousand people could sit in the upper story, and flagpoles more than 10 meters high rose from the lower story. Surrounding this were elevated pathways said to provide passage from the lower story of Epang Palace to the mountains to the south. According to *Guanzhong ji* (Record of Guanzhong [the Chang'an region]), "The summit of the Southern Mountains was designated to be the gate of the palace." Equally impressive was the elevated passageway that crossed over the Wei River to connect the Epang Palace with Xianyang. This was in imitation of a heavenly corridor described in *Shi ji* that leads from the Heavenly Apex star across the Milky Way to the Royal Chamber Star. *Guanzhong ji* also tells us: "[The halls of Epang Palace] were a thousand *bu* [1,350 meters] east to west and three hundred *bu* [about 400 meters] north to south. Ten thousand men could be entertained there." The Qin period is the earliest in China so far for which written texts and excavation seem to verify the claims of each other.

Epang Palace was said to be so large that when it was destroyed by conquering armies at the fall of the Qin, the fire burned for three months. Although this is probably an exaggeration, the site was certainly enormous. Archaeological surveys have shown the complex to be about 1,400 meters east to west by 450 meters north–south. In the back part, a pounded-earth foundation perhaps 7 or 8 meters high has been uncovered, showing a section of the rammed-earth platform on which the palace stood. These dimensions are close to those described in *Guanzhong ji,* but not so similar to those provided in *Shi ji*—perhaps because the local record was written significantly later. Moreover, only limited excavation has been possible. It is also conceivable that grander structures are yet to be found. If building platforms of 8 meters or more were standard in the back part of the palace complex, for example, one might assume that the front halls would be even higher.

The palaces featured ornate and varied tiles and ceramics. The tile patterns included sunflower designs, animals, leaves, and whorls. At least one floor tile had characters lauding the Qin with the saying "The whole empire is filled with subjects, the annual harvest has all ripened, may no person go hungry on the streets" (fig. 2.7). The costs for Epang Palace, in human labor and building materials in the third century B.C.E., must have been tremendous. But the undertaking fits the image of the First Emperor, documented in later texts and memorialized in the Great Wall, as unparalleled in his ambition, wealth, and quest for monuments to his importance.

The image of the emperor was further strengthened by the many detached "traveling palaces" built during the Qin dynasty, especially after the First Emperor had unified the seven states. Qin Shi Huangdi in particular embarked on frequent inspection tours of his empire, and he stayed at such palaces throughout the country. The number of these traveling palaces was staggering. It is known that he used remains of palaces in the six conquered states for this purpose, but he also built many palaces anew. According to *Shi ji,* "He built three hundred traveling palaces in Guanzhong [near Chang'an in the Wei River Valley] and four hundred beyond." The text continues: "Southward alongside the Wei River, and eastward from Yong Gate to the rivers Jin and Wei, were palatial rooms and scenic towers, all interconnected by elevated walks and covered ways. They were filled with beautiful women, draperies and wall hangings, bells and drums." The rules of the palaces were extremely strict. The women were assigned to specific palaces and forbidden to leave them, and "anyone revealing which palace the emperor was visiting at any particular moment was put to death."

Within two hundred *li,* or one hundred kilometers, of Xianyang were 270 palatial and official structures, all interconnected via covered ways *(fudao)* and paved passageways *(yongdao).* The architectural styles were varied, for "each time he conquered a prince, he erected a palace in imitation of the one he had acquired north of Xianyang." The discovery at Xianyang of ceramic roof tiles identical to those found at sites of the Chu and Yan states seems to confirm this claim.

The traveling palace farthest from the capital is in Jieshi on the shore of the Bohai Sea. Sites of Qin and Han palaces also have been uncovered at the seashore in Suizhong county of Liaoning. Among the remains there are pounded-earth foundations, hollow brick tiles, roof tiles, pieces of ceramic brick with patterns or other markings distinctive of the period, and watchtowers at Heishantou (fig. 2.8).

Figure 2.7. A brick floor tile, 27 by 31 centimeters by 4 centimeters thick, from Epang Palace of the Qin dynasty. Inscribed in relief on the tile are twelve characters that read "The whole empire is filled with subjects, the annual harvest has all ripened, may no person go hungry on the streets."

Figure 2.8. Remains of watchtowers at Heishantou, Suizhong, Liaoning province

Palaces of Western Han Chang'an

Of the six palaces shown in the plan of Han Chang'an in fig. 2.1, three are somewhat well known through textual records and excavation. The Changle Palace complex was begun in 202 B.C.E., the fifth year of the reign of Emperor Gaozu, on the ruins of the former Qin detached palace Xinglegong. The first formal palace of the Western Han dynasty, Changlegong took two years to complete, was 2.9 kilometers east to west and 2.4 kilometers north to south, and occupied one-sixth of the total area of the Western Han capital. Records show that the palace had a gate on each side and that the eastern and western gates were framed by towers. It also had a front hall for large public events and a back hall for residences, in keeping with the ideal layout proposed in the *Rituals of Zhou*. In 198 B.C.E., the court was moved west to Weiyang Palace, making it the political center of the Western Han dynasty, and Changlegong became the residence of the empress dowager.

The Weiyang Palace complex, which occupied one-seventh of the city's area, measured 2.25 kilometers east to west and 2.15 kilometers north to south. Although slightly smaller than Changle Palace, its buildings were far more grand. Like the Changle Palace complex, Weiyanggong seems to have had an entry gate at each side, with gate towers flanking at least two of them. At Weiyanggong there were forty or more halls, six hills, thirteen ponds, and about one hundred residential structures. Among them was a centrally located pounded-earth foundation about 200 meters by 350 meters, and 15 meters high. Believed to have been the front hall of the complex, it was situated alongside Longshou plain (fig. 2.9). The remains of palace complexes 2 and 3 are north and northwest of the front hall. Judging from objects excavated at the two sites, Palace 2 is thought to have been the residential space of imperial concubines and Palace 3 may have been offices for holding court. Of particular interest have been tunnels discovered underneath palace complex 2. Made with walls of mud and earth that were supported by wooden pillars and then whitewashed, and with floors paved in brick, these may have been the sort of underground passageways for imperial escape described in texts about the palace system of the later Eastern Han dynasty.

North and slightly west of Weiyang Palace was the Gui Palace complex. Its foundation was rectangular, approximately 800 by 1,800 meters. Constructed in 101 B.C.E., during the reign of Han emperor Wudi, it was a residence of the crown prince during the reign of Emperor Yuandi

(48–32 B.C.E.) and subsequently a home for the empress dowager. Among its halls were Hongning (Swan's Peace) Hall and Mingguang (Bright Radiance) Hall. An elevated passageway, presumably above the Zhicheng Gate thoroughfare, connected it to Weiyanggong. In addition to these elaborate administrative palaces, Han Wudi was an enthusiastic builder of detached palaces and parkland; his reign was a high point during the dynasty for such construction. Most of the detached palaces and other recreational spaces of the Western Han either had been used by Qin emperors or were rebuilt on former Qin sites.

The Jianzhang Palace complex, for example, was a place for the emperor's leisure situated outside the walls of Western Han Chang'an, to the city's west. Construction began in the last years of the second century B.C.E., more than two-thirds of the way through the reign of Han Wudi. The complex was connected to Weiyanggong by means of elevated corridors that passed above the outer city wall. The principal entry to Jianzhang Palace was a gate in its south wall. Within the complex were more than twenty halls besides the front hall, and a large body of water known as Taiye Pond. Three sacred islands there symbolized the isles of the immortals. Han texts, such as *Shi ji* and *Sanfu huangtu* (an illustrated description of the three imperial districts of the Han capital collated in the late eighteenth century), describe two platforms. Jiantai, the first, rose more than seventy meters, higher than any structure in the capital, and was where the emperor could make contact with the spirit world. On top of Shenmingtai, the second, was a bronze statue of an immortal holding a plate to catch dew from the "pure sphere beyond the clouds."

The emperor could also relax at Shanglin Park, located on the south bank of the Wei River. It had been parkland under the Qin dynasty, and continued to be used as such early in the Western Han period. During the reign of Emperor Wudi, however, the site was expanded. Historical records say it became 340 li square, with scores of palatial halls (one record says thirty-six, another says seventy). When complete, it was a huge detached palace complex with many natural scenic spots — hills, dense wooded areas, and lakes — for imperial rest and enjoyment. There the emperor could watch fish swim in the lakes, take in a dog or horse race, cheer on a favorite contender in an animal fight, and appreciate beautiful flowers and exotic trees. The largest body of water in Shanglin Park was Kunming Lake, which in former times had been used for naval training. Along the shores of the lake were many high buildings as well as stone sculptures of huge sea creatures and legendary Chinese heroes.

Figure 2.9. Remains of the foundation of the front hall of Weiyang Palace, Chang'an

According to literary sources, more than two thousand kinds of plantings were brought to Shanglinyuan from all over the empire (*yuan* means "park"). Shanglin Park was also a gathering place for creatures of the sea and land, so that besides being a place of natural beauty it was where the imperial family could hunt wild animals.

The foundations of Luoyang's palace complexes and of other structures inside the city walls have not been excavated. But texts inform us that the northern palace had more lakes and gardens, and thus was more popular, than the southern one. The Han emperors had residences in addition to the two main palaces inside this city, suggesting that, as was the case at the earlier Han capital, Luoyang's architecture was primarily imperial, although high-ranking officials were allowed to have residences inside the city walls. A granary and arsenal were located in the north of Luoyang, and most of the government offices were in the southeast. Luoyang had three main markets: a gold market northwest of the South Palace inside the city walls, a horse market outside the city walls to the east, and a third market, known simply as south market.

Sacrificial Temples and Ritual Structures of Qin and Han

Imperial worship and sacrifice in Qin and Han times were primarily devoted to heaven and the imperial ancestors, and remains of several ritual structures have been identified in both Han capitals. According to *Shi ji,* the Qin performed sacrifices known as *zhi,* which followed rituals established about four hundred years earlier. Dur-

ing the zhi, which probably were performed on high ground in forested areas, offerings were made to the four deities, each from a different direction and represented by the colors white, azure, yellow, and red. Sacrifices to the dynastic ancestors also were performed in the ancestral temple of the imperial capital.

After unification, Qin emperor Shi Huangdi transformed Xin Palace, located in Weinan, into Ji Temple, a ritual structure for ceremonial offerings to the heavens. Shi Huangdi's real objective, however, was to have the temple used for sacrifices to him. Furthermore, he had an underground passageway built to connect the temple to his funerary complex in Lishan, which was also constructed during his lifetime. Upon the First Emperor's death, his son and successor turned that structure into the Ancestral Temple for the Emperor and abolished the system that had existed in Zhou times of *tianzi qimiao,* or "seven temples for the son of heaven."

The Han added to the rituals and beliefs that the Qin had established. They built a group of ritual structures in the southern suburbs of each of their capitals. Han Gaozu, founder of the dynasty, added himself as Black Ruler to the four deities worshiped by the Qin. And a full spectrum of sacrifices was offered to gods of heaven and earth, mountains and rivers, the sun and moon, the stars and planets. Shamans are believed to have performed many of the various sacrifices.

During his reign, Han Wudi turned to intermediaries between the spirit world and himself for help in his quest for immortality. For this purpose he had numerous shrines built for worship of the spirits, and promoted the performance of sacrifices to them. In Later Han times, a circular altar for worshiping heaven was built in the southern suburbs, and in the north a square altar for worshiping earth.

Initially the Han emperors followed the Qin practice of sacrificing to the ancestors at temples located inside the capital city. Gaozu, for instance, built temples to the legendary emperors and to his own father in Chang'an. Under Han emperor Huidi, however, the ancestral temples were moved alongside the imperial tombs — a system that was maintained until the end of the Western Han dynasty. When Wang Mang seized the throne, he adopted a "nine temple system." Its remains may be the eleven rectangular foundations, arranged in three rows, excavated in the southern suburbs of Chang'an. In Eastern Han times the tablets with the names of each emperor were gathered in a single ancestral temple that was divided into rooms for each ruler. This system was followed by later dynasties.

Ritual structures known as Mingtang and Biyong,

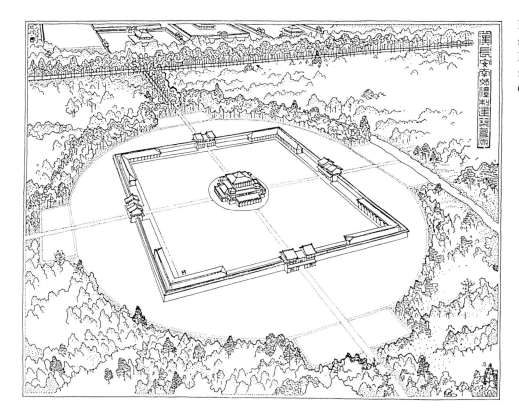

Figure 2.10. Proposed reconstruction drawing of the Mingtang and Biyong complex, from the Han period, found near Chang'an

sometimes translated as Hall of Light and Jade Ring Moat, were first built during the reign of Han Wudi to regulate the calendar and disseminate knowledge. With time, they came to be where the emperor was educated and offered enlightenment about texts. A building complex excavated in the southern suburbs of Han Chang'an, east of the remains associated with Wang Mang, has been identified as the composite ritual complex of Mingtang and Biyong (fig. 2.10). The exterior was a circular moat, and inside was a square enclosure surrounded by a wall. A gate opened at the center of each side of the square. In the very center was a twenty-sided bilevel structure elevated on a pounded-earth platform.

Han Religious Architecture

Daoism began at least as early as the Zhou dynasty, and was later associated with shamanistic practices and a quest for immortality. During the Han dynasty, Daoist buildings were constructed, though none so ancient has survived. By the end of the Han dynasty, Daoist schools of thought had been codified into a sort of religious system. Buddhism was also introduced to China during the last years of the Western Han dynasty. Han Mingdi (r. 58–76 C.E.) sent envoys as far west as India and welcomed the arrival of the Buddhist monks Kasyapa-Matanga (known in China as Zhufalan) and Gobharana

(Dharmaraksa, known to the Chinese as Shemoteng), Buddhist sutras, and Buddhist images. In 68 C.E., Mingdi established the Baimasi (White Horse Monastery) in his capital Luoyang. It has been said that its plan was based on an Indian Buddhist monastery, but there is no documentary evidence to prove this claim.

In the last years of the Eastern Han, Zhai Rong, a warlord who usurped power in Jiangsu, began a huge building program. In particular, he built a "pagoda shrine" in Xuzhou city of the province. Placed in the center of a monastery courtyard, the *stupa* (pagoda) had covered arcades and pavilions surrounding it. No fewer than three thousand worshipers are said to have witnessed the Bathing of the Buddha ceremony there. The architectural plan with its central pagoda is believed to have been imported from India, but the building materials and designs, which included timber-frame structures, seem to have been Chinese. Later, during the Northern and Southern dynasties, the central pagoda plan, or "pagoda courtyard" *(tayuan)* plan, was dominant in Buddhist architectural complexes in China, and was to inspire Buddhist construction in Korea and Japan.

Many rock carvings of Buddhist and Daoist images and inscriptions have been found on the walls of cliffs of Mount Kongwang in the vicinity of Lianyungang, Jiangsu province (fig. 2.11). Included there are Buddha images with nimbus flames behind their heads; a reclining image of the Buddha, probably a parinirvana scene, represent-

Figure 2.11. Cliff carvings at Mount Kongwang, Jiangsu
province, possibly depicting a standing Buddha and attendant

ing the death of the historical Buddha Sakyamuni; Buddhist disciples; as well as animals. At least some of these images were carved during the Later Han dynasty, making Mount Kongwang one of the earliest Chinese sites, if not the earliest, with rock-carved Buddhist imagery.

Mahao, Sichuan province, is a Later Han site with Buddhist imagery carved in a cave or cave-tomb. The site has fewer images than Mount Kongwang, but in contrast to the Jiangsu site, where many carvings are visible from the cliffs, the Sichuan site has images carved inside the caves. Both types of carvings, inside and outside, were derivative of Indian Buddhist cave architecture. Although Chinese artists continued both traditions for a long time, the carving of interior cave worship spaces eventually became the more popular.

Gardens

The private gardens of the Han nobility and wealthy merchants featured highly sophisticated landscape architecture. The Rabbit Garden of Prince Liangxiao of the Western Han, also known as East Garden, was one of the most famous. According to *Han shu* (Standard history of the Han), the garden was more than 300 li (150 kilometers) square with a great pond, palatial halls, and covered ways that joined the garden's architecture with that of the detached palace Pingtai more than 30 li away. Prince Liangxiao's own residence was northeast of the city of Suiyang. Liu Xin's (d. 23 C.E.) *Xijing zaji* (Miscellaneous notes on the Western Capital) tells us that inside Rabbit Garden were

> some one hundred "spirit mountains" composed of extraordinary stones, cliffs, and grottoes. There was also Yan Pond in which were Crane Isle and Wild Duck Islet. Palaces and towers were interconnected, all of them extending several tens of li. Exotic plantings, rare trees, and unusual creatures of the land, sea, and air filled his park. Day and night the prince and his guests went boating and fishing there. Besides palaces, towers, and other structures, the park was filled with many kinds of birds and beasts, as well as natural and perhaps man-made scenery.

Probably the most well-known Western Han garden belonged to Yuan Guanghan, a wealthy merchant. He built a garden four li east to west by five li north to south at the foot of Mount Beimang on the outskirts of the capital city, Chang'an. According to *Xijing zaji*, the park was spectacular. Rapids cascaded through man-made mountains taller than ten *zhang* (more than twenty meters), with eddies and whirlpools created in the river to form a home for nesting birds. Roaming throughout the park were rare and exotic beasts, including white parrots, purple mandarin ducks, yaks, and gray gaurs. The garden had an artificial mountain made of sand and pebbles, and ponds were surrounded by exotic trees and grasses. There were so many courtyards and causeways linking the buildings that one could scarcely maneuver through them. But the garden did not last. Yuan Guanghan was discovered to have been involved in criminal activity, forbidden from entering his garden, and eventually executed. Birds and beasts, plants and trees, all were confiscated by the emperor and removed for installation in Shanglin Park.

Although smaller than Rabbit Garden, the architecture, landscape, and plantings of Yuan Guanghan's private garden far surpassed the construction of Prince Liangxiao. Furthermore, Yuan Guanghan's garden had many more man-made features, including mountains, the sand-and-pebble beach, and waterways. Indeed, if the plantings and animals had not been of the highest quality and rarity, it is unlikely that they would have been moved to the emperor's own Shanglinyuan. Thus through the description of the garden of Yuan Guanghan we get a glimpse of imperial gardens of the Han, as well as an indication of the sophistication of landscape architecture at that time.

Han Residential Architecture

More is known about residential architecture of the Han than about that of any previous time period in China. In addition to building foundations uncovered at larger excavation sites such as cities, houses are depicted in relief sculpture that survives from Han tombs, and many models of houses have been excavated in Han tombs throughout China.

Most houses of the Han dynasty were not especially large. One house from the early part of the Western Han dynasty, for example, excavated in the western part of Luoyang, was nearly square, about 13.3 meters on each side, and enclosed by a pounded-earth wall 1.15 meters thick. The house had two entries, each about 2 meters wide. Just under the western wall inside the house was an earthen pit, probably used for cooking.

Han-period residential architecture has been uncovered in Niya in Xinjiang, where the foundation of an L-shaped house shows that it was divided into two rooms,

Figure 2.12. Funerary
pottery model of a
multistory building,
Han period, excavated in
Fucheng, Hebei province

Figure 2.13. Multistory
pottery tower excavated
from a Han grave in
Beijing

roughly north and south of each other. There were exterior and interior doors, each 1.25 meters wide. The north room had a small fireplace, whereas a larger, U-shaped fireplace was located in the south room. The larger heat source suggests that this was the main residential room.

From models, we know that the Xinjiang house was only one of many possible Han house plans. Various styles of buildings were constructed: square, I-shaped, corridor-enclosed, L-shaped, and north-and-south adjoining. Houses could have one or two rooms, multiple stories, and one or more courtyards around which rooms were arranged. Three varieties of post and lintel construction are believed to have been built: column and tiebeam (with a flat side facade beneath the roof eaves); column, beam, and strut, with gabled roof; and raised on stilts. Roofs could have one, two, or four sloping eaves projecting from the main roof ridge at the top of the building (figs. 2.12 and 2.13).

Hundreds of examples of relief sculpture and pottery models have been discovered in tombs near Chengdu, Sichuan province. Like all pictures in brick, these depictions are especially important because the tombs from which they come belonged not to emperors, or the highest-ranking nobility, but to Han China's upper middle class. Most of the Sichuan houses are two-chambered, with the principal room on the west and another on the east. A few, however, are more unusual. In one courtyard-style residence shown in a relief sculpture, the entrance is located on the west side of the south wall (fig. 2.14). Someone passing through the gate would first enter a front courtyard where animals were kept; to the east is a three-bay structure of column-and-tiebeam construction with a flat facade and overhanging eaves in front and back. Inside, two seated figures talk while eating. The two eastern courtyards show, in the north, a multistory tower, perhaps the artist's attempt to depict a structure that was actually attached to and projected beyond the courtyard

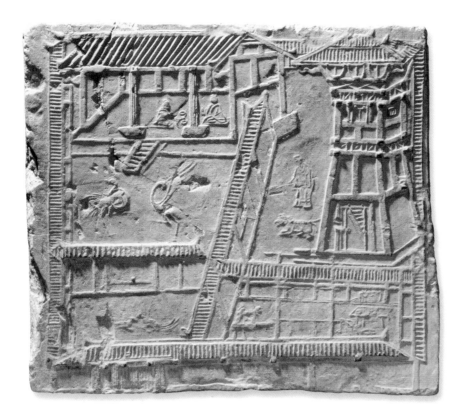

Figure 2.14. Relief sculpture showing a house with courtyards, from an Eastern Han tomb unearthed at Yangzishan, Chengdu

Figure 2.15. Detail of a painting from the wall of a Han tomb in Helinge'er, Inner Mongolia, second century C.E.

wall, and, in the south, the kitchen and additional storage space. The scene is probably a fairly realistic representation of the daily activities of a wealthy Han citizen.

The more well-to-do inhabitants of Han China probably had houses with gardens as shown in various relief sculptures and wall paintings from provinces throughout China (fig. 2.15). The biography of General Liang Ji of the Later Han dynasty in the history *Hou Han shu* (Standard history of the Later Han) describes one such home:

Ji constructed his residence using the top grade of wood. Both the public and private chambers had hidden and exposed parts. The rooms were so interconnected that they appeared like the interior of a cave. Pillars and walls were carved, with metal and lacquer filling in the spaces. The windows were covered with strips of the highest quality of silk, painted with floating clouds and immortal spirits. The platforms and pavilions were close enough together so as to see from one to the next. The flying beams and stone steps made it possible to cross between water and land. Gold, jade, and pearls, precious objects from exotic places, all were gathered here.

Some large residences of Han China were built like fortifications with high walls, corner watchtowers, and elevated passageways. These heavily protected homes probably would not have been permitted in China's big cities and towns.

The Tombs of Qin and Han

Qin Shi Huangdi's tomb, located in Lishan, southeast of the Qin capital Xianyang, is among the most well known and spectacular finds of Chinese archaeology. The hill beneath which the First Emperor of China was laid to rest has been known for centuries, and excavation in the area has been ongoing for more than twenty years. Much is known about the mausoleum complex, though to date Qin Shi Huangdi's corpse and the objects thought to be in its immediate vicinity remain untouched.

The funerary complex of the First Emperor of Qin was a doubly walled site oriented to the four cardinal directions. A tower was positioned at each corner of the outer wall. Along the center north–south line, south of the center, is the mound beneath which he is buried. It rises 76 meters and is 350 meters square; the orientation of the burial is believed to be east–west.

Although no wall parts survive today, we know that the outer wall of the complex measured 2,165 meters north to south and 940 meters east to west. Made of pounded earth, it was 6 meters thick. The main entrance was on the eastern side but each of the other walls also had a gate. The inner wall was 1,355 by 580 meters and had five entries, two at the north and one at each of the other sides. Four of them were in line with gates of the outer wall.

West of the funerary complex are pounded-earth foundations of various sizes believed to have been official and other auxiliary structures. To the north are the graves of more than twenty members of the Qin nobility. The most important excavations so far have occurred north of the road that leads to the east gate of the tomb. In the three burial pits, weapons, flagpoles, and life-size terra-cotta statues of those who served the emperor in life — his imperial bodyguard as well as cavalry and infantry — have been found (fig. 2.16). West of the mound another famous set of burial objects of the First Emperor was excavated: the exquisite gilt-bronze carriage, horses, and charioteer now in a museum adjacent the site of pit number 1. The grandeur, scale, and concept of the funerary complex built by the First Emperor initiated a new ideology of imperial burial in China that was to influence the tombs of all later rulers.

The emperors of the Western and Eastern Han dynasties are buried near their capital cities, Chang'an and Luoyang, respectively. The tombs of nine of the eleven emperors of the Western Han are spread along the north bank of the Wei River in the northern and eastern suburbs of Chang'an. The other two were built southeast of the capital. The names of each Han emperor's tomb and much about funerary rites in the Han dynasty have been known for centuries, because the information is preserved in historical and ritual texts. Excavation of the sites has shown as well that no two Western Han tombs were identical, although it seems that in general the Han royal mausoleums had square-shaped mounds enclosed by four-sided walls. Nor do any of the tomb remains follow exactly the spaces prescribed for rituals in front of the tumulus. All of the Western Han mausoleums were burned or pillaged when the dynasty fell, and little has been recovered from any of them.

Two general points can be made about the Western Han imperial burials. First, each emperor had his own funerary complex. This self-containment marks a clear separation from the burial system employed by Shang kings. Whether this was a Han innovation, an unfulfilled plan of Qin emperor Shi Huangdi, or a development undertaken by Zhou kings may one day be known if the Zhou rulers' burials are located and uncovered. For now these questions remain, although it is assumed that the Han emperors were aware of the burial customs of former dynasties.

Second, each Han empress was buried in a separate tomb alongside or near her husband's. In dynasties after the Han, we shall see imperial family cemeteries, individual imperial graves, and joint emperor-and-empress burials.

Liu Bang and his wife, Empress Lü, are buried beneath separate tumuli shaped like truncated pyramids, his to the northwest 280 meters from hers. His mound rose 32.8 meters and was 55 by 35 meters at the top sides; hers was slightly smaller. Each was enclosed by its own wall, and then by a common wall roughly 780 meters square. The enclosed space was known as a funerary park. Near the middle of the wall was a *sima* gate, the same name used to refer to gates of the outer walls of imperial cities, and at the wall corners were L-shaped towers. North of the "funerary park" and adjacent to it was a funerary city also enclosed by a wall.

Excavation of Han tombs so far suggests that each of the first seven Han emperors, at least, had a funerary town adjacent to or near his mausoleum. They were Gaozu's Changling, Huidi's Anling, Wendi's Baling, Jingdi's Yangling, Wudi's Maoling, Zhaodi's Pingling, and Xuandi's Duling. By the time Emperor Jingdi was buried in 140 B.C.E., just a few meters east of the Han founder's tomb, the funerary park had come to have front-and-back hall complexes, covered arcades, guardhouses, and gate towers. Although archaeological evidence has not yielded a plan of Jingdi's funerary town with walls that are as clearly defined as those of Han Gaozu's tomb, an entire underground funerary city definitely existed,

Figure 2.16. Part of the army of more than six thousand life-size terra-cotta warriors, found in pit number 1 of the tomb of Qin Shi Huangdi, Lishan, Shaanxi province

Figure 2.17. Funerary mound of the Western Han emperor Xuandi

populated by smaller versions of the renowned tomb figurines buried in Qin Shi Huangdi's funerary complex. Although a one-to-one correspondence between architectural remains and ritual is still impossible to establish, the ever more elaborate funerary parks and cities may be evidence that ritual sacrifices to the emperor known as *zhaomu,* once performed in the capital, may by this time have been moved closer to the tomb.

It also appears that Jingdi's tumulus was near the exact center of his funerary park. Thereafter this positioning became the tradition, though one that was not always followed. The mound of Jingdi's empress is northwest of the emperor's, in the same place with respect to her funerary park, but her complex was smaller. Jingdi's funerary town was two li east of his funerary park and contained five thousand households, most from the Guangdong region of southeastern China.

Records tell us, too, that members of rich and powerful families were moved to Han funerary towns from various parts of the country, and that some of the towns had as many as thirty thousand to fifty thousand inhabitants, or more. The funerary city of Han emperor Wudi, for example, is said to have had some three hundred thousand residents. By the time the seventh Han emperor, Xuandi, died in 49 B.C.E., funerary towns came to have government offices, shops, handicraft workshops, and even squarish-shaped wardlike divisions. It is unknown whether moving the population after the death of an emperor to a location so close not only to his tomb but also to the capital where his descendant ruled was a means of monitoring nobility who might potentially rise against the new ruler.

After the demise of Emperor Xuandi, the tradition of

funerary cities ended, although the site of Duling, his tomb, is one of the most completely excavated Han funerary complexes and has yielded extensive architectural remains. It is also one of the two tombs southeast of the capital city. Like the tomb of Han Jingdi, Xuandi's tumulus was located in the center of his funerary park (fig. 2.17). And like the earlier Western Han imperial tombs, there were sima gates to the funerary park near the center of each enclosing wall. Excavation has provided other details of the funerary complex, however, that for most other Han tombs are known only through written descriptions. South of the funerary park in which the tumulus lay was another enclosed complex that shared the eastern end of the larger complex's south wall. Known as the "residential" or "sleeping" park, the area was subdivided into a larger western precinct and a smaller, eastern one.

Along the main north–south line of the western enclosure was a main hall, the sleeping chamber that could be entered on the east and west sides, and a central front gate that joined the outer enclosure. This was probably a sacrificial hall. The western precinct contained several courtyards and buildings, arranged roughly symmetrically and believed to have been an administrative sector. The funerary mound of Xuandi's empress survives almost as it appeared in the last century B.C.E.

The tomb of Han Wudi is significant less for its scale and magnitude than as an example of the practice of rewarding deserving officials with burial close to the ruler they served. Such practices go back to at least the Shang royal tombs at Xibeigang, and it is likely that burials next to the tomb of the ruler had a continuous history through the Han dynasty.

In 117 B.C.E., in the twenty-fourth year of the reign of Han Wudi, the brilliant young military leader Huo Qubing died at the age of twenty-four. His military career lasted fewer than ten years, but during that time Huo led campaigns in the far west beyond Gansu province and into the Altai Mountains. Historical records indicate that he was responsible for the deaths of tens of thousands of China's enemies and that his military maneuvers led to the final Han victory against the Xiongnu. His funeral is said to have lasted a full day, with a cortege so long that it stretched uninterrupted from the capital to the tomb site.

For his services, General Huo was awarded a tomb site two kilometers northeast of the eventual site of his emperor's tomb, and some of Huo's relatives received burial rights near his. Moreover, the Han general had life-size stone sculptures erected at the approach to his grave, including the famous statue of the horse trampling a barbarian, symbolic of Huo Qubing's victories (fig. 2.18). Though the first appearance of sculpture along the approach to a tomb has not been determined, it certainly existed during the Han dynasty. Eventually the paths to Chinese imperial tombs were lined by monumental images of men, animals, and mythological beings, and became known as "spirit paths."

Figure 2.18. Statue of a horse trampling a barbarian, from the front of the tomb of Huo Qubing

The imperial tombs of the Eastern Han were destroyed so completely that excavation tells us little about their sizes or shapes. Located in the suburbs of Luoyang, they are divided into two groups, seven southeast of the city and four in the north. What little we know comes by way of historical records. Dimensions of the mounds of Later Han imperial tombs are recorded as between 136 and 380 bu (paces), and their heights ranged from 18.15 to 49.5 meters. Today their bases average about 10 meters on a side. Sleeping chambers and auxiliary buildings for guards were in the immediate area of the mausoleums. By this time, the practice of building funerary cities had ended. Compared with the traditions of the Western Han, the Luoyang imperial tombs were significantly smaller and humbler.

Besides the imperial tombs, there was a tremendous variety in nonimperial Han tomb construction: mausoleums ranged from earthen pits with wooden coffin chambers, to burial chambers carved into the walls of cliffs, to tombs built with solid and hollow brick and sometimes faced with decorated ceramic tiles, to combination brick and stone tombs, to stone tombs such as the one in Yi'nan, Shandong province (fig. 2.19). Often tombs had vaulted ceilings. One Eastern Han tomb of an unknown occupant in Luoyang has a chamber divided into two parts — a front part that includes a side room and a passage, and a rear part with a front hall and a rear room — as well as a partition between the parts. The tomb was built with hollow bricks (fig. 2.20). The front of

the pillar is engraved with designs of an azure dragon and a dragonlike animal. In general, commoners had the simplest tombs, often a single coffin placed into a dirt pit. Yet during the early years of the Han dynasty even members of the aristocracy were generally buried in simple pit tombs. The famous tombs of a Han marquis and his family excavated at Mawangdui in Hunan province, for example, in which two silk "guide to the soul" paintings were excavated along with thousands of other objects, were all simple pit tombs, though the coffins were made of lacquer and multilayered.

Tombs carved into natural rock are generally associated with Han nobility. The rock-carved tombs of Prince Liu Sheng and his wife, Dou Wan, date from the first half of the second century B.C.E. The inhabitants were interred in jade suits pieced together with gold thread. Tombs carved into natural rock are also found in

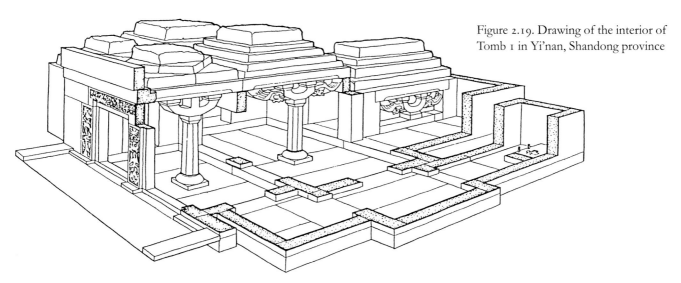

Figure 2.19. Drawing of the interior of Tomb 1 in Yi'nan, Shandong province

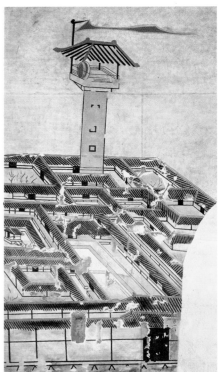

Figure 2.20 *(left)*. Chamber of an Eastern Han tomb at Luoyang

Figure 2.21 *(above)*. Mural showing city walls and gate tower in a Han tomb in Lujiazhuang, Anping county, Hebei province

Xuzhou, northern Jiangsu province, from the Western Han dynasty, and in Shandong province.

Brick tombs were built throughout the Han dynasty; subterranean tombs of hollow bricks were made even during the Warring States period. By the middle of the Western Han dynasty, bricks came to be smaller, segmented arches became common in ceiling construction, and tombs were often multichambered, with main chambers along the primary tomb axis and auxiliary rooms off it. Examples of the variety of brick tombs surviving in and around Luoyang include Han tombs noted for their richly painted interiors. Sometimes smaller or wedge-shaped bricks were mixed in with or lodged between larger ones to compensate for structural inadequacies; in other cases, segmented vaults were employed. In still other examples, stone slabs or stone strips were used in tomb construction, most often in Shandong and Jiangsu. Whether made of stone, brick, hollow brick (decorated tiles), or a combination, tomb interiors often were painted

or decorated with relief sculpture. The subjects of decoration were historical events, myths, legends, and scenes from the life of the tomb occupant. Important tombs had architecture aboveground as well as the underground chambers. Aboveground tomb construction included walls around the tomb precinct, gate towers at the entry, a line of monumental sculpture on either side of the approach to the tomb, stelae, and sacrificial temples.

Eastern Han tombs are some of the most extraordinary in Chinese history. It was not uncommon to have ten or more rooms arranged as three main chambers and connective corridors to side rooms. Tombs in the northern Chinese provinces of Hebei, Henan, and Inner Mongolia were covered with murals (fig. 2.21); those farther south in Shandong, Jiangsu, and Sichuan more often had relief sculpture carved into the interior walls or wall facings. Some of our most important information about Han urban and residential architecture survives in the form of wall decorations from these tombs.

Other Architectural Types of the Qin and Han Dynasties

Various other architectural forms are notable from these years. Gate towers were an important type of multistory architecture. They were often erected on either side of a road to mark the entry to a tomb, official building, altar, temple, palatial compound, pass, or even city. The exterior was composed of three parts: base, body, and eaves. Single-, double-, and triple-body gate towers were constructed, but those with three horizontally positioned bodies were built only for the emperor. The eave layer could be supported from underneath by diagonal struts or bracket sets. The support structures were often densely placed and very decorative. Gate towers were made of brick, earth, stone, or wood with earthen or stone cores. They were not intended to be climbed inside. Sometimes a set of eaves connected two of them, emphasizing their function as an entryway.

There are many references to such gate towers in Chinese literature. The southern entry to Qin Shi Huangdi's palace reportedly was framed by gate towers. And such towers at the Changle, Weiyang, and Jianzhang palace complexes of Western Han Chang'an are equally well known from literature. The earliest extant gate towers are from the Eastern Han dynasty. Actual gate towers survive, as do pictures of them in tomb painting and relief sculpture. Most of these examples and images are in Henan, Shandong, and Sichuan provinces.

The west gate tower from the tomb of Gao Yi in Ya'an county, Sichuan, is one of the most famous and best preserved. The upper section of the double gate tower rises 6 meters and is 1.6 meters wide and 0.9 meter thick (fig. 2.22). Including the body, or shaft, the gate tower is composed of thirteen stories from base to roof, each a different height. The lower section, without its base, is 3.39 meters high, 1.1 meters wide, and half a meter thick. Both the shaft and the upper section are carved with relief sculpture. The sculpture on the higher section begins with a procession, followed by mythological creatures above, then perhaps entertainers, and, highest, possibly another procession as well as animals and mythological beasts. The roof is a replica of a ceramic tile roof, including ridges, eaves, and eave tiles, as well as the bracket set and brace support system that would help hold up an actual roof.

In addition to gate towers, multistory timber-frame buildings probably first appeared in China during the middle of the Eastern Han period. Although no actual examples remain, pictures of such buildings survive in relief sculpture and tomb wall paintings, and small-

Figure 2.22. Double-body gate tower from the tomb of Gao Yi in Ya'an county, Sichuan province

scale versions have been found among excavated tomb objects. Most depict four-sided, probably square-based towers with three to five total stories (fig. 2.23). The existing technology probably limited construction to no more than five stories, although Han towers and pavilions, regardless of their actual heights, would make possible the technology required for Buddhist pagoda architecture in later centuries.

Illustrations, excavated objects, and the few extant remains together suggest that Later Han builders accepted not only the principle of narrowing the exterior size story by story toward the top of the structure, but also the existence of a superstructure marking each level on the exterior (presaging what came to be known as *pingzuo*) as well as the presence of simple hipped roofs with five ridges. In addition, there were probably bracket sets and braces to help support the weight of roof eaves, decorative balustrades on the pingzuo, lattice windows and doors on each level, and upturned roof eaves.

Figure 2.23. Pottery model of a multistory watchtower in Sanzhuang, Fucheng county, Hebei province

kets enclosed by walls on four sides, each with a centrally positioned gate (similar to any other city ward). The central tower is the most prominent and important feature of the brick tile. With two stories, its lower level was probably a government office and in its upper story hung the drum that was beaten to announce the opening and closing of the markets. The buildings inside the courtyard were positioned along the interior of the market wall. Presumably these were offices, residences of city officials, storage places such as granaries, and perhaps bathrooms. This layout for city markets was to be maintained through the Sui-Tang period.

Along with the various kinds of towers and pavilions, bridges are found in Han wall painting and relief sculpture. From the pictures and texts, it seems that at least two kinds of bridges existed in Han China. First were those bridges, either flat or segmented, supported by columns and beams built of both wood and stone. In either case, a wooden or stone pier was put into the water and the bridge was built on a frame above it. A rubbing of relief sculpture from the Wu Family Shrines in Shandong province shows a river crossing supported by a row of wooden posts.

In some illustrations a double line can be seen across the top of the bridge, probably indicating a two-lane road that made it possible for carriages to cross in opposite directions. Railings on either side protected those crossing the bridge from falling off. The Yangqu Stone Bridge, which spanned the Gu River in the Eastern Han capital, Luoyang, appears to have been of this type.

There are also pictures of segmented bridges, but from the side these looked more like a trapezoid than an arch. Such bridges could be ascended by a diagonal ramp from either side, and the central area, flat on top, was high enough for boats to pass beneath. From illustrations it is evident that high posts could be erected on either end.

Arched bridges constituted a second kind of bridge constructed during these years. A relief sculpture from a tomb in Sichuan province shows an arched bridge that was probably made in segments (fig. 2.25). The gradual curve made this sort of bridge easier to cross than those made of three straight parts. Segmented-arch bridges are not described in Han literature, but their depiction in sculpture suggests their use.

Connective roadways can also be considered a specialized architectural form of Han China. When elevated, they are called *zhandao* and *gedao*. Two other types of roadways, mentioned earlier, are yongdao and fudao. Yongdao, "connective passageways," were paved. When connective ways are underground, the Chinese term is

Areas for commerce and business had their own architectural needs. Details about marketplaces in Qin times are vague, but by the time Chang'an was the capital of the Western Han there were six markets in the western part of the city and three in the east, and Luoyang had three market areas (fig. 2.24). A brick tomb tile from Sichuan depicts a market divided by orthogonally arranged streets. This conforms closely with texts that describe Han mar-

Figure 2.24. Brick engraving of a market scene, showing a two-story tower, from an Eastern Han tomb in Sichuan

Figure 2.25. Brick relief showing a segmented-arch bridge, with horses, carriages, and acrobats

usually yongdao, whereas fudao, "covered ways," are usually aboveground. In both premodern and contemporary Chinese writings, however, yongdao and fudao, and occasionally gedao, may be used interchangeably.

Connective passageways in Han China had two main functions. Their primary purpose was to join one building to another. Texts tell us that zhandao and gedao, "elevated roadways," passed above city walls, supported from below by poles of different heights. Yongdao in Han Chang'an connected the Changle, Wei-yang, and Jianzhang palace complexes with the Gui and North palace complexes. These connective passageways probably were elevated high off the ground (in spite of the use of the term *yongdao* for them in texts), extended long distances to connect all the palaces, and were roofed and walled to protect those who passed through from sun, wind, and rain. Gedao are pictured in pottery models of wubao from tombs excavated in Gansu province. They had a railing on either side but were not roofed.

A secondary function of the roadways was to cross dangerous places safely. Yongdao also were constructed to make it possible to traverse hazardous cliffs and mountain passes, such as the crossing from the Qin to the Sichuan mountains. The passage was constructed by first cutting away a stone path one to two meters wide into the wall of the cliff. Then wooden beams and planks were laid on it. Another method of constructing passageways through mountains was to cut large holes horizontally into the cliff wall, about two meters apart, and then insert beams into the holes. The beams were supported from underneath by diagonal braces. Thick wooden planks were laid on the row of beams and fastened in place with iron chains or wooden railings fixed on the outer side of the roadway. Plank roads of this type were five to six meters across, wide enough to allow horse-drawn carts to pass over them. Some may have been roofed. Zhandao built close to the bottom of a valley were supported by straight poles instead of

Figure 2.26. Ceramic tiles used at the ends of roof eaves in construction of the Han period

braces. In certain instances this might have been advantageous, but such poles also risked being washed away by torrential rains.

A plank roadway to Sichuan constructed in Qin times was used through the late Eastern Han. The Ziwu Roadway joined the Chang'an region not only to Hanzhong and to Bao Roadway in the west but also to Dasan Pass; in addition it joined Luogu Roadway from Weigu to Tangguang. These were the main mercantile and military routes of Qin and Han China. In addition, Han emperor Wudi opened up Jidao Zhandao so that he could lead his troops into Sichuan and built the Caoyuan Zhandao to pass across the Sanmen Gorge on the Yellow River. Most of the plank roadways were destroyed in wars at the end of the Han era or during the subsequent period of the Three Kingdoms.

Achievements of Qin and Han Architecture

Both the Qin and the Han left important architectural legacies. The Qin created the Epang Palace, the First Emperor's mausoleum at Lishan, the Great Wall, and speedways to the interior of the country and the border regions — all achievements whose significance and influence lasted for hundreds of years. The Han designed and erected equally magnificent building projects, and many more of them during the course of their four centuries of rule. The greatest Han achievements in architecture were the capital city Chang'an, its Weiyang and Jianzhang palace complexes, Shanglin Park, and the transformation of the Chinese afterlife into an architectural world.

Major breakthroughs occurred in timber-frame construction during this period. The post and lintel system had several subtypes by this time, of which *tailiang*, or

column, beam, and strut, was the most important. Qin palaces almost certainly used the tailiang system whereby beams crossed columns perpendicularly in two directions and small vertical struts rose above the beams. The reconstruction of Palace 1 from Xianyang assumes that the tailiang system was used, and it was probably employed in Epang and all other grand Qin and Han palaces. In particular, it is thought that beams, or girders, were extremely long, perhaps spanning up to ten meters. Even the later palaces of the Tang dynasty (618–907), in its capital Chang'an, had beams no longer than these.

Although no multistory wooden buildings from the period exist today, Han China was sophisticated enough to produce such column-beam-and-strut architecture, and brick gate towers, relief sculpture in brick, and tomb wall paintings suggest that they were indeed built. Whether multistory wooden buildings supported by timber skeletons existed before the middle of the Eastern Han dynasty remains an open question. It is just as likely that the *jinggan*, or *ganlan*, system, whereby pieces of wood were laid one on top of another and crossed log-cabin style, was employed in the construction of tall wooden buildings such as those reportedly built by Han emperor Wudi.

Architectural developments also involved the use of a wide variety of brick and ceramic tiles. Floors and roads were paved with brick, walls were lined with brick, and ceramic tiles were placed at the ends of roof eaves (fig. 2.26). The drainage and sewage systems were made of the same materials. The most important place where brick and ceramic tiles were used, however, was in the subterranean tombs, including the pits of the First Emperor himself. Sometimes patterns were carved into tiles; at other times the patterns were stamped onto them. Clay was the main medium for funerary urns, and decorated ceramic tiles projected from the ends of roof

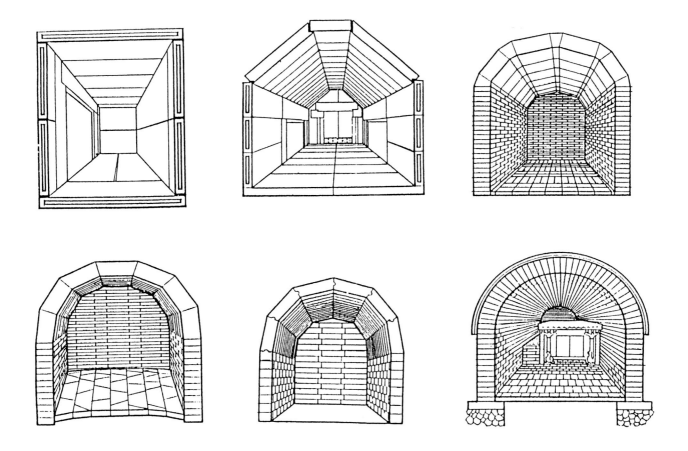

Figure 2.27. Forms of vaulting used in Han tombs

ridges. From pictures in tile and brick we have our ideas about tower construction in Han China. The bases of *que* (towers) also have led to the suggestion that they were raised on high foundations of alternating colors of brick, in checkerboard patterns, a feature evident in later Chinese pavilion architecture. Semicircular arches seen in underground tomb ceilings also are pictured on a few tall buildings preserved in relief sculpture.

Finally, Qin-Han China advanced the technique of vaulting, and vaults were used in such places as tomb interiors (fig. 2.27). Arches were made of flat and curved segments, of even and uneven sizes. Sometimes beams were lodged between the layers of arches, and other times mortar was used. In early Han China, trabeation, a column-and-tiebeam system supporting an arch on top, was the most common kind of construction. But during the Han period, arcuate construction appeared — that is, buildings came to be supported by the arch itself, with true curved lines that added a new contour to architecture of the Eastern Han.

CHAPTER 3

The Three Kingdoms, Western and Eastern Jin, and Northern and Southern Dynasties

FU XINIAN

From the third to the sixth centuries c.e., China experienced almost constant warfare. Still, the artistry and techniques used to create Chinese architecture continued to develop, fueled in part by technological innovation. Wooden buildings gradually replaced structures made of earth and wood; multistory buildings of wood, brick, stone, or some combination appeared in large numbers on the Chinese landscape; and rock-carved architecture reached unprecedented levels of sophistication. The simpler, starker, yet dignified structures of the Han thus began to evolve into the more fluid, vigorous, multipurpose buildings and decorations that were to flourish in Tang China.

Archaeology remains a key means of understanding and interpreting what we know about Chinese architecture during the four centuries after the fall of Han. Just a few buildings survive. The most intact aboveground are several pagodas — one of which, at the Songyue Monastery, may have been unusual or even unique for its time. We do know, however, that the period was one of acculturation, as Chinese leaders sought to unify their land after major conflicts and as cultural influences from beyond China's borders were blended into the religious, social, and architectural landscape. The principles

Details, figure 3.24 *(opposite)* and figure 3.19 *(above)*

of urban planning, which were fully established by this time, were used to create more coherent city layouts and to solidify a single-palace design for the capitals maintained by every kingdom, state, and dynasty. The southeast became a new, important center of Chinese culture, and in the north, trade and travel beyond China's borders brought innovative ideas, in particular, Buddhism.

The development and spread of Buddhism changed the look of Chinese architecture most dramatically during this period. Introduced in the Eastern Han period, Buddhism had gained tremendous momentum by the sixth century and had spread to every part of China. Given the strong palatial and funerary traditions in China, many of the architectural innovations made in the name of Buddhism, such as the pagoda and the idea of a monastery, carried over to these and other areas of Chinese architecture. Regimes of both the Southern and Northern dynasties built numerous Buddhist temples in their capital cities and in areas under their domain. During this time Buddhist pagodas and temples could be seen everywhere. More than 30,000 temples were reportedly built throughout the domain of the Northern Wei, with 1,367 in the capital city Luoyang alone. In addition, the rulers of the Northern dynasties expended fabulous amounts of money on digging grottoes and sculpting Buddhist images, as Chinese architecture continued to combine with Indian and Western Asian architectural forms and styles. By the late fifth and sixth centuries, Buddhist architecture had become Chinese architecture.

The non-Chinese origins of many of the rulers during these years, particularly those in north China, also affected architectural developments. The non-Han leaders brought with them none of the lavishness or embellishments of the Chinese building system, but they still endeavored to build great cities and palaces. Often they sought old forms, using Qin and Han as their models, perhaps as a means of asserting themselves as rulers in the Han Chinese tradition. The fifth- and sixth-century cities of Northern Wei Luoyang and Ye, for instance, maintained much of their pre-fourth-century Chinese building traditions.

Buddhism took hold in China during a complicated period; the frequently changing fortunes of particular powers are difficult to trace, as the unification of China under the Eastern Han gradually gave way to centuries of almost continuous warfare. The Eastern Han had been profoundly shaken by uprisings in the last decades of the second century C.E. In particular, leaders of the Yellow Turban Rebellion spread a popular religion that appealed to the mythical Yellow Emperor and the teaching of

Laozi. Cao Cao (155–220), a famous Han general, led a successful campaign against the Yellow Turbans in 184. At the same time, he adopted the son of the chief palace eunuch who had served at the court of the Han emperor Mindi. Eventually Cao Cao came to control the Han throne, married his daughter to the puppet emperor Xiandi, and established a power base for himself at Ye in southern Hebei province. Upon Cao Cao's death in 220, his son Cao Pi (187–226) declared himself emperor of the Wei Kingdom.

Meanwhile, in other parts of China, there were other uprisings against the collapsing Han. A provincial military general of Han, Liu Bei (161–223), established the kingdom of Shu in Sichuan. And Sun Quan (185–252) set up the Wu Kingdom at Nanjing. Thus, between the years 220 and 222, the period of the Three Kingdoms (Wei, Shu, and Wu) began in China. Later the period was the subject of rich historical folklore, enshrined in one of China's greatest literary classics, *The Romance of the Three Kingdoms*.

Shu was the first kingdom to fall, to the Wei in 263. Two years later, Wei, the most powerful of the Three Kingdoms, was taken over by Jin armies after a forty-five-year rule. The Jin were led by Sima Yan (236–290), who established his capital at Luoyang, site of the last Wei capital. In 280, Sima Yan defeated the last of the Three Kingdoms, Wu, and unified China. He became known as Jin Wudi.

Unification was brief. Upon Jin Wudi's death in 290, rebellion again broke out and peoples from the northern areas of China and beyond the northern border threatened. In 317, the Western Jin collapsed. Various kingdoms and dynasties were carved out of its former northern and western territories, while the last of the Jin fled south to the former Wu capital Jianye, which was renamed Jiankang. The year 317 marks the beginning of five successive dynasties whose capital was Jianye, today Nanjing in Jiangsu province of southern China. The dynasty came to be known as Eastern Jin (317–420) and its first emperor as Yuandi (r. 317–322). After 317, the unified Jin empire with its capital in Luoyang came to be referred to as Western Jin (281–316).

Between 316 and 420, sixteen different powers fought among themselves and against the Eastern Jin. These years are sometimes referred to as the Sixteen States. The period following, from 420 to reunification, is often called the Northern and Southern dynasties. The designation Six Dynasties, sometimes erroneously used for the entire period between Han and Tang, refers to the six powers, beginning with Western Jin and ending with Chen, that ruled southeastern China between 265 and 589.

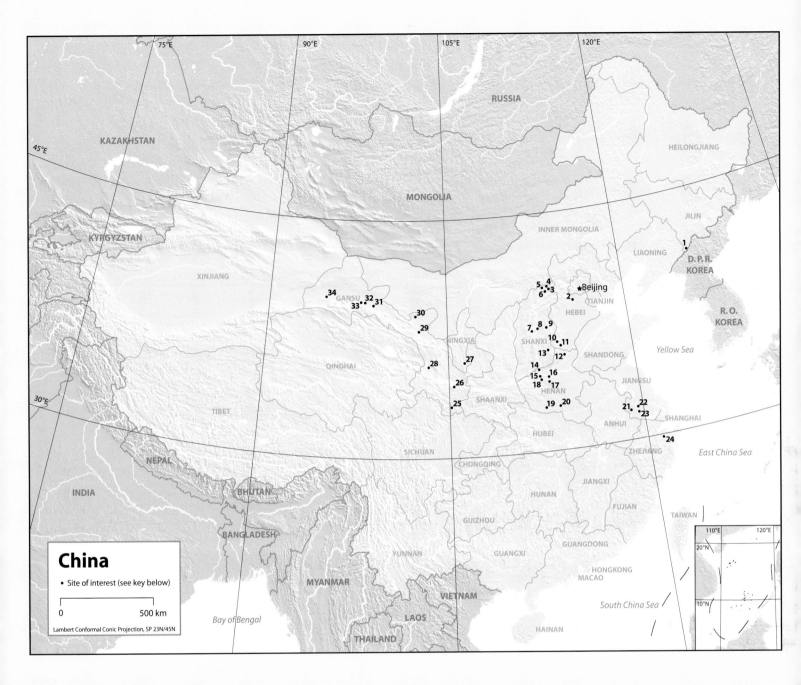

Map 3.
Three Kingdoms, Western and
Eastern Jin, and Northern and
Southern Dynasties Sites

In 420 Liu Song replaced Eastern Jin at Jiankang, and eventually three more powers ruled from Jiankang: Southern Qi (479–502), Liang (502–557), and Chen (557–589). Meanwhile, a dynasty called Northern Wei united north China in 439, ruling until 534 when it was split into Eastern Wei (534–550) and Western Wei (535–557). Subsequently those two dynasties were replaced by Northern Qi (550–577) and Northern Zhou (557–581), respectively. In 577, the Northern Zhou conquered Northern Qi, but their power was short-lived. Yang Jian (540–605), the man who was to become the first emperor of the Sui dynasty (581–618), conquered Northern Zhou in 581 and the southern dynasty of Chen in 589. Conquest of the south brought about the reunification of China.

Capital Cities

The practice of building only one palace in each capital emerged after the third century. One of the earliest examples of a single-palace capital city is Ye, Cao Cao's political center even before it became the Wei capital. By the time it had been established as the capital of the Wei Kingdom, it was a rectangular city, 2.4 kilometers east to west by 1.7 kilometers north to south (fig. 3.1). The city walls were made of rammed earth 15 to 18 meters thick. There were seven gates in the outer wall: three in the south, two in the north, and one each east and west. A major thoroughfare spanned the entire east–west distance of the enclosed city, dividing it into northern and southern parts. In addition, a main road ran north from the central gate of the south wall, bisecting the southern part of the city. The entire southern half of Ye was divided into residential wards, markets, and military barracks. The area north of the main east–west road also was divided into clearly demarcated sections: the eastern wards were residences for the nobility, and a palace area in the north center as well as an adjacent park to its west occupied the rest.

The garden and palace grounds together took up more than a quarter of the city area, all in the northwest. It is believed that the palace city stood on the site of a Han princely town. The closer a building was to the palace area, the more important it was considered by the imperial government. Government bureaus also stood just south of the east–west road that divided the city in two. No earlier Chinese city had such a clear central axis. The location of palaces and government offices along that line and the rigid lines of the ward system throughout the city—where larger streets enclosed areas divided by smaller, orthogonal ones—were to influence all later Chinese imperial city planning.

Construction of the palace building and government offices was the first initiative of the newly established Wei Kingdom for its capital at Luoyang in 220 C.E. The outer walls of the Wei city were kept the same as those of Eastern Han Luoyang, and all twelve gates and twenty-four major roads were preserved (albeit with new names). A significant change occurred inside, however: the North Palace was enlarged and became the sole palatial compound. Although Chinese emperors continued to build detached palaces, palaces in diverse locations for when they traveled, and auxiliary capitals with palaces, from this time on no imperial city would have more than one main palace compound (fig. 3.2). This single-palace system was not an innovation specifically of the Wei Kingdom, whose leaders had ruled from the single-palace city of Ye prior to their transfer to Luoyang. The single-palace system was also the norm among the Six Dynasties ruling in the Nanjing region. But it is true that beginning in the third century, due in part to the influence of the Wei Kingdom, the single-palace-city system was in use throughout China.

Several other features of the plan of Wei Luoyang were seen in its predecessor city, Ye. First was the long axial approach that begins south of the outer wall of the city and continues to the southern entry of the palace city. In order to approach the palace area directly, the main axis of Luoyang was moved west of what would have been a road that bisected the northern and southern walls. Second was placement of government offices due south of the palace city on either side of the main approach to it. (Eventually, Chinese rulers enclosed their administrative city in its own wall and named it *huangcheng*—literally, imperial city.) Third, the main hall of the Luoyang palace city, here named Taiji Hall (a reference to the North Star), was flanked by structures on its east and west. This feature was not maintained through the rest of imperial palace construction history in China, but it did appear in north China for several more centuries.

The official reconstruction of Luoyang's intramural architecture did not begin until 277, just three years before the transition to Western Jin. Palaces, temples, altars, and governmental offices were all modeled after the Ye plan. After the North Palace was enlarged, the South Palace of Eastern Han was officially abandoned, in accordance with certain rules of imperial planning prescribed in the "Record of Trades" section of the *Rituals of Zhou*. The altar of soil was on the western side of the city, and

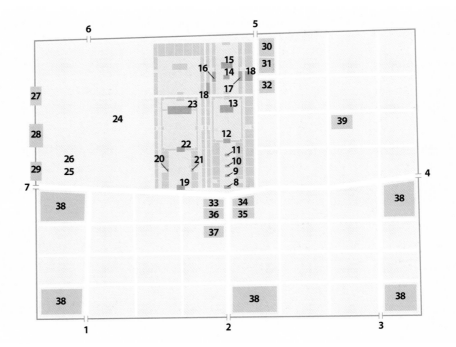

Figure 3.1. Plan of Ye, the first Wei capital, third century C.E.

1. Phoenix Sunlit Gate	12. Government Hall Gate	23. Hall of Literary Splendor	32. Chamberlain for Attendants
2. Central Sunlit Gate	13. Governing Hall	24. Bronze Phoenix Garden	Office
3. Broad Sunlit Gate	14. Warm Chamber	25. Stable of the Imperial	33. Counselor-in-Chief Office
4. Establishing Spring Gate	15. Illuminate Crane Hall	Coachman	34. Imperial Sacrifices Court
5. Broad Virtue Gate	16. Magnolia Quarters	26. Autumn Storehouse	35. Minister of Agriculture Court
6. Stable Gate	17. Catalpa Quarters	27. Golden Tiger Terrace	36. Censor-in-Chief Office
7. Golden Brilliance Gate	18. Resting Lodge	28. Bronze Phoenix Terrace	37. Court for the Chamberlain for
8. Outer Palace Gate	19. South Carriage Stop Gate	29. Icy Well Terrace	the Palace Revenues
9. Resplendent Sunlit Gate	20. Prolonged Autumn Gate	30. Court of Judicial Review	38. Military camps
10. Manifest Brilliance Gate	21. Eternal Spring Gate	31. Palace Interior Great Altar	39. Imperial Relative Ward
11. Producing Worthiness Gate	22. Principal Gate		

the ancestral temple was east of the main north–south thoroughfare (fig. 3.2, #15 and #16). Such records as Yang Xuanzhi's *Luoyang qielan ji* (Record of Buddhist monasteries of Luoyang), written from 547 to 550, and *Henan zhi* (Record of Henan), written seven and a half centuries later, during the Yuan dynasty, tell us that a bronze camel stood on the northern part of the main approach to the palace area. By Northern Wei times, this approach was named Bronze Camel Street.

During the Wei period, three small walled enclosures had been added in the northwest corner of the city. Two, known as Jinyongcheng and Little Luoyang, extended beyond the former northern wall (fig. 3.2, #19 and #20). The palaces of Wei were inside Jinyongcheng, a heavily fortified city with closely placed defensive towers on its walls. It is believed that this protected part of the city was modeled after the area of Ye known as Santai, or "three terraces" (fig. 3.1, #27, #28, and #29). Residences and markets of Luoyang were also enclosed in wards or walls,

but with time, as the city prospered, dwellings and commercial districts also appeared outside the city.

With the unification of China under the Western Jin, Luoyang became the national capital. Its most important palace area was in the northern center, the location of government offices, the ancestral temple, and the altar of soil flanking the main north–south street that approached the palace site. The rest of the city was divided into wards. The layout of Luoyang was essentially the same from the fall of Eastern Han through the period of the Sixteen States. The plan was of prime importance in the construction of all Chinese cities until the reunification of China under the Sui in 589.

Jianye, the capital of the Wu Kingdom, also illustrates the evolution of capital city construction during this period. In 210 C.E., Wu moved its capital from the location of today's Zhenjiang about fifty kilometers southwest, to today's Nanjing. At the same time, a military equipment storage area called Shitoucheng was built on

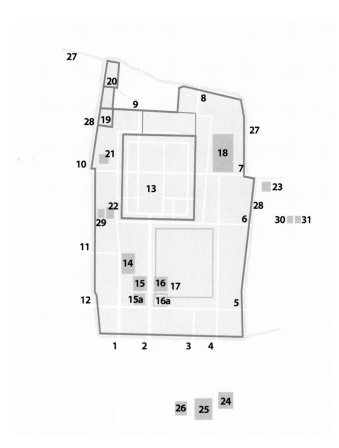

Figure 3.2. Plan of Luoyang under the Wei and the Western Jin

1. North of the Ford Gate (Gate of the Sunlit Ford)
2. Manifest Sunlight Gate
3. Peace and Prosperity Gate
4. Opening to the (Morning) Sun Gate
5. Clear and Bright Gate
6. East Sunlight Gate
7. Establishing Spring Gate
8. Broad and Boundless Gate
9. Great Xia Gate
10. Heavenly Purple Palace Gate
11. West Brilliance Gate
12. Broad and Sunlit Gate
13. Palace City (Northern Palace of Eastern Han)
14. Cao Shuang's Residence
15. Imperial Altar to the God of Soil
15a. New Imperial Altar to the God of Soil of Western Jin
16. Imperial Ancestral Temple
16a. New Imperial Ancestral Temple of Western Jin
17. Site of South Palace of Eastern Han
18. East Palace
19. Golden-Walled City (Jinyongcheng)
20. Little Luoyang

21. Treasury (gold storage)
22. Armory
23. Horse Market
24. Site of Imperial Academy of Eastern Han
25. Site of Luminous Hall of Eastern Han
26. Site of Imperial Observatory of Eastern Han
27. Gu (Grain) River
28. Yang Canal
29. Sima Zhao's Residence
30. Liu Chan's Residence
31. Sun Hao's Residence

the southwest bank of the Yangzi River. Northeast of the armory was a residence for the military general. In 229, a palace city was added beyond the general's residence, the main complex of which was named Taichugong. At this time, Jianye had no city walls. Its boundary was marked by wooden and bamboo fences, with earthen walls only at city gates.

In 247, Taichu Palace was renovated, and in 252, Zhaoming Palace was built to its east, with a park north of the two palaces. The entire northern half of Jianye was thus occupied by palaces, gardens, and granaries. A wide north–south thoroughfare, known as the imperial way, led to the palaces and gardens. The imperial way extended beyond the south gate of the city to Dahang Floating Bridge, which crossed the Qinhuai River and was flanked by government offices and military barracks. Residences were primarily in the southern part of the city. As in Ye and Luoyang, palaces were located in the northern part of the city and important buildings faced south.

Jianye was renamed Jiankang when it became capital of the Eastern Jin. Members of the Eastern Jin ruling class, who considered themselves successors of the unified Chinese empire of Western Jin, continued their government and institutions, including aspects of the plan of Wei-Jin Luoyang. For instance, the palace city of Jianye was enlarged and moved north and east, more in line with the location of the Luoyang palace city in the early fourth century, and the main thoroughfare south of the palace city was extended even farther than the bridge then known as Red Oriole Floating Bridge, so that it reached the southern suburbs where imperial sacrifices to heaven were performed (fig. 3.3, #36 and #34, respectively). The number of gates was increased to twelve from Luoyang's seven, although the gates were renamed in accordance with those used in Luoyang. A migration southward added to the population of Jiankang, and new residential districts were opened east of the city along Qing Creek.

In time, Jiankang became a hub of waterways protected by small walled towns and military barracks constructed all around. Positioned on the Yangzi and other rivers, its location meant that boats could go east and south from Qinhuai River to the various markets of the city. Soon after it was established, settlements for new immigrants appeared along the waterways, seeding what was to become a thriving, and sprawling, metropolis. The economy of the city flourished as Liu Song replaced Eastern Jin in 420, and was followed by the Southern Qi and Liang. Town after town developed in the adjacent prefectures, subprefectures, and command posts of the

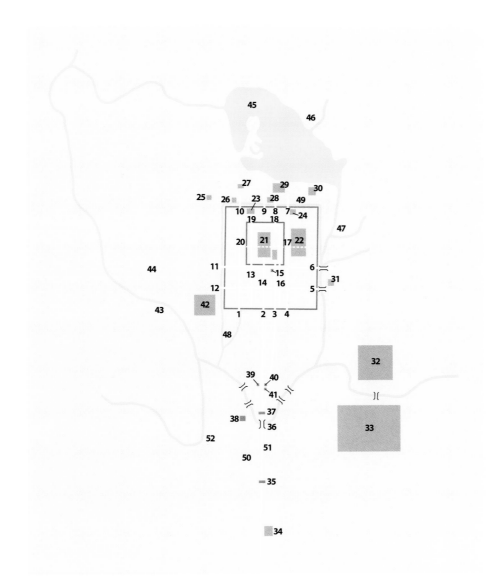

Figure 3.3. Plan of Jiankang
under the Eastern Jin

1. Ascending Sunlight Gate
2. Brilliant Sunlight Gate
3. Opening to the (Morning) Sun Gate
   Sunlit Ford Gate (Song)
4. New Opening to the (Morning) Sun Gate
   (added in 448)
5. Clear and Bright Gate
6. Establishing Spring Gate
7. New Broad and Boundless Gate
   (added in 448)
8. Peaceful and Prosperous Gate
   Received Brilliance Gate (name changed
   in 448)
9. Black Tortoise Gate
10. Great Xia Gate
11. Western Brilliance Gate
12. Heavenly Purple Palace Gate (added in 448)
13. Western Lateral Gate (Song, Qi)
14. Gate of Minister of War
15. Southern Lateral Gate (Jin)
    Heavenly Purple Palace Gate (Song)
    South Gate (Chen)

16. Eastern Lateral Gate (Song, Qi)
17. Eastern Lateral Gate (Jin)
    Myriad Spring Gate (Song)
    Eastern Flowers Gate (Liang)
18. Peaceful and Prosperous Gate (Jin)
    Broad and Boundless Gate (Song)
    Received Brilliance Gate (Liang)
19. Great Communication Gate
20. Western Lateral Gate (Jin)
    Thousand Autumns Gate (Song)
    Western Flowers Gate (Liang)
21. Terrace City, Palace City
22. Eastern Palace
23. Same Greatness Monastery
24. Garden Market
25. Yarn Market
26. North Market
27. Returning Kindness Monastery
28. Military exercise fields
29. Amusement Park
30. Nothern Suburban Altar
31. Straw City

32. Eastern Mansion
33. Danyang Commandery
34. Southern Suburban Altar
35. State Gate
36. Vermilion Bird Bridge, Grand Bridge
37. Vermilion Bird Gate
38. Salt Market
39. Imperial Altar of Soil and Grain
40. Imperial Ancestral Temple
41. National University
42. Western region
43. The Old Waterway of Yangzi River
44. Shitou (Boulder) City
45. Xuanwu (Black Tortoise) Lake
46. Shanglin (The Supreme Forest) Park
47. Green Creek
48. Canal (Little) Ditch
49. Tide Ditch
50. Yue City
51. Changgan ward
52. New Hostel

new empire — Shitoucheng, Dongfu, Xizhou, Yecheng, Yuecheng, Baixia, Xinlin, Danyangjun, Nanlangyajun, and others — giving way to residential and commercial settlements linked to one another by water on every side of the city. During the fifty or so years of Liang rule (502–557), especially in the 530s, Jiankang grew forty li (twenty kilometers) in every direction — west to Shitoucheng, east to Nitang, north to the Purple Forbidden Mountain Range (Zijinshan), and south to Yuhua Terrace — and it came to encompass a population of about two million. Although the city had no outer wall, only fences and fifty-six gates, it was the largest and most prosperous Chinese city of the age.

In 493, the Northern Wei established a capital once more at Luoyang on the Central Plain, marking the unification of north China under the rule of this dynasty of Xianbei origins, and in the same year they moved their primary capital there. Although the city walls and palaces of Luoyang were repaired during the last decade of the fifth century, no major changes were made to them. Perhaps the Northern Wei wanted to reaffirm themselves symbolically as successors to the imperial system of Han and Jin.

The major innovation of the Northern Wei capital was the extension of residential and market districts beyond the walls of Wei-Jin times to a city whose outer wall was 10 kilometers east to west by 7.5 kilometers north to south. Eventually the entire city was divided into wards and markets that extended on all sides of the old Wei-Jin capital, giving way to a true checkerboard plan of four-sided enclosed spaces, and exceeding the early Han capitals Chang'an and Luoyang in number and extent of wards and overall scale of the city (fig. 3.4). In order to reaffirm earlier principles of planning, such as a focus on the palace created by a north–south axis through the city, the main street leading from the southern city gate to the palace area was enlarged and extended. Government offices were located along this imperial way, still known as Bronze Camel Street.

Palace Architecture

None of the palace buildings created in third- through sixth-century China survives, but as was the case for Han, site excavations and textual records reveal much about the layouts of palaces built during these four centuries of disunion.

The city of Ye offers such clues to palace architecture of the time. Even before the Wei Kingdom was estab-

lished, Cao Cao and his forces had their power base in Ye. The palaces of Ye, too, had their origins in pre-Wei buildings. In the rebuilt Ye capital, the palatial sectors were located in the northwestern part of the city. The northwest corner (fig. 3.1, #24), east of Santai (three terraces, fig. 3.1, #27, #28, and #29) and west of the palaces, is the part of the city that some compare to the three small defensive cities of the subsequent Wei capital at Luoyang (fig. 3.2, #19 and #20, and fig. 3.4, #32 and #33), and indeed, military equipment was stored in the high foundations of each of the three tall structures, named Bronze Bird, Golden Tiger, and Golden Well. The eastern part of the northwestern quadrant of Ye was designated for palatial halls. Their arrangement was significant then, and had a far-reaching influence: the palace-city plan was to endure for centuries in China and in all likelihood influenced the architecture of Japan.

The Ye palace city was divided into two sectors of approximately the same size, east and west of each other. On the east were the residence of the king of Wei and places for official court business (fig. 3.1, #8–#18). West, at the focus of a parallel building complex, was Wenchang Hall (#23), the principal hall for imperial ceremonies. The main halls of each section, Wenchang and Tingzheng (#13), were arranged along north–south lines, facing gates at the southern end of the palace city (#8 and #19). The main north–south thoroughfare of Ye led from the main axis of the eastern sector of the palace city (beyond #8) through the rest of the city to the main south wall gate (#2).

As discussed earlier, when Wei conquered the former Han capital at Luoyang, the two palaces of Han were transformed into one enlarged palace area, following the precedent of the single palace-city system of Ye. The arrangement of palace architecture inside the Wei-Jin palace city, however, differed from that of Ye (fig. 3.5; compare fig. 3.1). The main part of the city in Luoyang faced south along the main north–south axis, west of center, and included the south gate of the palace city, Changhe Gate. In this area were buildings for the official business of the court and, north of these, the imperial residences. The arrangement fit the passage from the "Records of Trades" in the *Rituals of Zhou* that stipulated, "in front, halls of audience *(chao);* behind, sleeping chambers *(qin)."* The main hall, where the grandest public ceremonies of the Wei-Jin court were conducted, was named Taiji Hall (fig. 3.5, #11). Flanking Taiji Hall were East Hall and West Hall (#18 and #19), where the emperor lived and handled the daily affairs of the court. Southeast of the Taiji Hall complex, in their own enclosed court-

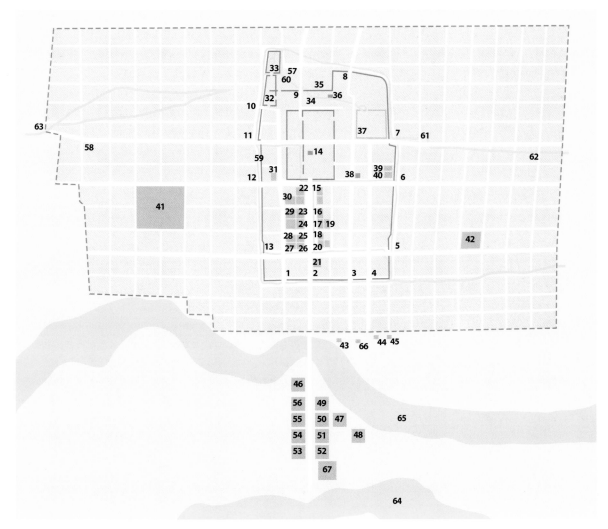

Figure 3.4. Plan of Luoyang under the Northern Wei

1. North Ford Gate
2. Manifest Sunlight Gate
3. Peace and Prosperity Gate
4. Opening to the Sunlight Gate
5. Green and Sunlit Gate
6. East Sunlight Gate
7. Establishing Spring Gate
8. Broad and Boundless Gate
9. Gate of Great Xia
10. Received Brilliance Gate
11. Heavenly Purple Palace Gate
12. West Sunlight Gate
13. West Brightness Gate
14. Palace City
15. Office of Left Guard
16. Office of Minister of Education
17. Imperial Supervisory of Academic Learning
18. Court of the Imperial Clan
19. Great Happiness Monastery
20. Imperial Ancestral Temple
21. Office of Capital Protector
22. Office of Right Guard
23. Office of Grand Commandant
24. Construction section

25. Nine-Rank Offices
26. Altar of Soil and Grain
27. Hutong Monastery
28. Station of Issuing Imperial Notices
29. Eternal Peace Monastery
30. Censorate
31. Armory
32. Golden-Walled City
33. Little Luoyang
34. Flowery Forest Garden
35. Jingyang Mountain of Cao's Wei (dynasty)
36. Lodge of Listening to Grievances
37. Eastern Palace reserved land
38. Office of Capital Construction
39. Imperial Granaries
40. Imperial Granaries Office Liason Office
41. Big market of Luoyang
42. Small market of Luoyang
43. Imperial Observatory Site of Eastern Han
44. Circular Moat Site of Eastern Han
45. National Academy Site of Eastern Han
46. Sitong Market
47. White Elephant Ward
48. Lion Ward

49. Jinling Chamber
50. Yanran (Mountain) Chamber
51. Fusang (Mulberry) Chamber
52. Yanzi (Mountain) Chamber
53. Admiring Justice Ward
54. Admiring Transformation Ward
55. Rejoining Virtue Ward
56. Rejoining Justice Ward
57. Military review field
58. Longevity Mound Ward
59. North Canal
60. Gu (Grain) River
61. East Stone Bridge
62. Seven-*li* Bridge
63. Changfen Bridge
64. Yi River
65. Luo River
66. Site of Luminous Hall of Eastern Han
67. Burial mound

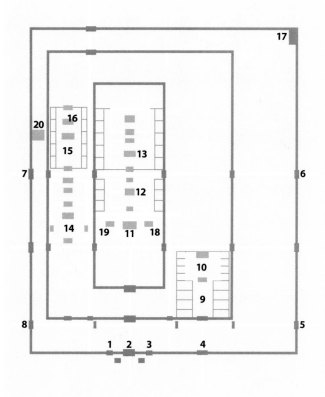

Figure 3.5. Plan of the palace city of Wei-Jin Luoyang

1. Lateral Gate	12. Morning Sunlight Hall
2. Heavenly Purple Palace Gate	13. Shiqian Hall
3. Lateral Gate	14. Establishing Beginning Hall
4. Commander-in-Chief Gate	15. Nine Dragons Hall
5. Eastern Lateral Gate	16. Good Fortunes Hall
6. Cloud Dragon Gate	17. Listening to Grievances
7. Spiritual Tiger Gate	Lodge
8. Western Lateral Gate	18. East Hall
9. Grand Secretariat	19. West Hall
10. Hall of State	20. Soaring to the Clouds Terrace
11. Great Ultimate Hall	

yard, were the Hall of State (*chaotang*, #10) and in front of it the office of the Grand Secretariat (*shangshusheng*, #9). The two were built along a secondary axis of the palace city that led to its second southern gate, Da Sima-men (#4).

The influence of the plan of the Wei capital at Ye can be seen in the structures north of the Taiji Palace complex (fig. 3.5, #12 and #13). Unlike at Ye, the important halls were not of equal size, but they did stand in a row. At Luoyang they were oriented to face Zhaoyang Hall (#12), the main residence of the empress. To the side of Zhaoyang Hall were residential halls for the empress and imperial concubines. After Zhaoyang Hall, the most

famous structure was Nine Dragons Hall (#15). A detail of a mural from Cave 127 at the Buddhist site Maijishan in Gansu province is believed to depict these and other palace buildings of Luoyang (fig. 3.6).

Defense seems to have been a primary concern of palace-city builders. All the important buildings of the Wei-Jin capital were elevated on platforms that were so high they resembled kiosks. To get to them it was necessary to ascend *gedao* (elevated roadways), by which some of the buildings were also interconnected. The outer walls also had many observation towers for defense. (The high elevations and towers also appear in fig. 3.6.) Finally, Lingyun Terrace—an arsenal that could supply three thousand troops—was positioned along the western wall of the palace city (fig. 3.5, #20).

The tradition of building imperial gardens continued during this period. Hualin Garden is said to have been behind the residential areas of the Luoyang palace city. There residents could enjoy man-made hills, lakes, pavilions, and kiosks.

In 330, the Eastern Jin rebuilt palaces based on the model of Wei-Jin Luoyang at their capital, Jiankang, which remained their most important city. Improved under the Liu Song and the Southern Qi, by Liang times Jiankang had the most magnificent palaces in China and was, in some ways, even more rigidly organized than Luoyang. The number of walls that enclosed it increased from one at Jianye to two and then three. The outermost wall surrounded the lowest-ranking officials and troops. Residences of middle-ranking officials were also there. Inside the second wall were the central administrative bureaus of the government, the court (fig. 3.7, #29) and, also on the east, the Grand Secretariat (*shangshusheng*, #28). A south gate led out of the southeastern sector of government offices and court buildings, an arrangement just like those at Wei-Jin Luoyang. On the western side of the second walled enclosure were the secretariat (*zhongshusheng*, #37), chancellery (*menxiasheng*, #36), imperial library (#35), and Yongfusheng, the Department of Eternal Blessings (#34).

The innermost walls enclosed areas for the emperor to hold court (#15–#27), and behind these were the rulers' homes. The courts included Taiji Hall (#19) and, to either side, Taiji East and Taiji West halls (#20 and #21). The inner quarters (*qinchu*) behind the public areas were Shiqian Hall (also known as Zhongzhai, #22) and Xianyang Hall (#25), residences of the emperor and empress, respectively, which were arranged around individual courtyards. All three palace compounds, Taiji, Shiqian, and Xianyang, had similar plans (three buildings in an east–west row). The main hall of each triplet was on

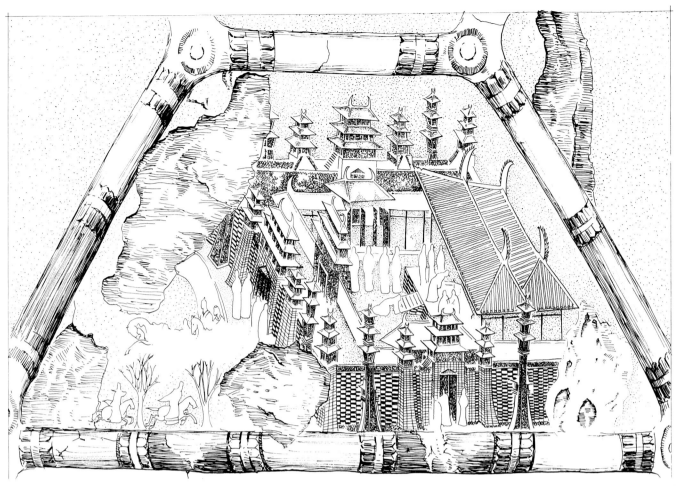

Figure 3.6. Drawing of a wall painting from Maijishan Cave 127, Gansu province

the central axis of the palace city, aligned with the back south gate of the innermost palace-city sector (#18) and the south (front) gates of all three palace-city walls (#15, #9, and #2). The imperial garden, Hualinyuan (#33), was north of the inner quarters.

As the economy of the Southern dynasties flourished, the palaces of Jiankang became more splendid. Especially sumptuous halls were built at the time of economic boom during the mid-Liang. When new palaces were constructed at the same time in Luoyang, which was by then the capital of the Northern Wei, the Northern Wei builders looked for inspiration to the architecture of both Wei-Jin Luoyang and Jiankang — but then surpassed these models. The emperor of Liang, in order to surpass the Northern Wei construction, rebuilt the two-story gates and towers of his Jiankang palace city as three-story structures and turned the twelve-bay Taiji Hall into a building of thirteen bays. In addition, he increased the height of the platform beneath the ancestral temple. Under the last of the Southern dynasties, Chen, the palaces were further beautified. The empress built three towers of fragrant wood that were to become

the most famous buildings of the Northern and Southern dynasties — Linchun, Jieji, and Wangxian — and had them decorated with gold, jade, and pearl ornaments. Despite this show of prosperity, Chen fell in 589 and the palaces and walls of Jiankang were leveled by war.

When the Northern Wei gained control over Luoyang and made it their capital, they continued the architectural traditions established in the earlier palace cities of Wei-Jin Luoyang and Eastern Jin Jiankang. The first change they made to Luoyang was to enclose it with three sets of walls, again following the precedent of the Eastern Jin (fig. 3.8). As at Jiankang, the highest-level administrative offices of the government, the grand secretariat, secretariat, and chancellery, were located within the second enclosure (mostly within the #12 and #13 complex), and the places where the emperor held court and lived were inside the third (smallest) boundary.

Again, Taiji Hall and the east and west flanking halls (#20, #21, and #22) were where large public gatherings occurred, and Taiji Hall was aligned with the main south gates of all three palace-city walls (#17, #14, and #1), on a street that led directly southward to Bronze Camel

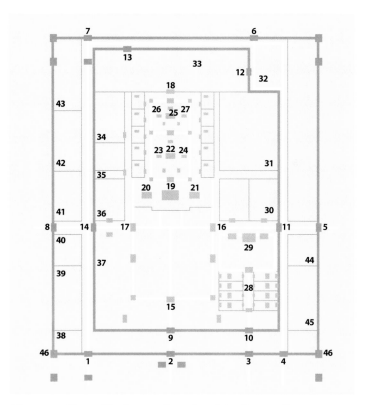

Figure 3.7. Plan of Jiankang, palace city of the Eastern Jin

1. Western Lateral Gate
2. Commander-in-Chief Gate
3. Southern Lateral Gate
4. Heavenly Purple Palace Gate (Song)
   Principal Gate (Chen)
   Eastern Lateral Gate (Song, Qi)
5. Eastern Lateral Gate (Jin)
   Myriad Springs Gate (Song)
6. Eastern Flower Gate (Liang)
7. Peace and Prosperity Gate (Jin)
   Broad and Boundless Gate (Song)
8. Received Brilliance Gate (Song)
   Great Communications Gate (Liang)

Western Lateral Gate (Jin)
   Thousand Autumns Gate (Song)
   Western Flowers Gate (Liang)
9. Southern Gate for Stopping Carriages (Jin)
   Receipt of Brilliance Gate (Liang)
10. Main Gate
11. Eastern Gate for Stopping Carriages
12. Eastern Pavilion of Flowery Forest
13. North Upper Pavilion
14. Western Gate for Stopping Carriages
15. Principal Gate (Jin)
   Solar Gate (Liang)

16. Cloud Dragon Gate (Jin, Qi)
   Eastern Cultural Splendor Gate (Song)
   Myriad Springs Gate (Liang)
17. Divine Tiger Gate (Jin, Qi)
   Western Cultural Splendor Gate (Song)
   Gate of Thousand Autumns (Liang)
18. Phoenix Manor Gate
19. Great Ultimate Hall
20. Eastern Hall of the Great Ultimate
21. Western Hall of the Great Ultimate
22. Respecting the Heavenly Way Hall (Central Studio)
23. Western Studio
24. Eastern Studio
25. Resplendent Sunlight Hall
26. Benevolent Voices Hall
27. Containing Rules Hall
28. Grand Secretariat
29. Court Hall
30. Scholarly Counselors Department
31. Empress Dowager Palace
32. Visitors Department (Bureau)
33. Flowery Forest Garden
34. Department of Eternal Blessings
   (Department for Provision of the Aged)
35. Imperial Archives (library)
36. Chancellery
37. Secretariat
38. Chamberlain for the Palace Garrison
39. Subordinate Secretariat
40. Right Guard
41. Subordinate Chancellery
42. Armory
43. Imperial Granaries
44. Left Granaries
45. Subordinate Department of State Affairs
46. Corner Towers

Street. A horizontal wall joined Taiji to the Taiji East and Taiji West halls. On that wall were gates called *shuanmen,* behind which were sleeping quarters for guards and others serving in the court. The principal halls of the two courtyards of buildings behind the Taiji Hall complex were, for the front group, Shiqian Hall (#23) and Xianyang Hall (#24), and for the back group, Xuanguang Hall (#27) and Jiafu Hall (#30). All four were in a line, each had flanking halls like the Taiji Hall complex, and each pair of halls was enclosed in its own courtyard. Small east–west alleys called *yong'gang,* which began on either side of Xianyang and Xuanguang halls, led through all three sets of palace-city gates and out of the city.

Although the layout of the Luoyang palace city under the rule of the Northern Wei did not change much com-pared with Jiankang, some buildings were used for differ-ent purposes. For example, in spite of their names and po-sitions the Shiqian and Xianyang palace complexes were no longer the residences of the emperor and empress dowager; they now were used for the daily affairs of the court. The principal residences of the emperor were instead located in the front hall complex of each of the two complexes behind Taiji Hall; and Xuanguang Hall (#27) and Jiafu Hall (#30), behind the alley that led out of the palace city, were the residences of the empresses and impe-rial concubines. These changes in building function were to be copied in the palace cities of Sui and Tang China.

In addition to the palatial halls, many multistory struc-tures elevated on high platforms were found inside the palace cities of the Three Kingdoms and the two Jins.

These structures, first made of a combination of earth and wood, were by the fifth century almost entirely timber-framed. Entries to palace complexes and individual halls had two- or three-story towers above them, all of extraordinary beauty. Watch towers projected from the walls of the palace cities and outer city walls, and every imperial city had arsenals, constant reminders of the rise and fall of rulers and dynasties during the period.

Funerary Architecture

By the last decades of the Han dynasty, funerals had become simpler than in earlier eras. The more frugal burials were a direct result of a monetary strain that plagued all levels of Chinese society during this time. Frequent warfare associated with the fall of the Han, the rise and fall of three kingdoms, and subsequent short-lived dynasties made sumptuous burials less and less feasible. Thus huge mausoleums, mounded tombs, sacrificial halls, funerary towns, and spirit paths were not built from the late third through most of the fourth century. More elaborate tomb construction began again under the Western Jin, but not on the scale of that seen before the last decades of the Eastern Han dynasty. Even after the Chinese capital moved southeast, the economic prosperity of the Western Han was not restored. Eastern Jin rulers in the vicinity of Nanjing (Jiankang), for example, were buried in a style commensurate with funerals for mere high officials of the earlier lavish period of the Eastern Han: their tombs were built into mountains and had underground chambers approximately seven meters long by five meters wide, covered by mounds more than ten meters high.

But when the economy again flourished during subsequent dynasties of south China, imperial tombs once again grew in size and grandeur. The tombs of rulers of Liu Song, Southern Qi, Liang, and Chen were large and distinctive. Investigation aboveground has taken place at most of the sites, and several of the tombs themselves have been excavated. Literary records confirm that the royal tombs of the Southern dynasties were built into hills with stretches of open ground in front of them. The chambers of most were dug into the hill about ten meters above ground level and were oval in plan, with brick walls and vaulted ceilings about ten meters high and six meters wide. A passageway led to the coffin chambers, which were reached through two stone doors. In accordance with texts describing funerary practices of the time, beyond the tomb chamber was an enclosing wall with a sealed door. Above the burial chambers, earthen

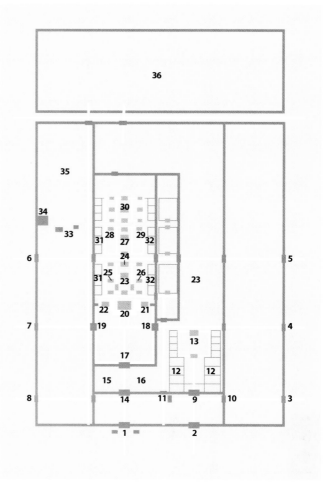

Figure 3.8. Plan of the Luoyang palace city of the Northern Wei

1. Heavenly Purple Palace Gate
2. Minister of War Gate
3. Eastern Lateral Gate
4. Cloud Dragon Gate
5. Myriad Years (Longevity) Gate
6. Thousand Autumns Gate
7. Spiritual Tiger Gate
8. Western Lateral Gate
9. Department of State Affairs Gate
10. Eastern Gate of the Department (of State Affairs)
11. Western Gate of the Department (of State Affairs)
12. Grand Secretariat
13. Hall of State
14. Southern Gate for Stopping Carriages
15. Chancellery
16. Secretariat
17. Principal Gate
18. Vermilion Flowers Gate
19. Heavenly Brilliance Gate
20. Great Ultimate Hall
21. Eastern Great Ultimate Hall
22. Western Great Ultimate Hall
23. Shiqian Hall
24. Resplendent Sunlight Hall
25. Benevolent Voices Hall
26. Embracing Rules Hall
27. Manifest Brightness Hall
28. Brilliant Brightness Hall
29. Shining Grandeur Hall
30. Good Fortunes Hall
31. Western Department
32. Eastern Department
33. Nine Dragons Hall
34. Rising Cloud Terrace
35. Western Forest Garden
36. Flowery Forest Garden

Figure 3.9. Stone qilin in front of the tomb of Emperor Wen of the Chen dynasty, Nanjing, Jiangsu province

Figure 3.10. Stone tianlu in front of the tomb of Xiao Jing, of the Liang dynasty, Nanjing, Jiangsu province

mounds were piled about ten meters high, sometimes as high as the hill into which the tomb was dug and other times to within five meters of the hilltop. The walls of the tomb chambers and funerary passageway were lined with stamped, decorated, or engraved bricks depicting animals, transcendent beings, or identifiable figures from Chinese history and legend, such as the Seven Sages of the Bamboo Grove.

Much is also known about tomb architecture near the capitals of north China. Although so far only the tomb of Northern Wei emperor Xuan Wudi (r. 500–515) has been excavated, the sites of some other imperial tombs have been identified, and the tomb of Empress Dowager Wenming has been the subject of scholarly research. Some regions have yielded exceptional finds. Discoveries of tombs and artifacts in the Datong area, the vicinity of the Northern Wei capital before Luoyang, and in regional centers of smaller states and kingdoms at China's borders — in particular the Hexi corridor (Jiayuguan-Jiuquan region of Gansu), Guyuan in Ningxia, Ci county in Hebei, and tombs of the Korean kingdom of Koguryo in present-day Jilin province — have made it possible to reconstruct in detail aspects of the daily lives of officials and nobility of the fourth through sixth centuries. Luoyang, which was a capital for most of the period between Han and Tang, has also yielded tombs, but so far none as noteworthy as those farther from the Central Plain. From the thousands of tombs now known from this period, those selected for discussion here were chosen because of excellent preservation inside and because they represent many other tombs of similar type.

Among the most notable of the tombs are those in the Nanjing region. The motif of the Seven Sages of the Bamboo Grove appears there with some frequency in funerary decorations in both official and imperial tombs, including a brick tomb dug into a hill at Huqiao, seventeen kilometers northeast of Danyang. Roughly oval in shape, the concealed space of that tomb is 15 meters long, 7.2 meters wide, and 4.5 meters to the top of the vaulted ceiling. Atop the lintel over the stone double door that provided access to the tomb is an inverted V-shaped brace, a structural and decorative feature that is associated with timber-frame architecture of the Northern and Southern dynasties.

Aboveground, the royal funerary architecture of the Southern dynasties is distinctive. Some earlier traditions were kept, such as sacrificial temples and gates at the approaches to tombs, but new ones were added: the spirit paths were lined with mythological creatures, columns were erected with animal-shaped capitals, and stelae were

Figure 3.11. Stone tianlu from the tomb of Liang emperor
Wendi, Danyang, Jiangsu province

used. The occupants of more than thirty tombs from the Southern dynasties with spirit paths are now known and about a dozen more, so far, await identification. A creature named *qilin,* one of a male-and-female pair of winged, lean felines with a long tongue whose name has sometimes been translated "unicorn," is found only on the spirit paths of emperors. The largest extant qilin stands 3.3 meters long and 2.7 meters tall in front of the tomb of Emperor Wu (r. 502–550) of the Liang dynasty. It is similar to the slightly smaller and later sculpture in front of the tomb of Emperor Wen (r. 560–566) of Chen (fig. 3.9). The *tianlu,* also winged and with a long tongue and shorter neck, is more feline, has a less decorated body, and is found at the tombs of princes (fig. 3.10). Also striking is a stone tianlu from the tomb of Liang emperor Wendi (fig. 3.11). Most intriguing are the fluted stone

The tomb of Empress Dowager Wenming, who died in 490, just three years before the transfer of the Northern Wei capital, is particularly noteworthy. She was buried at Fangshan (today Liangshan) in a tomb whose construction had begun in 484 at a hilly site twenty-five kilometers from Datong. The locations of her tomb, Yonggu, other royal tombs in the same area, and funerary temples have been known for centuries. Excavation took place in 1976.

The mound above the empress dowager's tomb was 22.9 meters high and squarish at the base, which spanned 117 meters north to south and 124 meters east to west. The tomb was directly beneath the mound and consisted of a diagonal ramp leading down from ground level, an antechamber, a connective passageway, and a large burial chamber. The roof of the antechamber was a simple barrel vault, but the back chamber had a cupola ceiling, vaulted but flat on top. Orientation was only four degrees east of due north–south, with the entry to the tomb at the south. The total interior length was 17.6 meters, making it larger than any known tomb of the Jiankang region and one of the largest tombs of the Northern or Southern dynasties unearthed thus far, and the interior walls were carved with relief sculpture. Texts tell us that the stone Hall of Eternal Resoluteness (Yonggutang) stood six hundred meters south of the tomb, that the approach was lined with animal sculpture and stelae, and that the funerary precinct was enclosed by a wall whose entry was marked by *que*— freestanding gate towers.

Several other tombs from the early period of Northern Wei rule have been excavated in the Datong area, all with brick underground chambers and some with a pyramidal, or truncated pyramidal, vaulted ceiling. The tomb of Sima Jinlong and his wife, uncovered about 6.5 kilometers southeast of Datong in 1965, has become well known because of the painted lacquer panel screen depicting scenes of feminine filial piety taken from the text *Admonitions of the Court Instructress*.

Sima Jinlong's tomb is extremely large, nearly fourteen meters from the beginning of the ramp leading down to the tomb to the northern end. It consists of front and back chambers joined by a connective passageway and a side chamber east of the antechamber. All were roughly four-sided. The front and back chambers had pyramidal vaulted ceilings and the side, or "ear," chamber *(ershi)* had a simple barrel-vaulted ceiling.

As has been the case for tombs near Nanjing, the sites of mausoleums of Northern Wei emperors and empresses who ruled when their capital was in Luoyang have been known for centuries. (Information about prob-

Figure 3.12. Column at the tomb of Xiao Jing of the Liang, Nanjing

columns raised on bases with animals on the capitals. The bases of these columns vary and include one in the shape of a pair of hornless dragons. Lion-like animals on lotus petals are found on capitals too, and an inscribed placard identifying the tomb occupants is sometimes carved onto the column (fig. 3.12). In general, three pairs of creatures line the spirit paths: qilin, columns, and stelae at emperors' tombs, and *bixie* (a variant form of qilin or tianlu), columns, and stelae at princely and official tombs. Each of these statues is carved from a single piece of stone.

Northern Wei tombs are also of considerable importance, and those created during the period before the Northern Wei moved their capital to Luoyang in 493 are striking.

able spirit paths approaching these tumuli has been much more difficult to find.) Specific details about some of the sites became known from stelae with funerary inscriptions found in Mangshan, the mountainous region north of the capital where most of these rulers were laid to rest. It was locations identified on these same stelae that led the way to looting of tombs in the years before the establishment of the People's Republic. Not until the 1960s was limited excavation begun, in the vicinity of Mangshan.

Nonimperial tombs have been uncovered around Luoyang, but many of these have been looted as well. Robbers made their way into the simple single-chamber tomb of Yuan Shao, an official of the Northern Wei, by way of a tunnel that led directly into the burial chamber, a passage almost as wide as the shaft originally dug for access to the tomb.

Single-chamber tombs were fairly common for Northern Wei nonroyal burials. The tomb of Sima Yue, excavated in Meng county, Henan, was a single-chamber tomb with an unusual approach. The brick tomb, oriented north–south with a paved brick floor and vaulted ceiling, was approached by a forked road, each prong of which was about a meter long, preceding the more standard straight approach to the tomb. (Although the reason for this unusual approach is unclear, some have speculated that it may have been intended to foil robbers.)

Other tombs of considerable importance have been found in Gansu province. Two towns about twenty-five kilometers apart on either side of Beida River in the saharan part of Gansu province known as the Hexi corridor — Jiayuguan (or "Jiayu Pass"), where beacon towers and other parts of the Great Wall survive, and Jiuquan — have yielded hundreds of tombs from the third to early fifth centuries. The distinguishing feature of the Jiayuguan group is paintings depicting daily life, which were created using wet and often casual brush strokes on the brick interior walls. Many of the brick tiles have been removed to the Gansu provincial museum or other museums. Tombs with intact walls show that the painted tiles were interspersed among smaller plain ones. The placement of decorated tiles among undecorated ones also occurred in other parts of China during the period of disunion, including at a sixth-century tomb excavated in Deng county, Henan.

A two-chamber brick tomb excavated near Dingjiazha, eight kilometers northwest of Jiuquan, believed to have been built during the Later Liang (386–399) or the Northern Liang (401–433) kingdom, offers a striking contrast to Jiayuguan tombs in terms of quality and an overall plan for the paintings. The walls of the Jiuquan

Figure 3.13. Desert fortress painted on the wall of Dingjiazha Tomb 5, near Jiuquan, Gansu province

tomb, known as Dingjiazha Tomb 5, show scenes of daily life, including, on the lower areas, a rare painting of a desert fortress (fig. 3.13) and, on the ceiling, a painting of the world of the deities. As for the structure, the floor plan of the two-chamber tomb is similar to plans of imperial tombs in the Jiankang region, thousands of kilometers away. So is the barrel-vaulted ceiling over one chamber and pyramidal arch above the other.

Tombs from a family cemetery excavated at Qijiawan on the eastern side of Gansu, 3.5 kilometers west of Dunhuang and dated to the Western Jin and Sixteen States era, include single, double, and more complex arrangements of subterranean chambers. As in Jiuquan and Jiayuguan, the two-chambered tombs have one room with a barrel-vaulted ceiling and another with a pyramidal vault. At nearby Foyemiaowan, decorated and undecorated bricks were set into interior walls in the manner employed at Jiayuguan.

The Xianbei tombs are of a rather different sort from those of the Northern Wei. Xianbei is the name of one of many peoples from north of the Great Wall who entered China and established states and dynasties during the period between Han and Tang. The Xianbei are viewed as a conglomerate of tribes, and thus far it has not been determined which tribes created the tombs discussed here. Tombs with Xianbei occupants have been uncovered in Henan, Shanxi, Hebei, and Ningxia. Although they are exclusively single-chamber structures, interior decoration suggests that all belonged to people of political importance in fifth- to sixth-century north China.

Five Xianbei tombs have received considerable attention because of what was found inside. Two are in Guyuan, Ningxia, one is in Ci county, Hebei, and the other two are in Shanxi province. The earliest of these is probably the Northern Wei tomb in Guyuan in which lacquer sarcophaguses of a Xianbei ruler and his wife were uncovered. Paintings presumed to represent the tomb occupant were found alongside paintings of Buddhist divinities, Chinese paragons of filial piety, and the Queen Mother of the West and King Father of the East, divinities native to China. The combination illustrates the manifold ideological systems in north China under Northern Wei rule. Yet nothing of the non-Chinese origins of the occupant is reflected in the structure of the Guyuan tomb. Rather, it is a single-chamber tomb with a pyramidal-vaulted ceiling, approached by a long ramp from ground level.

This same plan was employed in the tomb of Li Xian, a member of the local gentry buried in the same county in 569, almost certainly later than the Guyuan tomb occupant. Li Xian's tomb is known for the gilded-silver ewer of Sasanian origin that was found in it. The tomb of a female, nicknamed the Ruru princess, buried in Ci county, Hebei, in 550, similarly has an extremely long approach ramp to a single chamber with pyramidal-vaulted ceiling. An unusual feature of this tomb is its floor, on which patterns resembling the border of a carpet were painted. The two Xianbei tombs in Shanxi, in Shouyang and Taiyuan, belong to Kudi Huiluo and his wife and Lou Rui, respectively. Lou Rui, whose biography is in the *Standard History of Northern Qi,* is shown in the exquisite paintings of men on his tomb walls.

The period of the Northern and Southern dynasties was one in which elements of Chinese architecture were adopted by peoples at China's borders. Non-Chinese people from the Liang kingdoms in Gansu and the Xianbei, as well as from the northeastern side of China, used Chinese tomb architecture in their own official burials. Koguryo, in what is today Jilin province of China and North Korea, provides a good example of this cross-fertilization. One of the three kingdoms into which Korea was divided from roughly the first century C.E. to 668, Koguryo has yielded more than twelve thousand tombs from this six-century period, most with stone interiors. The majority of these tombs have one or two underground rooms. Those with double chambers, such as the Twin Pillar Tomb in North Korea, or Changchuan Tomb 1 in Ji'an county, Jilin, have the same floor plans and ceiling structures as tombs of

north and south China from the fifth and sixth centuries C.E. A variation on the cupola ceiling that is common here, in which the rise between the walls and the flat ceiling top is achieved in step fashion rather than a smooth curve, originated in Eastern Han construction.

Only in south China, west of the territory of the Six Dynasties in provinces like Sichuan, Yunnan, Hunan, and Guizhou, does one occasionally find tombs with materials or plans strikingly different from those described already. Tombs excavated into natural rock at ground level or on cliffs are found in Sichuan and Gansu. In one double tomb, each chamber of which is rectangular and made of stone, an earthen mound was placed above each burial. Each compartment had a flat ceiling. The tomb was entered via two doors of stone, behind which was the stone-paved ramp up to the burial area. As is the case in so many brick tombs, the stone walls were painted.

Empress Yifu, wife of the Western Wei emperor Wen, was buried in 540 in a cliff tomb at Maijishan, near Tianshui, Gansu province. These cliffs are best known as the site of Buddhist worship caves from this period through the Tang dynasty; Empress Yifu's tomb is beneath Cave 43. Two attendants are buried with the empress in the three-bay structure. Overhead is a carved image of the Buddha, and ornately carved capitals support a simple hipped roof (fig. 3.14).

Burial in Buddhist grottoes may have been widespread among royalty and nobility of the Eastern and Western Wei and Northern Qi. The powerful Eastern Wei general and eventual ruler Gao Huan, who died in 547, has a false tomb among the Xiangtangshan caves northwest of the Northern Qi capital at Ye, located due south of the former Wei Kingdom capital Ye. Gao Huan's remains are actually in a nearby Buddhist cave at Gushan, the specific location of which has eluded archaeologists so far. (It has been conjectured that Gao Huan's empress Lou and his son, Gao Yang, are buried at Xiangtangshan.) The use of Buddhist caves as tombs during this period would be a natural progression. The spread of Buddhism during the Northern and Southern dynasties encouraged a considerable crossover of architectural features between cave temples and the common tomb plan of the period.

Buddhist Architecture

Buddhism originated in India and was introduced to China in the early years of the Eastern Han dynasty. The earliest Chinese Buddhists are believed to have been

Figure 3.14. Drawing of entry to the tomb of Empress Yifu,
Maijishan Cave 43, Gansu province

members of the upper echelons of society; only in the last years of Han rule does Buddhism seem to have spread beyond this group to the general population. During this initial period of influence, and during the subsequent century of the Three Kingdoms, Wei, and both Jins, China experienced nearly constant warfare. The mood in China, among all levels of society, was one of uncertainty and anxiety about the future. It was at this moment of vulnerability that Buddhism and the eternal salvation it preached moved full speed into all parts of China.

The earliest recorded Buddhist monastery in China was White Horse Monastery, built in Luoyang when it was still the Eastern Han capital. Nothing of the Han building complex survives, but it is said to have been modeled after an Indian plan, with a pagoda as the main structure. By the

time of the Western Jin, Luoyang had forty-two monasteries and temples to the Buddhist faith.

As has been mentioned already, Jin unification was short-lived. Upon the breakup of that empire, Buddhism had an even stronger appeal for people at every level of society. Desperate emperors, perplexed aristocrats, and the suffering masses turned to Buddhism as a way of extricating themselves from the abyss of misery that encompassed China. The rulers Shi Le of Later Zhao, Fu Jian of Former Qin, Yao Xing of Later Qin, Zhang Gui of Western Liang, and Juqu Mengsun of Northern Liang (all small kingdoms that existed during the Sixteen States period) were devout Buddhists. They received instruction from Indian monks, built temples, and had scriptures translated from Sanskrit into Chinese, but primarily their purpose

Figure 3.15. Pillar-pagoda inside Cave 39, Yungang, Shanxi province

image could not be placed in the center; instead, smaller imagery was positioned on the four sides of the central pillar. The lack of a central image may have detracted from the desired solemn and focused mood and may be the reason the pagoda was eventually superseded by large halls that could both house sculpture and provide additional devotional space.

Meanwhile, under Northern Wei rule, certain monks suggested to the emperor that he was an incarnation of the Buddha. Although the suggestions may have been nothing more than idle flattery, the same Northern Wei emperor had huge gilt-bronze images of the Buddha Sakyamuni cast. Those images were too large for pagodas, so halls were built to hold them. Palatial halls of the Chinese capital became models for the Buddhist halls of important monasteries and, not coincidentally, the emperor was the builder and patron of both. No wooden buildings survive from this time, but the front facades of caves at Maijishan, the Buddhist site where Empress Yifu was to be buried in the next century, are believed to represent the type of huge Buddha hall constructed under emperors of the Northern Wei.

Both front facades and relief sculpture inside Buddhist caves at Yungang, on the outskirts of the capital Datong, and at Maijishan, offer a glimpse of wooden Buddhist architecture of the Northern Wei (figs. 3.15, 3.16, 3.17, and 3.18). Sculptural relief in Caves 12 and 39 are fine examples. These show fully developed timber-frame structures, elevated on platforms, approached by stairs, and divided into bays by columns. Although we have no proof that columns of Buddhist halls were elaborated with imagery as they appear in the cave sculpture, the simple bracket sets consisting of blocks and arms only in the direction of the building facade, the inverted V-shaped struts between these bracket sets that together supported the weight of roof eaves, the two sets of roof rafters, the ceramic tile ends that decorated the rafters, and the curving ornaments that were named "owls' tails" by Chinese builders are believed to resemble actual structures.

Aside from relief sculpture or paintings of Buddhist buildings — countless examples of which remain on the walls of Mogao caves in Gansu province, the Longmen caves in Henan, and such other cave sites as Maijishan — knowledge of Buddhist architecture of the dynasties of north and south China is restricted to descriptions in texts or excavated evidence (figs. 3.19 and 3.20). Both have provided a wealth of information about the monasteries of Luoyang when it was the Northern Wei capital.

was personal salvation. At this early stage, through the fourth century, Buddhism was essentially a religion of meditation, sutra recitation in front of images, and symbolic pagodas said to house Buddhist relics. It was only when a large enough body of iconography came to be part of the temples — in their images and wall paintings — that dissemination of Buddhism really became possible.

As long as the pagoda remained the focus of Buddhist worship, worship space was limited. The pagoda was small, and moreover much of its interior was taken up by a central pillar that ran through it, for structural stability as well as perhaps symbolic reasons. A main devotional

Figure 3.16. Ceiling of Cave 12, Yungang

Figure 3.17. Decoration above door lintel showing bracket sets,
roof rafters, and roof ridge decoration, Cave 12, Yungang

Figure 3.18. Drawing of the front facade of Maijishan Cave 4,
Gansu province

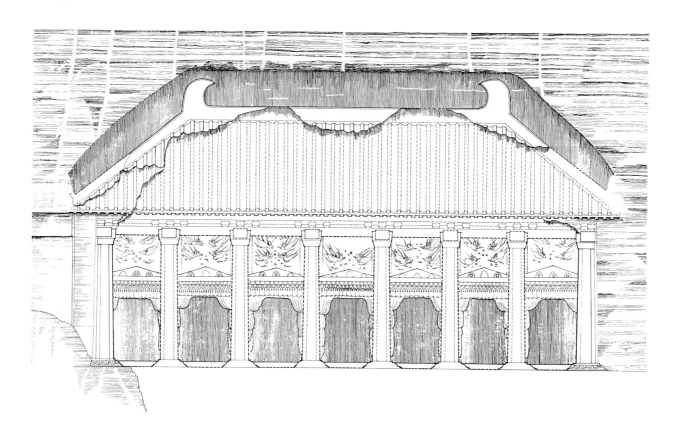

Figure 3.19. Wall painting of Buddhist buildings in Mogao Cave 420, Gansu province

Figure 3.20. Lotus-ceiling cave, Longmen grottoes, outside Luoyang, Northern Wei period

Major Monasteries of Northern Wei Luoyang

Yang Xuanzhi's *Luoyang qielan ji* (Record of Buddhist monasteries of Luoyang) is the major document detailing the more than thirteen hundred monasteries and temples in the Northern Wei capital. Of these, Jingming Monastery and Yongning Monastery, built around 500 and in 516, respectively, were the most important. Jingmingsi had a seven-story pagoda; Yongningsi had one with nine stories made of wood. (The suffix *si* means "monastery.") According to the text, Yongningsi was enclosed by a rectangular wall with a gate on each side. The main gate, at the south, was three stories, 66 meters high, and resembled Duan Gate of the Northern Wei Luoyang palace city. The gates of the other three walls were similar, but only two stories high. At the center of Yongningsi was the nine-story wooden pagoda, 161 meters tall, elevated on a base 46 meters high. The pagoda had nine bays on each side — that is, it was supported by ten pillars that defined the nine intervals of the facade. Each side had three doors and six windows. The doors of this pagoda, perhaps the most magnificent of the Northern Wei, were of vermilion lacquer and used gold nails. Golden bells hung from the corners of each level. Directly north of the pagoda was the Great Buddha Hall,

which was said to be modeled after Taiji Hall of the palace city. Inside was a golden Buddha 3 meters high. In front of the pagoda was the south gate, known as Shanmen in a Buddhist monastery, which joined the enclosing wall of Yongningsi. Within this monastery wall were more than a thousand bays of structures, including monks' quarters, towers, and pavilions. The description confirms that imperial architecture had been adopted — and sometimes adapted — for religious uses.

Extensive excavation at Yongningsi began in 1979. It is now known that the pounded-earth wall that enclosed it was 212 meters east to west by 301 meters north to south and an average of 3.3 meters thick. The south gate was a seven-bay, multistory structure whose foundation was 44 by 19 meters. The pagoda was slightly south of the true center of the monastery and was raised on a pounded-earth platform 2.2 meters high and 38.2 meters square and surrounded by a stone balustrade.

The investigation of the Yongningsi pagoda has provided some of the most important information to date about early Buddhist architecture in China (fig. 3.21). The timber frame was composed of two perimeter rows of columns that define nine bays on each of the four exte-

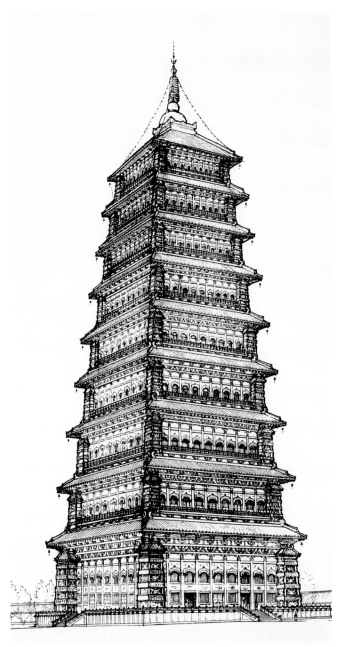

Figure 3.21. Reconstruction drawing of Yongning Monastery Pagoda, Luoyang, Henan province, circa 516

bricks. The interior core, in fact, occupied a space five bays square. It is believed that the technology of timber-frame architecture of the time was not sufficient to support a nine-story pagoda of this magnitude and thus the earthen center was necessary.

Using the excavation, documents, and details of contemporary architecture known through relief sculpture or murals in Buddhist caves of the period, Yongningsi pagoda has been theoretically reconstructed. Five niches for Buddhist images are suggested on the south, east, and west sides, and the unadorned north side is reserved for a staircase to the upper levels. The ogee-arched exterior details, inspired by a decorative feature above doors and windows of early Indian Buddhist architecture, are found in images painted on cave walls at Yungang. It is believed that the exterior was predominantly red.

The thirteen-bayed great hall of Jingzhou's Yuquan Temple no longer exists, but because it had only two rows of columns and the continuous beam that joined them was a dozen or more meters long, it was certainly a wood-framed structure. Many wooden pagodas built during the Liang dynasty probably had three, five, seven, or nine stories and most were square-shaped. The frame of the multistoried pagoda was formed by wooden pillars that rose to the top, where there was a gilded bronze vase or a multilayered disc. At least this is what is detailed in the literature, a description that nearly matches two extant ancient pagodas in Japan: the five-story pagoda of Hōryū-ji and the three-story pagoda of Hokki-ji, both constructed at the end of the seventh century in Nara prefecture, Japan. Both of those have a large base in the middle, on which a central pillar stands to support the timber frame. Each level has eave posts resting on horizontally placed beams. The two Japanese pagodas are small in comparison to the Yongningsi pagoda, but their proportions give us some idea of how the seven-story pagoda of Dayuanjingtai Monastery and the nine-level pagoda of Tongtai Monastery in Jiankang might have been built during the Southern dynasties period.

Related to the process by which Buddhism was sinicized was the donation by religious patrons of residences for conversion into temples. This practice was extremely popular in Northern Wei Luoyang. When the donated homes were too small for the needs of monastery architecture — some, for instance, were too small for a pagoda — the transformed religious complex might consist only of a front hall for the Buddha and a back hall for preaching. (In other words, Buddhist complexes without pagodas existed at this time.) Some of the converted residences had other differences, too: for example,

rior sides. The next ring of columns was aligned with the columns that were not on the corners, to create seven bays. The two rows of columns created an outer ambulatory, a feature that appears in later Chinese pagodas made of either timber-frame or brick. The floor of the ambulatory was made of wood and could be reached via a ramp (mandao) leading to the center from each of the three gates on the sides of the pagoda. Four pillars on pedestals were placed at the center of the pagoda, their locations along the lines defined by the centers of the ramp approaches and entries behind them. The space between the pillars, however, was solid, made of sun-dried mud

there are those that kept their private gardens. The abundance of these urban monasteries, in all of their various forms, greatly contributed to the rapid popularization of Buddhism, especially in China's cities.

Meanwhile, in the south, a similar transformation to a predominantly Buddhist state was under way. In 471, Emperor Ming of Liu Song converted an imperial residence into Xianggong Monastery. In 507, Emperor Wu of Liang built Guangzhai on the site of a former residence. Buddhism peaked in north and south China at the same time, with the Northern Wei in the north and the Liang in the south. By the end of the Northern Wei, 1,367 Buddhist building complexes stood in Luoyang, and 13,727 were spread across their empire. In Jiankang under Liang rule, nearly 500 monasteries stood in the capital, and the number of Buddhist establishments in the empire is recorded as 2,846. In both north and south, architectural forms from regions west of China, directly from India or by way of development in Central Asia, had to be further transformed into structures that the Chinese could build with native materials and that they felt could be accommodated on their already architecturally defined landscapes.

Figure 3.22. Relief sculpture in Cave 12, Yungang, Shanxi province

The Sinicization of Buddhist Architecture

Three fundamental stages describe the adoption and adaptation of Indian worship forms and spaces by the Chinese. First was the construction of a building to house the relics of the Buddha (the pagoda). Second was the addition of a Buddhist worship space separate from the pagoda. This brought about the concept of the Chinese monastery, the origins of which are traceable to India. Third was the replacement of the pagoda with the Buddha hall as the focus of worship. The first two phases were accomplished during the Northern and Southern dynasties, and by the time several more centuries had passed the Buddha hall reigned supreme in Chinese monastery space.

The three fundamental architectural forms of early Indian Buddhism are *stupa, vihara,* and *caitya.* Each presented a concept foreign to Chinese architecture. Nevertheless, all three found places in the Chinese building system before reunification in 589.

Stupa to pagoda is the best studied of the architectural transformations. The original stupa was an earthen relic mound with an egg-shaped dome beneath which the relics of the historical Buddha Sakyamuni are said to have been buried. Variations on this form came to be made in stone with a high finial during the early centuries of Indian Bud-

dhism, before the Eastern Han dynasty. The form was elongated as it crossed Central Asia on its path eastward. By the time it reached China, probably near the end of the Han dynasty or just after, it was a decidedly tall structure by Chinese standards. The only tall building in China at the time of Buddhism's entry there was the *que* (tower). Thus it was the blending of the stupa and the que that brought about a standard early pagoda form like the one that stands at the center of Cave 10 in Yungang: the circular plan of the Indian stupa became four-sided and the high structure became higher, but it was divided into stories (as was the Chinese multistory structure named *lou*), with Chinese architectural components articulated on each story. The Chinese were masters of relief sculpture by this time, having honed their skills in Han funerary art. For these craftsmen, it was a simple exercise of carving to articulate columns, bracket sets, intercolumnar struts, and roof tiles in stone. Yet the distinctive stories are significant (fig. 3.22).

The excavation of Yongning pagoda shows that Chinese builders had not yet mastered the art of a tall timber-frame structure — rather, the early pagoda was made up of stacked single-story buildings. There was no question that a proper Buddhist pagoda should be tall. Throughout its history in China, the pagoda towered above the low walls that enclosed the rest of Buddhist worship space, ever a reminder to the Chinese that this was an imported religion whose buildings had been accommodated to fit Chinese architectural patterns.

Figure 3.23. Yicihui pillar, Dingxing county, Hebei province, built in 569

One of the most curious monuments of sixth-century Buddhism is the Yicihui pillar that stands alone in Dingxing county, Hebei (fig. 3.23). The closest comparable structures might be the pillars that heralded the approach to tombs of the Southern dynasties. The comparison is not totally farfetched, for the lion atop the pillar in front of Xiao Jing's tomb in Nanjing is as much a symbol of Buddhism as the Buddha meditating in a hall at the top of the column in Dingxing county. It is uncertain if the unique pillar was inspired by pagoda architecture or was conceived as a pillar, perhaps one of a pair, that supported a Buddha hall at its summit.

Besides the composite layers of halls that composed the pagoda at Yongning Monastery or the one in Cave 10 at Yungang, two other pagoda forms were present in sixth-century China. One, mentioned earlier, is the pagoda of Songyue Monastery on Mount Song, Henan, dated 523 (fig. 3.24). Its twelve sides may represent an attempt to join the Chinese world of straight edges with the circular plan of Indian Buddhism.

The other pagoda form associated with the sixth century is four-sided and has a single story. Although

restored in 611 during the Sui dynasty and so discussed in Chapter 4, Simenta (Four-Entry Pagoda) of Shentong Monastery in Shandong province is believed to be based on an Eastern Wei structure. It is an important building that may help us understand what the sixth-century brick or stone pagodas recorded in texts looked like. The Northern Wei are said to have built a three-story stone pagoda in Datong in 367 and a "stone chamber" at Yonggu, Fangshan, in 481. Between 477 and 493 they built a five-story stone pagoda and Zhiyuanshe Stone Hall. Because none of these stone structures have been found, brick pagoda architecture remains our best possibility for imagining the forms of these buildings.

The early Indian Buddhist architectural form vihara probably originated in a courtyard-style house. In India, monastic courtyards were enclosed by cells in which monks dwelled, carved into the enclosure on three sides of a hall. When residential spaces were converted into religious areas in China, courtyards similarly came to be enclosed by monastic cells. Vihara thus embodied two concepts, enclosure and monasticism. Both of these ideas were fairly easily accommodated in the Chinese architectural system. Since very early on, Chinese architecture had consisted of courtyards surrounded by covered arcades, and division of the arcades by pillars could be suited to monastic cells. Moreover, monastic cells were frequently not created in China; instead monks often resided and studied in Chinese-style dormitories located off the main axis of a monastery, or even sought meditational space in nearby grottoes.

These larger grottoes, initially rock-cut worship spaces known as caitya halls in India, found their only native Chinese counterpart in rock-cut tombs. Unlike the well-documented transformation from stupa to pagoda, it is not clear that the Chinese rock-carved funerary architecture inspired Buddhist worship caves. It is certain, however, that during the period of disunion, tremendous amounts of energy and money, including huge amounts of imperial funds, were spent in every part of China on excavating caves for Buddhist worship. Because of the permanence of stone in comparison to wood, much more is known about the forms and arrangements of Buddhist caves than is known of monastery structures and plans.

The word *caitya* is also used in the context of a caitya arch. In that case, it is a form imported to China as a decorative, pointed, horseshoe-shaped lintel carved above an entry or window, or framing a Buddha image that originated on the exterior facade or entry to Indian Buddhist caves in the late centuries B.C.E.

Figure 3.24. Pagoda of Songyue Monastery, Mount Song,
Henan province, built in 523

Figure 3.25. Entry to Cave 16 at Tianlongshan, Shanxi province. Roof rafters are painted red under the eaves on the facade.

Chinese Buddhist Cave Temples

Cave temples are a fundamental form of Buddhist architecture in China. They were carved and remain in most parts of China, notably Xinjiang, Gansu, Ningxia, Shaanxi, Henan, Shanxi, Hebei, Shandong, Liaoning, Qinghai, Sichuan, Yunnan, Guangxi, Jiangsu, Zhejiang, and Jiangxi. Wherever there were Buddhists, if it was possible to carve caves such spaces were created for worship and meditation.

Most of the Buddhist cave-temple sites trace their histories to the period between Han and Tang. Sculpted and painted Buddhist imagery survives in most of them, and the majority also document examples of period architecture in relief sculpture. In addition, the arrangement of chambers within single caves and the arrangement of caves in groups inform us about other types of Chinese architecture from the same time period.

The cave temples considered most important for the study of Chinese architecture of the Southern dynasties are Qixia Monastery in the vicinity of Nanjing and the Great Buddha Cave in Xinchang, Zhejiang. Many more caves survive in north China. Among these, especially important for the investigation of Buddhism at this time are Liangzhou, in Wuwei county, Gansu; Binglingsi in Gansu; the Mogao caves near Dunhuang, Gansu; Maijishan in Gansu; Yungang near Datong in Shanxi; Tianlongshan near Taiyuan in Shanxi; Longmen near Luoyang; Gongxian in Henan; and Xiangtangshan in Hebei.

Together with representations of architecture in Buddhist cave temples discussed already, details from three other cave temples are especially important for understanding Buddhist architecture of the Northern and Southern dynasties. One, the entry to Cave 16 at Tianlongshan, is an example of several features noted already in this period's architecture, namely the combination of simple bracket sets and inverted V-shaped struts across a lintel and underneath the roof eaves; the tradition of entering the Buddhist hall via a one-bay deep porch, which sometimes was attached in wood to the Buddhist cave temple; the use of octagonal columns (which can be traced back at least as far as the Eastern Han dynasty); and the polychroming of the exterior of buildings as heavily as is done today (fig. 3.25).

Other important details can be gleaned from Mogao Cave 248, an example of a central-pillar cave temple. The central pillar had more functions than support of a ceiling. The pillar was a stupa, and around that stupa — which was sometimes a repository for images of four quadrants of the Buddhist world, at other times a backboard for one image, and at still other times a space for the "thousand Buddhas" representing the myriad world of the Buddhist faith and its deities — a worshiper could circumambulate in ritual devotion. As in Indian and Central Asian Buddhist caves in Xinjiang province (Xinjiang Uyghur autonomous region), the pillar could be placed in the center or near the back wall. The diameter of the pillar could decrease from base to roof or be of uniform exterior dimensions — much as we see in pagodas in the round. At the Songyue Monastery pagoda, for example, the perimeter narrows from base to top, whereas at the Simenta, the perimeter size remains constant. In multistory central pillars, a set of roof eaves projected from each story.

Finally, we come to a worship cave interior such as that of Cave 3 at Maijishan. Here we have a fully developed Buddhist worship hall, probably resembling one from the first centuries of Buddhism in China. On the back wall, a main image sits under a canopy and caitya arch, and images and paintings re-create the rest of a Buddhist world of deities in relation to the main Buddha. Also important is the ceiling, a canopy or pyramidal-vaulted one of the kind observed in contemporary tombs. Cave temples like this suggest that temple and tomb shared both architecture and iconography in fourth- to sixth-century China. That is, although it was typical for a Buddhist to be cremated, the pervasive funerary world of Han China may have resulted in the creation of tombs for Buddhists of the fourth, fifth, and sixth centuries that were modeled after Buddhist cave temples or halls. The burial of Empress Yifu in a rock-cut tomb at a Buddhist cave site is an example of this phenomenon. Structural details such as inverted V-shaped brackets and pyramidal-vaulted ceilings, which were shared by funerary and religious architecture, are thus better understood as period-style features than as specifically religious or secular. The palace and Buddha hall are as architecturally intertwined as the cave temple and tomb.

The similarities between tomb and temple architecture illustrate one way in which Chinese Buddhist architecture had separated itself from its Indian origins. The Chinese also blended the traditions by creating a dodecagonal pagoda and enshrining a Buddha in a hall at the top of a towering pillar. After the reunification of China, yet another offshoot of traditional Indian Buddhist architecture was to emerge: fully planned and richly developed aboveground monasteries.

CHAPTER 4

The Sui, Tang, and Five Dynasties

FU XINIAN

The thriving economy and international culture of the Sui and especially the Tang dynasty stimulated a period of tremendous architectural creativity. These two dynasties form the earliest period from which an outstanding example of every type of Chinese building — palace hall, Buddhist hall, pagoda, tomb, cave temple, and bridge — exists or can be reliably reconstructed. Sites from this time include the earliest extant Chinese wooden halls and architecture from not only China's great cities but also faraway towns and isolated pilgrimage sites, allowing us to compare metropolitan and provincial modes of construction. Examples of high-ranking and more humble construction also survive in their earliest versions from the Tang dynasty, making it possible for the first time to differentiate architecture by rank through both textual and actual evidence. Paintings of architecture, too, survived in far greater quantity than before, and, unlike earlier artwork, they can be viewed alongside actual buildings.

China had extensive associations with other countries during this era. Trade brought men of the Tang across Central Asia and the Pamir mountains, to Afghanistan and Persia, and indirectly into contact with the Byzantine Empire. With such interchange came elements of foreign cultures, including religion, painting, sculpture, music, dance, household utensils, and customs.

Details, figure 4.36 *(opposite)* and figure 4.37 *(above)*

Architectural influences were part of this mix, but because China's building system was already well developed and deeply rooted, the greatest changes probably occurred in decorative designs, carving techniques, and new colors. Many ornaments from other countries — such as the crocket, string bead pattern, and eight-petal lotus design — were adopted and turned to suit Chinese taste.

Accelerating the emergence of a distinctive Chinese architectural style was the internal political unity of the time. This became more evident after 589, when General Yang Jian (540–605) overthrew the Chen (557–589), the last of the Six Dynasties that had ruled from the city of Jiankang after the fall of Han. The rise of the Sui dynasty, with Yang Jian as its first emperor, Sui Wendi, meant that for the first time in more than 350 years China was united.

Like the Qin, Sui was a short-lived dynasty. It endured only thirty years, falling during the reign of its second ruler, Wendi's son Sui Yangdi (r. 605–617). But its brevity is only one of the reasons that Chinese historians like to compare the Qin and Sui dynasties. Of particular architectural significance was the vision the two dynastic founders brought to their rule. Like China's First Emperor, Sui emperor Wendi viewed cities and their architecture as an inseparable aspect of legitimizing imperial rule.

The city was where an emperor could most clearly display the wealth and splendor of his empire. In a mere three decades, both Chang'an and Luoyang were built anew as cities of unequaled size and grandeur, while borrowing much from China's urban past. The Sui were also responsible for the construction of the Grand Canal, which for centuries was the key commercial link between north and south China.

The Tang dynasty that followed the Sui was to define an era of great cultural splendor and commercial and political power. It was a period of national prosperity and unity, expanding frontiers and international contacts. Imposing palaces, imperial gardens, and official mansions were built in the capital Chang'an and the eastern capital Luoyang. A great number of Buddhist temples and Daoist temples were built in the Tang capital and elsewhere, and the carving of grottoes continued. Four temples dating to that time are known to exist today.

The Tang empire collapsed in 907. This time, disunion lasted only fifty-four years. Yet from this relatively short period of Chinese history, decades of constant warfare during which five dynasties and ten kingdoms vied for power, more wooden structures survive than from the previous three centuries of Sui and Tang rule. These humbler halls of short-lived states mark the final legacy of the Tang building tradition.

Capitals and Other Cities

Like the Han, the Tang dynasty (618–907) built on cultural and governmental models from its short-lived predecessor. Having learned from the mistakes of Yang Jian and his son, the more cautious founder of Tang, Li Yuan (565–635) established an imperial system that endured for nearly three hundred years. During that time, Chang'an became the greatest city in the world, with a truly international population. Remarkably complete documentation and continued excavation through the second half of the twentieth century have allowed the reconstruction of almost every imperial building in the Tang capital city, true to the location, size, and many architectural features of the originals.

In its day, the Sui-Tang capital Daxing-Chang'an was the largest city in the world, and the eastern Sui-Tang capital, Luoyang, built according to the same model, was the second largest. The Heijō capital in Japan, at what is now Nara, and at least nine other capital cities in Japan and in the Korean peninsula followed the urban pattern of the Sui-Tang capitals. Equally well planned but different in design was the greatest Tang city in southeastern China, Yangzhou. Concessions to the dominant Tang scheme in city planning were made in China's western regions, but even there the most fundamental aspects of Chinese urbanism were implemented.

In 582 Sui emperor Wendi began what has been called the greatest feat in urban planning of the premodern world at a site ten kilometers southeast of the former capital of the Western Han dynasty, Chang'an. The Sui ruler named his city Daxing, or "great flourishing." Covering an area of 84.1 square kilometers, it was the largest city thus far in the history of China. Although built on a new site, when the Tang dynasty was established, the name of the capital returned to the name of the primary city of Han China, Chang'an. Tang Chang'an was surrounded by a rectangular wall made of pounded earth that spanned 9.7 kilometers east to west and 8.6 kilometers north to south (fig. 4.1). The space encompassed by that wall was known as the outer city. Inside, in the north center of Chang'an, were two more walled enclosures north and south of each other, occupying an area of 9.4 square kilometers (2.8 kilometers east to west by 3.3 kilometers north to south). The southern one, known as the imperial (or administrative) city, where the offices of the Tang central government were housed, measured 1.8 kilometers in length. Due north and extending 1.5 kilometers was the palace city. In Sui and early Tang times, the imperial residence, the offices that supplied provisions and otherwise

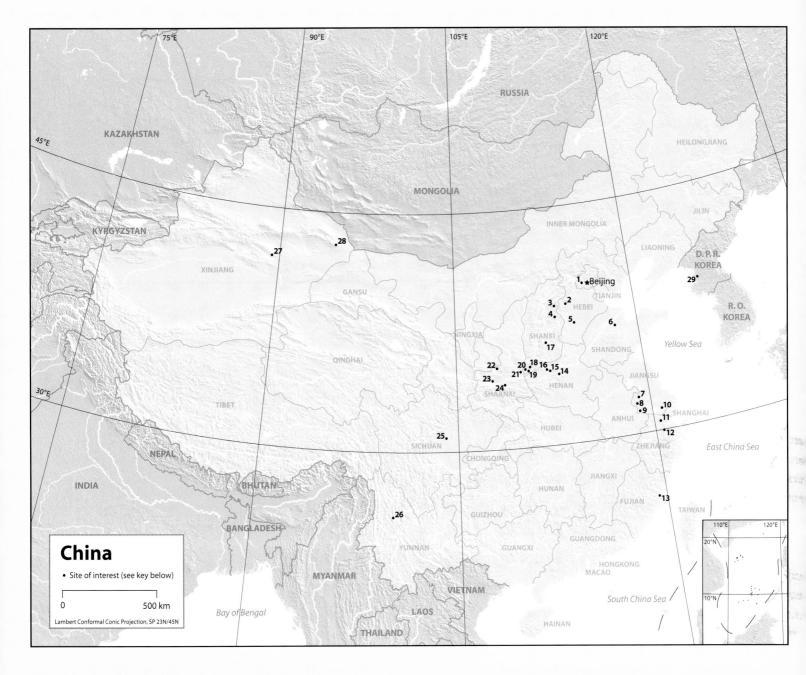

Map 4.
Sui, Tang, and Five Dynasties Sites

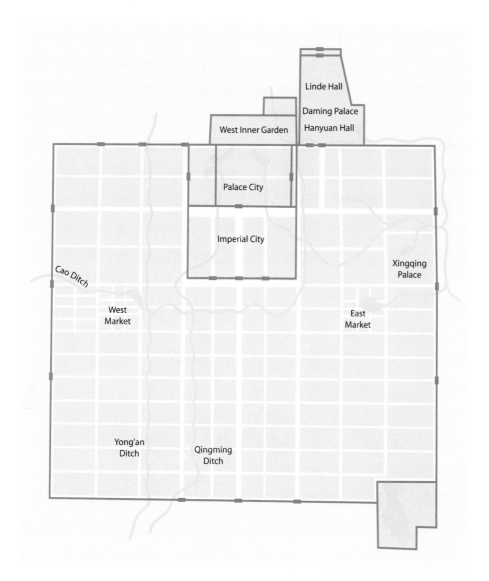

Figure 4.1. Map of Chang'an, capital of the Sui and Tang empires

serviced the palace, and the residence of the crown prince were located in the middle, west, and east, respectively. Bordering the northern wall of the outer city, the central portion of which was shared by the palace city, were imperial gardens and imperial parkland. Beyond the imperial and palace cities but within the outer city wall were wards, most of them residential but some occupied by religious institutions, markets, and commercial districts and, in one case, another imperial palace.

The positions of the wards were determined by major streets that originated at fourteen gates in the outer city wall, five on the north side and three on each of the other three sides. Between the streets, which were aligned with the city gates, additional avenues ran the length and width of Chang'an. In all, nine major streets cut across the city north to south and twelve traversed it east to west. These twenty-one streets defined the walled boundaries of the 110 wards (sometimes thought of as 108 wards because each of the markets, one on the eastern and one on the western side of the city, occupied a ward); twenty-six wards

were on the eastern and western sides of the palace and imperial cities, and the rest were to the south. Although the wards were not perfectly uniform in size, their consistent arrangement made for a "checkerboard" city plan.

Each gate of the Sui-Tang Chang'an outer wall had three entryways. The central one was reserved for imperial passage, and the outer two were for the entrance or exit of officials and commoners. Similarly, all main thoroughfares were divided into three lanes, the middle of which was restricted to imperial usage. These streets were lined with *huai* (locust trees), and beyond the trees were open drainage ditches.

The width of Chang'an's streets is impressive even by today's standards. The widest street in the city, 220 meters across, separated the palace city from the imperial city, and the main north–south street of Chang'an was 155 meters wide. No street on the outside of a ward was fewer than 100 meters in width. The streets were reportedly made broad to provide easy passage for the officials who needed to race through the city on government errands. Quick passage was possible through every ward as well: most had streets between forty and sixty meters wide that bisected each other in the center of the district. The larger wards had three east–west and three north–south streets, which created sixteen interior divisions.

In purely residential wards with these sixteen interior sectors, houses lined both sides of the three lanes in both directions. Officials and nobility, however, had significantly larger plots of residential space. Mansions could occupy a sixteenth, quarter, half, or occasionally even an entire ward. Each of the double-ward-sized eastern and western markets occupied more than a square kilometer of the city. Two gates provided access to the market wards from each direction, with shops built along either side of the major north–south and east–west thoroughfares.

Chang'an contained many religious institutions. In the early eighth century, there were ninety-one Buddhist and sixteen Daoist temple complexes. Monasteries built by national or official patronage, such as Ci'ensi and Xingshansi, could span half or even an entire ward. The huge resident and mercantile foreign population also had its own residential sectors and religious structures. Nestorian Christians, Zoroastrians, and worshipers of other Persian faiths, for example, had religious buildings in Chang'an.

The strict axiality of the urban plan was inherited from earlier Chinese capital cities. Yet in one way, the Sui-Tang imperial city was markedly different from its predecessors. Although the palace city and the imperial city were still contiguous and shared a wall, for the first time in Chinese urban history they were separate entities. This change may have been anticipated in the period after Han, particularly in the initial post-Han plans of Ye and Luoyang at the time of the Wei Kingdom (220–265). Under the Wei ruler Cao Pi, for example, the city of Ye was designed with a single palace area, a plan followed in urban schemes at Luoyang from the third century on. Similarly, the design of Jianye during the rule of the Wu Kingdom (222–280) had consisted of a single palace area. Indeed, a marked change in imperial city planning in the third century C.E. was the termination of multiple palaces, such as those in Qin-Han China. By the establishment of Sui Daxing, however, the size of the bureaucracy and complexity of the government had so increased that it was deemed preferable to position government offices adjacent to the imperial family and household, but each inside its own walled sector. Thus the concept of an administrative city, or imperial city, was born. Similarly, the positions of markets became fixed during this era: whereas in the times of Han, the Three Kingdoms, and the Northern and Southern dynasties markets were located at various spots throughout the capitals, now they were set

symmetrically east and west of the main north–south axis of the city, also enclosed by their own walls.

Yet even though the roots of many aspects of the great Sui-Tang capital plan can be found in pre-sixth-century China, Chang'an of the seventh through ninth centuries was still a landmark achievement in Chinese urban planning. Besides the separation of palace and imperial cities, the ward system, introduced in the third century B.C.E., was taken to an unprecedented level of organization. In addition to the strict ward system and two markets, other features anticipated in earlier imperial planning have come to be considered trademarks of imperial ideology by this time: a park due north of the palace city and a bilaterally symmetrical plan divided by a major and extremely long thoroughfare, the widest north–south in the city, called Red Oriole Road.

Luoyang

The eastern Sui capital at Luoyang was founded by Wendi's son Yangdi in 605. Its nearly square outer wall measured 7.3 kilometers on the east, 7.3 kilometers on the south, 6.1 kilometers on the north, and 6.8 kilometers on the south, with a perimeter of 27.5 kilometers. The Luo River ran right through the city from southwest to northeast, dividing it into districts known as "north of Luo" and "south of Luo."

In spite of original intentions to replicate the plan of Sui Daxing and construct a bilaterally symmetrical city, the topography northeast of the Luo River proved somewhat restrictive, so the palace and imperial cities were constructed farther northwest within the scheme (fig. 4.2). Another incentive for the location of the palaces was Yique, about ten kilometers south and west of the palace city, where water flowed between two mountains. Although the spot was scenic, construction of wall-enclosed wards in that area was impossible. Instead, the city wards were east, south, and southeast of the palace and governmental areas. Still, Luoyang followed the imperial plan initiated by the Sui in the separation of the palace and imperial cities, the location of Taoguang Park north of the palace city, and the width of Red Oriole Road approaching the imperial and palace cities. In addition, like Chang'an and many of its post-Han predecessors, the gates of the palace-, imperial-, and outer-city walls were aligned, as were three bridges that spanned the Luo River south of the imperial city and north of the outer-city wards. One of the bridges, Tianjinqiao, was a pontoon bridge. Because of the number of necessary

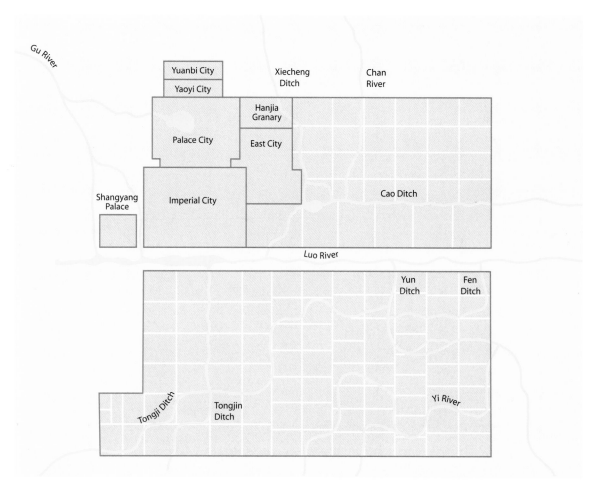

Figure 4.2. Map of Luoyang, Sui and Tang capital

wards and the concentration of wards east of the palace and governmental sectors, wards were constructed north of the northern boundary of the palace city and even north of the garden north of that. Furthermore, two additional walled sectors, Yaoyicheng and Yuanbicheng, were constructed north of Taoguang Park and the northern outer wall. The city could not have extended much beyond these spaces, however, because the mountain range Mangshan lay to the north.

Through careful planning, 104 wards, nearly the number at Chang'an, were fit into the Tang eastern capital. Even though the palace area was not in the north center of the whole, and even though there was a third market, a checkerboard system of streets was again achieved because the wards were more consistently sized than those at Chang'an. Seventy-five residential wards were laid out south of the Luo River, three of which were used for the two markets in this area of Luoyang. Twenty-four wards were located north of a tributary of the Luo River called Cao Canal that emanated from the boundary between the palace city and the imperial city. The canal was the transport mechanism for goods in and out of the palace and

administrative areas. Five more wards were placed between the Luo River and Cao Canal. Thus the total number of wards north of the river was twenty-nine, one of which was used for a market. Finally, a sector called East City and the Hanjia Granary were located between the northeastern residential wards and the imperial city, palace city, and Yaoyicheng-Yuanbicheng areas.

A study of measured drawings of Chang'an and Luoyang in Sui-Tang times shows that the dimensions of the palace and imperial cities were used as modules in planning the respective capitals. It may well have been modular planning that made it possible to construct these magnificent urban spaces on such an unprecedented scale and in an astonishingly short time. Each city was built in just two years.

Ward and Market System in Sui-Tang Cities

The organization of space outside the imperial and government sectors of Sui-Tang Chang'an was anticipated in the urban designs of earlier Chinese capital cities. Indeed, every Chinese capital since the Han dynasty had been designed with some sort of internal subdivision in mind. By Tang times, however, the organization of city space into four-sided enclosed areas was a feature of urban planning outside the capitals as well.

As mentioned above, a typical residential ward of Tang Chang'an was surrounded by earthen walls with gates on at least two and often four sides and with between four and sixteen internal divisions. The wards, which were most often longer east–west than they were north–south, functioned as small fortresses, their gates opening at dawn and closing at the night curfew so that the population's entrance and exit could be controlled. Only nobles and officials were permitted to have their gates directly facing the streets. Soldiers patrolled the streets at night and even officials were prohibited from coming out before their gates were opened in the morning, unless they had a special reason such as a summons to the court.

Inhabitants could buy their daily necessities within their own residential wards but went to the markets for larger commercial activities. Like the residential wards, marketplaces were small walled compounds accessible only through guarded and regulated gates. At the center of each market was a building for its administrative officials. Streets radiated out from the center, with shops arranged so that stores with similar trade were in the same area. Market wards were open from noon to sunset.

No Tang texts describe the feelings of residents who lived in such highly organized cities. From the vantage point of a city planner, one could hardly conceive a more neatly arranged and ordered urban space. Yet such rigid organization must have hindered the easy flow of goods and people, as well as, ultimately, economic growth. Indeed, Chang'an and Luoyang were the last Chinese capitals to be so severely structured or regulated. It was probably no accident that the breakdown of the checkerboard plan coincided with the unprecedented economic and commercial growth experienced in Chinese capitals of the Song dynasty from 960 onward.

Ideally, every Tang provincial and prefectural capital was designed in accordance with the ward system implemented in China's national capitals — that is, so that homes of the general population were kept separate from not only the residential architecture of a prince (or other highly positioned controller of a lesser capital), but also government offices, official residences, storehouses, and military barracks. But in fact the ward system began to break down outside of the Chinese capitals before the end of the Tang dynasty. The plan during the Tang era

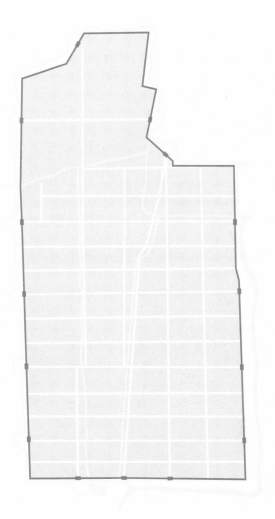

Figure 4.3. Plan of the city of Yangzhou during the Tang dynasty

for Yangzhou, one of several flourishing commercial centers in southeastern China, had strict north–south and east–west streets defining the residential wards of the populace, the city ruler's residential sectors, the government administrative spaces in the north, and the moat that surrounded the city walls (fig. 4.3). As the city evolved, however, the functions (and architecture) of some wards spilled over into other areas, weakening the absolute divisions of the original scheme and encouraging a far more fluid and dynamic city environment than that suggested by the neatly defined divisions.

Tang Planning Beyond China's Borders

The association between the rigid, orthogonal city plan and Tang China could not have been stronger. It was perhaps the most obvious and easily recognized symbol of the powerful East Asian monarch and his imperial system.

Thus the city plan was one of the fundamentally Tang Chinese images that was imitated beyond China's borders when rulers in Japan and on the Korean peninsula sought models for their own imperial governmental systems.

In early eighth-century Japan, for example, the establishment of the Nara period coincided with the founding of the Heijō capital according to the Sui-Tang model. That city, today at Nara, and another, the late-eighth-century capital of the Heian period, today at Kyoto, are the best known. But in fact six capitals were built in Japan between the mid seventh and the late eighth century, and all of them owed their designs to Sui-Tang China. In addition to the Heijō and Heian capitals, built in 710 and 794, respectively, the Fujiwara capital, today at Asuka, and the Naniwa capital, today at Osaka, were constructed in the second half of the seventh century; and the Kuni and Nagaoka capitals were founded between the construction of the Heijō and Heian capitals. Excavation suggests that, especially in the Asuka region, imitation of Chinese models in the design of cities and architecture may have predated the seventh century.

On the Korean peninsula, excavation has confirmed that architecture and building complexes at the capital of the Koguryu kingdom at today's Pyongyang (427–668) followed Sui-Tang patterns. So did the upper, central, and eastern of the five capitals of the Bohai (Parhae) kingdom, which date from the second half of the eighth century until no later than the fall of the kingdom in 926.

The influence of Tang urbanism was felt in the farthest reaches of the empire. Although the commanderies and garrisons of Tang China's western regions (today in eastern and central Xinjiang Uyghur autonomous region) were constructed with local materials and mostly by builders who had only heard of the great cities of Tang, these structures also bore the stamp of Sui-Tang. Inside the mud-earth walls of Gaochang and Jiaohe, for instance, rulers' spaces were separate from those of the rest of the population, and the layout of streets in parts of the cities was orthogonal.

Palatial Architecture

Within a year after the founding of the two Sui capitals, a palace city was completed at each. The palace complex at Daxing was named Daxinggong; that at Luoyang was called Ziweigong. Although the names were changed, to Taijigong and Taichugong, respectively, both sites continued to be used after the establishment of the Tang dynasty. In addition, the Tang built two new palace complexes at Chang'an. In 662, Daminggong was constructed

by the third Tang emperor, Gaozong, adjacent to Chang'an but northeast of the outer city in former parkland, and Tang emperor Xuanzong built the Xingqing palace complex inside the Longqing ward in 714. Moreover, both dynasties had detached palaces. Sui detached palaces included Jiangdugong, Renshougong, and Fenyanggong, whereas Cuiwengong, Jiuchenggong, Shangyanggong, and Hebeigong were built under Tang rule. Due to superior record-keeping and excavation, detailed and reliable information exists about the plans and about many of the structures in the palaces of both dynasties.

The southern entrance to Taijigong, Daxinggong of the Sui, was the terminus of Red Oriole Road of the Tang capital. It was one of three parts into which the Tang palace city, 2.8 kilometers east to west by 1.5 kilometers north to south, was divided. East of Taijigong was the palace of the crown prince, known as the Eastern Palace. It measured 833 meters east to west. West of Taijigong were storage areas for goods that supported the needs of palace life, living quarters for the women, and a few official bureaus. This area measured 703 meters across at its widest point.

The central sector of Taijigong was the imperial court, known as Danei, the imperial palace or "great inner" (fig. 4.4). It was 1.3 kilometers wide and covered an area of 1.9 square kilometers. Danei was itself divided into three parts: the court, residential area, and gardens. These were the most important spaces in the Tang imperial system. The court, symbol of state power, was the location of grand ceremonies and the place where affairs of state were decided. The residential sector represented the authority of the royal family.

The ceremonial space of the emperor extended slightly south of Taiji Gate, the main entrance to the court and palace area. Between it and Chengtian Gate, the entrance to the entire Taijigong complex, ceremonies dating back to Zhou times were enacted. These included rites of the New Year and the winter solstice. Northward, in the courtyard between Taiji Gate and Taiji Hall, the emperor held court on the first and fifteenth days of each lunar month and on the occasion of a syzygy. These rituals also were traceable to the Zhou, when they were known as the rites of the central court and the daily court.

The courtyards in front of and behind Taiji Hall, or Taijidian, were enclosed by covered arcades, with a gate on the eastern and western sides. The eastern gate led to offices, the chancellery, the Office of Historiography, and the Institute for the Advancement of Literature, the western gate to the secretariat and Hanlin Academy.

Directly behind the back gate to the Taijigong rear courtyard was the dividing line between the court and residential areas of Danei. This was the main east–west thoroughfare across the palace city. The residential area consisted of two main palace complexes. In the southern one, Liangyidian, the first Tang emperors held court every other day, following the Zhou custom. To the east and west were the palace complexes of Wanchun Hall and Qianqiu Hall. Like Liangyi Hall, each was enclosed by a covered arcade that created a courtyard in front of it.

Behind the second cross street in the palace city was the residential area of the empress and concubines, its entrance flanked by Rihua Gate on the east and Yuehua Gate on the west. No official was permitted to enter here. The main hall, Ganludian, was similar in plan to the Liangyidian complex in front of it, and was bounded on either side, east and west, by Shenlong Hall and Anren Hall. Each hall was in its own courtyard defined by covered arcades. Each of the main residential halls was part of a two-part structure: the front hall or buildings for public situations, and the back structures for private ones. The bipartite arrangement of each complex, in which the main front building was larger than the structure directly behind it, was carried throughout the central, eastern, and western sectors of Taijigong. In addition, all buildings were arranged in accordance with the cardinal directions, in an ultimate extension of the concept of orthogonal planning implemented in the outer city.

Beyond Rihua and Yuehua gates were more palatial halls and offices of lesser importance in the imperial bureaucracy than those adjacent to the Taijidian complex.

Only in the gardens of Taijigong were the symmetry and organization broken. There, too, halls and pavilions were fronted by courtyards or enclosed by covered arcades, but the buildings were fit into spaces defined by ponds and waterways. At the center of the back wall was Xuanwu Gate, in line with every main hall and gate of Chang'an itself. Xuanwu Gate provided imperial access to the private parkland next to the capital city outer wall.

Since premodern times, each reconstructor of the Tang palace city has had to rely on his best judgment for such details as the number of entries to a gate, because original texts are not explicit. Today the palace city of Chang'an is buried beneath the city of Xi'an.

The palace city of the Tang capital at Luoyang (Ziwei-gong of Sui times, and alternately known as Luoyang-gong in the Tang) stood in the northeastern area of the Sui-Tang capital. Measuring 2,080 meters east to west by 1,052 meters north to south, Taichugong, like its Chang'an counterpart, was divided into three parts. Danei, the central area, locus of the imperial court, was 1,030 meters wide. The Eastern Palace was on the east, and west

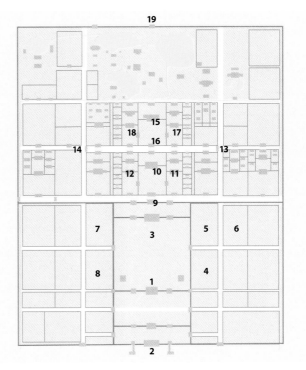

Figure 4.4. Plan of Taijigong, the palace city in the Tang capital, Chang'an

1. Taijimen (Great Ultimate Gate)
2. Chengtianmen (Continuing Heaven's Mandate Gate)
3. Taijidian (Great Ultimate Hall)
4. Chancellery
5. Office of Historiography
6. Institute for the Advancement of Literature
7. Secretariat
8. Palace Visitors Bureau
9. Back Gate of Taijigong
10. Liangyidian (Heaven and Earth Hall)
11. Wanchundian (Myriad Springs Hall)
12. Qianqiudian (Thousand Autumns Hall)
13. Rihuamen (Sun Splendor Gate)
14. Yuehuamen (Moon Splendor Gate)
15. Ganludian (Sweet Dew Hall)
16. Ganlumen (Sweet Dew Gate)
17. Shenlongdian (Divine Dragon Hall)
18. Anrendian (Peace and Benevolence Hall)
19. Xuanwumen (Black Tortoise Gate)

was "west city," each 340 meters wide. Beyond each were narrow walled-in regions, 190 and 180 meters in width.

Taichugong's Danei was divided into front and back sectors: the front was the location of the imperial court and the back was where the royalty lived. The approach to its main hall was Yingtian Gate, on top of which was a two-story gate tower. A watchtower was positioned on either side. Although of the same form, Yingtian Gate was larger than Chengtian Gate, its counterpart at Chang'an. Directly behind Yingtian Gate was Qianyang-dian, the largest hall in Luoyang. It spanned thirteen bays across the front and soared fifty meters in height. A covered arcade with a gate on each side surrounded it.

Between Yingtian Gate and Qianyang Hall, on the same axial line, was Qianyang Gate. Streets ran east and west from the gates of the covered arcade around Qianyang Hall. To the north was Wencheng Hall, and north of the western street, Wu'an Hall. They formed a line with Qianyang Hall, as did the corridor-surrounded arcades that enclosed each of the three. To the south was the chancellery on the east and the secretariat on the west. North of the three halls was the first east–west thoroughfare through the palace city providing access to the narrow walled areas on the outlying regions and separating the court from the residential quarters of Taichugong.

The main structure of the residential area was named Daye Hall. The emperor held court there every other day. To its east and west were rows of halls, and halls in their own courtyards. The second cross street of the palace city was to the north, and beyond it were the bedrooms of the empress and concubines. As at the Chang'an palace city, officials were not permitted to enter this area. Huiyoudian was the main hall of the female residential area. It stood on a line with Qianyang and Daye halls and was flanked by halls to its east, west, and north. All were building complexes composed of two main halls, the larger in front and smaller in back, and all were enclosed in their own arcades and had courtyards in front.

In the northern portion of the western narrow, enclosed sector was Jiuzhou Pond, inside the imperial garden. North of the pond was a princely residence and south was a row of five halls used for large banquets. Huge pavilions were also in this area.

Four major changes can be observed from the two previous centuries. First, the palace area of Sui can be seen as a three-part complex—court area, residential area, and gardens in a line from south to north. The palaces of Jiankang, Northern Wei Luoyang, and Eastern Wei Ye, by contrast, consisted of three concentric walled areas. Second, Sui Daxinggong and Ziweigong placed Taijidian, a single hall for holding court, as a focal point of the city. Third, the secretariat and sima gates that since Wei-Jin times had been southeast and on the four sides of the Taiji Hall complex, respectively, were separated from it, thereby abolishing the secondary axis that these structures had formed on the eastern side of the palace city. Last, the great rites enacted in Taiji Hall since Wei-Jin times were moved to Chengtian Gate, the main south gate of the palace city. The daily court and rites of the first and fifteenth days of the lunar months were held instead at Taiji Hall and Liangyi Hall behind it, no longer in the halls directly east and west of Taijidian. In other words, the axis of imperial primacy in the palace city had shifted from east–west to north–south.

Daminggong

Daminggong, or the Palace of Great Light, was situated northeast of the palace city of Chang'an, outside its outer wall. Excavation done since the 1950s has revealed that its outer wall had a rare trapezoidal shape, 1,135 meters east to west along its north side and 1,370 meters along its south wall, which also formed part of the north wall of Chang'an. Measuring 2,256 meters along its straight western side, the Daming palace complex was 3.11 square kilometers (fig. 4.5). Daminggong can be seen as a four-part complex. Southernmost, just beyond the entry to the complex across a waterway, lay a square 500 meters on a side. At the north end of the square, rising 15 meters from ground level, was the first and main hall, Hanyuandian. In some ways, Hanyuandian was equivalent to Chengtian Gate of the Taiji palace complex: there the grand imperial rites were performed and a pavilion stood in front of it on either side. The first interior wall of Daminggong continued east and west of Hanyuandian.

Three hundred meters behind Hanyuan Hall was Xuanzheng Hall, from whose two sides extended the second interior wall of the complex. Enclosed by a covered arcade, Xuanzhengdian was more than three hundred meters wide. Beyond its arcade were offices of the central government: the chancellery and Office of Historiography on the east, and the secretariat and Department of Palace Administration to the west. Xuanzhengdian was where the emperor held court on the first and fifteenth days of each lunar month. Between the two main halls was the central administrative area of the Tang court. Behind Xuanzheng Hall was Zichen Gate, and beyond it Zichen Hall. This was where the emperor held court every other day. It was the equivalent of Liangyidian, the main imperial residential hall of Taijigong. Due east of Zichen Hall were halls for bathing and steam baths, and due west were Yanying and Hanxiang halls. The emperor went to these when he was not holding court.

The third cross street of Daminggong was north of the Zichendian complex. Beyond it were the sleeping quarters of the empress and imperial concubines. The main sleeping chamber, Penglai Hall, was due north of Zichen Hall, and Hanliang Hall was directly behind it. More minor halls were arranged along north–south lines east and west of the two main sleeping chambers. Farther north was Taiye Pond, with an islet known as Mount Penglai rising from it. Halls were built on all sides. Two large building complexes, Lindedian and Taifudian, were built on the west. The Linde Hall complex, excavated more than thirty years ago,

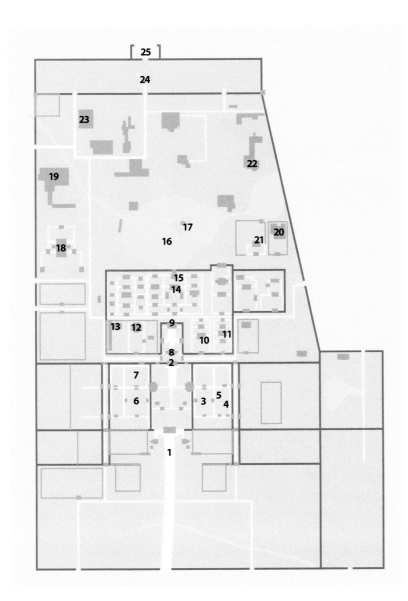

Figure 4.5. Plan of Daminggong, the palace complex just outside the walls of Chang'an, the Tang capital

1. Hanyuandian (Enfolding Vitality Hall)
2. Xuanzhengdian (Manifest Government Hall)
3. Chancellery
4. Office of Historiography
5. Institute for the Advancement of Literature
6. Secretariat
7. Department of Palace Administration
8. Zichenmen (Purple Palace Gate)
9. Zichendian (Purple Palace Hall)
10. Bathing halls
11. Warm Chamber Hall
12. Yanyingdian (Prolonged Brilliance Hall)
13. Hanxiangdian (Enfolding Heavenly Bodies Hall)
14. Penglai Hall
15. Hanliangdian (Enfolding Coolness Hall)
16. Taiye Pond
17. Mount Penglai
18. Lindedian (Unicorn Virtue Hall)
19. Taifudian (Grand Happiness Hall)
20. Taihedian (Grand Harmony Hall)
21. Qingsidian (Clear Thinking Hall)
22. Dajiaoguan (Grand Horn Tower)
23. Sanqingdian (Three Clarities Hall)
24. Xuanwumen (Black Tortoise Gate)
25. Chongxuanmen (Double Profoundness Gate)

was for banquets and less formal receptions than those held in the halls of the first two courtyards of Daminggong. Taihedian and Qingsidian were smaller complexes where the Tang emperors went for entertainment and recreation. North were two Daoist temple complexes, Dajiaoguan, also known as the Temple of Emperor Xuanyuan (Laozi), and Sanqingdian. (Daoist architecture was common in the Tang palace complexes because the religion was popular among Tang rulers.) And beyond the Daoist structures was the north wall of Daminggong, whose central gate was Xuanwumen. The entire area north of Penglaigong and Hanlianggong can be thought of as the garden area of the palace complex.

The most extensive excavation at Daminggong so far has taken place at the sites of several of the hall complexes. Hanyuan Hall was raised on a high mound, more than ten meters aboveground at its front (fig. 4.6). Approached from the south by way of a brick ramp, this ascent was

called Dragon Tail Way. Above the foundation mound was a double-layer platform, the upper section of which was called *bi* and the lower section *jie,* both Chinese words for stairs. An exquisitely carved stone balustrade enclosed the approach and foundation on all sides.

The hall itself stood on the upper section of the platform (fig. 4.7). Fifty-eight meters across the front, the eleven-by-four-bay hall was further enclosed by a one-bay-wide veranda on all sides. It projected a simple hipped roof, the type reserved for China's most eminent structures. At Hanyuan Hall, covered arcades stretched eleven bay-lengths across the front and back sides and four bay-lengths in depth. Arcades whose roofs curved upward joined the side arcades at ninety-degree angles, leading to triple-bodied pavilions in front of the hall. The approaches to the pavilions, sometimes called flying corridors, resembled the curve of a rainbow, a common form in Tang architecture. Triple-bodied pavilions,

Figure 4.6. Reconstruction drawing of Hanyuan Hall (Hanyuandian), the main hall of Daminggong

with those closest to the hall having the broadest dimensions and those farthest, the shortest, were also constructed frequently in the Tang period. Those on the east at the Hanyuan complex were named Xiangluange; on the west were Qifengge. Each structure was elevated on its own tall foundation platform, and the group was raised on a marble platform the same height as that of Hanyuan Hall. From east to west the entire area of the complex was about two hundred meters.

Looking down from the front of Hanyuan Hall, the emperor could see the east and west audience halls, southeast and southwest of Xiangluan and Qifeng pavilions. Each was fifteen bays across the front. It was said that at the time of grand ceremonies, tens of thousands of people could gather in the square in front of Hanyuan Hall. Even though only the ground level of the Hanyuandian complex can be confirmed, the site provides the best view so far of the grandeur and elegance of imperial Tang architecture.

The Linde Hall (Lindedian) complex, where the emperor gave banquets and held informal audiences, was on a two-layer platform raised on high ground west of Taiye Pond. Nicknamed "triple hall," it was composed of three interconnected structures (fig. 4.8). All had at

least nine bays across the front, placed so that the pillars defining the bays as well as the arcades formed single lines. It is believed that the middle hall had two stories and the front and back halls were single-story structures. The total east–west span was 58.2 meters and the depth was 86 meters. As can be seen in the reconstruction drawing, all three halls are believed to have had eminent yet simple hipped roofs.

A square pavilion projected from either side of the middle hall. North of the pavilions, on either side of the back hall, were Youyi and Jielin towers, each raised on a brick platform to the level of the upper story of the middle hall, that is, to seven meters high. Covered "flying corridors" led east and west, and then turned southward on the west side and northward on the east side to connect with a building on the east side and with the enclosing arcade on the west. That building, Huiqing Pavilion, was said to hold three thousand guests during banquets. "Flying corridors" also joined the back end of the front hall of the Lindedian complex to the arcade, which enclosed the entire precinct. Texts record that theatrical performances were held in the arcades and polo matches took place in front of the first hall. Although reconstructions are still in part theoretical, the excavated evidence for Lindedian as

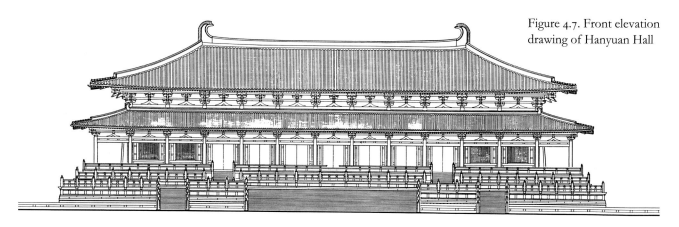

Figure 4.7. Front elevation drawing of Hanyuan Hall

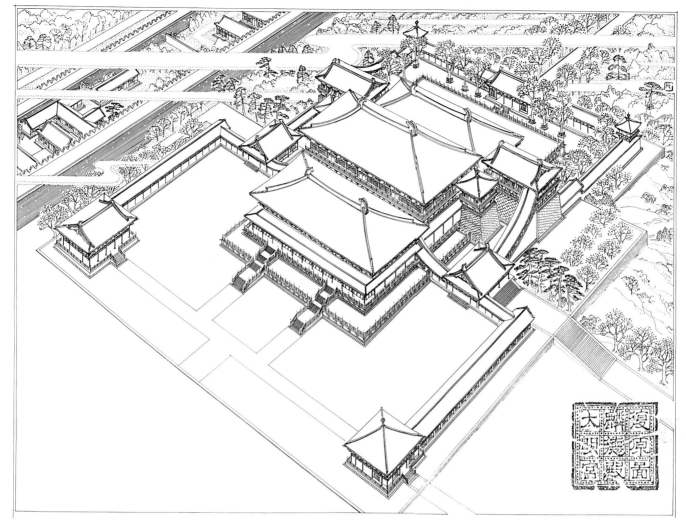

Figure 4.8. Reconstruction drawing of Linde Hall (Lindedian), in Daminggong

well as textual records not only offer us a glimpse at the lives of the Tang court but also indicate that a variety of architectural schemes were used in palatial complexes built at the same time.

Sanqingdian, or Hall of the Three Purities, was one of two Daoist building complexes at Daminggong. Located in the northern part of the palace complex in its own precinct, north of Taiye Pond and south of the north gate Qingxiaomen, Sanqing Hall was raised on an enormous earthen platform, 73 meters north to south by 47 meters east to west and 14 meters in height. It is believed to have been a multistory hall with a simple hipped roof that could be approached from two sides. The 14.7-meter-long southern approach was stepped, and the approach on the northern part of the west side of the hall was 44.3 meters, suggesting a magnificence comparable to Dragon Tail Way at Hanyuandian. Like Dragon Tail Way, the second approach was made of patterned brick and lined with a stone balustrade.

Extensive excavation has also taken place at the Xuanwu and Chongxuan gates (fig. 4.9). Xuanwumen was the central gate of Daminggong's north wall. Beyond it to the north was *jiacheng*, a "sandwich city," 156 meters north to south, that was squeezed between this gate and Chongxuanmen. (Beyond it, to the north, was imperial parkland.) Excavation has shown that Xuanwumen and Chongxuanmen were of similar size. Moreover, both were raised on foundations of pounded earth that supported timber structures. Wood was also used to frame the opening for passage through the earthen base. Wooden posts were placed in closely spaced lines on either side of the passageway, and beams were laid on top in a trapezoidal arrangement. The wooden superstructure above was supported by a layer of posts and bracket sets lodged into beams. A balustrade enclosed the wooden structure, five bays by two, that projected above the earth-faced city walls, which continued around Daminggong from either side of the gate.

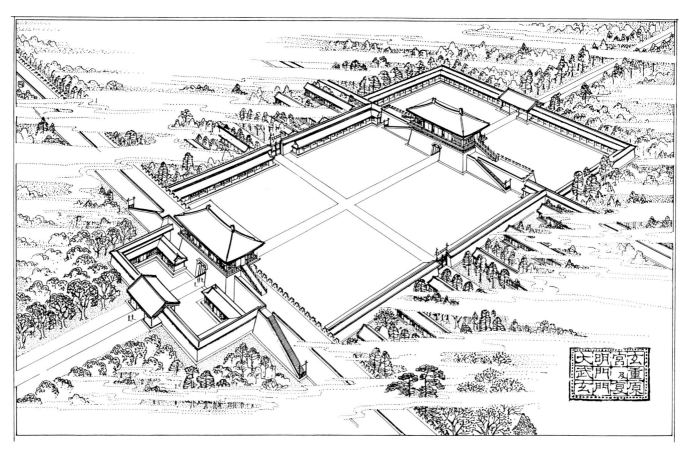

Figure 4.9. Reconstruction drawing of Xuanwumen (Xuanwu Gate) and Chongxuanmen (Chongxuan Gate), in Daminggong

Directly south of Xuanwu Gate was a courtyard enclosed by a covered arcade, with a small three-bay, single-story gate in front of it. Similarly, a small three-bay gate joined a covered arcade around a courtyard north of Chongxuan Gate. The two small and two large gateways stood at the northern end of the axial line that ran from the front gate of Daminggong, through Hanyuan, Xuanzheng, and Zichen halls, the residential palaces of the empress, and Taiye Pond. One explanation for the many gates in this part of Daminggong was the need to quarter troops there for guarding the palace.

It is believed that every main hall of the Daminggong complex was elevated on a pounded-earth platform faced with brick and stone and was surrounded by a stone balustrade. It is also thought that when they were first constructed, beginning in 634 during the reign of the second Tang emperor, Taizong (r. 627–649), a combination of earth and wood was used, employing the building techniques of the Northern and Southern dynasties and the Sui. The east, west, and north walls of Hanyuan Hall were made of pounded earth, as were the one-bay walls on the sides of the three structures of Lindedian. When rebuilt, halls were supported entirely by timber frames.

Floors were paved with brick or stone, and stairs and ramps were brick with patterns molded into them. The walls were still earthen, but lacked brick facing; rather, they were painted red or white. Indeed, information from excavations at dated halls suggests that beginning in the mid-Tang, architecture became more colorful overall. Red-brown was the main color used for the timber frame, bracket sets were painted in warmer tones, and bright vermilion was the color of doors. Window slats were green, roof tiles were made of dark gray tiles, and sometimes green-glazed ceramic tiles were appended to the purlins and eave ends. In the later halls of Daminggong, yellow, blue, and green ceramic roof tiles were used.

Xingqinggong in Xingqing ward was the second of Chang'an's palace complexes located beyond the walls of the original palace city. Its origins are traced to the year 701, when it was built as the residence of five princes. The third of these princes was to become the famous Emperor Xuanzong (r. 713–755), whose reign is associated with the glorious period known as the High Tang. It is different from every Chinese palace complex constructed until this time in two ways: it is primarily associated with one man, and it was located within the outer wall of his capital, but outside the boundaries of the palace city. Eventually it was enlarged to include parts of Yongjia and Shengye wards. Like Daminggong, Xingqinggong has been the site of fairly intensive excavations, which confirm much of what was known about the site from the extensive textual and illustrated premodern records. A stone rubbing made from a stela of 1080 shows the plan of the palace (fig. 4.10).

In 714, the year after Xuanzong acceded to the throne, the Residence of the Five Princes was renamed Xingqinggong. Measuring 1,250 meters north to south and 1,080 meters east to west, the outer wall of this palace complex suggested nothing extraordinary. The interior configuration was distinct from Taijigong and Daminggong, however, because so much of it was occupied by Dragon Pond. Further, the palace complex was joined by a covered road to Fuyongyuan, renowned as Chang'an's most beautiful garden and the preferred residence of Xuanzong's illustrious concubine, Yang Yuhuan (Guifei).

The implication is that this was a place of beauty where Xuanzong could enjoy his greatest privacy when in the capital city. But by the time Xuanzong had made Xingqinggong his main residence, in 729, audience halls had already been constructed there. Xingqinggong was also joined to Taijigong and Daminggong by covered private roads.

Shangyanggong was another major palace complex of the Tang period. Located in the southwestern part of the Luoyang imperial city, on the eastern side of private imperial gardens, this was where Tang emperor Gaozong lived and conducted governmental affairs during the last years of his life. Thereafter, Shangyanggong became an important palace of the Luoyang capital, on a par with Daminggong of Chang'an. Although it remains unexcavated, a plan of it is preserved in the fifteenth-century encyclopedia *Yongle dadian*.

In recent years, important evidence has come to light about a detached palace of the Sui and Tang. Known as Renshougong during the Sui dynasty and as Jiuchenggong in Tang times, its remains lie in Linyou county of Shaanxi province, about 163 kilometers from the capital Daxing-Chang'an. In addition to its distinction as the only Sui-Tang excavated palace complex that is actually detached (separate from the capital), its designer is known. Yuwen Kai is in fact one of the only "architects" whose name has been preserved in Chinese records. He is also said to be responsible for the designs of Daxing and Luoyang in Sui times, and for construction of the Grand Canal and Anji Bridge (discussed later in this chapter).

Figure 4.10. Plan of Xingqing Palace, Chang'an, from a stone rubbing

Sui emperor Wendi ordered Yuwen Kai to build Renshougong between 593 and 595. The palace was destroyed when the Sui fell in 617, but in 631, Tang emperor Taizu commanded that it be reconstructed, again as a detached palace, and work was completed the following year. Taizong made five trips there and his successor, Gaozong, visited eight times, once changing its name and then changing it back again. Excavation has shown that the Sui and Tang palace complexes were different. At least two of the architectural complexes believed to be from the Sui period had the U-shaped combination of "flying corridor" and covered arcade constructed at Tang Daminggong. One was a gate tower that joined a wall and bridge around the complex; the other was the main hall complex, Renshoudian.

One well-recorded and studied monument from the city of Luoyang is believed to have been built in Tang palatial style: the Mingtang (a ritual building sometimes called a Hall of Light) constructed by concubine-turned-empress Wu Zetian. She usurped the throne from her husband, the emperor Gaozong, following his death in 683, and her bloody path toward legitimate rule of the Tang empire included the execution of numerous

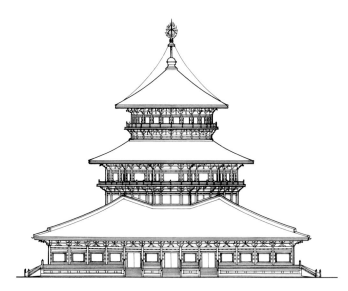

Figure 4.11. Reconstruction drawing of the Mingtang (Hall of Light) in Luoyang, eastern Tang capital

descendants of Gaozong and other relatives who might have been successors to the throne. In architecture, her desire to be perceived as a Chinese monarch was symbolized by the construction of a Mingtang in her preferred capital, Luoyang (fig. 4.11).

Although descriptions of Mingtang survive in Chinese texts of the first millennium B.C.E., even by Han times it was unclear if the patterns of former structures were maintained. There is evidence that the structure believed to be the Mingtang built in the early first century C.E. by Wang Mang, usurper of the Han throne, probably was the hall for imperial rituals, but no one has definitely confirmed this belief. The evidence for the Mingtang constructed in Luoyang by the Tang usurper empress is better.

In the spring of 688, Qianyuan Hall of the Sui dynasty was torn down and in its place Empress Wu raised her Mingtang. Towering 86.4 meters and occupying an area of 88.2 meters square, the three-story hall took twelve months to complete. Several reconstructions of this building have been proposed. The most current is a hall that, although square at the base, had a dodecagonal second story and a twenty-four-sided top level. We do know that in the original, a 2.94-meter-high iron phoenix soared from the center of the rooftop and the second and third stories had circular or conical ceilings.

Later, a five-story Heavenly Hall was constructed north of the Mingtang on the site of the former Daye Hall of the Sui dynasty. Its purpose was to house an enormous image of the Buddha. The Mingtang and the Heavenly Hall, two of the tallest wooden structures built during the Tang dynasty, were some twenty meters higher than other wooden architecture of the time. Their tremendous height and complicated ceilings represented the greatest achievements in timber-frame architecture of the Tang period, and the technology used to create them influenced all later wooden construction in China. Moreover, the skyline of the Chinese city was forever altered. Now buildings soared above its outer walls.

Tombs

Unification and the economic prosperity of the long, stable rule of the Tang are reflected in tomb construction. Tombs of the seventh through ninth centuries were larger and more extravagantly designed than those of the previous three and a half centuries of disunion. Nevertheless, officially at least, tomb construction was still governed by sumptuary laws and regulations. Emperors' tombs were in their own class and subject to no real limitations. But tombs of nobility and the aristocracy, and those for nonnobility but not commoners, were constructed according to seven grades. The ranking system stipulated the height of the mound aboveground, the number and types of stone animals on a spirit path, the shape and height of funerary stelae, and the dimensions of the underground portion of the tomb. An official of first rank was permitted a tomb of about 103 square meters, for example, whereas officials from the seventh rank were allowed to build a tomb only one-hundredth that size.

The tombs of the Sui and Tang dynastic founders followed the systems of imperial tombs of the Northern dynasties (386–581). Sui emperor Wendi and Tang emperor Gaozu were buried, in 604 and 626, respectively, in graves dug deep underground with huge earthen mounds shaped like truncated pyramids on top, two sets of walls surrounding them, and a gate opening on each side of each wall.

The second Tang emperor, Taizong, initiated the practice of using a natural mountain, Jiuzong, for his tomb. Of the eighteen tombs of Tang emperors, fourteen were built with natural mountains serving as mounds, which not only saved construction of an earthen mound but offered a natural, majestic grandeur. All of the Tang rulers continued the Northern Wei practice of satellite tombs whereby close relatives and meritorious officials were awarded tombs near the emperor's. A drawing of the tomb of the third Tang emperor, Gaozong, and Empress Wu, published in a fourteenth-century record of Chang'an, shows the natural mound, two enclosing walls and their gates, sculpture of their spirit paths, and satellite tombs.

Like the tomb of Gaozong and Wu Zetian, most of

Figure 4.12. Spirit path at Qianling, tomb of Emperor Gaozong
(d. 683) and Wu Zetian (d. 705), Qian county, Shaanxi province

the Tang imperial tombs had double-wall enclosures. Generally speaking, the inner wall was square and its four gates were named after the four directional spirits: Green Dragon on the east, White Tiger on the west, Black Warrior on the north, and Red Oriole on the south. Beyond each gate was a pair of earthen *que* faced with brick and a pair of stone lions. Just inside Red Oriole Gate on the south was an offering hall. The several-kilometer-long spirit path was due south of Red Oriole Gate. Lining it, from south to north, were pairs of stone columns, winged horses, horses, stone stelae, and stone figures of officials (fig. 4.12). Several kilometers southwest of the mound were the "palaces," nearly four hundred bays of rooms arranged according to the system of having the court in front and residential architecture behind, with all to "serve Him in death as in life." Indeed, there were storage areas for things left behind by the emperor, and each day eunuchs and female attendants would prepare his burial garments, provide water for him to wash and three meals a day, and perform regular sacrifices.

Ruyuan, the area contained by the outer wall of a Tang imperial funerary setting, was a forbidden area overgrown with cypress trees, known informally as "cypress city." Boundary markers were set up beyond the outer wall to designate it as a protected (or "sealed-off") area where trespassing was prohibited. This was where the majority of satellite tombs were built.

Qianling, the tomb of Gaozong and Wu Zetian located in Qian county, Shaanxi province, is often considered the archetype of the eighteen Tang imperial tombs. The tomb, which is in a better state of preservation and situated on a more ideal site than most of the thirteen others constructed around natural mounds, is centered on the dominant peak of the Liangshan range. The path leading down to the burial chambers begins about halfway up the mountain, beyond statues of the officials positioned outside Zhuque (Red Oriole) Gate.

Completed in 684 after the death of Gaozong (and reopened when Empress Wu was laid to rest after her death in 705), the inner walled enclosure stretched 1.45 kilometers east to west and 1.5 kilometers north to south. A gate with its own pair of towers and lions distinguished each side, and L-shaped towers projected atop the four corners. The foundation of the offering hall inside Red Oriole Gate survives. South of that gate, a hill began at the foot of the main peak, creating a ridge along which

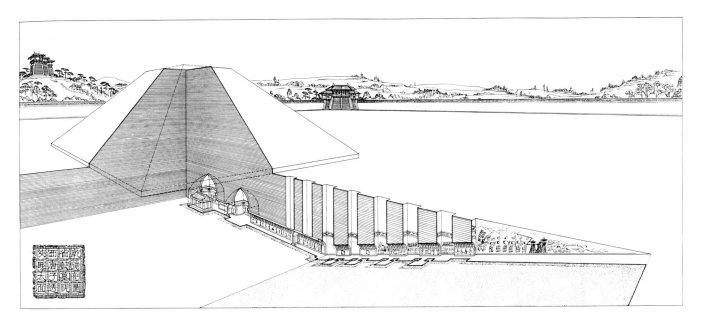

Figure 4.13. Reconstruction drawing of the tomb of Crown Prince Li Zhongrun, satellite tomb to Qianling, Qian county, Shaanxi province, circa 706

the spirit path led. At the southern terminus of the ridge were two small hillocks, east and west, each with a gate tower framing the south gate of the outer wall of Qianling, which also formed the boundary of "cypress city." The southernmost pair of que were 2.85 kilometers south of the hillocks. Made of earth, they marked the start of the "sealed-off area" in which the seventeen satellite tombs were located.

Unlike the imperial family, nobility of the Sui and Tang period were not allowed to use natural mountains or build tombs alongside natural hills. Instead, their mounds were man-made and burial chambers were completely underground. Their tombs could be enclosed by a wall, but only one gate, on the southern wall, was permitted. Children of emperors were allowed mounds in the shapes of truncated pyramids, but high-ranking officials and lesser tomb constructors could have only conical mounds.

To reach the tombs during construction, ramps were built underground. The tombs of high-ranking nobility were about seven to eight meters below ground, necessitating a very long, deep entry path. Therefore, the lower half of the ramp was usually a tunnel dug through a shaft. The higher the rank of the tomb occupant, the longer the diagonal passageway and thus the greater the number of shafts, up to seven. The shafts were generally referred to as ventilation shafts, the tunnels cut between the ventilation shafts were known as compartments, and the spaces exposed by the ventilation shafts were called air wells. Just before reaching the tomb

chambers, the diagonal path leveled off. The tomb chambers themselves tended to be square with brick walls and vaulted brick ceilings. Large tombs consisted of two chambers, in front of and behind each other, connected by a corridor. The approach ramps, walls, ceilings, and connective passageways of Sui and Tang tombs were covered with paintings of, among other subjects, scenes from the life of the tomb occupant and pictures of those who had served him or her in life. Architecture of the era was often depicted as well. Indeed, some of the most detailed representations of architecture survive on the walls of the tomb of Crown Prince Li Zhongrun, son of Emperor Gaozong, who was among the many members of the royalty executed when Empress Wu usurped the throne (fig. 4.13). Gate towers of the capital city, including multiple-bodied que like the ones whose foundations were suggested in excavation of Hanyuandian, were painted on the approach to his tomb, and the top of the entry gateway was painted above the door to the front chamber.

The layout of architecture painted in the murals of Li Zhongrun's tomb is said to have resembled the plan of the Eastern Palace, residence of the crown prince, in the Chang'an palace city. Similarly, the number of underground chambers, ventilation shafts, compartments, and air wells have been seen as indications of the number of courtyards, main halls, rooms, and corridors in residences of tomb occupants when they were alive. Thus the plan and paintings of Tang tombs not only describe the

Chinese concept of "in death as in life" and identify the social status of the interred, but at times may even illustrate the architectural layout in which the deceased had lived.

Three excellent examples of imperial funerary architecture survive from the first half of the tenth century. Two are the tombs of Li Bian and Li Jing (fig. 4.14), a father and son who ruled the Southern Tang kingdom at Nanjing, and the third is the tomb of Wang Jian, emperor of the kingdom of Former Shu in Sichuan. In addition, an extraordinarily well preserved nonimperial tomb remains in Quyang county, Hebei province.

The Southern Tang royal tombs are of considerable interest. Although Li Bian had the same name as the ruling family of Tang, he was not a descendant. Rather, in 937, the year in which he established his kingdom, he changed his name as part of his claim to imperial rule. Both his tomb and his son's are built into natural rock with mountains behind them. Excavation of their burials began in 1950, making them among the first imperial tombs to be uncovered after the founding of the People's Republic.

Each of the tombs has three square chambers along a nearly north–south line. A niche joins the front two rooms at either side, and the burial chamber, the back one, has three niches on either side at Li Bian's tomb and two at the tomb of his son. The walls are made of brick-faced mud and the floor is stone. The tomb interiors display an exquisite microcosm of the world of the living, through a combination of architectural relief, paintings of architecture, wall and ceiling paintings (including depictions of the constellations on the ceiling), and drainage canals carved into the floor.

Compared with excavated tombs of Tang royalty such as Li Zhongrun, the Southern Tang tombs have more underground rooms. It may be that when the tombs of Tang emperors are excavated they will resemble those of Southern Tang rulers with three (or more) main rooms and side chambers, rather than those of their prince and princess children. The third and last ruler of Southern Tang, who endured only until 975 and whose kingdom was by 961 subordinate to the Song dynasty (960–1279), was not given a royal tomb.

Only a quarter mile outside the western gate of

Figure 4.14. Interior of the tomb of Li Bian (r. 937–943), Jiangning county, Jiangsu province

Figure 4.15. Interior of the tomb of Wang Jian, Chengdu, Sichuan province, 918

Chengdu, the tomb of Wang Jian (847–918) was found in 1939 and excavated several years afterward (fig. 4.15). Like the Southern Tang royal tombs, Yongling has three chambers, but in this case the front and back ones are only about half the length of the middle one. Structurally, Wang Jian's tomb is unique. The ceiling consists of thirteen double arches of red sandstone (5.5 meters at their highest point), with stone slabs between. The underground structure is reinforced on its exterior by brick. A huge red lacquer door ornamented with bronze provides entry to the tomb. Each chamber is three steps lower than the one in front of it. Although Wang Jian's tomb was robbed (probably within ten years of his burial), archaeological treasures remain. In the center of the 11-by-6-meter central chamber is a stone pedestal on which the coffin was placed. Around the pedestal stand twelve armored warriors, shown only from the waist up, as well as ten musicians, dancers, and dragons. Wang Jian's own portrait, made of red sandstone, is on a platform in the back chamber, and originally the walls and ceiling were painted.

Another important tomb excavation is that of Wang Chuzhi, a military governor who died in 923 and was buried on Xifen Hill, Xiyanchuan, in Quyang county,

Hebei. The stone tomb consisted of an entry ramp, a connective passageway between it and the main chamber, a back chamber where Wang and his wife are buried, and east and west side niches joining the main chamber (fig. 4.16). The interior walls are covered with relief sculpture and painting. Among the paintings are re-creations of architectural framing, panels resembling screen paintings of birds and flowers, and a large landscape painting that is the focus of the northern wall of the front chamber.

Buddhist Architecture

No Buddhist monastery survives intact from the Sui, Tang, or Five Dynasties periods. Nevertheless, through superior examples of halls, pagodas, and cave temples, as well as excavation and documents, we know more about Buddhist architecture of the Tang than any period before it. For example, Buddhist monasteries of the Tang period can be divided into two main groups, those that received imperial sanction (national monasteries), and those that were private. Private monasteries could be built anywhere, in urban, village, or isolated settings, whereas the majority of nationally decreed monasteries were in cities or on sacred peaks visited by the emperor. Among nationally patronized monasteries, those built for emperors and empresses were of the highest grade. Monasteries of the lesser, second grade, such as Da Yunjingsi, built by Empress Wu, and Kaiyuansi, built by Emperor Xuanzong, were constructed by imperial order but under the direction of prefectures rather than the central government. Architecturally, the buildings of these two grades of monasteries followed standards for palace halls. Imperial monasteries of the third grade were built with funds raised by princes, princesses, nobles, high-ranking officials, and wealthy merchants. Standards for these monasteries were similar to those for residences of nobility in the imperial capital, and similarly were linked to the rank of the patrons. Private monasteries, considered the lowest grade, most often followed the design principles of residential architecture and, as we shall see,

were easily distinguishable from imperial religious architecture in the way that imperial and nonimperial tombs could be easily differentiated by anyone familiar with architectural features of the time.

The major monasteries to receive imperial patronage of the Sui in Daxing were Daxingshansi and Dachandingsi. Daxingshansi stood on high ground on the east side of Red Oriole Road. Occupying an entire city ward, it stretched 562 meters east to west by 525 meters north to south, an area of 29.5 hectares. Daxingshansi means Monastery of the Mountain of Great Flourishing. Named after the capital, it was the most important temple complex in the greater Sui city.

Dachandingsi was divided into two parts, an eastern monastery and a western one. Both were designed as places to pray for Sui Wendi and his empress after their

Figure 4.16. Interior of the tomb of Wang Chuzhi, Quyang county, Hebei province

deaths. Larger than Daxingshansi, Dachandingsi occupied all of Yongyang ward and half of Heping ward, an area of 97.5 hectares. A wooden pagoda in the eastern monastery rose ninety-seven meters, more than ten meters taller than the pagoda built by Empress Wu in Luoyang and certainly the tallest structure in Sui Daxing.

The major monasteries of Tang imperial patronage in Chang'an included Ximingsi, Ci'ensi, and Zhangjingsi. Ci'en Monastery was built by the man who would become Emperor Gaozong in 648 when he was the crown prince, for prayers to his mother after her death. After he acceded to the throne, it became one of the great national monasteries. Consisting of 1,897 bays of buildings arranged around more than ten courtyards, Ci'ensi occupied the eastern half of Jianchang ward, an area of 26 hectares. The brick pagoda in one of the western courtyards is the famous Great Wild Goose Pagoda (discussed later in this chapter).

Ximingsi, one-quarter of Yankang ward and 12.2 hectares in area, had been the residence of the powerful Sui minister Yang Su. Upon the founding of Tang it became the residence of Li Tai, Prince of Wei, the favorite son of Emperor Taizong. In 658, Taizong's successor, Gaozong, turned it into a monastery that included more than 4,000 bays of rooms divided among thirteen major halls and arranged around ten courtyards. One of the halls that has been excavated, which is thought not to be the main hall, measured 51.5 by 33 meters, nine bays by six. (Excavation began at Ximingsi in the 1980s.) In addition to its status as a major imperial monastery of the capital, Ximingsi is famous as the residence of the Japanese monk Kūkai (774–835) when he was in the Chinese capital from 804 to 805 studying Buddhism of the Zhenyan sect. Zhangjingsi was established outside Tonghua Gate by Emperor Daizong in 767 to memorialize his mother, Empress Wu. Zhangjingsi had more than 4,130 bays of rooms and a staggering forty-eight courtyards of buildings. This is the largest number recorded for any monastery known in China.

As had been the case in Northern Wei Luoyang, it was common practice in Sui-Tang Chang'an for residences of high-ranking officials, princes, princesses, and even the crown prince to be converted to monasteries as well as for new temple complexes to be built. In 705, for example, Xingtangsi was converted by Princess Taiping as a posthumous monastery for Wu Zetian. In 662, Princess Chengyang established Guanyin Monastery, and Prince Zhanghuai built Qianfusi in 674. All were large, occupying between one-sixteenth and one-quarter of a ward. Of these three, Guanyinsi is the most important, for it later became the famous Qinglong Monastery.

Along with Ximingsi, Qinglong Monastery is one of the few monasteries of Tang Chang'an that has been excavated. Like Ximing Monastery, Qinglongsi is associated with Kūkai, the Japanese monk who came to the Chinese capital at the beginning of the ninth century to study Zhenyan Buddhism with Chinese and Indian masters and who thereafter transmitted teachings of the sect to Japan, where it is known as Shingon. Although Qinglongsi is not as large as Ximingsi, more extensive digging has taken place there.

Qinglongsi occupied an area of about 13.3 hectares, or one-quarter of Xinchang ward, and was composed of at least three courtyards of buildings. The precinct on the west measured approximately 98 by 140 meters and was enclosed by a covered arcade that had gates on the north and south sides. In its front center was a pagoda whose foundation was 15 meters square. Behind was a main hall, thirteen bays by five, or 52 by 20.5 meters. With pillars forming two rows along the hall's perimeter, its dimensions were almost the same as those of Hanyuan Hall of Daminggong. As discussed, arranging a pagoda and hall in a line in their own courtyard had been the standard in Chinese Buddhist architecture since the period of the Northern and Southern dynasties (Yongningsi in Luoyang is a good example).

Extraordinary ruins have been excavated at site 4 of Qinglongsi. There, building foundations from before and after the year 847 reveal two different ground plans for a Buddhist hall. The earlier, with front and back hall sections, resembles the plan of a hall uncovered at Ximingsi. That plan has been associated with the space in which a Zhenyan Buddhist priest such as Kūkai would have been ordained. A different plan was used in the later rebuilding, however. The architectural style of the Buddhist hall rebuilt in the western precinct of Qinglongsi in the aftermath of Buddhist persecutions that ravaged Chinese monasteries in the 840s is believed to be the same as that of the East Hall of Foguang Monastery, built in 857 and discussed later.

Major Features of Sui-Tang Monastery Plans

Although evidence is far from complete, certain generalizations can be made about Tang monastery plans in comparison to those of the Northern and Southern dynasties. In addition to courtyards in which a pagoda and hall, one behind the other, were the focus, courtyards with pagodas as the central focus were prevalent in north

Figure 4.17. Wall painting from Mogao caves, near Dunhuang,
Gansu province, showing Buddhist buildings

and south China during the period of disunion and
continued to be built in Sui and early Tang times. One
Sui-period example of a plan centered on a pagoda is
Dachandingsi, mentioned earlier. More common in the
Tang period, however, were plans in which a Buddha hall
was framed by a courtyard. This plan is believed to have
been influenced by the prevalent design in Tang palace
architecture. All courtyards were enclosed by covered
arcades and had at least north and south gates. The larger
ones had east and west gates as well. In addition, also following the arrangement in the Tang palace cities, some
monasteries had two main halls, one in front of the next.
In these cases there were two courtyards, in front and
back of each other, that shared an interior wall; together
they formed a shape like a domino. Then there were the
more complicated monastery plans that, like palatial
architecture, were built along multiple north–south and
east–west axes, with each hall usually still within its own
courtyard and surrounded by a covered arcade. The
largest courtyard housed the most important Buddha
hall. Our evidence for all of this is taken primarily from
paintings of Buddhist architecture. Based on paintings
from the walls of Mogao caves near Dunhuang and
paintings on silk found in the Dunhuang repositories, a

variety of Tang Buddhist monastery plans have been proposed (figs. 4.17 and 4.18).

Buddhist monastery space also lends itself to association with the plans of imperial-patronized architectural
complexes such as the ancestral temple *(taimiao)*. There,
too, we know from texts that the main hall was in the primary courtyard of the complex, and subsidiary halls were
within their own courtyards, or precincts *(yuan)*.

In imperial architecture, including Buddhist, courtyards were often named for their principal buildings.
Written texts often refer to the pagoda courtyard (or
precinct), Chan (meditation) courtyard, Vinaya (disci-
pline) courtyard, Pure Land courtyard, True Awakening
courtyard, Three Levels courtyard, storage courtyard,
and Mountain Pavilion courtyard, among others.

The similarity between Buddhist and palatial architectural complexes seems to have been one reason for the
ban on Buddhism and for the Huichang Persecution —
the widespread destruction of Buddhist architecture that
occurred in 845, the fifth year of the *huichang* reign period of Tang emperor Wuzong. Emperor Wuzong is said
to have been opposed to an earlier imperial decree that
stated, "monastery halls were to be constructed and
decorated like residences of the imperial palace." This

Figure 4.18. Drawing of a Buddhist monastery in Mogao Cave 219, Tang dynasty

Figure 4.19. Roof eaves and rafters of the main hall at Nanchan Monastery, Mount Wutai, Shanxi province, 782

imperial vendetta against Buddhism is often given as the explanation for the dearth of extant wooden architecture built before 850. Whether due to sponsored destruction or natural causes, only four timber structures remain from the Tang period.

Fortunately, more survive from the fifty years after the fall of Tang. The earliest extant dated Buddhist hall is the main hall of Nanchan Monastery, located in an isolated setting on the sacred peak dedicated to the bodhisattva Manjusri, Mount Wutai, in Shanxi province (fig. 4.19). It has been suggested that the remote setting is the reason it escaped destruction in 845 when some forty-six thousand buildings are said to have been pulled down. That may also explain why Chinese architectural historians were not aware of it until the 1950s.

The main hall of Nanchan Monastery is a three-bay-square building, 11.75 meters across the front and 10 meters deep. It is supported by twelve peripheral pillars, above which span beams and crossbeams. The longest crossbeams span the entire length of the building, perpendicular to all five roof rafters, in what is known as a four-rafter span (actually four-rafter "distances," with a distance defined as the space between two rafters), and penetrate the columns (fig. 4.20). As a simple hall, there are no interior columns and no ceiling, just a frame for the hip-gable roof. The form of hall is called *tingtang* in Chinese, a name denoting its lesser eminence in contrast to *diantang*, usually, although not here, the form of main halls.

The dates of the main hall at Nanchansi are established by inscriptions on members of the timber frame. A crossbeam in the western side of the central bay of

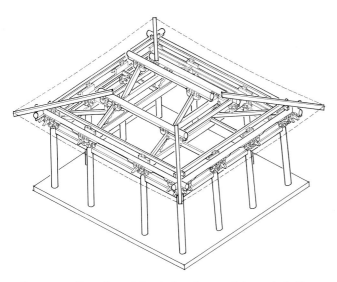

Figure 4.20. Drawing of the timber frame of the main hall at Nanchan Monastery

Figure 4.21. East Hall at Foguang Monastery, Mount Wutai, built in 857

the hall was inscribed *jianzhong sannian* (third year of the jianzhong reign period), or 782, at a time of repair. The hall is believed to follow the style of that date. A date translating to 1086 appears on another horizontal beam of the hall, placed there during subsequent repairs. At that time, all but four of the originally four-sided columns were replaced by circular ones.

The East Hall of Foguang Monastery is dated 857, the eleventh year of the *dazhong* reign period and a time when Buddhism resurged in the Tang empire. Located on the opposite side of Mount Wutai from Nanchansi, the distinction "east hall" for the main hall makes note of the east–west orientation of the monastery. The structure of the timber frame and the exterior of Foguangsi's main hall offer a clear contrast with those of the Nanchansi hall. It is important to keep in mind that the differences

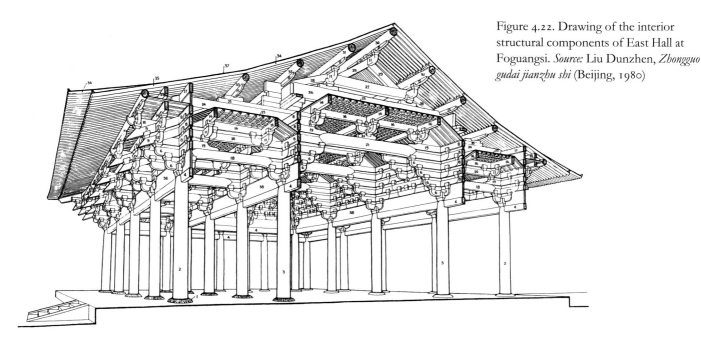

Figure 4.22. Drawing of the interior structural components of East Hall at Foguangsi. *Source:* Liu Dunzhen, *Zhongguo gudai jianzhu shi* (Beijing, 1980)

1. Plinth
2. Eave column
3. Interior or hypostyle column
4. Architrave or connecting beam, lintel, girder
5. Capital block
6. Transverse bracket arm
7. Longitudinal bracket arm
8. Tiebeam or axial tiebeam
9. Down-pointing cantilever
10. Wooden member parallel to and on topmost transversal bracket arm, intersecting eave purlin, with front end exposed
11. Longitudinal bracket arm of intermediate length
12. Longitudinal bracket arm of shortest length
13. Longitudinal bracket arm of longest length
14. Luohan tiebeam
15. Wooden support between longitudinal bracket arm and eave purlin
16. Paneled ceiling tiebeam
17. Wooden member on which the main beam rests
18. Exposed tiebeam
19. Semi-camel's-hump-shaped support
20. Plain tiebeam
21. Four-rafter exposed tiebeam
22. Camel's-hump-shaped support
23. Lattice ceiling
24. Rough tiebeam
25. Wood support above rough tiebeam
26. Four-rafter rough tiebeam placed above ceiling
27. Crossbeam
28. Side brace connecting crossbeam with purlin
29. Inverted V-shaped brace
30. Ridge purlin
31. Upper purlin
32. Intermediate purlin
33. Lower purlin
34. Rafter
35. Eave rafter
36. Flying rafter or cantilever eave rafter
37. Roof board
38. Board onto which bracket sets adhere
39. Ox-spine tiebeam

have more to do with one being a more eminent structure than with the seventy-five years that separate them.

Foguang Monastery's East Hall is our best example of a high-ranking hall of the Tang dynasty (fig. 4.21). Seven bays by four (34 by 17.7 meters), it was supported by inner and outer rings of columns that divided the hall into an interior space, or inner *cao,* and an outer cao — the formation uncovered in the post-847 hall from Qinglongsi. The exterior boasted a hipped roof, simpler in construction than the hip-gable form employed above the main hall at Nanchansi but reserved for more eminent structures nevertheless. (The roofs of palace buildings at Daminggong, as described earlier, are believed to have been hipped.) Other features that bespeak its high rank are the huge and complicated bracket sets, one half the height of the columns above which they are positioned, or one-third the distance from the floor to the roof eaves of the front

facade; the seven fundamental constituents of bracket sets, including two diagonal lever-arms or cantilevers *(ang);* the replicas of bracket sets between columns that help support the large and heavy eaves; and the lattice ceiling (fig. 4.22).

It is important to remember that the purpose of the main hall of a monastery was to house Buddhist images (fig. 4.23). Both the Nanchansi and Foguangsi main halls had altars for the display of images, and most images in the halls today have been preserved from the Tang dynasty. The other two timber-frame halls that survive from Tang times, both tingtang, are also in Shanxi, the province in which most pre-fourteenth-century Chinese wooden architecture is found. Five Dragons Temple, alternately known as the Temple of Prince Guangren, is in Longquan village of Ruicheng county. Dated 833, it has five bays across the front and a hip-gable roof. The main hall of Tiantai'an in Pingshun county similarly has a front facade of three bays and a hip-gable roof, but no inscription has provided a date more specific than that it is from the Tang period (fig. 4.24).

The number of extant wooden halls built in the tenth century or later is so great that it would be impossible to discuss all of them. The process of identifying and studying old buildings in China is very much ongoing, and although lists of important and extant buildings exist, none is definitive, for more halls with early dates will probably be found. Most of the recent discoveries have been in mountainous regions of southern Shanxi. Usually the buildings are small and survive amid other, later halls without stelae that provide dated inscriptions. Several buildings that came to light in the past two decades initially were thought to be Song (960–1279) but through subsequent scholarly investigation — comparison with dated, extant structures or discoveries of records at the site or in texts — have been redated more specifically to the tenth or eleventh century. Discussed here are four buildings that represent current knowledge about Chinese architecture from the decades between Tang and Song. They were chosen because at this time more is known about these wooden halls than about others from the Five Dynasties and Ten Kingdoms periods. Thus they have also been used as a basis for comparison by architectural historians studying newly identified early halls.

Ten Thousand Buddhas Hall of Zhenguosi is one of the two most important extant structures of the period (figs. 4.25 and 4.26). In part this is because it is the only extant hall of the short-lived Northern Han (951–979), a kingdom founded by a general of Shatuo Turkic descent who played the newly founded Song empire against his Liao (947–1125) allies before falling to the Song in 979. Yet the hall also has structurally impressive features. Three bays square (11.6 by 10.8 meters) with twelve peripheral columns and none on its interior (like the humble main hall of Nanchan Monastery), in sharp contrast to the Nanchansi hall, Ten Thousand Buddhas Hall has enormous and complicated bracket sets, comparable to those of the eminent East Hall of Foguangsi. The bracketing may have been an attempt to render status to an otherwise insignificant building from a dynasty striving to survive. The date of the hall, 963, is given in a record of Pingyao prefecture in Shanxi.

The other extremely important wooden structure, the main hall of Hualin Monastery, is similarly small with similarly enormous and complicated bracket sets. Dated 964, just a year later than Zhenguosi's hall, it is also the only architectural remnant of a short-lived kingdom, Wu-Yue (907–978), which endured in Fujian during the

Figure 4.23. Stone pillar inscribed with Buddhist scripture, Foguang Monastery

Figure 4.24. Main hall of Tiantai'an, Pingshun county, Shanxi province, Tang dynasty

Figure 4.25. Corner eaves and bracket sets of Ten Thousand Buddhas Hall, Zhenguo Monastery, Pingyao county, Shanxi province

first decades of Song rule. It is also the earliest wooden hall that survives in southeastern China.

The hall that one sees today on an active street in Fuzhou, capital of Fujian province, has been restored to its tenth-century form and no longer bears signs of the restorations it underwent during the Ming (1368–1644) and Qing (1644–1911) dynasties. Its large bracket sets are marks of the Tang period; in subsequent centuries such bracket sets decreased in size compared with the height of the columns above which they sit. The bracket sets of the main hall, also known as Daxiongbao (Great Buddha) Hall of Hualin Monastery, are further distinguished by the presence of three cantilevers—a feature that remained popular in Buddhist architecture of southeastern China through the Song dynasty. Different from the small halls of north China built at the same time, Hualinsi's mid-tenth-century hall was three bays wide, four bays deep (15.9 by 14.7 meters), and had four interior pillars. Like all of the Buddhist halls, Daxiongbao Hall originally had an altar with images, but in contrast to the two Tang buildings on Mount Wutai and Ten Thousand Buddhas Hall, none of the images survive.

The two other dated wooden buildings with pre-Song dates are in mountainous areas of Pingshun, the same county of southeastern Shanxi province as Tiantai'an of the Tang period. Great Buddha Hall of Dayunyuan is the only known example of architecture of the Later Jin kingdom (936–947). The hall was built in 940, two years after the founding of the monastery. (The suffix *yuan* in the name of the monastery is the same character, as described above, used to denote a courtyard or a precinct of a *si*, or monastery; it is an alternative word for *si* that is encountered again in later architecture.) Dayunyuan may have been a large monastery by tenth-century standards: an inscription of 983 refers to more than one hundred bays of buildings. Three bays square (11.8 by 10.1 meters) with a hip-gable roof, Great Buddha Hall itself is similar to what we have seen in contemporary architecture, but it did have two interior pillars (figs. 4.27, 4.28, and 4.29).

The West Side Hall of Longmen Monastery was identified in 1973 and dated 925. Recent investigation suggests that the simple and unobtrusive hall was part of a sizable monastery consisting of four main courtyards along an axial line, three of which had a Buddha hall in the back and adjacent east and west side halls. The extant hall joined the middle of the three main halls.

Pagodas

Pagoda architecture continued to flourish during the Tang period. One difference between earlier Chinese pagodas and those of the Tang is their placement in the monastery. Central pagodas, whether the focus of monastery space or on an axis shared by one or more Buddha halls, became less common. More prevalent were twin pagodas, located either in the main courtyard but in front of the main Buddha hall or in their own precincts southeast and southwest of the main courtyard. The majority of pagodas, wooden and brick, are believed to have been four-sided in plan.

In addition, countless funerary pagodas were constructed during the Sui-Tang period. They consisted of one or more stories and were circular, square, hexagonal, and octagonal in plan, in wood, brick, or stone. Elevated on pedestals, some had an entry in the shaft or below it that opened into the center of the pagoda.

Our knowledge of wooden pagodas, some of which have been described already, comes exclusively from written records. In addition to the great seven-story, ninety-seven-meter-high pagoda of Dachandingsi built in Daxing in 611, a timber pagoda forty-four meters high was constructed at Jingfasi in Yankang ward of the Sui capital in 590; Sui Wendi's empress built twin pagodas of the same height at Fajie Nunnery in Fengle ward; and in 629 a nine-story pagoda, also forty-four meters

Figure 4.26. Interior of Ten Thousand Buddhas Hall, Zhenguo
Monastery, built in 963

Figure 4.27. Dayun Monastery,
Pingshun county, Shanxi
province, founded in 938

Figure 4.28. Great Buddha Hall
of Dayun Monastery

Figure 4.29. Corner bracket set,
interior of Great Buddha Hall,
Dayun Monastery

Figure 4.30. Four-Entry
Pagoda, Shentong
Monastery, Licheng county,
Shandong province,
restored in 611

high, was constructed at Huirisi in Huaide ward of Tang Chang'an.

For extant pagoda architecture, we turn first to those built in stone, and then to brick pagodas. Most stone pagodas from the Sui and Tang periods had only one story. They survive all over China in a variety of shapes. Sui-Tang stone pagodas are generally made by one of two techniques: either stone blocks are put together or stone slabs are laid in layers. The most famous single-story stone pagoda is Simenta (Four-Entry Pagoda) at Shentong Monastery in Licheng county, Shandong province (fig. 4.30). Dated to the year of its restoration, in 611, regularly sized stone blocks form the lower part and above them smaller stone blocks were laid in strips to form its single story. Measuring 7.3 meters wide and 15 meters high, it had a pyramidal roof. A ground plan shows that the structure consisted of an outer wall and inner core, both made of stone and separated by a 7.7-meter corridor. The eaves were made of corbeled stone, and stone was laid in the reverse direction for the roof. The roof was supported by triangular stone beams placed on top of diagonal stone slabs above the corridor.

A small pagoda at Yunju Monastery in Fangshan, Hebei, is in several ways a typical single-story stone pagoda (fig. 4.31). Its foundation platforms, eaves, and roof components were laid with flat stone slabs. The shaft of the pagoda was made up of four upright stone slabs. The decorative lintel above the doorway is in the form of a pointed horseshoe-shaped arch. Seen frequently in relief sculpture of architecture in Buddhist caves of the Northern and Southern dynasties period, in particular at Yungang in the late fifth century, the decorative lintel is a remnant of the *caitya* arch common in early Indian Buddhist architecture.

The reliquary pagoda at Qixia Monastery is an example of the type of stone pagoda in which layers of stone slabs were laid on top of one another (fig. 4.32). The structure rises about fifteen meters all together, and each layer of stone — pedestals, shaft, eaves, layers between the eaves, and even the *harmika* (spire) on top — was carved in relief.

Unlike stone pagodas, the majority of those in brick are funerary. They survive in almost every Chinese province, with famous examples at Huishan Monastery in Dengfeng, Henan, Foguang Monastery on Mount Wutai, and Baoguo Monastery in Yuncheng in southern Shanxi, built in 822 (fig. 4.33). Each of the structures has a high base and multilayered superstructure but is considered to have only a single story. Although in the Tang period no stone pagodas that completely imitated wooden structures are known, all brick pagodas replicate features of a timber building — bracket sets at the Foguangsi funerary pagoda, for example, and door and window frames at the pagodas from Huishansi and Baoguosi. The replication of details of the Chinese timber frame in brick or stone is a standard feature of pagoda architecture that pre- and postdates the Sui-Tang period in pagodas of all shapes and forms, but the heights of brick-carving at the time are evident in Sui-Tang funerary pagodas. Columns, beams, bracket sets, gates, windows, eaves, and spires of single-story funerary pagodas were laid with precut or prefired bricks or with bricks pre-engraved with relief sculpture.

Multistoried brick pagodas can be divided into two groups, *louge* and *miyan*. Some believe that the louge form was an imitation of Chinese wooden pagoda forms, whereas the miyan variety derived from an original Indian form whose shuttle-shaped exterior lines offered a unique and beautiful image in Chinese construction history.

Louge is a combination of the Chinese characters for multistory structure *(lou)* and pavilion *(ge)*. The most famous extant pagoda of Tang China, the Great Wild Goose Pagoda (Dayanta) of the great Ci'en Monastery, is an example of louge construction (fig. 4.34). Louge structures consist of clearly differentiated stories, with the lowest story the tallest and the ascending stories successively shorter. Dayanta was built in Sui times and restored by Tang emperor Gaozong in 648 to commemorate his mother. This and other well-known pagodas of the Tang capital, such as the pagoda built to memorialize the Buddhist monk Xuanzang at Xingjiaosi in 669 and the pagoda of Xiangji Monastery, are all of the louge variety.

Miyan means, literally, densely placed eaves, and refers to the narrow and numerous layers of eaves above the shaft of a pagoda. Densely placed eaves are part of the decoration of some louge-style pagodas, but two features distinguish a pagoda of the miyan variety. First, the lowest story is the tallest, as is the case in a pagoda of louge form, but although the layers above the first one usually diminish in height toward the top, they are more similar in length to one another than those of the louge type. Second, as for the densely placed eave layers, instead of having a decreased perimeter of each layer from bottom to top, as in the louge style, the outline of the eaves in a miyan-style pagoda is parabolic. This feature is very noticeable in the Small Wild Goose Pagoda (Xiaoyanta) of Jianfu Monastery, built in 707 and restored in the Ming dynasty (fig. 4.35). Qianxun Pagoda of Chongsheng Monastery in Dali, Yunnan, is also an example of the densely placed eave style (fig. 4.36).

Although different on the exterior, both louge-style and miyan-style pagodas had hollow cores with wooden stories on the inside. Indeed, the main differences had to

Figure 4.31. Pagoda at Yunju Monastery, Fangshan county, near Beijing, Tang dynasty

Figure 4.32. Pagoda at Qixia Monastery, near Nanjing, Jiangsu province, 601

The Grand Canal

do with the shape of the pagoda itself. Octagonal pagodas of the louge style, for example, appeared in China in the tenth century. This new shape in the brick pagoda required the installation of a brick central column, which was separated from the outer wall by a corridor. Every story of the exterior of an octagonal brick pagoda had its own brick columns, beams, bracket sets, gates, windows, eaves, and railing. On the inside, the core pillar was connected to the outer wall by a layer of bricks, approximately one meter thick, which supported the floor of the layer above it. At the center of each level, passageways in either direction crossed each other, forming a fairly spacious central chamber at the point of the cross. An excellent example of this type of pagoda is the Tiger Hill Pagoda at Yunyan Monastery in Suzhou.

Some structures of this period, such as bridges or canals, required more civil engineering than did buildings or building complexes. Although such projects had a history in China before the Sui dynasty, unprecedented examples were constructed during this period. The Grand Canal, for example, was one of the greatest engineering feats in the history of China, a unique project that had as profound an effect on Chinese society as the Great Wall had a millennium earlier.

Even before the Sui unified China, they created canals. These projects continued after unification, culminating in the Grand Canal that extended more than two thousand kilometers, from Hangzhou in the south to Zhuo prefecture, just south of Beijing, in the north, and to Daxing in the west. Records show that the canal, con-

Figure 4.33. Funerary pagoda of Chan master Fanzhou,
Yuncheng, Shanxi province

Figure 4.34. Great Wild Goose Pagoda, Ci'en Monastery, Xi'an, restored in 648

Figure 4.35. Small Wild Goose Pagoda, Jianfu Monastery, built in 707, with later restoration

ceived by architect Yuwen Kai, was sixty meters wide, with an imperial way (for the emperor's passage) lined with willow trees on either side. To check the depth of the water, wooden geese with iron feet were released from the upper reaches of the canal and the distance they traveled was measured. If a bit more water was needed, sluice gates could be opened. In places where there was great discrepancy in water levels, however, it was necessary to build earthen dams with gradually sloping sides and install capstans on either side. These were turned by cattle, using them to drag boats over the dams through a passage on which mud slurry had been spread as a lubricant. Indeed the ways in which passage was aided and ensured were as ingenious as the Grand Canal itself.

Bridge technology also made several significant advances during the periods of Sui and Tang. The most extraordinary bridge of the day was Anji Bridge, which spanned the Nanjiao River in Zhao county, Hebei. Yuwen Kai, the same man who designed both the Grand Canal and the Renshou Palace complex, came up with the segmented-arch, open-spandrel bridge design that in China was first implemented at Anji Bridge. The bridge's

twenty-two stone segments, each 1.03 meters wide, were laid together to form a continuous arch, pierced by two small and two large spandrels on either side (fig. 4.37). The span of the structure is 37.2 meters and its rise is 7.23 meters. The spandrels on either side helped both to reduce the load borne by the stone arch and to allow water to pass through at times of potential flood. Anji Bridge predates open-spandrel bridges in Europe by an astonishing twelve hundred years.

All major bridge projects in the Tang dynasty were initiated and controlled by the state. There were eleven of them, including pontoon bridges, stone bridges, and wooden bridges supported by piers. The largest bridge in Tang China was Pujin Pontoon Bridge in Yongji, southern Shanxi province. About three hundred meters long, it spanned the Yellow River all the way to Chaoyi prefecture in Shaanxi. Originally the bridge was composed of several hundred boats linked by bamboo cables, but the cables could not withstand floods and freezing and so were replaced by iron chains in 724 during the reign of Tang emperor Xuanzong. In addition, four iron oxen and two iron piers were cast on each end of the bridge to act

Figure 4.36. Three pagodas of Chongsheng Monastery, Dali,
Yunnan province, with Qianxun Pagoda in foreground; second
half of Tang period, with later restoration

as anchors. Each ox weighed seventy tons, and beneath its belly an iron pillar was poured three meters below ground to anchor the iron chains. The strength of the iron chains was superior to that of bamboo, allowing greater space between floating boats and thus alleviating damage caused by floods and ice. Tremendous wealth was spent on this enormous casting and forging project. It was one of the great construction projects of Emperor Xuanzong, and a great feat of engineering in Chinese history.

Major Architectural Developments of the Sui-Tang Period

During the stable three-hundred-year period of the Sui and Tang dynasties, major improvements were made in every type of structure and building material used in China. Although many of the achievements of the Sui-Tang period must be attributed to designs, techniques, or initiatives of previous centuries, every form now associated with traditional Chinese architecture came to fruition during this period and, furthermore, set patterns for future construction principles and practices.

Some of the most significant achievements in Chinese architecture of the Sui-Tang period can be observed in the timber frame, literally the backbone of all Chinese construction. Much of what we understand about the Tang timber frame is known only through later texts. Most important among these is a thirty-four-*juan* (volume) architectural treatise titled *Yingzao fashi* (Building standards). Presented to the Song throne in 1103, it describes elements of Tang wooden architecture. According to the *Yingzao fashi,* there are four kinds of timber-frame structure: *diantang,* a high-ranking hall; *tingtang,* a simpler hall; *yuwu,* subsidiary structures; and *tingxie,* pavilions. The complex timber frame of Foguangsi East Hall is a diantang structure, for example, and the simpler Nanchansi main hall is a tingtang; the difference is clearly illustrated by a comparison of figs. 4.22 and 4.20, respectively. Five Dragons Temple and the hall from Tiantai'an were tingtang as well. Side halls of large building complexes — such as those that flanked main halls of the Chang'an and Luoyang palace cities, warehouses, army barracks, and buildings attached to covered arcades that enclosed palatial-style halls — all were yuwu, and multistory pavilions on the periphery of large complexes such as Xiangluan and Qifeng of Hanyuandian were tingxie (fig. 4.6). Although no extant writing of the Tang dynasty explains these forms, the correspondences between existing structures and criteria for the four forms in *Yingzao fashi* sug-

gest not only Tang implementation of the system but also that it was already codified by that time.

Not surprisingly, the most eminent extant Tang hall, East Hall at Foguangsi, is the one where the closest correspondences between the Song text and the structure have been found. The columns of East Hall, for example, are all the same height, approximately five meters. That length is just four centimeters short of the width of the central front facade bay of the structure, in accordance with the stipulation in *Yingzao fashi* that the height of a column must not exceed the length of any of a structure's bays. (The front facade central bay is the widest at that hall.) Similarly, the cao system mentioned earlier in reference to Foguangsi's main hall, in which the building is divided into inner and outer spaces defined by rows of columns one bay in from the exterior columns, is articulated in *Yingzao fashi.* So is the system for describing bracket sets, which is treated in greater depth in Chapter 5.

Two general statements about Chinese architecture can be drawn from this discussion. As we have observed in the planning of cities, official construction in China has a textual basis. In addition, Chinese architecture at every level — from city plans to details of bracket sets — is based on a modular system. Even though so far no Tang or Song building looks exactly like any structure described in the *Yingzao fashi,* impressive implementation of the system has been proved by measuring building elements of Tang and later Chinese construction, including those of structures beyond China's borders but based on Chinese models, for example, of eighth-century Japan.

In *Yingzao fashi,* the modular method for building components is called the *cai-fen* system. *Cai* is the measure of the section of a bracket arm, the most basic element of the modular system, for which eight grades are possible. *Fen* is one of fifteen submodules into which cai is divided. It is now believed that rudiments of the cai-fen system existed during the Northern and Southern dynasties, although proof is nearly impossible due to the lack of extant wooden architecture. By Tang times, the width, length, and depth of large and small building components, from bay measurements to column heights to roof ridges to beams, architraves, and bracket set parts, all could be generated, at least theoretically, by the measurement of cai. At a structure like Foguangsi's East Hall, exemplary of a high grade of cai, the height of the columns was 250 fen, the depth of columns was 220 fen, the space between rafters was half that, or 110 fen, and the spacing between bracket sets was half the height or depth of a column, either 125 or 110 fen. At the lower-ranking Nanchansi main hall, the grade of cai was lower and thus the actual measurements were smaller.

Figure 4.37. Anji Bridge on the Nanjiao River, Zhao county, Hebei province, 605–616

The modular system offers numerous benefits. First was the structural advantage. Because the size of materials was determined by the eight grades (there were eight in Song times, and we believe, but still cannot prove, that there were also eight during the Tang dynasty), the stress on large and medium-sized materials was the same, provided the submodular intervals (fen) between building parts were followed. Indeed, the modular intervals controlled stress for all building components from largest to smallest. Second, the cai-fen system offered tremendous convenience to artisan-builders, who needed nothing more than a measuring stick divided into fen of the required grade to construct almost every part of a structure. Knowing the formulas for intervals by heart, the labor force not only worked fast, they could be illiterate and still construct a stable structure. The system was much easier than the metric or any other system that required both blueprints and calculation while building.

The placement of columns in a building and the arrangement of structures in a building complex also were prescribed in the *Yingzao fashi*. For individual halls, so far we have seen the inner and outer cao configuration at Foguangsi East Hall and at Qinglong Monastery and we have seen the front and back (or "inner" and "outer") division of two adjacent spaces in the pre-840s structure and in the hall excavated at Ximingsi.

These two building plans are named in Chinese by characters that they imitate, *hui* and *ri*. Hui, two concentric squares, is the groundplan of inner and outer cao. The ri form, which was described earlier as a domino shape, already has been observed in the plans of Xuanwu Gate and Chongxuan Gate at Daminggong of Tang Chang'an (fig. 4.9) and is the scheme of the earlier Qinglongsi hall and the hall from Ximingsi. An expanded version of the Chinese character ri, the *mu* plan, consists of three courtyards, each with a main hall enclosed by or attached to a covered arcade, and is part of the arrangement of halls in the Sui-Tang palace cities of Daxing-Chang'an and Luoyang and in the three main hall complexes of Daminggong, each of which follows the ri plan (fig. 4.5). We also have observed the U-shaped plan in the Hanyuan Hall complex from Daminggong and at Renshougong.

Octagonal buildings, again a feature that has pre-Sui-Tang sources, were also built during this period. An octagonal pavilion foundation has been uncovered at a Tang palace site in Luoyang. Framed by eight peripheral columns and supported by another four interior columns spaced at the midpoints of four sides of the exterior ring, this hall follows the structure of the octagonal hall at the Buddhist monastery Eizan-ji in Nara prefecture, Japan, which was constructed in the second half of the eighth century. Architraves that joined the four central pillars provided a square wooden frame on top of which were placed eight posts connected to eight exterior pillars under the eaves. Eight diagonal beams, also supported by the eight columns and bracket sets above them, emerged from the center. Part of their weight was borne by posts. Above the wooden structure an octagonal, pyramidal roof was supported. Octagonal plans were also prevalent in brick and stone pagoda architecture. If octagonal structures had specific symbolism in Tang China, it so far has not been explained.

As was the case with the timber frame and perhaps the modular system, elements of individual hall structure that are readily apparent in extant buildings of the Tang dynasty trace their origins to construction during the Northern and Southern dynasties. Among them are batter, rise, curvature of roof eaves' corners, and concave roof. Batter, a translation for *cejiao* in Chinese, is the slight incline of peripheral columns toward the center of a structure. Rise, or *shengqi* (not present at Foguangsi's East Hall), refers to the progressively longer lengths of pillars, proceeding out from the center, across the front facade of a structure, so that the shortest columns in the front of a hall are on either side of the center front bay and the tallest are underneath the front corner eaves. The third element, curvature of roof eaves' corners, is sometimes noticeable. Concave roof means simply that the roof line forms a concave curve. All these features are evidence of a kind of control over a structure's outline that appears to have been perfected and standardized in Tang architecture so that a straight line could curve gracefully at its ends without an apparent break. As for specific features, both octagonal and shuttle-shaped columns, curved beams known as "rainbow-shaped" beams, and the overhanging roof eaves whose weight was borne by bracket sets on the exterior of a structure are examples of this kind of graceful control of straight to curved surface. In addition, a technique of column construction known as *juansha*, often translated as "entasis," in which the column bulged just above its center, was introduced by the Tang period. That too added to the graceful, curved effect of a Tang wooden hall. Rarely did a curve in any part of a Tang structure appear to have been accomplished in segments.

Of all the locations of curvature in a Tang building, most distinctive was the concave curve of roof eave ends, which remains a trademark of Chinese wooden architecture. That curve is present in most Chinese roofs, of which the simple hip, hip-gable combination, overhanging gable, pyramidal, and conical forms are believed to have appeared by the Sui-Tang period.

Standardization in color also is believed to have occurred

by the Sui-Tang period. Colors during this era were, first of all, bright. Except for the gray cement tiles, Chinese architecture was alive with vibrant hues: roof ridges and eaves' tiles were glazed yellow and green, pillars were red, window frames were green, and walls were white. These colors are accurately rendered in paintings of architecture preserved on the walls of tombs and Buddhist caves.

Significant progress and standardization were also achieved in the arrangement and grouping of buildings in space. A smaller structure could be added to any side of a main hall. Rooms attached to the right or left were known as *xiewu* (literally, "armpit rooms"). Rooms that joined to the front or back of a larger hall were called *duiliu* (opposite eaves). A part that projected outward, front or back, was called *guitouwu,* or the "tortoise-head room." Extension from the main structure in the form of, for example, a "flying corridor," also was possible in a multistory structure. Famous examples of this feature are the Lindedian and especially the Hanyuandian complexes of Daminggong (fig. 4.6). Projection from a structure of more than one story is also evident in paintings of architecture. What we might call composite structures, in which subsidiary halls were attached to a main one, were considered by the Tang to be more structurally pleasing than an independent hall, regardless of whether the main hall had straighter or more curved eaves or more than one story, or was large or small.

The placement of halls relative to courtyards also was a consideration of Tang builders. It became standard practice for a gate to stand directly in front of a main hall. That gate joined a corridor, which continued along the front and surrounded the hall, forming a courtyard, and subsidiary halls stood right and left of the main one. Just as one hall was clearly the primary one in a building complex, in large palaces or monasteries composed of many courtyards, the principal courtyard, the focus of the architectural group, was always evident. Courtyards provided a private setting so that a hall almost never faced directly onto the street. Courtyards also offered mood, such as open or private, quiet or serious, or a space for lively entertainment. The number and placement of gates, connective passageways, and corridors could enhance or alter any mood. Just as the slope of roof eaves was the most distinctive feature of the individual hall by Tang times, the courtyard was the most distinctive spatial feature, one that, like the roof eaves, was to remain a symbol of traditional Chinese construction for the rest of its history.

In terms of the general features of larger spaces such as cities and parts of cities, or smaller spaces like courtyards of building complexes, the dominant spatial principle is four-sided enclosure. In every Chinese urban scheme, longitudinal and latitudinal space is clearly laid out, and in capital cities the spaces formed by the north–south and east–west streets were wards. Although the urban scheme might be perceived as monotonous, every person knew his or her place in relation to the whole as clearly as he or she understood the placement and relation of main and auxiliary structures. Systematic and hierarchical planning inside four-sided enclosures, from single courtyards to cityscapes, should be considered supreme elements of the Tang aesthetic.

Four-sided enclosure and rigid planning, however, did not override natural features of topography. Rather, Tang architectural settings strove to use natural features to their best advantage. On the elevated middle section of Red Oriole Road, for example, the Sui built their largest Buddhist monastery, Daxingshansi, and the Tang constructed Xuanduguan, their largest Daoist monastery. In the very low southwest of Daxing-Chang'an, a wooden pagoda rose more than a hundred meters. In cities of southeastern China where it was impossible to avoid water running through at least part of the city, such as Suzhou and Yuezhou (today Shaoxing), the water was incorporated right into the city by constructing multistory residences alongside the riverbanks and wharfs. Bridges with red railings crossed the waterways. Thus, beginning in Tang times, the interplay of high and low, land and water, red and blue, worked together to create a unique aesthetic for Chinese cities adjacent to water in the Jiangnan region of southeastern China.

Sui-Tang Architecture Abroad

Sui-Tang architecture definitely influenced architecture beyond China's borders. Following the introduction of Buddhism to Korea in the fourth century and to Japan in the sixth, architecture was transmitted eastward along with the other Buddhist arts and countless aspects of Chinese civilization. The same was true to varying extents at each of China's borders, for China during the seventh, eighth, and ninth centuries was the dominant influence in Asia from Gaochang to Nara, not only politically but also economically, militarily, scientifically, technologically, and in literature and art. Through trade, official embassies, and proselytizing, China and its people were known throughout Asia, and people came from all over to live and work in the Sui and Tang capitals. By far the greatest evidence of the influence of Chinese architecture and urban planning beyond China's borders is found in the city plans, palatial complexes, and monasteries of the Korean peninsula and Japan. Because the survival rate has sometimes been better to China's northeast than in China itself, architectural historians have looked to Korea and Japan to understand aspects of Chinese construction. But as more Chinese structures, including Tang ones, have been identified and studied, as additional relief sculpture and paintings of architecture have been found in Chinese caves, and as we expand our knowledge about traditions and dates of buildings in Korea and Japan, our understanding of construction in all three countries has been refined.

During the sixth century, Chinese-style wooden architecture entered Japan via the Korean peninsula and directly from China across the sea. Chinese construction principles had influenced Korean palatial, Buddhist, and funerary architecture during the pre-Sui centuries, and the influence of pre-Tang architecture on Japanese buildings is now thought to have been considerable. The Buddhist monastery Hokki-ji, for instance, south of Nara, where a pagoda survives from the late seventh century, was begun in 588. The monastery Shitennō-ji, in Osaka, rebuilt in this century, retains its plan of 593. Hōryū-ji, the most famous of Japan's early Buddhist monasteries, has four wooden structures built before the eighth century. All these monasteries preserve elements of pre-Tang Chinese and Korean architectural styles.

Upon the establishment of the Sui dynasty, relations between China and Japan were formalized further. In 607, Japan sent an ambassador to the Sui court, and the first Japanese ambassador to China after the founding of the Tang dynasty came in 630, establishing official relations between China and Japan. Between then and 894, Japan sent eighteen official embassies. The most profound influence of these exchanges is seen in the plan of the Heijō capital, Heijō-kyō (today the city of Nara), constructed in 710. Occupying an area of 20.2 square kilometers (4.2 kilometers east to west by 4.8 kilometers north to south), or about one-fourth the area of Sui-Tang Daxing-Chang'an, it was modeled after the Tang capital. Heijō-kyō's palace city was at the north center, the terminus of Red Oriole Road, which began at Rajōmon (Red Oriole Gate), in the center of the south end of the city. The city was divided into east and west districts like Tang Chang'an. Three north–south roads ran the entire course on either side of Red Oriole Road, and eight major thoroughfares crossed the entire city as well.

The Heijō capital was divided into seventy-two wards, among which the palace city occupied four, and one market was established in a ward on each side. Subsequent to completion, twelve wards were added northeast of the city and three half-wards were added north of the outer wall on the west side of the city. These areas came to be known as the outer city. Different from Chang'an, in the Japanese capital, every ward (jo) was square, 530 meters on each side and divided by three north–south and three east–west streets, each 4 meters wide, into sixteen sectors called tsubo. The streets that divided the seventy-two wards were each 24 meters in width. Each tsubo was the size of a commoner's home, whereas residences of the nobility occupied one-fourth of a ward. Like the Sui-Tang capitals, the Heijō capital had major monasteries. Yakushi-ji, Gangō-ji, and Daian-ji each occupied between twelve and fifteen tsubo. There was, however, one major difference between the capital of Nara Japan and Chinese capitals: Heijō-kyō had no formidable outer wall. Rather, except for a small portion of outer wall on either side of Red Oriole Gate in the south, the city limits were marked by streets. One might say that the Japanese adopted and adapted those elements of the Tang capital plan that best suited both their needs and their topography. Not only did neither walls nor moats surround the Nara capital, but also its eastern and western boundaries were determined by preexisting hills rather than a predetermined measurement.

In 794, a Japanese capital even closer to a perfect Tang model was constructed. This was the Heian capital, today Kyoto, perhaps the most perfect implementation of the ideal Chinese city plan ever built. The historical record, *Engi-shiki,* of 927, informs us that in formulating the administrative regulations of the city, those for Tang Chang'an were consulted.

No Japanese wooden hall follows a Tang plan as closely as either of these capital cities resembles Daxing-Chang'an. Nevertheless, every Japanese monastery known today from the Asuka (552–645), Hakuho (645–710), and Nara (710–794) periods is built around a courtyard scheme whose origins can be traced directly to China or to China by way of Korea. The main structures at the core of each monastery — the main hall, pagoda, front (south) gate, and covered arcade — are consistent with those of contemporary Chinese monasteries, but their arrangements vary. The Shitennō-ji, from the Asuka period, had its pagoda and main hall lined up one behind the other and gated on the front and back, a plan that originated in China by the Northern Wei period and evidence of which is preserved at Yongningsi in Luoyang. At the Hōryū-ji, by contrast, the pagoda and main hall are side by side in the main courtyard.

By the Nara period, it was common to see twin pagodas on either side in front of the main hall. Such a layout survives at the Yakushi-ji in Nara, among other places, and is believed to have had seventh-century precedents. A variant of this plan remains at the Tōdai-ji, also in Nara from the Nara period, in which the twin pagodas were moved into their own precincts south of the main Buddha hall courtyard. Built in the middle of the eighth century, the Tōdai-ji occupied an area 0.8 by 1 kilometer due east of the outer city of the Heijō capital. The huge size of its main Buddha hall — eleven bays (88 meters) across the front when first constructed — corresponded to that of Qianyuan Hall in the palace city of Sui-Tang Luoyang. (The hall found there today is a reconstruction built on a smaller scale.) Similar plan layouts of Chinese monasteries are represented in wall paintings in Buddhist caves.

Occasionally Japanese buildings bear a direct likeness to a particular form of Chinese construction. Japanese Buddhist halls constructed under the direction of the monk Kūkai, who studied in Chang'an at the beginning of the ninth century, are good examples. Another is the Heijō capital monastery Tōshōdai-ji. Its main hall, built under the supervision of a Chinese Buddhist monk named Jianzhen (Ganjin in Japanese), similarly exhibits clear signs of Chinese style. (Its roof was rebuilt after 1650.) Evidence of shared construction in an octagonal hall excavated in Tang Luoyang and the eighth-century octagonal hall at Eizan-ji in Nara prefecture has also been noted.

For the rest of Buddhist history in East Asia, architectural styles of Chinese Buddhist sects were transmitted to Korea and Japan along with religious doctrines. Never again, however, was the influence of Chinese architecture as pronounced or as widespread — perhaps because reunification in 960 by the Song dynasty failed to reinstate a single, China-centered political and cultural power that matched the strength and splendor of the Tang empire.

CHAPTER 5

The Liao, Song, Xi Xia, and Jin Dynasties

GUO DAIHENG

The collapse of the Tang dynasty led to more than three hundred years of conflict among competing ruling dynasties, which fought for power from different areas of China. The Liao (947–1125) were centered in Liaoning and eastern Inner Mongolia and occupied sixteen prefectures of northern Hebei and Shanxi. The Song (960–1279) controlled the historic heartlands of China, but an area much smaller than that ruled by the Tang empire. And the Jin (1115–1234), originally centered in Heilongjiang but extending to Jilin, Liaoning, and Inner Mongolia and occupying the northern half of China, reigned as far south as Henan province. A fourth power, the empire of the Tanguts, or Xi Xia (Western Xia), ruled western Inner Mongolia, Tibet, parts of Gansu, and Ningxia from the mid eleventh century through the first quarter of the thirteenth century.

In 960 C.E., Zhao Kuangyin founded the Song dynasty and became its first emperor. After that, the area encompassing the Central Plains of China to south of the Yangzi River was largely at peace. But Liao and Western Xia regimes in northern and western China continued to battle with the ruling Northern Song.

The Jin dynasty, whose founders were a Tungusic people known as the Jurchen or Jurched (Nüzhen in Chinese), emerged from the forests of

Details, figure 5.49 *(opposite),* figure 5.46 *(above)*

northeast Asia in 1115. Its armies overran the final Liao resistance in 1125, and the last Northern Song capital fell to the Jurchen in 1127. Song emperor Huizong (r. 1101–1125), out of whose court would come the most influential architectural treatise in Chinese history, spent the rest of his days in the north in Jin captivity. His ninth son, however, managed to escape capture and reestablish the Song dynasty in the south at Lin'an (Hangzhou) in 1127. Thereupon Southern Song (1127–1279) rule was initiated. Contention between Song, Jin, and Xi Xia endured for another century. All three fell to the most powerful military force in Asian history, the Mongols, between the 1230s and 1270s.

Under Song rule, the Chinese economy grew as never before. Art and literature flourished and attracted unprecedented numbers of patrons at the Chinese capital. The Song court equalized the tax system, ordered huge irrigation projects, and saw an enormous urban boom even while promoting farming. International trade, including sea trade with the Indian subcontinent, expanded dramatically. Education became a priority, and a learned bureaucracy burgeoned. Not only was the Song dynasty a great age for Chinese scholar-officials, some of the most important of China's inventions — the compass, gunpowder, and movable type — occurred during Song rule. These three items — as well as paper, which had been invented earlier in China — were later introduced to Europe.

Confucianism, Daoism, and Buddhism flourished side by side in Song China. In fact, a certain amount of fusion occurred among the three faiths. The most significant philosophical development was what is known as Neo-Confucianism, in which the Confucian classics were reinterpreted and expounded in light of much more recent thinking, particularly Buddhism.

The strong economy, better educated society, court sponsorship of the arts, and new philosophies all influenced the architecture of the Song empire. The many buildings (and accompanying gardens) of the royal and private families of the Song dynasty led to styles even more artistic, exquisite, elegant, poetic, and self-conscious than previous dynasties had aspired to create.

A startling change also occurred in urbanism: the rigidly bounded ward system broke down in favor of more open cities in which commerce could thrive, and the population was encouraged to enjoy life more fully. Shops and business centers were spread through the capitals, and designated cultural-entertainment centers known as *wazi* emerged. The breakdown of closed wards meant that commerce could flourish day and night, and night markets sprang up to provide meeting and shopping areas for nighttime revelers. The Northern Song scroll *Qingming Festival on the River,* which is usually interpreted as depicting the city during the annual spring cleaning of ancestral tombs, beautifully captures this burgeoning city life with its rows of shops, jostling crowds, and endless stream of horses and carriages (fig. 5.1).

Architectural changes also occurred in temple complexes, in part because of the considerable fusion of Buddhism and Daoism, and in part because of the influence of newly popular sects with specific architectural needs. The emphasis on education in Song China led to government and privately sponsored schools and academies both in cities and in the countryside. And new wealth gave way to more lavish residences and private gardens.

The Song courts were not only great patrons of the arts, including architecture, but also renowned compilers and codifiers of their tradition. The oldest complete architectural manual, *Yingzao fashi* (Building standards), was commissioned by Emperor Huizong and presented to the throne in 1103. The book details a high level of standardization in use in Song dynasty construction, especially imperial building projects. Besides palace and monastery building, Song bridge-building techniques were the most advanced in the world at the time. Indeed, the architectural, engineering, and construction arts were in full bloom during this dynasty.

Equally amazing architectural feats were achieved in construction north of Song China. The Liao were responsible for building the tallest and oldest extant wooden pagoda, the famous Timber Pagoda in Ying county, Shanxi. In addition, they were masters of wood joinery who created more different forms of bracket sets than are known from any other Chinese dynasty. Liao builders were virtuosos of wooden ceiling construction as well. Their tomb designs are the first to approach the complexity and diversity of Han funerary architecture since the fall of Han. Fifteen Liao wooden Buddhist halls, one of which was rebuilt in 1140, as well as more than sixty brick pagodas, survive. By the end of the twentieth century, more than 350 Liao tombs had been excavated.

The Jin are usually considered successors to the Liao architectural tradition — in part because they returned to many Liao city and monastery sites, reusing or rebuilding what had survived from former times. But although Jin wooden and funerary architecture still stands (mostly in Shanxi province), no Jin halls survive that compare in magnitude or complexity to those of the Liao. The Jin, however, did improve on Liao techniques of ceiling design

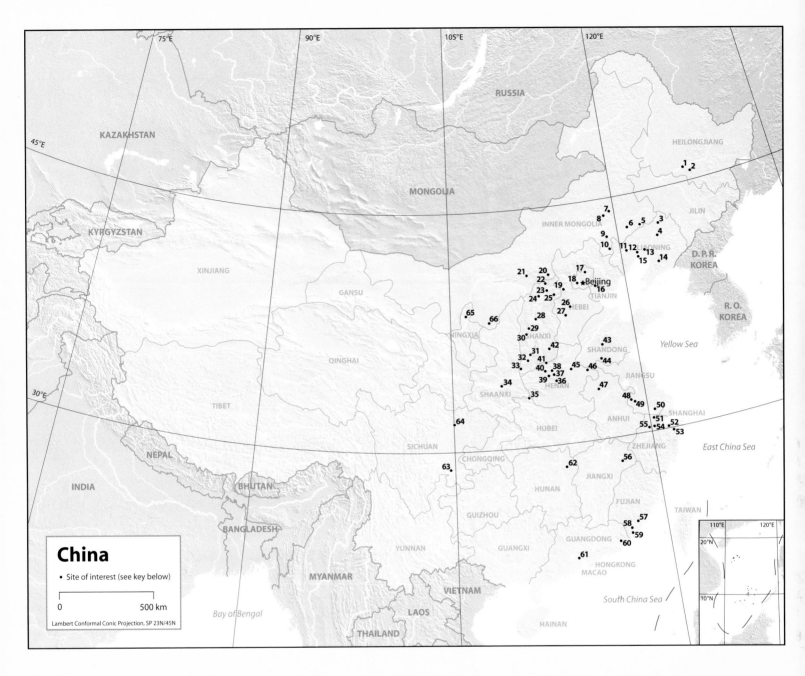

Map 5.
Liao, Song, Xi Xia,
and Jin Dynasties Sites

Figure 5.1. Detail from *Qingming Festival on the River,*
eleventh–twelfth century, Palace Museum, Beijing

and enhanced builders' ability to support ceilings with only a few interior hall pillars.

Like the Song, Liao, and Jin, the Xi Xia rulers also built cities and monasteries. Their greatest architectural masterpieces are the tombs in their royal necropolis outside of Yinchuan, in the Ningxia Hui autonomous region.

National and Prefectural Capitals and Commercial Cities

Like their predecessors, the Song officially ruled from multiple capitals. But in fact during each major period one capital dominated all administrative and cultural activity. During the Northern Song it was the "eastern capital" Dongjing (also known as Bianjing, Bianzhou, and Bianliang), today the city of Kaifeng in Henan province. In the Southern Song it was Lin'an, today Hangzhou in Zhejiang province, then and now one of China's most beautiful cities.

The Liao and Jin, by contrast, used a multiple capital system. The five Liao capitals were Shangjing, Dongjing, Nanjing, Zhongjing, and Xijing. Shangjing, which liter-

ally meant "upper capital" and was sometimes known as the Superior Capital, was located at Lindong (or Balinzuoqi) in Inner Mongolia, and was established in 918, even before the dynasty was officially founded. Dongjing, the eastern capital, was founded at the city that is today Liaoyang, Liaoning province, in 919. Nanjing, the southern capital, which today lies beneath Beijing, was established in 947. Zhongjing, the central capital, today Ningcheng in Inner Mongolia just kilometers from the Liaoning border, was designated a capital in 1007. And Xijing, the western capital, today Datong, was established in 1044. The Jin similarly had a five-capital system. Their first capital, also called Shangjing, founded during the reign of Wuqimai (1123–1135), was about thirty kilometers southeast of Harbin in Heilongjiang. As the Jin power base moved south, so did their capitals, and their first Shangjing was eventually abandoned. In 1125 Wuqimai established a Jin western capital at the site of the Liao western capital, and nineteen years later the Liao eastern capital became the Jin eastern capital. Three more Jin capitals were established in 1153: one at the former Liao central capital, which became the northernmost Jin capital (replacing the first Shangjing), one at the

Liao southern capital, which became the Jin's central capital, and one at the former Song imperial city Dongjing (Bianjing), in Henan province, now the Jin southern capital.

Song Imperial Capitals

The history of Dongjing of the Northern Song dynasty extends back to the Spring and Autumn period (770–476 B.C.E.). During the Tang dynasty it was a provincial capital and later it was the primary capital of the Later Zhou dynasty (951–960), whose leaders named it Bianjing. Guo Wei (904–954), first ruler of Later Zhou and known for his purge of Buddhist monasteries, carried out a major urban building plan in Bianjing in the mid-950s. He opened up new streets and roads, widened old ones, repaired and opened canals and dikes, and lengthened and fortified the outer walls of his city.

Upon unification of China by the Song dynasty, it was determined that Bianjing would make a suitable capital — its topography was auspicious, its location had potential for political stability, and it had good access to trade and commerce with south China. Thus the city was named Dongjing, eastern capital of the Song dynasty. In 963, the fourth year of the reign of the Song founder, Zhao Kuangyin, large-scale expansion and renovation began.

Song Dongjing was a triple-walled city (fig. 5.2). The innermost wall contained the palace city, in some texts referred to as *huangcheng* (imperial city). Enclosing it on four sides was the second wall, or "inner city," and then came the outer city, sometimes referred to as the "spread-out city" *(luocheng)*. The exact locations of the innermost and second walls have not been determined. Texts record the palace city to have been located northwest inside the second wall. Though many and somewhat varying plans of Song Dongjing have been published between the fall of the Northern Song and the twentieth century, it is agreed that the outer wall, which had no right-angle corners, extended approximately 7.7 kilometers on the east, 7.6 kilometers on the west, 7 kilometers on the south, and 6.9 kilometers on the north. It had four northern wall gates, three wall gates on each of the other sides, and ten sluice gates.

As was the case in earlier Chinese imperial cities, major roads emerged from and led to outer-wall gates. The most important thoroughfare in Dongjing was the triple-lane Imperial Way. Two hundred meters wide, it ran north–south between the south gate of the palace city and the south center gate of the outer wall. The other two imperial ways in the city were the east–west avenue that spanned the entire city just south of the palace city, and the north–south avenue that extended from beyond the northern outer wall into the middle walled area. Other major roadways in the Northern Song capital extended north–south and east–west, but not with the rigidity that had imposed a ward system on the Tang capitals.

More than in any past Chinese capital, riverways were crucial to the economic pulse of Dongjing, "the city through which four rivers flow." These four rivers — the Bian, Cai, Wuzhang, and Jinshui — all flowed into the moat that surrounded the outer city wall and filled canals built beyond the capital. Transport by water became important to the city's economic well-being — food and goods from the east and south were shipped to the city exclusively by water. Jinshui (Golden Water) River had an additional purpose: it enclosed the walls of the palace city and supplied water for its imperial gardens.

Beginning the decade before the establishment of the Song dynasty, when the city (then named Bianjing) was the Later Zhou capital, it had no defined wards. This meant that, unlike in the Tang capitals, commerce could happen nearly anywhere. As a result, the Imperial Way bustled with business activity, as did the entire area within the second

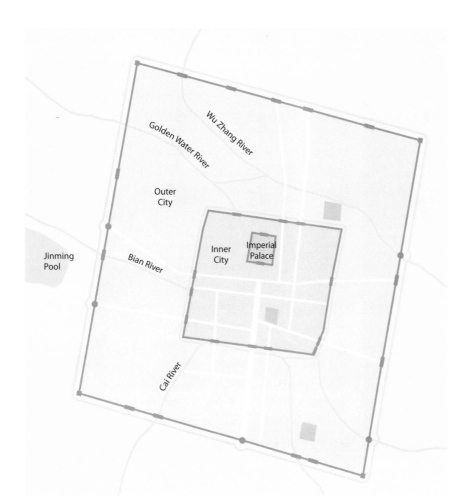

Figure 5.2. Plan of Dongjing, eastern capital of the Northern Song; schematized rendering. In fact the outer wall was not as straight as depicted here.

city wall and right up to the gates of the palace city. Commerce also took on a new look in the Song city: shops lined long streets that passed through the city, rather than roads inside four-sided enclosures. In some areas of the city, there seemed to be a clear division between residential and shopping zones. The area north of Zhou Bridge was exclusively residential, for instance, whereas the area to the south was a shopping district, and Panloujie, the street that ran east–west through the second city wall, was an especially vibrant shopping area. Yet on Mahang Street both residences and shops could be found, and in other locations markets coexisted with commercial districts. More than anything else, Song Dongjing bustled with economic prosperity. Thousands of merchants engaged in business there.

Some of Dongjing's markets were famous. As many as ten thousand people could squeeze into the main courtyards and side corridors of Wa Market at Great Xiangguo Monastery. And a well-known night market on Mahang Street stayed open until midnight and reopened at 4 A.M. Some restaurants and wine shops never closed at all. Perhaps the best places to enjoy the economic and cultural offerings of this prosperous city were in the five or six wazi (entertainment districts). There one could watch dramatic or acrobatic performances or visit a teahouse, wine shop, or brothel.

By the end of the Northern Song dynasty the population of Dongjing is estimated to have been between 1.3 and 1.9 million. Like Tang Chang'an, it was the largest city in the world during its time — a political, cultural, and economic center — and many of its achievements and most notable characteristics were a direct result of the collapse of the ward system.

In 1138 the Song household moved its capital south to Hangzhou, renaming it Lin'an. The city had served as the capital of the Wu-Yue kingdom (907–978) during the Five Dynasties and Ten Kingdoms period, and had a history of prosperity that made it an attractive choice as the Southern Song capital. The Song enlarged the palaces of the Wu-Yue kingdom, added ritual halls and altars, dredged rivers, added roads, improved transportation, and further developed business, handicrafts, and trade. Lin'an thus became the political, economic, and cultural center of the remaining part of China that belonged to the Song empire. It was the Chinese capital for 138 years before it fell to the Mongols in 1276.

Lin'an remains one of the most beautiful cities in

Figure 5.3. West Lake, with the octagonal Six Harmonies Pagoda in the foreground, as it appeared when Hangzhou was the capital of the Southern Song dynasty; Hangzhou, Zhejiang province

China. Nestled against Phoenix Mountain to its south, facing West Lake on the west, and with plains on the other two sides, the city was an irregularly shaped narrow rectangle with palaces built along the ridge of Phoenix Mountain (fig. 5.3). The Southern Song capital was different from all previous Chinese imperial cities in that its palaces were built in the southern part.

Correspondingly, the Imperial Way of Lin'an progressed southward through the entire city, beginning at the north central palace-city gate. About 4.5 kilometers long, it was the busiest part of Lin'an. To its south were the offices of the city government and the courts, and at its center was the business district, where market streets and some of the wazi, including a pleasure district, hummed with activity at all hours. East of the southern part of the Imperial Way were residences of high officials and more of the business district. Just beyond the commercial area off the central part of the Imperial Way were additional official resi-

dences. The official industrial area and warehouses were located in the northern part of the city.

Inside Qiantang Gate, northwest of West Lake, were the imperial academy, schools of higher learning, and military college. Although much of Lin'an was occupied by commerce and handicrafts, the city was renovated in harmony with its beautiful surroundings: many gardens and miniature parks were contained in it.

Extensive roadways were essential to Lin'an's economic success. In addition to the Imperial Way, there were four streets that ran north–south, four spanning the city from east to west, and secondary roads as well. All roads had three lanes, with a central section for imperial passage. Appropriate to the topography of the city, a network of large and small roads, some of which ran diagonally, linked every part of Lin'an. Some of the streets may have had the word *fang* (ward) in their names, but the rigid ward system had long since vanished.

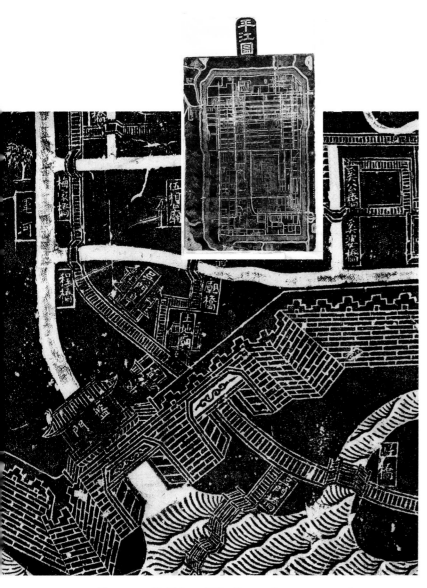

clustered somewhat. Although private handicraft businesses could be found anywhere, such official ones as Wulinfang and Zhaoxianfang were concentrated in the north of Lin'an. Imperial porcelain and ceramic kilns were centered at the foot of Phoenix Mountain in the south. And silk and other textiles were both manufactured and sold in a district near Peng Bridge, the largely residential central section of the Imperial Way. (Lin'an's largest book shop and the printing district were there as well.)

Pingjiang, the Song name of a prefectural capital that later became Suzhou, is representative of some of the smaller thriving cities that developed during the Song dynasty. Located on a fertile plain south of the Yangzi River, it was a vital hub of communication with both north and south China, as well as an important regional center in the Southern Song dynasty. The city was known for its handicrafts as well as for mercantilism.

Pingjiangtu (Map of Pingjiang), which was inscribed on a stela usually dated 1229, shows the city to have been rectangular in shape, about four kilometers north–south by about three east–west with five city gates (fig. 5.4). The network of waterways was as important as the roadways in Pingjiang. The four main north–south rivers and the three east–west ones are all shown on the engraved plan. The major streets and roads ran parallel to the rivers. Added to these were smaller streets and waterways, which made transportation by land or water easy. Houses and shops, many of which are also shown on the map, faced the street and were backed by water. A moat surrounded the entire city.

Figure 5.4. Rubbing of Pingjiangtu from a stone stela, 1229

Like Northern Song Dongjing, there were four main waterways in the Southern Song capital, the most important of which was Yanqiao River. Many markets and businesses were located along the banks of this major transportation route through the city. In addition, numerous rivers outside the city walls linked Lin'an to the Grand Canal, forming a network of waterways crucial to its economic vitality.

According to the contemporary record, Wu Zimu's *Record of Dreams of the Splendors of the Capital* (Mengliang lu, written during the Southern Song dynasty), "From Hening Gate to Guan Bridge not a family could be found who did not own a business." Along the Imperial Way, one could find a range of these family-owned specialty and general stores. Wazi, the districts of teahouses, restaurants, wine shops, and entertainment, were spread through every commercial and mercantile area. Other specialty shops were

Representative Liao Capitals

The non-Chinese dynasty Liao was organized as a confederation in the first decades of the tenth century by Abaoji (872–926). An amalgamation of the tribes of Qidan (Khitan) and of other races on the Mongolian plain and in today's Liaoning, the dynasty was officially established in 947, the last year of the reign of Abaoji's son Deguang (902–947).

The earliest Liao capital, Shangjing, is an example of a double city, a form associated with Liao and Jin construction. Walled in 918, Shangjing consisted of a northern section known as the imperial city and a southern section called Hancheng, literally "city of the Han population." The imperial city, a squarish enclosure whose sides each measured between 1,470 and 1,580 meters, included palaces for the imperial family. Hancheng was primarily for non-native inhabitants, including the Han

Chinese. Smaller and less fortified than the imperial city, each of the walls of Hancheng except the northern one, the one shared with the imperial city, was between 1,000 and 1,150 meters in length.

Architecture of this first Qidan capital reflected a blending of Qidan, Han Chinese, and other peoples' lifestyles that was to be characteristic of the Liao empire. Inside the imperial city, the government buildings and religious architecture of non-nomadic peoples of East Asia were made of permanent materials. The Qidan population, however, lived in tents. Structures of the southern city reflected the lifestyles of the countries of origin of its inhabitants — Koreans, Bohai, Uyghurs, Han Chinese, and others. Indeed, one purpose of the two walls may have been to separate the native Qidan population from the rest of the city's inhabitants.

From what we know about the second Liao capital, which was called Dongjing and was captured from the non-Chinese kingdom Bohai (Parhae) in 919 and established by the Qidan in 938, it seems that its plan was similar to that of Shangjing.

The Liao central capital, Zhongjing, also had multiple walls. Although it retained elements of the two earlier Liao capitals, Shangjing and Dongjing, it showed itself to be more a part of the imperial tradition of north China and the Central Plain than were its two predecessors. Divided into northern and southern cities, each with its own palace sector, the northern city contained two walled areas, a palace city and an imperial city. The palace city was situated in the north center of the imperial city, similar to the plan of palace and imperial cities in Tang Luoyang. Furthermore, an imperial way ran approximately two kilometers through the northern city's palace city, beginning at a south wall gate named Red Summer Gate.

Although not the most important of the Liao capitals, the southernmost, Nanjing, also known as Yanjing, may be considered the most influential in the history of Chinese urbanism (fig. 5.5). Its remains lie beneath the city of Beijing today (figs. 5.6 and 5.7). Even though the history of urbanism at Beijing dates to the second millennium B.C.E., Beijing's history most often is written beginning with its years as the Liao capital.

Figure 5.5. Reconstruction plan of the capital city known as Nanjing under the Liao dynasty and Zhongdu under the Jin dynasty, which later became Beijing

1. Yuanhe Hall
2. Palace city
3. Imperial city
4. Outer city

Figure 5.6. Remains of the Jin central capital (Zhongdu) in southwest Beijing

Figure 5.7. Brick and tile from the Liao dynasty excavated in Beijing

Built on the foundation of a city that dated from Tang times known as Yuzhou, Liao Nanjing was a multiple-walled city whose imperial city was in the southwest corner and whose palace area was in the south center of it. One gate was shared by all three cities (palace, imperial, and outer), and the outer city and imperial city also shared a gate. The most important areas of the palace city were the palaces and imperial gardens. The palaces lay in the east, extending even beyond the palace-city wall. The south gate was known as South Section Gate. The gates facing east and west, respectively, were

Zuoye (later known as Wanchun) Gate and Youye (later known as Qianqiu) Gate.

East of the palace area was South Orchard, and west were the Yao Pond palace gardens. The palace gardens were vast and Yao Pond contained Yao Islet, on top of which was Yao Pond Hall. The residences of the Liao rulers were built beside the pond.

With the imperial city located in the southwest, only two streets traversed the entire space, one running east–west, and the other north–south. Two more main streets began at outer wall gates but ended at the imperial city. There were also some smaller streets.

The area outside the imperial city was surrounded by wards and contained several Buddhist and Daoist monasteries, from which a few structures survive today. Fayuansi, for instance, was known as Minzhongsi during the Liao dynasty. The pagoda at Tianning Monastery was part of Tianwangsi in the eleventh and twelfth centuries.

Jin Capitals

Four Liao capitals became the sites of Jin capitals, and as far as anyone knows the eastern and western capitals retained the plans of former times. In addition, the original and the second northern capitals, both known as Shangjing, of the Jin dynasty were double cities, the former with a plan resembling Liao Shangjing's and the latter built on the ruins of Liao Zhongjing, the double city with features of Tang imperial urbanism. The fifth Jin capital, the southern one, was also rebuilt on the ruins of a former city, Song Bianjing. And the last Jin capital, the central capital Zhongdu, is considered the most important for the same reasons that so much attention is given to the Liao city Nanjing on which it was built.

There are notable differences between the Liao and Jin versions of the southern capital city, called Nanjing in Liao times and Zhongdu during the Jin dynasty. When the Jin established their central capital at the site of the former Liao southern capital, they greatly expanded it. The palace and imperial cities were repaired and, more important, came to be located more in the center of the city. The perimeter of the outer wall was now 17.6 kilometers. *Jin tujing* (Pictorial record of the Jin) tells us that the nearly square capital had twelve outer-wall gates, three on each face, with the main one in the center of each side. Late in the Jin dynasty, a thirteenth gate was added in the northeast so that the ruler could have access to Daning palace complex on Qionghua Island.

The three north-wall gates were opposite those of the south wall, and the east-wall gates opposite those on the west. Roads emanated from the wall gates, but only three actually crossed the entire length or width of the city. Two of these ran east–west; the complete north–south street stretched southward beyond Liao Nanjing's longest thoroughfare. The roads that began at the other six gates of Jin Zhongdu extended to the imperial city.

Another change that occurred between Liao and Jin times had to do with the ward system. From what is known about the Liao southern capital, it appears the city was divided into nine main wards in the manner of Tang urban patterns. When the Jin expanded the city, the ward system did not break down as fully as it had in Song Bianjing, but streets and lanes did cut through wards such that the four-sided enclosure of neighborhoods that had defined the Chinese *lifang* (ward) system was loosened and a more casually arranged array of streets and roads prevailed. Historical records tell us that Jin Zhongdu had sixty-two neighborhoods, some of which were divided in two.

Yet another difference between the Liao and Jin capitals was the increased commercial activity in Jin Zhongdu. Although the Jin capital could never be compared to a Song city in the number and complexity of its stores and transactions, it had much more in common with a Chinese city than with a large settlement of seminomadic tribesmen. This was due in part to the Jin's being the second of the "conquest dynasties," or foreign groups, to establish empires on Chinese soil in the aftermath of Tang, and in part to the strong spirit of commercialism that prevailed in China as a result of Song rule. The area around Tanzhou Street, the major east–west thoroughfare, was like a downtown — a place to buy and sell goods from Jin China, greater China to the south, and other non-Chinese territories in the northeast. A new market area opened by the Jin was Xinbi, located in the Kaiyang neighborhood in the southeast area of the city.

Three aspects of the Jin central capital are particularly reminiscent of Chinese imperial planning. First was the location of the palaces near the center of the city. According to the biography of Jin emperor Shizong (r. 1161–1189) in *Jin shi* (Standard history of the Jin), Renzheng Hall of the old Liao southern capital became the initial focus of the Jin palace city. As the capital was expanded, however, the palaces, as in Song Bianjing, were positioned inside an imperial city and the palace and imperial cities were centralized relative to the outer city wall.

The centrality of the palace city also followed the prescription for imperial urbanism put forth in the "Record of Trades" section of the *Rituals of Zhou*. The palace city was surrounded on four sides by the imperial city, which was itself enclosed on all sides by the outer city. The government offices and imperial gardens were inside the imperial city but outside of the palace city. In addition, the Jin adopted the Chinese tradition of having an imperial way, which ran north–south through the city. The Imperial Way passed through the south central gate of the imperial city, Xuanyang Gate, and the south central gate of the palace city, Yingtianmen, dividing the capital into east and west sides. On the east were the ancestral temple *(taimiao)*, fields for playing ball games, and Laining Guest House.

The secretariat, the offices of the six government ministries, and the Interpreters Institute, a guest house for foreign envoys bringing tribute, were on the west. A similar distribution on either side of the main north–south thoroughfare through the city had existed at Bianjing when it had been the capital of the Later Liang dynasty (907–923). The positioning of the ancestral temple on the east and administrative and supervisory offices on the west also follows the stipulations of the "Record of Trades."

Finally, in addition to the ancestral temple, Jin Zhongdu had standard altars of a Chinese capital city that had not been present in Liao Nanjing. These included altars for worshiping the heavens, earth, wind, rain, sun, and moon.

Ports and Commercial Cities

Around the middle of the Tang dynasty, warfare between the Uyghurs, Tibetans, and others, sometimes involving the Song, prevented overland travel across the so-called Silk Road. Another way to transport goods from China to India and back had to be found, and via water became the most feasible solution. Consequently, cities on the south Chinese coast — including Guangzhou in Guangdong province, Quanzhou in Fujian province, and Mingzhou in Zhejiang province — experienced rapid growth and development.

These three cities had three features in common. First, none had even a trace of a ward system; rather each developed freely in response to economic concerns. Quanzhou, for example, was irregularly shaped, a polygon with an area of ten square kilometers. Guangzhou was enlarged ten times, and its initial stages of growth can be seen as those of three cities, central, eastern, and western. Only in the early Ming period did the three consolidate and the city expand to the north and south.

The second feature shared by the three port cities was an excellent traffic system by land and water. All were linked to the major inland and coastal urban centers of China, and in some cases beyond. Quanzhou, for instance, had two main roads that crossed near the center, following the system of a Tang provincial capital. These main roads made it possible to reach the gates of the outer city wall, all four of which had been built anew in Song times. The southern part of the road system was also added in Song times. Mingzhou was fully covered by its network of waterways, three rivers and six streams. The main east–west river flowed through the entire city, including the inner *zicheng*, location of the local ruler's residence and offices of the regional government.

Third, each city had a resident population from the countries with which it traded. Guangzhou, for instance, where merchants from more than fifty countries traded during the Southern Song dynasty, had a staggeringly large foreign population: 120,000 non-Chinese are said to have been there as early as 787, centuries before the Southern Song dynasty. Guangzhou also had a mosque, the Huaishengsi, whose minaret still stands.

Song and Jin Palaces

Although no buildings from the palaces of the Northern and Southern Song capitals survive, much is known about them from historical records. Similarly detailed descriptions exist about the palaces of Jin Zhongdu. Little is known, however, about the palace complexes of any of the Liao capitals, even Liao Nanjing, or about those of Jin capitals north of Zhongdu.

Once the Song had decided to make the capital of the Later Zhou dynasty (and before them, the Later Liang) their primary capital, they initiated a large-scale expansion of the palace complexes within. They began by repositioning the main north–south axis so that it formed a straight line from Zhou Bridge through Red Oriole Gate (the main south gate of the imperial city) and southward to Nanxun Gate (the central south gate of the outer city wall).

More details are known about the palace area of Northern Song Dongjing (also known as the palace city or the "great inner") from the *Standard History of Song*: "The palace city was four to five li [2–2.5 kilometers] in perimeter. On the south were three gates, the central of which was named Qianyuanmen [renamed Xuandemen in 1032]. The east gate of the south wall was Zuoyemen and the west gate was Youyemen. The gates on the east and west sides of the palace city were named Donghua and Xihua, respectively. The single north gate was named Gongchenmen" (fig. 5.8).

The Dongjing palace city included the outer court, inner quarters, back garden, scholars' academy, and various government offices. The principal structure of the outer court was Daqing Hall, where the emperor held grand audiences. The complex, which was nine bays across the front with east and west side halls of five bays each, was enclosed by sixty bays of corridors. It was large enough to accommodate tens of thousands of guests.

Wende Hall, the focus of a complex of buildings west of Daqingdian, was where the Song emperors conducted the most important governmental affairs. North of Daqing Hall was the Zichen Hall complex, where the emperor per-

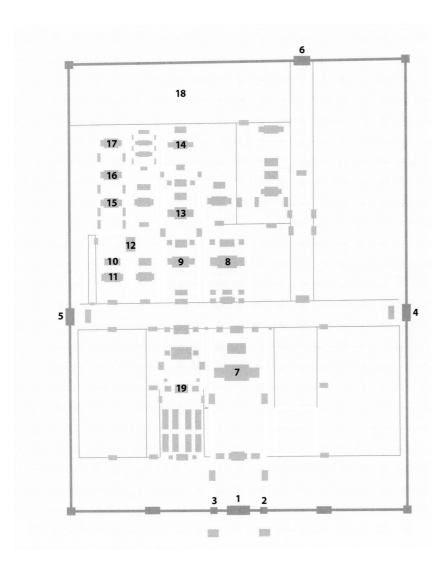

Figure 5.8. Plan of the Dongjing (Bianjing) palace city, Northern Song

1. Xuandemen (Manifest Virtue Gate)
2. Zuoyemen (Left Lateral Gate)
3. Youyemen (Right Lateral Gate)
4. Donghuamen (Eastern Splendor Gate)
5. Xihuamen (Western Splendor Gate)
6. Gongchenmen (Military Gate)
7. Daqingdian (Grand Celebration Hall)
8. Zichendian (Purple Palace Hall)
9. Chuigongdian (Governing by Nonaction Hall)
10. Xuyundian (Hoping for Clouds Hall)
11. Jiyingdian (Gathering the Talented Hall)
12. Shengping (Ascendant Peace) Tower
13. Funingdian (Bliss and Tranquillity Hall)
14. Kunningdian (Maternal Tranquillity Hall)
15. Longtuge (Dragon Diagram Pavilion)
16. Tianzhangge (Heavenly Grandeur Pavilion)
17. Baowenge (Precious Pattern Pavilion)
18. Rear garden
19. Wendedian (Literary Virtue Hall)

formed grand ceremonies during festivals. West of Zichen Hall was the Chuigong Hall complex, where audiences and banquets were held for foreign envoys. Farther west was the Xuyun Hall complex, and just south of it the Jiying Hall complex. Northeast of these was Shengping Tower, where worthy scholars received from the emperor *jinshi* degrees (the highest in the Chinese system) and where plays were performed and banquets held.

North of the outer court, behind Chuigong Hall, were the residences of the emperor, empresses, and imperial concubines. Among its halls were Funing and Kunning. The imperial libraries Longtuge, Tianzhangge, and Bao-wenge were also here. So were the places where the emperor held banquets and inspected provincial affairs. North of the outer court were the imperial gardens, and late in the Northern Song period a Mingtang (Hall of Light) was built in the southeastern part of the palace city.

The most striking feature of the plan as a whole is that the main architectural complexes are not built along a single axial line. This may be a result of the reuse of palaces of the former dynasties of Later Liang and Later Zhou. Yet because they did not provide nearly enough space for the enormous and complex Song imperial household and government, more palace buildings had to be added where they would fit. The main axis of the Northern Song capital can be thought of as passing through the Daqing Hall complex and the gate in front of it; this was the locus of grand audiences. The Wende Hall and Chuigong Hall complexes, which were extremely important structures due to the ceremonies and affairs conducted in them, formed the second most important axial line in the capital. The offices of government were in front of them and next to Daqingdian. Although we have learned of parallel axes of imperial construction at the palace city of Tang Chang'an and earlier in imperial cities of the Northern and Southern dynasties, here the arrangement of buildings should be attributed more to the reuse of an old site than to other causes.

Nevertheless, certain features of pre-Song imperial planning prevail. One is the nearly ubiquitous employ-ment of the *gong* (I-shaped) plan, seen not only in the Daqingdian complex but also in Wendedian, Zichendian,

Figure 5.9. Song emperor Huizong (r. 1101–1125), detail from *Auspicious Cranes*, ink and colors on silk, Liaoning Provincial Museum, Shenyang

Chuigongdian, Funingdian, and elsewhere. Each of these palace complexes is, moreover, surrounded by a covered corridor with a large courtyard in front. Daqingdian, like other eminent main halls of earlier Chinese palace complexes (and later ones), was nine bays across the front with more narrow side halls (each five bays wide) and pavilions connected to the covered arcades in front. As if securing the Daqingdian's historical reputation as the model imperial Song hall complex, sixty bays of covered arcade enclosed it, a gate by the same name was directly in front of it, and to either side of that gate were Right and Left Rijing gates. Unfortunately, nothing survives of Daqing Hall except two-thirds of its foundation, which forms an inverted-T shape that measures about eighty meters east to west and over sixty meters at its longest north–south point. All of these palace complexes were destroyed in 1127 by Jin invaders.

Two images help give a picture of a palace complex at Song Bianjing. One is a detail from the painting *Auspicious Cranes* attributed to Song emperor Huizong, which is now in the Liaoning Provincial Museum (fig. 5.9). The other, in the same museum, is engraved on a bronze bell, depicting a gate with five entries and triple-bodied gate towers at its end (fig. 5.10). Like Hanyuan Hall of the Tang palace complex Daminggong, Xuande Gate, entrance of the Dongjing palace city, had an inverted U-shaped plan and triple-bodied *que* (gate towers) at each front end. Like the engraving on the bell, it is said to have been a seven-bay

wooden structure with five entries and a hipped roof. Also like Hanyuan Hall, diagonal covered arcades are thought to have emanated from the sides of the main entryway to the front towers. Xuandemen is said to have had green glazed roof tiles, red-painted doors, and golden nails, and between the doors on the walls were stone carvings of dragons and phoenixes flying among the clouds.

Lin'an, the other great Song capital, had been designated the temporary capital (Xingzai) in 1132, a name that alluded to Song aspirations to recapture the northern portions of their empire and return the capital to Bianjing. Marco Polo's name for Lin'an, the city we today call Hangzhou, was Quinsai, his version of *xingzai*, which he must have heard when he was there. The same word is found in local records of the thirteenth century.

Bounded on the west by the foot of Phoenix Mountain and on the north by the side of Mount Wansong, on the east by the south bank of Zhong River and on the south by territory north of the Fantian Monastery (built in the Five Dynasties period), the palace area of the Southern Song capital drew on the designs of structures and styles that had been prominent in the Northern Song. The late-Ming period prefectural record, *Qiantang xianzhi*, claims that the Southern Song palace city had thirty palatial halls, thirty-three smaller halls, four studios, seven multistory structures, twenty pavilions, one gallery, six platforms, one observatory, and ninety kiosks. In addition, north of the palace city were a palace for the crown prince,

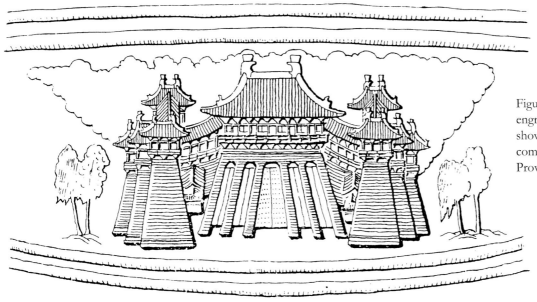

Figure 5.10. Drawing of engraving on a bronze bell showing part of the palace complex of Bianjing, Liaoning Provincial Museum, Shenyang

called the Eastern Palace, and Deshou Palace, a residence for the emperors Gaozong (r. 1127–1162) and Xiaozong (r. 1162–1189) after each had abdicated the throne.

The palace city consisted of five parts: the outer court, inner quarters, Eastern Palace, scholar's academy, and back gardens. In general, it conformed to the age-old stipulation of court in front and private spaces behind.

The palace city was surrounded on four sides by the imperial city. The gates of the imperial city, which lined up with those of the palace city, were Lizheng in the south, Hening in the north, Donghua in the east, and Fuhou in the west. Most of this information about the layout of the city is published in a revised 1867 edition of the *Record of Lin'an.*

Records also tell about the outer court. It contained four palace complexes, some of whose names were the same as those in the earlier Song capital Bianjing: Daqingdian, Chuigongdian, Yanhedian ("Back Hall"), and Duanchengdian. Daqingdian, where grand audiences were held, stood just inside the south gate. Chuigongdian was just north of the west side of Daqingdian, and Back Hall was north of it. East of Back Hall was Duanchengdian. Of these three, Chuigongdian was where daily affairs of the palace were conducted, Back Hall was where the emperor retired to greet the winter solstice and celebrate the first day of the lunar calendar, and Duanchengdian was where the emperor rested and fasted as part of his preparation for imperial rituals. Duan-

chengdian was multifunctional; in fact, its name on the placard above the lintel at the entry changed to reflect its various functions. When it was used for suburban rituals of the Mingtang it was known as Duanchengdian, when titles were conferred on officials there it became Jiyingdian, when banquets were held there for foreign envoys it was Chongdedian, and when appointments of military officials were made in it, it was Jiangwudian.

There were many different structures in the inner quarters. The emperor's own apartments were called Funingdian and Qinzhengdian, and his dining hall was Jiamingdian. The residential apartments of the empress included Nonghuadian, Kunningdian, Ciyuandian, Renmingdian, and Shoulidian. The emperor and his officials discussed state affairs in Xuandedian. The Chongzhengdian complex was for scholarly discourse and housed the imperial library. The structures of the Eastern Palace included Xinyitang, where the crown prince studied, and Yizhai Studio, where he slept. (Cining Hall, used by the empress dowager, was also there.) Garden architecture of the inner quarters included Boya Tower and Xiuchun Hall.

The back garden was northwest of the inner quarters. Its major structures were Cuihantang, Guantang, Lingxue Tower, Qingrui Hall, and a number of pavilions and kiosks. Following the Tang practice, the academy of scholars in the Southern Song capital was positioned in the northern part of the palace city, just inside Hening Gate. Although we can get from texts an idea of the size of the complex, or at least the number and relative positions of main hall complexes, we lack the kinds of measurements available for the Dongjing palace city.

Palaces of Jin Zhongdu

In 1151, the Jin began to construct their central capital and palace city. The palace city was located in the center of the imperial city and had three parts. In the middle were the emperor's hall of audience and sleeping chambers. On the east was the Eastern Palace, which, as in all other Chinese capitals, was where the crown prince and empress dowager lived, and was as well the location of the Department of the Imperial Household, which served the personal needs of the emperor and his family. The third section, west of the hall of audience and the emperor's residence, was the imperial garden, which included Qionglinyuan, Penglaiyuan, and the residences of the imperial concubines. According to *Jin tujing* (Pictorial record of the Jin): "When the Emperor of Jin, Wanyan Liang [Hailing Wang, 1122–1161], determined to establish a capital at [Liao] Yanjing, he dispatched artisans and painters to the capital of the former Song dynasty [at Bianjing], ordering them to make pictures of the construction system of palaces and halls. He changed some dimensions, made some corrections, and then presented them to his Minister of the Left, Zhang Haobei, ordering him to make emendations according to the picture." Based on descriptions in the three most important records about the palaces at Jin Zhongdu, *Jin tujing, Beixing rilu* (Diary of a journey northward), and Fan Chengda's *Lanbei lu* (Record of grasping the reins), one can conclude that the layout of the main hall of the Jin palace city at Zhongdu was almost identical to that of Daqing Hall of Song Dongjing, except that the Jin buildings were larger.

Da'andian, the main hall of the Jin palace city, was eleven bays across the front with side halls of five bays each on each side. Song Bianjing's Daqing Hall, one recalls, was only seven bays across the front. Each was enclosed by a covered arcade of some sixty bays. In front of Da'an Hall was Da'an Gate, nine bays across the front, with Rihua and Yuehua gates to its left and right, respectively. The equivalent structures of Song Dongjing were Left and Right Rijing gates. In front of Da'an Gate was the U-shaped Yingtianmen, the main gate of the palace city. Its equivalent at Song Bianjing was Xuande Gate. Both had city wall towers above, side towers, and pavilions joined to them by covered corridors east and west.

The only difference was that Yingtianmen was eleven bays across and Xuandemen was only seven.

Renzheng Hall, which was used for daily audiences, was also the focus of a courtyard-enclosed-by-a-corridor building group with some thirty bays of covered arcades. Three-bay pavilions named East and West Shanggemen stood on both of its sides, and bell and drum towers were built inside the courtyard. North of Renzheng Hall was Zhaominggong, which was oriented toward Zhaoming Hall and Longhui Hall, the residences of the emperor and empress, respectively.

Most of the structures of the Jin Zhongdu palace city were built during the Jin dynasty. Given the arrangement of structures in the center, and what kinds of buildings stood there, it seems clear that the Jin affirmed in their imperial planning the Chinese concepts of centrality and "hall of audience in front, private chambers behind." Similarly, the placement of residences of the empresses, concubines, and crown prince can be said to have consciously followed Chinese imperial city patterns. We shall see in Chapter 6 that the imperial cities of Yuan and Ming China owed much of their plans to Jin Zhongdu. Indeed, had the Jin central capital not been built as it was, today's Beijing might have a different plan.

Scholars have been intrigued to learn of an almost one-to-one correspondence between the plan of the Jin palace city as described in *Lanbei lu* and the plan derived from paintings of Buddhist paradises on the walls of the south hall of Yanshan Monastery in Fanshi county, Shanxi. The south hall is a humble building even by Jin standards, yet inside are extraordinary murals signed by Wang Kui, a court painter who completed them in 1167 (fig. 5.11). If literary descriptions and texts work hand-in-hand to confirm our understanding of twelfth-century Chinese architecture, then the many examples of paintings of architecture from the Tang dynasty, especially those on the walls of caves in the Dunhuang region, might offer significantly more clues about Chinese architecture than is often believed.

Altars, Temples, and Shrines

In the Song dynasty, as in earlier times, altars, shrines, and temples were erected for sacrifices and for veneration. The Chinese word *tan,* often translated as "altar," refers to an exposed structure where sacrifices were performed. Like all Chinese structures, however, tan were part of architectural complexes that could include roofed buildings. The character *ci* can be translated as "shrine." Also part of large building complexes, ci were constructed in premodern China for the veneration of deities or deified mortals. *Miao,* translated here as "temples," similarly were constructed for the veneration of mortals, demigods, and natural spirits. But Chinese architectural terminology is not always precise and, moreover, none of the three buildings was intended originally for the worship of deities. Altars, shrines, and temples are not religious structures as much as loci for the performance of native Chinese rites and rituals or for the veneration or deification of spirits, heroes, or demigods recognized by the Chinese people.

The primary purpose of an altar in China is sacrificial. Altars were roofless architectural forms used for sacrifices to heaven, earth, the sun, and the moon. Their size, height, number of stories, and shape differed according to the focus of the sacrifice. Certain altars were reserved for sacrifices by the emperor himself. Those had associated structures, such as one where the emperor fasted before performing the rituals.

In the Song dynasty, the altar for sacrifices to heaven was called Nanjiaotan, or Southern Suburban Altar. Located in the southern suburbs of the capital, it was a three-story circular structure whose measurements were multiples of nine, the number symbolic of the Chinese emperor. The lowest level of the Song altar for sacrifices to heaven, for example, had a diameter of 81 zhang (267 meters), the second tier was 54 zhang (178.2 meters), and the highest one was 27 zhang (89 meters). The height to the top of the uppermost tier was also 81 zhang. Steps led to the altar on each of four sides. Enclosing it were three walls.

The altar for sacrifices to earth was called Fangzetan. In contrast to the Altar of Heaven, the Altar of Earth was located in the northern suburbs of the capital, had two tiers, sat on a square base, and was built with even-numbered measurements. Besides these two forms of altar, there were altars in which more than one type was grouped together. For example, the Altar of the Spirits of the Nine Palaces, for sacrifices to the wind and rain, had a square altar on the lower level and nine small altars on top of it.

A temple, unlike an altar, was constructed primarily for commemoration and veneration, although sacrifices were also performed in miao. From Song times on, the most famous of these was the Temple to Confucius in Qufu, where Confucius was philosopher of the state of Lu in the sixth and fifth centures B.C.E. Its construction during the Song dynasty is described in *Song Quelimiao zhitu,* or "Song-dynasty construction drawings for the temple of Queli"

Figure 5.11. Mural from interior of the main hall of Yanshan Monastery, Fanshi county, Shanxi province, believed to follow the plans of architectural complexes painted by court painter Wang Kui in 1167

(Queli here refers to the village of Confucius's birth). Reportedly this Song Confucian temple had two parts: a western section for sacrificial offerings, and an eastern area that was the temple and Confucian residence. The architectural complexes of the eastern part were clearly differentiated by rank. The principal hall had seven bays across the front with a double-eave, hip-gable roof. The next most important halls, the imperial library and the Hall of the Lady of Yunguo (the wife of Confucius), had five bays, and the rest of the halls were three bays across. The sizes of courtyards corresponded to the sizes of their halls. The courtyard in front of the main hall, for example, was built according to the "courtyard enclosed by a covered arcade" style, which had been employed for the most eminent halls since the Tang dynasty.

During the Jin dynasty the Confucian temple expanded in all four directions, although the focus of the complex remained the same main hall. Other changes were made as well. A small building was erected on Apricot Terrace (where Confucius had lectured his disciples), and the imperial library was expanded and named Star of Literature Pavilion (Kuiwenge). At the main building, the Hall of Great Achievement (Dachengdian), a green glazed-tile roof was added, as were azure-painted bracket sets, vermilion-painted balustrades, and carved dragons winding around the stone pillars. Dachengdian and the Hall of the Lady of Yunguo behind it were joined into a gong-shaped structure. After this Jin-period expansion, the Dacheng Hall nucleus became an even more prominent part of the plan. Several stela pavilions survive from the Jin period; other structures of the Confucian temple in Qufu are from later periods.

Another noteworthy temple was Houtumiao, a structure in Wanrong, Shanxi province, that was first established in 163 B.C.E. and was devoted to the Earth Goddess. From the Han through the Tang dynasty, emperors went in person to sacrifice to the goddess. Beginning in 1007, the ritual was elevated to *dasi,* a great offering. Three years later, in 1010, the Houtumiao was renovated. The "Temple Image Stela," carved in 1137, preserves one of the earliest plans of a Chinese temple complex, and although it was recarved in 1556 and again in 1632, the image is believed to show the original layout of Houtumiao (fig. 5.12). According to the inscription, the Song site consisted of eight courtyards extending about 1,102 meters north to south by 524 meters east to west. All of the principal halls were placed on the main north–south axis. A wall with three straight edges but a semicircular northern face and a tower at each corner enclosed the entire site. As seen on the stela, the main structures from south to north were the main gate Lingxingmen, Taning Temple, Cengtian Gate, Yanxi Gate, Kunrou Gate, Kunrou Hall, a sleeping hall, and the Altar Where Xuanyuan (the Yellow Emperor) Swept the Earth. Auxiliary halls stood on either side of the axis.

The Temple to the Earth Goddess was structurally magnificent. The main hall, Kunroudian, was nine bays across the front with two hipped roofs, in the style of the grandest halls of Tang imperial cities such as Hanyuandian. The approach to the hall passed through five courtyards, the same number used in imperial palace architecture. The courtyard in front of Kunrou Hall was enclosed on four sides. Kunroudian and the sleeping chamber behind it were joined by a covered corridor, with the three structures forming the gong plan also characteristic of Chinese imperial construction. With numerous multistory structures

and the combination of circular and square forms in its outer wall, the Temple to the Earth Goddess in Wanrong represented the best of Chinese architecture at the time.

The Jin Shrines in Taiyuan, Shanxi province, are of great significance, even though the date of their initial construction is unknown (fig. 5.13). The earliest documented shrine on the site was built to commemorate Prince Shu Yu of Tang, second son of King Wu of the Zhou dynasty. Shu Yu was considered the ancestor of the state of Jin and was renowned for achievements in agriculture and water conservancy. In 979, the second Song emperor, Taizong, rebuilt the shrine to Tang Shu Yu. Between 1023 and 1032, during the Renzong reign, Shengmudian (Sage Mother Hall) was built to honor the mother of Prince Shu Yu. In 1168, during the Jin dynasty, an offering hall *(xiandian)* was constructed in front of Sage Mother Hall. Additions and rebuilding continued through the Yuan, Ming, and Qing dynasties, giving way to the huge building complexes about twenty-five kilometers south of Taiyuan today. Sage Mother Hall and the offering hall are the only extant pre-fourteenth-century structures.

Sage Mother Hall, centerpiece of the Jin Shrines, is seven bays across the front, six bays deep, and has a double-eaved, nine-ridge roof (fig. 5.14). Structurally, it is an example of the most eminent hall type in medieval China, the *diantang.* The center four columns on the front facade support beams that are three rafter lengths in depth, creating a wide veranda with additional open space for sacrifices to the Sage Mother. Wooden dragons were carved around the front facade columns in 1087 (fig. 5.15). They are the oldest extant dragon columns in China. The bracket sets, by contrast, are of multiple styles, representing numerous repairs made to the hall in the eleventh and twelfth centuries (figs. 5.16 and 5.17). The upward curve of the roof eaves is gentle and graceful, characteristic of Song style. Statues of the Sage Mother and forty-two female attendants dominate the interior of the hall. Slightly less than life-size and carefully molded to give each individual features, they represent the height of Song sculpture.

In front of Shengmudian is a fish pond fed by spring water. The pond is spanned by a cruciform-shaped bridge roughly 5 meters east to west by 3.5 meters north to south. Beneath the bridge are thirty-four pillars, also arranged in the shape of a cross. The pillars support wooden beams, rafters, and the floorboards of the bridge, called Flying Bridge. Located in front of the bridge, the offering hall is three bays square with a nine-ridge roof and bracket sets similar to those preserved from the twelfth-century repair of Sage Mother Hall.

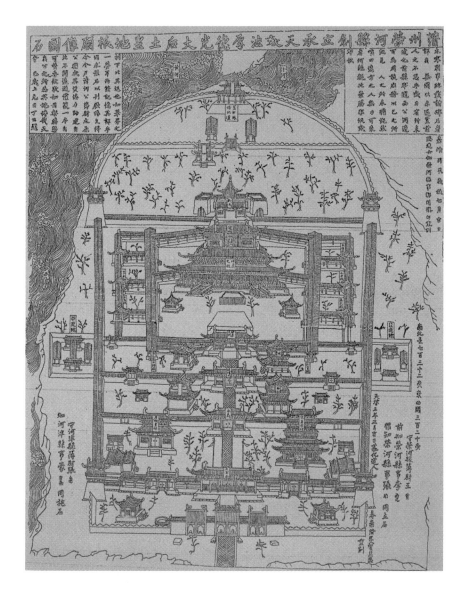

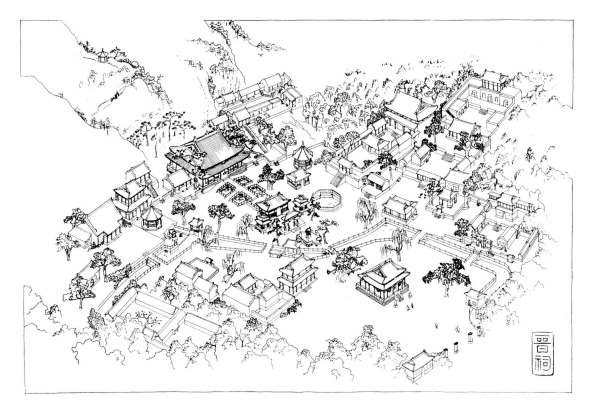

Figure 5.12. Drawing of the Temple Image Stela, Houtumiao (Earth Goddess Temple) in Wanrong, Shanxi province, 1137

Figure 5.13. Jin Shrines, Taiyuan, Shanxi province

Figure 5.14. Sage Mother Hall, Taiyuan, Shanxi province, 1023–1032

Figure 5.15. Pillars in the front of Sage Mother Hall

Funerary Architecture

The tombs of all but the last emperors of Northern Song and Liao and many of the emperors of the Xi Xia dynasty remain, as do countless aristocratic and humble graves of the tenth through thirteenth centuries in all parts of China. Each of the major dynasties of these centuries accorded their rulers royal tombs. Those of Northern and Southern Song and of the Xi Xia were restricted to one area. The Liao, by contrast, clustered the tombs of their rulers, but no one site can be called a Liao dynastic necropolis. Only fragments remain of the Jin royal tombs. The first Jin rulers were buried near the site

of their first capital, Shangjing, and later reburied with other Jin emperors south of their central capital, about ten kilometers northwest of Fangshan, in the city limits of Beijing today. Jin emperor Xuanzong (r. 1213–1224) was buried at the southern Jin capital, today Kaifeng.

Seven of the nine emperors of the Northern Song dynasty have mausolea in Gong county, Henan province. So does the father of Zhao Kuangyin, the dynastic founder. Besides these eight tombs, twenty-one empresses are buried in Gongxian, as are some three hundred relatives (including children) of the imperial family. The area of the funerary complexes is about sixty square meters. Based on a geomantic principle to which the Song ruling family attributed some of their success, the funerary area was higher in the southeast (the location of the mounds) and lower in the northwest (the actual burial ground). The eight male tombs were arranged in three groups, with no more than five kilometers between any two of them. Indeed, this Northern Song tomb group is sometimes considered the first royal Chinese cemetery because even in the

Figure 5.16. Front corridor of Sage Mother Hall

Figure 5.17. Sage Mother Hall showing two sets of roof eaves

Western Han dynasty and under the Six Dynasties' rule in the southeast (when the emperors' tombs were all in the vicinity of Chang'an and Nanjing, respectively), tombs were placed much farther from one another than in Gongxian.

Each royal tomb has nearly the same form: they are all oriented about six degrees east of north–south and originally were enclosed by wattle-and-daub walls. All of the emperor's tombs consisted of aboveground architecture and underground chambers known as the underground palaces. Similarly, empresses' tombs had aboveground and underground components. Each imperial tomb was complemented by auxiliary burials, and special caretakers guarded each enclosed tomb area. Inside the enclosures, the cutting of firewood and grazing of cattle were prohibited. Beyond the walls were a few individual princes' tombs, traveling palaces for emperors when they came to pay their respects at the tombs of their ancestors, precincts in which blessings to the dead could be recited, and residences of the tomb caretakers.

The aboveground portions of the Northern Song imperial tombs were as important as the underground architecture. A high mound was at the core of each. Four gates provided access through the walls enclosing the burial ground, which had four corner towers. Beyond the gates were offering halls where memorial prayers to the deceased were recited. Small, subsidiary buildings flanked the sacrificial halls. Originally, the mounds above the burials were elevated on three earthen platforms of diminishing size, the lowest of which was eighty-seven meters square. Cypress trees were planted on the platforms, and the burial chamber was located directly beneath. Each of the eight imperial tombs has different dimensions from the others, with the distance from mound to floor of the burial chamber ranging from nineteen to thirty-four meters. South of the triple earthen platforms and the south sacrificial hall were the spirit paths for the tomb of each emperor and of Zhao Kuangyin's father, each a passage approximately three hundred meters long lined by memorial gateways, stone animals, mythological creatures, and stone men of Chinese and non-Chinese origin (fig. 5.18).

At empresses' tombs, the aboveground portions were generally the same as those of emperors, except that each element tended to be smaller. The underground chambers were northwest of the tumuli, and were used to store imperial portraits and objects used by the empresses in life. Tomb guards were stationed nearby, and offerings were directed toward the *xiagong* (underground palaces). The principal structures of a Northern Song empress's tomb were the main hall, countenance hall (where portraits were hung), abstinence hall (for vegetarian feasting), hall for clothes washing, kitchen where the sacrificial

Figure 5.18. Spirit path at the tombs of Gongxian, Henan province, Northern Song dynasty

animals were prepared, hall for the tomb caretaker, hall for the palatial attendants, and storage areas.

The only Northern Song imperial tomb that has been opened is that of Empress Li, wife of the second emperor, Zhao Guangyi (939–997). After she had been buried in 998, her tomb was robbed and was subsequently unearthed. The length of underground chambers, including the ramp down into the tomb and connective causeway to the main chamber, was 50 meters. The mound on top was 8 meters high. The main chamber was circular in plan, 7.95 meters in diameter and 12.26 meters from ground level to the highest point of its vaulted ceiling. Ten pillars were lodged into its brick interior walls, along with carvings in brick between the pillars that depicted doors and windows as well as figures seated at tables. Murals with architectural details of palaces and pavilions joined the relief sculpture, and white clouds and celestial bodies were painted on the ceiling. A U-shaped coffin bed remained in the chamber. The interior resembled that of the contemporary aristocratic tombs excavated in Baisha and Luoyang (discussed later).

Enough monumental sculpture survives along the spirit path approaches to Northern Song imperial tombs to differentiate between earlier and later period styles. Sculptures in front of the earliest tombs are simple and straightforward compared with the more realistic mid-Song images. Sculpture from the latest Northern Song royal tombs is the most lively and most skillfully carved, and offers the greatest detail.

Believing that their capital city in Zhejiang province was temporary, the Southern Song rulers were buried with the assumption that their graves would be moved to Gongxian after the full size of the empire was restored. (In fact, in the official record their tombs were named *cuangong,* or temporary tombs, rather than suffixed with *ling* like the royal tombs of Chinese emperors of the previous millennium.) Consequently, their tombs were of a smaller scale than those of the Northern Song, with mounds about two meters high and five meters in circumference — and with no spirit paths leading to them. Still, the Southern Song were responsible for one innovation in imperial tomb architecture. The two parts of Northern Song tombs known as the "upper" (aboveground) and "lower" (underground) palaces were positioned in a row. This was to become a tradition in Ming and Qing imperial architecture.

Like so many Chinese dynasties, the Liao dynasty was able to give all but its final ruler a fitting imperial burial. But unlike these other dynasties, the Qidan tribes brought with them to China burial practices that bore witness to their seminomadic heritage. Evidence of these Qidan burial rites, discussed later, has been revealed through texts and confirmed by excavation.

Aboveground, however, remains of Liao imperial graves have much in common with those of contemporary Song royalty. For example, based on the existence of a spirit path in front of the tomb of Yelu Cong, a relative of the imperial Liao clan who was buried in 979 in Chifeng county, Inner Mongolia, it is believed that pairs of men and animals lined the approaches to tombs of Liao emperors. Spirit paths are suggested at tombs of three Liao emperors by the exceptionally long approaches to the tomb in Qingzhou, Chifeng county, but no remains have confirmed their existence.

Known as the eastern, central, and western mausolea, the site of the tombs of the sixth, seventh, and eighth Liao rulers who reigned from 982–1101, more than half the duration of the empire, is sometimes called Qingling. Each tomb consisted of at least six underground chambers approached from the surface by a diagonal ramp. The two main rooms were along an axial line defined by the entry ramp, and in the case of the eastern mausoleum, an antechamber might be considered an additional space in front of the two main rooms. Side rooms were joined by passageways to the central and back rooms. The shape of each room was circular or octagonal. All three mausolea were completely painted inside, although only murals from the eastern mausoleum have been preserved. Their subjects include landscapes of the four seasons; portraits of Chinese, Qidan, and other officials who served the Liao empire; and replicas of wooden architecture (fig. 5.19).

Among the earlier royal Qidan tombs, that of the dynasty's founder Abaoji has attracted the most attention even though the site identified as his tomb, Zuling, has never been confirmed. Interest in Abaoji's tomb is part of a more general curiosity about Zuzhou ("ancestral prefecture"), the walled city with which it is associated, and a structure in it known as the "stone house," where excavations have led to speculation that Abaoji used the dolmen-like building as his ancestral temple. The other

Figure 5.19. Detail of interior of the eastern mausoleum, Qingzhou, Chifeng city, Inner Mongolia, Liao dynasty

Figure 5.20. Xi Xia necropolis, near Yinchuan, Ningxia Hui autonomous region, 1038–1227

Liao rulers were buried in Huaizhou, about thirty kilometers from Zuzhou, and Xianzhou and Qianzhou, both near Beizhen in Liaoning province.

The royal tombs of the Tangut, or Xi (Western) Xia, emperors are located at the eastern foot of the Helan mountain range in the western suburbs of Yinchuan (formerly Xingzhou) in the Ningxia Hui autonomous region (fig. 5.20). The nine emperor tombs and seventy auxiliary burials, spread over fifty square kilometers of dramatic desert landscape, have much in common with those of the imperial cemetery in Gongxian. The tomb of Weiming (Li) Zunxu (r. 1211–1223), for example, has been excavated. Aboveground its approach was marked by a pair of gate towers and a pair of stela pavilions. Behind them were two walls, just as at the tomb of Tang Gaozong and Empress Wu, which enclosed an area of 183 by 134 meters. Continuing along the approach between the two enclosing walls, pairs of statues of civil and military officials formed a spirit path. Also aboveground were the sacrificial hall as well as gates and corner towers that adjoined the wall.

Behind the offering hall a diagonal path, west of the main north–south axis of the approach, led to the subterranean region. Behind it, also aboveground, was an octagonal burial mound of which seven layers remain. Each side of the octagon is about 12 meters, and its pres-

ent height is about 16.5 meters. It seems that each layer of the mound, including the top, was originally covered with wooden eaves on top of which were green glazed tiles, and that the mound was painted reddish brown. In other words, its color and form imitated those of timber-frame architecture.

Apparently the passage to the tomb was never sealed. Underground were one main chamber, 24.9 meters below ground level, and two symmetrically positioned side chambers. The main chamber measures 5.6 meters by between 6.7 and 7.8 meters at the base. The underground chambers were excavated right out of the yellow loess earth; no brick was used, but wooden panels were placed on all four walls.

A large variety and number of nonimperial tombs both north and south of the Northern Song's borders with Liao and Xi Xia were also constructed between the Five Dynasties period and the fall of Song. Among the more than 350 nonimperial Liao tombs that have been excavated, some distinctions can be made between the tombs of the Han Chinese and those of the Qidan aristocracy within Liao territory. In Song and Jin China, wealthy citizens, merchants, and perhaps aristocracy had tombs with splendid interior decoration. Twelve tombs or cemeteries are chosen here to represent funerary construction between the tenth and thirteenth centuries. Among them are tombs with as many as nine subterranean chambers; burials in stone, wooden, and multilayer sarcophaguses; coffin beds, sometimes for sarcophaguses and other times for less well contained remains; and cremation tombs, or burials of ashes in underground architectural complexes.

Although excavated some four decades ago, the three tombs at Baisha, Yu county, Henan province, remain outstanding examples of Song funerary construction. All have roughly the same plan: a ramp leading into the tomb from ground level (mudao), an underground ramp that extends from the tomb entry down to the level of the tomb floor (or to nearly that level), an antechamber (more pronounced in Tomb 1 than the other tombs), a connective causeway (guodao) joining the front and back chamber, and the back chamber, which is the main chamber in Tomb 1. Baisha Tomb 1 was excavated right into the loess of the earth, but once its shape was carved out, the walls were faced with brick and the main chamber was covered with a vaulted brick ceiling. A narrow space existed between the brick facing and the earthen wall. The small antechamber was rectangular in plan, 1.84 by 2.28 meters, and rose 4.22 meters in height, but the rear chamber was hexagonal, a burial-chamber shape that became fashionable in Song and Liao China, with sides between 1.26 and 1.3 meters and a dome 4 meters above the floor.

Figure 5.21. Ceiling and walls of an octagonal chamber from a tomb in Xin'an, Henan province, Northern Song dynasty

Spectacular paintings and relief sculptures on brick walls ornament the Baisha tombs. Included in Baisha Tombs 1, 2, and 3 are architraves, bracket sets, eave rafters, roof ridges and roof tiles, doors, and windows that imitate their timber counterparts. After all these were in place in brick, actual wooden doors were installed at the entryway. Another common feature in Song tombs that appears at Baisha is a female figure looking out a partially open door. Scholars have offered a range of interpretations of this image: it may represent a last look of the departed or identify the location of the occupant, who is always buried in the chamber behind the woman. Often, and present in all three Baisha tombs, the occupants are depicted in paintings as seated at a set table with servants behind them. The scenes of banquets and other entertainment for the deceased are themes observed in tomb decoration since the Han dynasty.

A six-chamber tomb excavated in Shangluo, Danfeng county, Shaanxi, has one of the most unusual plans known among Song tombs. Five four-sided chambers radiate from each side of the central hexagonal room except for the entryway on the south. The main room, 4.5 meters in height, measures 2.9 meters north–south and 3.1 meters east–west. A brick tomb with a single four-sided burial chamber excavated at Jiuliugou, Yanshi, Henan, includes

interior architectural decorations that rival the magnificent ornamentation in Baisha. So do decorations in a tomb with an octagonal chamber uncovered in Xinle, Henan (fig. 5.21).

One of the best-known Southern Song tombs is the joint burial of Zhang Tong and his wife in the Huangyue mountain range, Jiangpu county, Jiangsu. A rectangular pit tomb, its ceiling was made of stone, on top of which small bricks were joined to form a vault with an arch fifty-four centimeters high. A partition wall divided the main chamber into two parts, the left side for Zhang Tong's burial and the right for his wife's. Burial goods were placed in niches in the walls of both parts of the room.

Tombs from the Song dynasty have yielded beautiful examples of art and architecture, but few true surprises. The excavation of Qidan tombs, by contrast, has uncovered aspects of Liao society never imagined from texts alone. It has, furthermore, confirmed details of difficult-to-believe burial practices described in texts. Over the past fifty years, the world of the Qidan has emerged as a complex society whose multinational population drew from Chinese literature, folklore, and predynastic Qidan rites in creating its funerary practices. The tombs discussed here exhibit the range of styles and customs preserved below ground.

The joint burial in 1018 of the Princess of Chenguo,

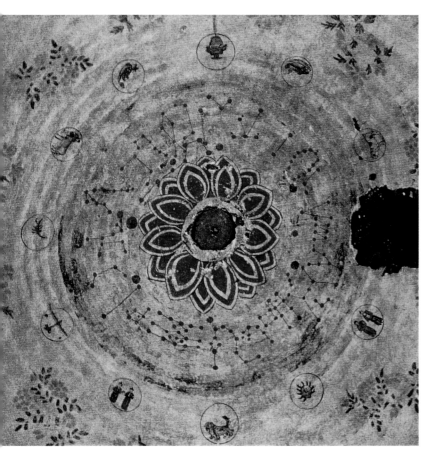

Figure 5.22. Ceiling from the tomb of Zhang Shiqing, Xiabali, Xuanhua county, Hebei province, 1116

daughter of Emperor Jingzong (r. 969–982), and her husband, brother-in-law of Emperor Shengzong (r. 982–1031), in Qinglongshan, Naiman Banner, Inner Mongolia, has attracted more attention in recent years than any other Liao tomb. In large part this is because of the gold, silver, and amber objects buried inside. Among them were suits of metal netting that covered every inch of the bodies, as well as golden death masks and crowns, and silver and gold boots. Texts also describe this manner of burial for the second Liao emperor, Taizong, but his tomb has not yet been excavated.

The bodies of the princess and her husband were placed on a funerary bed along the back wall of the circular brick burial chamber, which was 4.38 meters in diameter and just under 4 meters high. Two side niches, also circular in plan, were joined to it by corridors. The stone epitaph was placed in a four-sided antechamber. The tomb was covered with murals: on the ceiling was an expansive painting of the sun, moon, and stars against the night sky.

The bodies of the princess and her husband have not been examined, but the corpse of an unidentified female similarly buried in a six-piece suit of metal netting in a stone single-chamber octagonal tomb in Haoqianying,

Qahar Right Wing Front Banner, Inner Mongolia, has been studied. Her body appears to have been posthumously punctured in the chest and shoulder for drainage of bodily fluids and then refilled with vegetable matter. The same process is described by a Song writer for the preparation of Liao emperor Taizong's corpse. Such death rituals also were enacted in the first millennium B.C.E. by peoples of North Asia who were perhaps very distant forebears of the Qidan.

Two Liao sites provide evidence of family cemeteries. One, believed to belong to members of the Xiao family, a consort clan of the emperors who took Yelü as their family name, was uncovered in Kulun Banner, Inner Mongolia. Eight Kulun Banner tombs have been dated to the reigns of the three emperors buried in the cemetery in Qingzhou. The Kulun Banner plans exhibit a range of burial chamber types. Although all but Tomb 1 had a single main chamber with a long approach to it, room shapes were circular, octagonal, and four-sided. Those with side niches had circular, octagonal, hexagonal, and four-sided plans, which usually matched the shape of the main chamber. Each of the tomb interiors was covered with murals and featured replicas of wooden architecture in brick and paint. A few Chinese themes such as landscape and bird-and-flower painting were present, but the great majority of painted subjects were Qidan men and women. One fascinating exception to these themes is found in ceiling murals from tombs in the family cemetery excavated at Xiabali, Xuanhua county, Hebei. In addition to the sun, moon, star groups known as the twenty-eight *xiu* (lunar lodges), and twelve calendrical animals common in Chinese funerary art, signs of the Western zodiac are painted on the ceilings of several of the tombs, including Zhang Shiqing's (fig. 5.22).

Although associations can be made between burial practice and ethnicity (so far, for example, no Chinese living under Liao rule has been found buried in a metal wire suit), it is not clear that Liao tomb structure evolved over time. Indeed, some of the oldest Liao tombs are architecturally the most complicated. One example is the joint burial of Zhao Dejun and his wife in the southern suburbs of Beijing. He was buried in 937 and she in 958. Oriented eastward, their tomb consisted of nine circular chambers. The largest, 4.12 meters in diameter, was the main central room that contained the coffins. Eight pillars joined by tiebeams, bracket sets, doors, windows, and lintels decorated its walls, and the entire interior had been painted. A single-chamber tomb, 22.5 meters in length and dated to 923, uncovered in Baoshan, Chifeng city, Inner Mongolia, in 1994, and believed to be the grave of a Qidan, was similarly covered with architectural deco-

Figure 5.23. Architectural model used as an outer coffin, from Tomb 7 at Yemaotai, Liaoning Provincial Museum, Shenyang, late tenth century

Figure 5.24. Entry to the Duan family tomb, Ma village, Jishan, Shanxi province

ration. Its wall paintings included Chinese females and even a scene of a meeting between Han emperor Wudi and the native Chinese deity, the Queen Mother of the West.

Finally, a few Liao excavations provide important evidence of the timber-frame tradition. One is Tomb 7 excavated at Yemaotai, Faku county, Liaoning, in 1974. Inside the tomb, which consisted of a main chamber and three small rooms in front of it, all four-sided, was a cypress-bark architectural model. It was the outer of two coffins (the inner one was made of stone). Two silk scrolls hung on its interior walls.

Now in the Liaoning Provincial Museum in Shenyang, the wooden structure was three bays by two (fig. 5.23). Its central front bay, 123.7 centimeters across, was occupied by a double-panel door. Windows were created in the upper portions of the two side bays, each just over half the length of the central one, and ten four-sided pillars supported the structure. Ten posts supported a balustrade around every side of the structure except its front, central bay. Two steps led to the balustrade opening. The roof was a nine-spine, combination hip-gable type that projected out at a forty-five-degree angle on each of the four sides. This outer sarcophagus is almost identical to a structure called *jiuji xiaozhang,* a nine-ridge small-scale container described in the "small-scale carpentry" section of the Song architectural treatise *Yingzao fashi.*

Despite the non-Chinese ancestry of the dynastic family, Jin tombs embellished the patterns and decorations of Northern Song burials. More than twenty tombs in southern Shanxi province, many located in towns and villages along the Fen River, such as Houma, or Ma village, are exemplary. Although most are single-chamber tombs, they nevertheless have domed ceilings and interiors that

Figure 5.25. Woman looking out a door, interior of Duan family tomb

Figure 5.26. Detail of relief sculpture in Duan family tomb

Figure 5.27. Brick carving in imitation of wood, side wall of Duan family tomb

are more decorated than any known Song tomb. Among the relief sculpture and paintings that cover their walls are imitations of a great variety of wooden architectural details, including further examples of the small-scale carpentry described in *Yingzao fashi*, portraits of the deceased, depictions of entertainers and musicians, and a female looking out a partially open door (figs. 5.24, 5.25, 5.26, and 5.27). Some believe this last scene symbolizes the passage between the world of the living and the world of the tomb.

Garden Architecture

It is written that 150 imperial and private gardens were created in the Northern Song capital. It is not known how many gardens graced the Southern Song capital, but they must have been breathtaking: texts claim that in this natural beauty spot of hills and lakes, the most spectacular scenery was offered by the manmade gardens. In the capitals of Liao and Jin, too, rulers, aristocrats, officials, and scholars are said to have built such places for celebrating the outdoors.

The most important imperial gardens of the tenth through thirteenth centuries, and those we know most about, are located in the two Song capitals and Jin Zhongdu. Two Northern Song gardens exemplify the contrast in imperial designs of the period. One is dominated by a mountain, the other by water.

Genyue, a manmade garden located in the northeastern part of the capital, took its name from the trigram *gen* from *Yi jing* (Book of changes) and *yue*, often translated "peak." Construction began in 1117 and was not completed until 1122, just a few years before the fall of the dynasty. Longevity Mountain stood in the northeastern part of Genyue. It took the form of the character for mountain, *shan*, with a 150-meter-high peak in the center and the lower Ten Thousand Pines peaks on either side. Cleansing Gorge flowed between them. A half kilometer southeast of Longevity Mountain was the town of Furong, and to the southwest was the Lake District. The water flowed through Hui Xi (Returning Brook), cutting it into two streams. One of these flowed into the mountain stream, and then into a square pond called Yanchi (Wild Goose Pond). The other wound around Ten Thousand Pines peaks and emptied into Phoenix Pond.

Sprinkled throughout the garden were about forty structures: imperial verandas, lodges, towers, platforms, and simple, rustic huts. Each building was unique. In addition, in the western part of Genyue were an inner and an outer garden named Yaoliao and Xizhuang, said to imitate farm scenery. Rare flowers and trees, including some that bore fruit, were the predominant feature of this section of Genyue, which also had scenic spots named for their ornamental plants — for example, Plum Ridge, Apricot Hill, Lilac Cliff, Cypress Slope, and Mottle Bamboo Foothill. Among the trees were innumerable exotic birds and beasts.

The layering of peaks in Genyue was ingenious. Longevity Mountain was high and steep, a sharp contrast to the flanking Ten Thousand Pines peaks. Rows of cliffs were formed in layers that resembled curtains. High and low spots in the garden were also formed by stone paths, walkways, plank-road pavilions, and grottoes. Land and water were truly integrated to create a complete and beautiful environment.

By contrast, as its name suggests, Jinming Lake was a garden in which water was the most important element. Located north of the main road that led out of the capital from Xinzheng Gate, the site had been a training ground for the imperial navy. At the end of the Northern Song dynasty, halls and dwellings were built and trees were planted, turning it into a water park. This was the location of the annual dragon boat regatta. Performers competed for prizes and the emperor himself came to watch. There were only a few structures in the garden. The Baojin Tower group was south of the lake, and a banquet hall was beyond it to the south with an archery hall and Hall for Reflecting on the Water at its side. Heart of the Water Hall was in the middle of the lake. Zhang Zeduan's painting *Jinmingchisi biaotu* (Guide map to Jinming Lake Monastery) is thought to be a portrait of this garden (fig. 5.28).

The gardens of the Southern Song capital, renowned for their beauty, were at least as famous as those of Northern Song Dongjing. The back garden of the palace city of Lin'an was located west of Phoenix Mountain in the southern part of the capital. With its high elevation and cool breezes, it became a popular summer resort of the imperial family. Workmen soon created the famous Little West Lake, about 6.6 kilometers square and joined to the palace by a 180-bay covered corridor. According to *Nandu xinggong ji* (Record of the detached palace of the southern capital [Lin'an]), Little West Lake was at the center of the garden. A few buildings were scattered above and below Phoenix Mountain, including an unpainted hall and building with a thatched roof. Flowers and trees were planted to create scenic spots famous for their plants, including Plum Hill, Little Peach Garden, Apricot Depression, and Cypress Garden.

Figure 5.28. Zhang Zeduan, *Jinmingchisi biaotu*, eleventh–twelfth century

Imperial gardens separated from the palaces were located mainly around Little West Lake, which was accessed by a painted pleasure boat. Jifangyuan and Yuhuyuan were north of the lake, Pingshanyuan and Nanyuan were south of it, Jujingyuan was to the east, and Yanxiangyuan was to the west. In addition, the Deshou (virtue and longevity) palace garden and Cherry Garden were in the neighborhood of the palace city, and west of the city at the foot of Santianzhu Peak was Tianzhu imperial garden. The most striking garden, however, was that of Deshou, which was divided into four parts, each with different scenery. The eastern section was primarily for appreciating flowers, whereas the western was a scenic spot for viewing and admiring the entire landscape: hills, waterways, pools, artificial mountains, layered rockeries, each in its own place. A pavilion of every variety was in the northern section of Deshou palace garden, and in the south were places for archery, horse racing, and ball games as well as the Recording Delight Hall, which was used for banquets.

Between 1191 and 1208, gardens also flourished at the Jin central capital. Approximately twenty imperial gardens were built inside and outside the city. Most famous were those at two detached palaces, Daninggong (today beneath Beijing's Beihai Park) and Yuquanshan. Daninggong had a manmade lake carved out of the marshes with Qionghua Island rising from the center of the lake. Guanghan Hall was constructed on the island, and according to documents there also were artificial mountains and tremendously high piles of rocks that had been taken by the Jin from Genyue when they had plundered the Northern Song capital Dongjing.

Private gardens were also of considerable importance and beauty, and during the Song dynasty they were built throughout China. The *Record of Famous Gardens of Luoyang* by the Song writer Li Gefei documents that during the Song period there were eighteen famous private gardens in Luoyang, which was also a Song capital. Some were of the pond-and-hill variety, either one pond with two hills such as Fuzheng Garden or one hill with two ponds such as Huanxi Garden. Others were of the flower-garden type, such as Guiren Garden, where not only peony, herbaceous peony, peach, and plum blossoms grew, more than a thousand of each variety, but also a large bamboo forest. Among these private gardens, that of scholar-official Sima Guang (1019–1086), author of the expansive history of China *Zizhi tongjian*, was striking. Named Duleyuan (Garden for Solitary Joy), the garden, according to Sima Guang's own record of it, *Duleyuan ji,* had large areas of herbal and floral plantings and contained a scholar's hall with five thousand volumes. To the north of this hall was a pond, and from the center of the pond rose an artificial island with bamboo planted along its entire perimeter. Bamboo Studio, with earthen walls and a thatched roof, was also north of his hall of learning. To its south was Enjoyment of Water Veranda, which had its own pool in the middle. The covered ditch that channeled water to the pool was divided into five streams known as Tiger's Paw Spring. The interplay of water and land continued once the water had flowed out of the veranda; at that point it divided into two smaller brooks that poured into the large pond in the north.

Not all gardens were this large or elaborate. In the Southern Song capital, Lin'an, some residents had small gardens next to their homes. Wu Zimu's *Record of Dreams of the Splendors of the Capital* informs us that the Jiang residence had such a garden. Occupying only several hectares, it had pavilions, platforms, flowers, and trees. Peach Village, Apricot Inn, and Wine Shop all contributed to the scenery of a rustic village garden.

Another kind of private garden was the villa, many of which were found in the hills near West Lake and on the beaches of Qiantang River. Villas varied greatly in size. The South Garden of high-ranking official Han Tuozhou, near Long Bridge at the southwest corner of West Lake, had ten kinds of pavilions and kiosks of

Figure 5.29. White Pagoda, Qingzhou, Chifeng city, Inner Mongolia, built in 1049

unequaled craftsmanship, as well as archery fields, horse racing corridors, mountain grottoes, magnificent halls, and pools for floating cups while composing verse. A few shops and country inns added to the scenery.

The cities of Suzhou and Wuxing also had numerous private gardens. Southern Song literatus Zhou Mi wrote in *Wuxing yuanling ji* (Record of the gardens of Wuxing) that the city had thirty-six, of which the largest covered more than a hundred acres and the smallest were the size of a single residence. His contemporary Fan Chengda (1126–1193) wrote in *Wujun zhi* (Record of the city of Wu [Suzhou] and its districts) that this city had more than ten private gardens. Some of these, including Canglangtingyuan, or Garden of the Blue Sea Waves Pavilion (which was actually begun in the period of the Five Dynasties), and Wangshiyuan (Garden of the Master of the Fishnets), can still be seen.

Monasteries

One could write convincingly about the importance of approximately one hundred religious buildings of the Song, Liao, and Jin that either survive today or were thoroughly studied prior to their recent destruction. Remaining monasteries, which stand in almost every Chinese province, number about half that. Still, enough Chinese architecture survives from the second half of the tenth century onward that it is not possible to do justice to every important or significant structure. Instead, eight buildings or sites with truly extraordinary features are discussed here.

Buddhist monasteries of Song, Liao, and Jin were built according to five fundamental plans. Monasteries in which the pagoda was the focus appeared in China during the Han dynasty, when Buddhism was introduced, and flourished through the eleventh century. This arrangement of a pagoda towering in the center with a main hall for Buddhist images behind it was especially prevalent in Liao times. One of the finest examples is Fogong Monastery, a temple complex in Ying county, Shanxi, dominated by a 67.3-meter-high structure named Timber Pagoda (discussed more fully later). The same plan was employed in Qingzhou, Chifeng city, Inner Mongolia. Its similarly impressive brick pagoda, constructed in 1049, goes by the name White Pagoda, as do several other extant Liao pagodas (fig. 5.29). As at Fogongsi and in Qingzhou, only the pagoda, built in 1057, survives at Daguangji Monastery, in Jinzhou, Liaoning. There, however, halls originally stood in front of and behind

the pagoda. Dahaotiansi, a monastery of the same type in which the dominant pagoda was positioned between a nine-Buddha hall and a Dharma Hall (a hall for preaching the dharma, or Buddhist law), is described in the tenth chapter of *Quan Liaowen* (Complete writings on Liao). Although this style is not limited to the Liao period, more monasteries with a dominant pagoda on the main axis survive from the Liao than from Song or Jin China.

The pavilion *(ge)* is a second tall, multistory structure common in Liao Buddhist monasteries. Not as tall as a pagoda, the pavilion was often featured on the main axis or appeared with another pavilion. When the pavilion is on the main axis, it can be the central focus of the monastery or stand in front of the main hall. The most famous monastery with a pavilion is Dulesi in Ji county, Hebei, and the most famous pavilion from the tenth through thirteenth centuries is Dulesi's Guanyin Pavilion from the Liao dynasty (fig. 5.30).

The pavilion and Shanmen (front gate) from Dulesi, both dated 984, are the only two Liao-period buildings at the monastery today. It is possible that Dulesi resembled another Liao monastery with a pagoda on its central axis, Fengguosi in Yi county, Liaoning, which has been reconstructed based on monastery records. In both, a nine-bay hall containing seven Buddha images, a Dharma Hall, and a pavilion to the bodhisattva Guanyin are believed to have stood along the main axis together with the front gate. Pavilions to the Three Vehicles (Triyana) and Amitabha stood to the east and west, respectively, and elsewhere in the monastery were an enclosing corridor of 120 bays known as the Grottoes of the Four Worthy Sages, a hall for the monks (Sangharama), an abstinence hall, an abbot's quarters, dormitories, and a kitchen.

Unlike Liao monasteries, where the pavilion is often the single focus or at least the central feature in front of the main hall, Song monasteries often featured the main hall in front of the pavilion. An example of this arrangement is Longxing Monastery in Zhengding county, Hebei, originally founded in the Sui dynasty (fig. 5.31). Construction by order of the emperor during the Northern Song dynasty resulted in the plan with these buildings along the central axis: front gate (built during the Jin dynasty), Hall to the Sixth Patriarch (built between 1078 and 1085 and now destroyed), Moni Hall (built in 1052 and dedicated to the Buddha Sakyamuni), Dabei Pavilion (also known as Foxiang Pavilion, dedicated to the bodhisattva Guanyin), and twin buildings from the Song period, the Pavilion of the Revolving Sutra Cabinet and the pavilion dedicated to the bodhisattva Cishi (Maitreya), in front of Dabei Pavilion on either side. In spite of the monastery's founding

Figure 5.30. Guanyin Pavilion of Dule Monastery, Ji county, Hebei province, 984

date, Dabei Pavilion was constructed in 971 and has been restored in recent years. A nine-bay lecture hall behind it, however, has been destroyed.

One of the longest Chinese monasteries north to south, Longxingsi varies from wide to narrow along its main line as a way of accommodating the size of each structure and the spaces between. The architectural climax is the three-pavilion group at the back of the monastery. A similar monastery with a pavilion at the back was Daxiangguosi, also built by imperial patronage, in the Northern Song capital Bianjing. At Daxiangguosi, the multistory structural group consisted of the Pavilion for Supplying the Sacred Ones (Zisheng) at the back, with

twin pavilions to Manjusri (Wenshu) and Samantabhadra (Puxian) in front of it.

The Shanhua Monastery in Datong, Shanxi, built in the Liao-Jin period, is a wonderful example of twin pavilions in front of a Buddha hall. Along the main axis of the monastery from front to back are the front gate (Shanmen), Hall of the Three Sacred Ones (Sanshengdian), and the main Buddha hall (Daxiongbaodian). The pavilions on either side in front of Daxiongbaodian were dedicated to the bodhisattvas Manjusri and Samantabhadra; both structures were attached to the covered corridor that enclosed the monastery. Today Manjusri Pavilion and the corridor are gone; Samantabhadra Pavilion was rebuilt in 1953.

The Liao, Song, Xi Xia, and Jin Dynasties 167

Figure 5.31. Longxing Monastery, Zhengding county, Hebei province

A similar design was adopted at Huayan Monastery, also in Datong and also begun in Liao times. Today the monastery contains structures built after its founding, and because of the uneven ground on which it stands it is named according to its two main parts, the upper and lower monasteries. A record of 1162 known as the "Record of Repair of the Bhagavat Sutra Repository" informs us that in 1140, nine-bay and five-bay halls were built on their former sites, and that other buildings included pavilions to Cishi (Maitreya) and Guanyin, Hai-hui Hall, the Sutra Repository, a bell tower, the Shan-men, and "ear" halls (doudian, or small halls attached to either side of the main building). Volume five of *Datongxian zhi* (Record of Datong prefecture) states, "In olden times, there were north and south pavilions at Huayansi." (Because the orientation of the monastery is east–west, the north and south pavilions would have been in front of the main hall.)

It is also recorded that Dahaotian Monastery in the Liao southern capital (Nanjing) had "a broad hall rising in the center with a multistory tower to either side."

Based on these three examples, the plan that features a main hall with twin pagodas in front of it is associated with Liao construction.

According to *Anzhai suibi* (Miscellaneous writings from peace studio, part two, section 14), monasteries of Chan Buddhism had seven halls. Under the Southern Song, the Ten Monasteries and Five Mountain Monasteries of the Chan sect (a meditational sect established between the tenth and thirteenth centuries at Mount Jing, North Mountain, and South Mountain in Hangzhou and Mount Ayuwang [Asoka] and Mount Taibo in Ningbo) were influenced mainly by the seven-hall plan. *Da Song zhushan tu* (Illustrated [record] of mountain monasteries of the great Song), a text by the Japanese monk Gikai dated 1247–1256 and stored at the monastery Tōfuku-ji in Kyoto, includes diagrams of three of the Ten Monasteries: Lingyinsi, Tiantongsi, and Wanniansi.

Most noticeable in those drawings is the arrangement of buildings along strict north–south and east–west lines. Indeed there are seven structures pictured along the north–south axis of Lingyin Monastery. From south to north, they are the Shanmen (front gate), Buddha Hall, Vairocana Hall, Dharma Hall, Front Abbot's Quarters, Abbot's Quarters, and Room for Seated Meditation. On either side of the Buddha Hall are a Storage Hall precinct and Monks' Hall. The buildings are arranged so that the front gate is opposite the Buddha Hall and the precinct with the Storage Hall faces the Monks' Hall. The illustrations of Tiantong Monastery and Wannian Monastery similarly show a front gate, Buddha Hall, Buddhist Law Hall, and abbots' quarters along the main axes, and halls for the monks and storage on the subsidiary axis. It seems, then, that a standard arrangement for a Chan monastery in Southern Song China was to have structures for worship or sacred activities along the main axis and buildings for more mundane affairs on either side of it. In earlier Chan monasteries, residential space for monks was scattered throughout the monastery. With time, however, the abbots' quarters came to be located on the same line as the halls that housed Buddhist images, thereby revealing the elevation of the monks' status at this time.

Typical Buildings in a Buddhist Monastery

Every Buddhist monastery has halls dedicated to the Buddha. Usually the most important images are contained in a main hall, most often known as *dadian* (great hall), *zhengdian* (true or authorized hall), or Daxiongbaodian (Hall of the Great Strong Preservation). The most spectacular examples of main halls from this period are discussed later. Another hall dedicated to the Buddha and containing images is the Dharma Hall (for expounding the Buddhist law, or dharma). Law or lecture halls can also be used for preaching or teaching dharma.

Besides these, five structures are found, almost without exception, in Buddhist temple complexes of the Liao, Song, and Jin. The front gate, called Shanmen — literally "mountain gate" and sometimes translated as gatehouse because it is a building rather than a freestanding door — marks the entry to Buddhist space. The three-by-two-bay

Figure 5.32. Shanmen, Dule Monastery, Ji county, Hebei province, 984

Figure 5.33. Timber Pagoda, Fogong Monastery, Ying county, Shanxi province, 1056

Figure 5.34. Detail of an exterior corner of the Timber Pagoda

Shanmen from Dule Monastery is one of the smaller examples extant from this time period (fig. 5.32), whereas the front gates of Daxiangguo Monastery in the Northern Song capital, Bianjing, and of the Song Monastery Tiantongsi in Ningbo, Zhejiang — which are no longer standing — were seven bays across the front and three stories high.

Much has been said already about the importance of tall buildings, pagodas and pavilions, in tenth- through thirteenth-century Buddhist monastery space. The design and size of multistory buildings differ according to their function and position in the monastery, but it is rare to find a monastery in north China without one. Those on the central axis of the temple complex are the tallest, have the most complicated structures, and are the most important buildings in their monasteries. The tallest extant wooden structure is the 67.3-meter Timber Pagoda of Fogong Monastery in Ying county, Shanxi, the unambiguous focal point of its monastery (figs. 5.33 and 5.34). Equally famous and prominent in their monasteries are Dabei (or Foxiang) Pavilion of the Song monastery Longxingsi in Zhengding, Hebei (fig. 5.35), and Guanyin Pavilion of Dulesi in Ji county, Hebei, which was built in 984 in Liao territory. Each is an exceptional structure, even though Dabeige has been restored. Seven bays across the front and five deep, with a porch that extends five bays beyond the first story, Dabeige houses a 21.3-meter statue of the bodhisattva Guanyin positioned on an altar that rises 2.35 meters from the pavilion floor. It is estimated that in an earlier stage the pavilion may have risen 37 meters and been four stories. The Timber Pagoda and Guanyin Pavilion of Dule Monastery are both among the technically most sophisticated timber-frame structures known in China. It is probably because of the structural sophistication that both have withstood earthquakes and other natural disasters for more than a millennium.

Simpler and smaller are the paired pavilions that stand on either side of the main north–south axis of a monastery. Generally two stories, Puxian Pavilion of Shanhua Monastery in Datong, as well as Cishi and the Revolving Sutra Cabinet pavilions of Longxing Monastery, are all examples of this type of multistory structure. Paired pavilions were usually three bays across the front with a mezzanine layer inside (fig. 5.36).

During the Southern Song dynasty, monks' halls were an important feature of Buddhist monasteries of the Chan. Their purpose, housing for resident monks, remained unchanged since earliest times, but during the Southern Song period they grew tremendously. For

Figure 5.35. Dabei (or Foxiang) Pavilion, Longxing Monastery, Zhengding county, Hebei province, built in 971

Figure 5.36. Puxian Pavilion, Shanhua Monastery, Datong, Shanxi province, rebuilt in 1953 following Liao-period style

instance, Thousand-Monk Pavilion was built at Mount Jing Monastery in Lin'an in 1140 and Great Monk Hall was constructed at Tiantong Monastery between 1132 and 1134. Great Monk Hall contained Buddhist images as well as a long, continuous bed where the monks sat in meditation or slept. No examples of such large monks' halls survived natural disasters of the Yuan dynasty. During Ming times, each of the monks' halls had a separate function: meditation, dining, or residence.

In Song and Liao monasteries, it was common to find images of the Five Hundred Luohan, or monks (*arhat* in Sanskrit), in the front gate or the upper story of a pavilion. One exception was Jingci Monastery in Lin'an, where, according to the *Can Tiantai Wutaishan ji* (Record of a visit to Tiantai and Mount Wutai), written by Cheng Xun (1011–1081) in 1072, such depictions of the Luohan were featured near the Great Buddha Hall. In the Five Hundred Luohan Precinct were two stone pagodas, each nine stories and about ten meters in height. Images of the five hundred Luohan were carved on the pagodas, which were inside pavilions of unspecified size.

Covered corridors enclosed all the principal halls of monasteries created during this period. At Fengguo

Monastery in Yi county, Liaoning, the length of the enclosing arcade was 120 bays. It was nicknamed the "grotto of the four worthy sages." The length of the enclosing corridor at the Daxiangguo Monastery in the Northern Song capital was some three hundred bays, and at the Mount Jing Monastery, a long corridor with towers enclosed its buildings. The covered corridor of Shanhua Monastery in Datong from Liao-Jin times is one of the best preserved of the period. At times, Buddhist narratives were painted on the corridor walls.

Daoist Architecture

The Song emperors were great patrons of Daoist architecture. Promulgating the belief that Daoist transcendants had come down from the heavens to transmit heavenly writings, they frequently enacted the drama of the "Descent of the Ancestral Sages." Song emperor Zhenzong (r. 998–1023), for example, enacted a ceremony in which he received the heavenly teachings and ordered the construction of Daoist monasteries named Tianqingguan throughout the empire. Later, Emperor Huizong (r. 1101–1125) titled himself "the emperor who is a Daoist master" and ordered construction of a Hall for Welcoming Truth to greet the heavenly spirits. Huizong kept up the flurry of Daoist construction, which continued without a break even after the Southern Song took over. In Lin'an alone, more than thirty Daoist monasteries were built within a hundred years of the transfer of the Song capital there. The Jin dynasty saw the rise of several new Daoist sects whose structures would form important monasteries during the next dynasty, Yuan. And even though the Xi Xia were not avid builders of Daoist architecture, the religion was protected under their empire.

Most Daoist monasteries of the Song period have six areas: *shendian,* a spirit hall, for sacrificial rites; *zhaiguan,* a hall where believers can eat vegetarian meals in their quest for enlightenment *(xiuzhen);* scripture repositories; halls for preaching Daoist law; guest halls; and gardens. The architecture of Daoism resembles that of Buddhist monasteries because since earliest times it had developed in the context of the Buddhist tradition.

Two of the most famous Daoist monasteries of the Song period were Chongfugong on Mount Song in Henan province and Zongyanggong (renamed Dongxiaogong in 1021) on Mount Dadi in Lin'an. Both were built on mountainous terrain amid streams, grottoes, ponds, and cliffs. The approaches to mountain monasteries wound through mountains and forests: at Dongxiaogong, for example, the approach stretched an astonishing nine kilometers from the front gate to the main hall. Daoist monasteries in more urban settings were smaller. Examples are Bixiasi on Taishan in Shandong; Tianshifu at Shangqing in Guixi, Jiangxi; the Temple of the Jade Emperor in Jincheng, Shanxi; the Temple of the Eastern Peak in Xi'an; and Penglai Pavilion in Shandong. Of these, Song architecture remains only at the Jade Emperor Temple in Shanxi, where the Middle Hall and Hall of the Jade Emperor survive from 1076. Other places where Daoist architecture from the Song period can still be seen are Xuanmiaoguan in Putian, Fujian, site of a hall dated 1016; Xuanmiaoguan in Suzhou, where the main hall stands from 1176; the Monastery of the Two Immortals (Erxianguan) in Jincheng, Shanxi, whose main hall is dated 1107; and Yunyansi in the Douchui Mountains, Jiangyou county, Sichuan, site of Chitiancang Hall and Feitian Hall, from the Song era.

Famous Religious Architecture

Far too many wooden structures remain from the Liao, Song, and Jin periods to give attention to them all. But the eight religious structures chosen for discussion here are some of the most exquisite timber-frame halls built anywhere in the world at any time. No other builders in the history of the world have achieved the innovation, design, or structural stability that became the trademark of the Song, Liao, and Jin.

Sakyamuni Pagoda of Fogong Monastery was built in the year 1056 and is superlative in so many ways that it is often referred to in China simply as Timber Pagoda. Octagonal in plan, at 67.3 meters it is the tallest standing pagoda in China. Its wooden shaft makes up 51.35 meters of that height, and the sides of its base are each 5.58 meters long. From the exterior the pagoda of Fogong Monastery appears to be five stories tall, with two sets of roof eaves on the lowest story. In fact, it is a unique nine-level structure: four interior mezzanine levels are concealed between the five levels apparent from the outside. In addition, the

Figure 5.37. Moni Hall, Longxing Monastery, Zhengding county, Hebei province, 1052

Figure 5.38. Cishi Pavilion, Longxing Monastery

columns that support each level of the pagoda are arranged in two concentric rings such that the structure appears to be a pillar-supported octagonal hall surrounded on all sides by a covered arcade. Columns and beams form a truss between each pair of interior and exterior columns of the surrounding arcade, where diagonal braces are also employed. The support system of the four concealed stories is more rigid than that for the five stories: its components resemble girdle beams used in construction today. Each level was shorter and narrower than the one below it, and bracket-set formations were adjusted accordingly.

Fifty-four different bracket-set clusters are used at the Timber Pagoda, more than are found in any other single Chinese building. The result is a dynamic structure, the epitome of Chinese timber-frame architecture.

Guanyin Pavilion of Dule Monastery may have anticipated the Timber Pagoda. Built in the year 984 in Ji county, Hebei, it survives with the Shanmen (front gate) as the only Liao structures at the monastery, which was continually renovated through the Qing dynasty. (The hipped-roof structure on a low platform is the only extant gate from the Liao dynasty.) With huge bracket sets, deep

Figure 5.39. Interior of the Revolving Sutra Cabinet Pavilion, Longxing Monastery, showing the sutra cabinet, Song dynasty

Figure 5.40. Daxiongbao Hall, Shanhua Monastery, Datong, Shanxi province, eleventh century

eaves, a shallow roof slope, and columns slightly higher at the corners than those that define the center bay, it probably retains the flavor of a Tang structure.

Like the Timber Pagoda, Guanyin Pavilion conceals part of its structure. Five bays wide and four deep, it is two stories on the exterior with a hidden mezzanine level between them on the inside. Guanyin Pavilion is also a structure with an inner space *(cao)* enclosed by an arcade (outer cao) defined by two rings of columns. Guanyin Pavilion, however, rises only twenty-three meters, one-third the height of the Timber Pagoda. Yet the pagoda has a sculptural program on each interior level, whereas the hexagonal second-story interior of the pavilion is opened to house a sixteen-meter sculpture of the bodhisattva Guanyin. To help support the ambitious interior, diagonal braces and slanting beams were added at the corners, between columns, and around the octagonal ceiling frame. During the Qing dynasty, posts were propped under the exterior eaves to help support the structure.

Every building that survives from Song times at Longxing Monastery in Zhengding, Hebei, is noteworthy, but two are extraordinary. Begun in 592, Foxiang Pavilion (also known as Dabei Pavilion) and its 21.3-meter-high image of Guanyin were rebuilt by order of the founder of the Song empire, Emperor Taizu (r. 960–975). The pavilion was reconstructed in 1942 and repaired again at the end of the twentieth century.

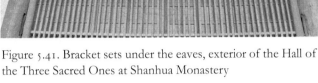

Figure 5.41. Bracket sets under the eaves, exterior of the Hall of the Three Sacred Ones at Shanhua Monastery

Figure 5.42. Corner bracket set and eaves, Daxiongbao Hall, Huayan Monastery, Datong, Shanxi province

The most unusual hall at Longxing Monastery is Moni Hall (Monidian), seven bays long in each direction and cruciform in plan. A portico with hip-gable roof projects outward on each side (fig. 5.37). The twin pavilions Cishige and the Revolving Sutra Cabinet Pavilion, mentioned earlier, also survive from the Song dynasty at Longxing Monastery (figs. 5.38 and 5.39). Like Guanyin Pavilion, each conceals a mezzanine level inside. Yet the timber frames of the Longxing Monastery pavilions are not identical. Cishi Pavilion is the only Song structure with a pillar that rises from the ground to the roof frame. And the Sutra Pavilion has columns sized to each level, standard in Liao and Song construction, but its revolving sutra cabinet is the only one of its kind that remains from the Song dynasty.

Established in Tang times and severely damaged at the end of Liao, much of Shanhua Monastery in Shanxi province was rebuilt in 1123. As described earlier, three structures — a Shanmen, Hall of the Three Sacred Ones, and main hall (Daxiongbaodian)—stand on the main axis, and a pair of pavilions as well as two "ear halls" joined the enclosing corridor at this monastery of the western capital of Liao and Jin. Of the original pair of pavilions, only Puxian Pavilion, on the west side, remains.

Daxiongbao Hall of Shanhua Monastery is one of the buildings that survive from Liao times (fig. 5.40). Seven bays by four with a hipped roof, its structure blends elements of the two fundamental hall types —*diantang* and *tingtang*, high-ranking hall and simpler hall, respectively — whose forms are articulated in the architectural manual of the Song court. To make room for the altar, which held Buddhas of the five directions (north, south, east, west, and center), columns that would otherwise have formed a perfect column grid were eliminated. This strategy became a standard practice beginning in Liao times.

The Hall of the Three Sacred Ones at Shanhua Monastery is a Jin structure. There, columns were moved out of alignment with those of the exterior but not eliminated, a common practice in Liao-Jin architecture. The front gate is also a Jin-period structure. Both buildings exhibit fan-shaped bracket clusters, a characteristic of Liao-Jin buildings in the western capital (fig. 5.41).

The Liao-Jin monastery Huayansi, also located in Datong, was the one later subdivided into upper and lower monasteries. Daxiongbaodian, the main hall of the upper monastery, was constructed in 1140 (figs. 5.42 and 5.43). Nine bays by four, it was one of the largest halls of the time, with a ground plan that covered 1,560 square meters. The elimination of pillars led to a huge open interior space, and the hipped roof and enormous size of the structure created a solemn and impressive exterior. Bhagavat Sutra Repository, part of the lower monastery, was constructed in 1038. Its unimposing exterior, five bays by four with a hip-gable roof, stands in sharp contrast to the ornate cabinetry inside used to store scriptures. Recessed in the four walls are thirty-eight bays with miniature carved structures, including the superlative multistory "palace of heaven." Thirty-one statues inside the hall, many from the Liao period, are of the same superior quality as the cabinets.

Baoguo Monastery in Yuyao county, near Ningbo, Zhejiang province, was first constructed in the Tang dynasty and rebuilt between 1008 and 1016. Its main hall, Daxiongbaodian, was built in 1013 (fig. 5.44). It is five bays square today, but only the three middle bays were built in the Song dynasty; others were added in Qing times. Two features, the descending cantilever of the bracket sets and the melon-wheel-shaped columns made of joined pieces of wood, are described in the architectural treatise *Yingzao fashi*. The three *zaojing* (cupolas) in the ceiling are, like the melon-shaped columns, unique among surviving Song architecture (fig. 5.45).

Chuzu'an (Hermitage of the First Patriarch) at Shaolin Monastery in Dengfeng county, Henan, is said to have been visited in 537 by Bodhidharma, the legendary founder of Chan Buddhism. The main hall was built in

1125. Three bays square and supported by sixteen vividly carved stone columns and naturally curving beams, it is a tingtang structure with a straight-edged door, bracket sets, and windows. Among the 227 brick and stone pagodas in the "forest of pagodas" at Shaolin Monastery are two from the Tang period, two from the Song, and eleven from the Jin dynasty (fig. 5.46).

Yunyan Monastery in Sichuan province was constructed by virtue of Tang imperial edict between 874 and 879 and was converted during the Song dynasty into a Daoist establishment. Feitian Sutra Repository, named after a winged Buddhist divinity, was constructed in 1180 during the Southern Song as a small multistory pavilion. Inside was an octagonal prism, in the center of which rotated a wooden column. When pushed, the pavilion moved. Ten meters high and 7.2 meters in diameter, Feitiancang is made up of three parts: a pedestal *(cangzuo)*, shaft *(cangshen)*, and "heavenly palace pavilion" *(tiangong-louge)*. Six layers of magnificent bracket sets of twenty different varieties were positioned between the shaft and the heavenly palace pavilion. The doors and windows are exquisite.

Figure 5.43. Daxiongbao Hall, built in 1140, Huayan Monastery

Figure 5.44. Daxiongbao Hall, Baoguo Monastery, Yuyao county, Zhejiang province, built in 1013

Figure 5.45. Melon-shaped columns and zaojing from the interior of Daxiongbao Hall, Baoguo Monastery

Figure 5.46. Forest of pagodas at Shaolin Monastery, Dengfeng county, Henan province

Figure 5.47. Great Pagoda, Great Pagoda Monastery, Ning-cheng, Inner Mongolia, Liao dynasty with later restoration

Figure 5.48. Liaodi Pagoda, Kaiyuan Monastery, Ding county, Hebei province, 1055

Masonry Pagodas

The Song, Liao, and Jin dynasties were the climax in the history of masonry pagoda architecture in China. Close to one hundred masonry pagodas survive, and they show greater variety of form, more ambitious interior and exterior structures, and more elaborate exterior decoration than do pagodas of any previous or later time. Initially, pagodas were square, hexagonal, and octagonal (and in the case of Songyue Monastery pagoda, dodecagonal), but beginning in the mid–Northern Song period, the octagonal plan dominated. Three forms are prevalent in tenth- through thirteenth-century pagoda architecture: the *miyan* (densely placed eaves) style, the *louge* (multi-story) style, and the *huashu* (bouquet) style. The first two varieties were also common in Tang architecture; the huashu style was new.

Pagodas with densely placed eaves were the most popular kind built during the Liao and Jin dynasties. A superior example is the Great Pagoda of Great Pagoda Monastery in Ningcheng, Inner Mongolia (fig. 5.47). Multistory pagodas consisted of both masonry superstructures, with plinths supported by bracket sets beneath the first level built in wood, and completely stone or brick buildings. Bouquet-style pagodas resembled pagodas of this earlier style in their lower portions, but bulged from an indrawn waist to a bouquet structure on top.

Louge-type pagodas branched dramatically from their earlier forms. Although some followed the construction patterns of Tang times, with a single outer wall and interior, four new structural forms appeared. One of these, the central-pillar-block pagoda with an outer wall, had a brick periphery. Between the inside core block and the exterior wall floors were interior stories connected to the outer wall by layers of bricks or bracketing. Pingzuo on the exterior of the pagoda provided a place for standing for those who climbed it by way of stairs that wound around the pagoda between the inner and outer walls. An early example of this form is the Renshou Pagoda of Kaiyuan Monastery in Quanzhou. A later one is Liaodi Pagoda of Kaiyuan Monastery in Ding county, Hebei (fig. 5.48).

The double-walled pagoda has both inner and outer surrounding walls, with stairs between for access to the top of the structure. Each story of the pagoda is covered with an arched brick ceiling. Examples of octagonal versions are Tiger Hill Pagoda of Yunyan Monastery (fig. 5.49) and the Bao'en Monastery Pagoda, both in Suzhou, and Six Harmonies Pagoda in Hangzhou (seen in fig.

Figure 5.49. Tiger Hill Pagoda, Yunyan Monastery, Suzhou, Jiangsu province, 959

5.3). The nine-story Bao'en Monastery Pagoda, brick but with wooden pingzuo and wooden eaves, rises seventy-six meters with approximately seventeen meters between its walls (fig. 5.50).

Thick brick walls made it possible to install longer-lasting brick stairs instead of wooden ones. There were two methods for making brick stairs. One was to install them inside the thick walls, bending the stairway to follow the wall shape. This was how the seven-story, hexagonal, louge-style Wanfo Pagoda in Mengcheng county, Anhui, was constructed in 1105. The same method of stair instal-

lation was used in a pagoda with a completely different exterior, the thirteen-story, square White Pagoda of Jiuzhouba in Yibin county, Sichuan, built in the miyan style between 1098 and 1109. In another variety of thick-walled pagoda, the stairs penetrated the wall. In this construction, the pingzuo, which were offset from the exterior levels by half a story, served as stair landings. Finally, the octagonal bouquet-style Liurong Monastery Pagoda in Guangzhou, fifty-seven meters high and rebuilt in 1134, had nine exterior stories and seventeen interior ones.

The solid-core brick pagodas came in two varieties

Figure 5.50. Bao'en
Monastery Pagoda,
Suzhou, Jiangsu province,
1131–1163

and were of the miyan or louge style. One form featured spiral stairs with openings to the outside for ventilation and lighting. An example is the Iron Pagoda of Yougou Monastery, built at the Northern Song capital Bianjing in 1049 (fig. 5.51). Octagonal in plan, thirteen stories and 54.66 meters high, its name comes from the brown-glazed brick facing, which from a distance looks like iron.

Some solid-core pagodas were built without stairs in Liao times. One form was raised on a platform and had a high shaft, with layers above made in the densely placed eaves style. Examples of solid-core pagodas of this type are the octagonal nine-story pagoda of Tianning Monastery from the Liao period in Beijing and the octagonal thirteen-story Great Pagoda in Ningcheng. The Great Pagoda rises seventy-four meters. This kind of pagoda, most often square or octagonal, has an extremely high base known as a Sumeru altar, with the shaft the lowest of the stories above the base. The octagonal, seven-story, fifty-meter White Pagoda in Qingzhou is an example of a solid-core louge-style pagoda. Wanbu Huayan (Avatamsaka) Sutra Pagoda in Hohhot (Huhehaote), Inner Mongolia, seven stories and forty-three meters in height, is another (fig. 5.52). Sometimes this kind of pagoda had a small chamber at its base known as the *tiangong* (heavenly palace) and a chamber below it called *digong* (underground palace) in which sutras, relics, and other Buddhist objects were stored.

Finally, there were several special pagoda forms constructed during the tenth through thirteenth centuries, many of which blended construction systems, materials, and new forms. One of these was the Liao pagoda at Yunju Monastery in Fangshan, Hebei, whose hemispherical body is unique among extant architecture of the period.

Schools

In Song China there were two kinds of schools, official and private. The official schools were the National Academy, prefectural colleges, and county schools, all of which were supported by their respective governments. Examples of private schools were academies of classical learning *(shuyuan),* family-run schools *(jiashu),* home schools *(sheguan),* and educational societies *(shuhui).*

The architecture of the official schools included a temple for homage to Confucius and the sages of the classical age, a pavilion where the imperial edicts were kept, lecture halls, administrative offices, dormitories, and

Figure 5.51. Iron Pagoda, Yougou Monastery, Kaifeng, Henan province, 1049

Figure 5.52. Wanbu Huayan Sutra Pagoda, Hohhot, Inner Mongolia, Liao period, repaired in 1162 and later

ous 125 bays of rooms, with a great variety of buildings. Southernmost was Banbi Pool. To its north was Lingxing Gate, behind which were four courtyards, one after another. Along the central axis were the buildings that defined the courtyards: Propriety Gate, Dacheng Hall, Mingde Hall, and the Royal Library Pavilion. In the Royal Library Pavilion, the upper level was for books, and the lower level was a meeting place for teachers and students. Classroom space began behind Mingde Hall, and dormitories were located both east and west of Dacheng Hall. Teachers' rooms were beyond the western wall of the complex, and archery grounds were farthest to the back.

Among private schools, the earliest academy of classical learning was White Deer Grotto Academy, established in 940 on Mount Lu in Jiangxi during the Southern Tang (937–978), one of the Ten Kingdoms. Other famous Northern Song academies were Yuelu in Changsha, Hunan province, Songyang in Dengfeng, Henan province, and Suiyang in Shangqiu, Henan province. The number and varieties of academies increased greatly during the Southern Song era. They came to be built in some of the most picturesque locations in China, sometimes in the vicinity of Buddhist and Daoist monasteries. Unfortunately, not a single building survives.

An illustration of an academy of learning is included in *Jingding Jiankang zhi*. There, Mingdao Academy is shown as an urban school made up of two groups of buildings that followed the gong scheme so prevalent in imperial architecture. The front group, Chunfengtang, consisted of the lecture hall and library pavilion. The back group, called Zhujingtang, was where students and teachers congregated. Offices and living spaces were on either side of the back group. In front of Chunfengtang was a veneration shrine for Cheng Mingdao, founder of the academy. The school also included a lotus pond and vegetable garden.

athletic fields for archery or other physical exercise. The layout of these structures varied: in some official schools the temple was in front of the other buildings, and in others they were side by side. In an illustration of a prefectural college in *Jingding Jiankang zhi* (Record of Jiankang [Nanjing] during the Jingding period [1260–1264]), the temple is in front of the educational buildings.

Jiankang Prefectural College, predecessor of the Confucian Temple in Nanjing, was first built in 1029. Destroyed by war, it was rebuilt in 1135. At that time it had a gener-

Commercial Architecture

When the ward system that had characterized Chinese urbanism before and during the Tang dynasty broke down in Song times, businesses and shops came to be built right on the main streets of cities. Some shops of similar type were built in the same area, but others were famous enough to stand independent of competition. The doors and windows of all shops faced directly onto the street, without courtyards or gates in front. Most impressive of the commercial structures in Song cities were restaurants.

Northern Song Dongjing had more than seventy-two restaurants and countless wine shops. The largest restaurant was Fanlou, a three-story structure of five interconnected parts. Elevated bridges and balustrades made it possible to pass from one to the other at any time of day or night. It was rebuilt between 1119 and 1125, shortly before the fall of the dynasty.

According to the record of the Northern Song capital, *Dong jing menghualu* (Dreaming of past splendors in the eastern capital), entrances to restaurants and wine shops throughout the city were decorated with colored ornaments. In addition, the ceilings of entryway corridors were decorated with intricate lattice woodcarvings, and in the evening the spaces above and below the latticework were brightened by the light of lanterns and candles.

There were two main types of restaurants in the Northern Song period: those converted from residential space and those that had been gardens. The ones that had formerly been houses still faced the street but had courtyards in the back. These restaurants usually had smaller rooms, with flowers and bamboo growing at the windows. Wine shops tended to be in renovated gardens. Yanbinlou Restaurant, for example, was a garden wine shop in which customers could enjoy themselves at the pavilion, pond, boat, or swings.

Restaurants were distinct from other buildings in the Northern Song capital not only because they were more than one story but also because silk hung from wooden frames in front of them. In addition, some had red railings and others had hanging from their front gates curtains trimmed with pink lace or red lanterns shaped like gardenias. All these decorations are illustrated in the famous painting of the capital, *Qingming Festival on the River.*

In the Southern Song capital Lin'an, besides restaurants like those described at Bianjing, there were teahouses decorated with works by famous calligraphers and painters. Overall, though, their architecture does not seem to have been as elegant or graceful as that of the restaurants.

Of all the shops in the city, those that sold silk and medicine were the most distinctive. Silk stores were located amid shops that sold gold, silver, and textiles. They were grand, with formidable front gates. Apothecary shops were even taller, so that they could be spotted from a distance, and the main room of these shops was at least seven bays across the front. *Qingming Festival on the River* also shows that these shops had their own workshops in their back courtyards.

Bridges

The Song were tremendous builders of bridges, and the four discussed here are famous worldwide for their overall design or innovative features. Structurally, the Song bridges can be divided into two groups: beam *(liang)* bridges and arch *(gong)* bridges. The arch bridges have a semicircular profile, with curved edges and open spandrels. Both types were made of bamboo, wood, and stone. A few pontoon bridges and chain bridges were also built during this period, but only the stone beam and stone arch bridges have survived.

Luoyang Bridge spans the Luoyang River, ten kilometers northeast of Quanzhou in Fujian province. Five hundred forty meters long and seven meters wide, the bridge was made of huge blocks of stone. Because the bridge lay at the mouth of the Luoyang River, with tidewater dashing against its underwater structure, it was difficult to keep the piers steady with only the weight of the stones themselves. The construction, which took six years (1053–1059), thus occurred in stages: First, big blocks of stone were thrust onto the river bed along the central line of the bridge, building a foundation. Next, oysters were planted among the stones. (Oysters were known to propagate in every direction, and thereby could cement the stones into monoliths.) Once a steady foundation for the bridge had been formed, forty-six piers were built on top. During high tide, stone beams were floated on rafts onto the piers, and stone slabs were laid atop the beams.

Anping Bridge, also known as Wuli Bridge, in Anhai, Jinjiang county, Fujian, was constructed between 1138 and 1151. A stone bridge of the beam style, it spanned 2,500 meters, making it the longest bridge in Chinese history up to that time (fig. 5.53). The underwater foundation of the bridge was raft-shaped, and the piers were built with stone slabs one on top of another in alternating longitudinal and transversal layers. Some of the piers were rectangular and some were boat-shaped. The floor of the bridge was laid with huge stone beams. Following damage by hurricanes, tidal waves, and earthquakes, the bridge has been repaired six times. During these repairs the bridge was shortened to 2,070 meters because the river it spans had filled in somewhat over time.

Built between 1165 and 1173, Xiangzi Bridge, also known as Guangji Bridge, spanned Exi (Evil Stream), east of Chaozhou in Guangdong province. The waters of the aptly named river were so torrential that piers could not stand in the middle. The creative solution for this problem was to erect beam bridges on the east and west

Figure 5.53. Anping Bridge, Jinjiang county, Fujian province,
1138–1151

sides of a pontoon bridge, to create a total length of 518.1 meters. The pontoon bridge was made of eighteen boats, connected with steel cables, and the bridge floor above was made of wooden planks. This pioneering effort successfully solved the traffic problems in areas of rapids and shoals. In 1958, the pontoon bridge was replaced by a bridge of reinforced concrete with three openings.

Another major bridge was built in 1192 (during the Jin dynasty) to span the Yongding River 13 kilometers southeast of Beijing. Lugou Bridge, a continuous-arch structure with twelve open spandrels, extends 265 meters and is 8 meters wide and about 10 meters high. The front sides of the piers, which faced the torrents, are pointed and the backs are square. The foundation of the piers that support the bridge is made of alluvial sand mixed with gravel and reinforced with short wooden posts. Lugou Bridge is famous for the beautifully carved stone panels of its railing and for the posts of its balustrade, which are graced by stone lions (fig. 5.54). Marco Polo marveled at the bridge and its lion carvings in his *Description of the World*. The structure's nickname, Marco Polo Bridge, came about because of his description and stands in sharp contrast to "Lugou," which means black moat (an alternate name for the Yongding River). Repaired in 1444 and 1698, the bridge was the site of the Marco Polo Bridge Incident on July 7, 1937, the official beginning of anti-Japanese resistance. In 1975, a platform transport truck carrying 429 tons crossed the bridge, proof of its capacity to withstand the stress of modern times.

Yingzao Fashi and the Standardization of Architectural Forms

Yingzao fashi (Building standards) is an architectural manual first issued in 1103 at the court of the Song emperor Huizong and reissued in 1145 after the dynasty had moved south. The purpose of the book was to establish national regulations for construction. It begins with two historical chapters, entitled "General Terminology," in which passages from classical and historical texts preceding the Song dynasty are cited to define forty-eight architectural terms. Chapter 2 ends with a paragraph about rules for calculation of the corvée, the amount of tax required in exchange for labor in the building industry.

Next are thirteen chapters that deal with "Rules of Operation," the technical standards and regulations for building that encompass construction techniques for full-size timber-frame buildings, small-scale wooden buildings, and building parts including doors, windows, balustrades, niches, and cabinets; methods for making stone building components and suitable subjects for stone carving; rules for building residential foundations, walls, fortifications, and trenches; the art of surveying; guidelines for decorative painting, including patterns and pigments; subjects and techniques of woodcarving; specifications and techniques for the use of the lathe; regulations for sawing according to the modular system and for economizing in the use of wood; as well as rules for tiling, brick masonry, mortar, and the use of bamboo and pottery kilns. Fifteen chapters follow that deal with standards and quotas of manpower and materials for each type of work. And the final six chapters contain a total of 193 illustrations of various details of construction and materials (figs. 5.55 and 5.56).

Yingzao fashi was published against the backdrop of sweeping political, civil, economic, social, and educational reforms proposed by the official Wang Anshi (1021–1085). Wang hoped that the architectural treatise would strengthen the administration of the state-run building industry. In 1097, the official Li Jie was given the task of compiling it, and the work was completed in 1100.

Figure 5.54. Lugou Bridge, near Beijing on the Yongding River, built in 1192

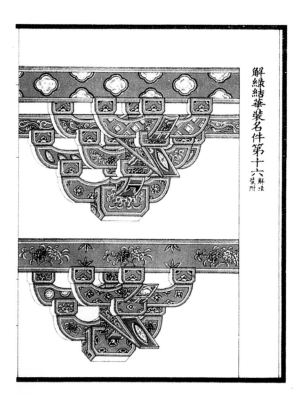

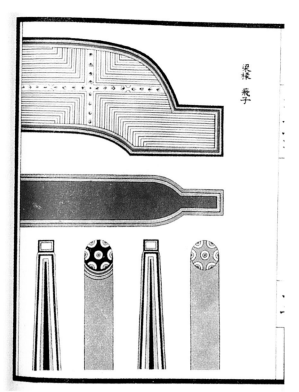

Figure 5. 55. Illustration from *Yingzao fashi,* published in 1103; reissued in 1145

Figure 5.56. Black-head gate (or "crow's-head door"), illustration from *Yingzao fashi.* The name derives from the tops of the posts, which are painted black.

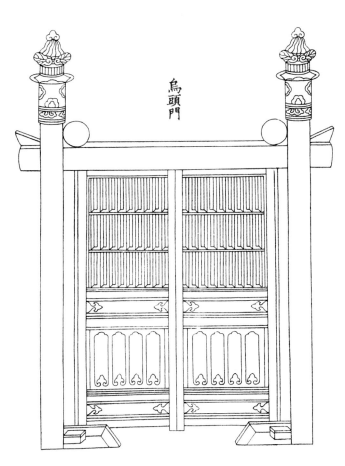

After approval by the emperor, the book was published and its guidelines were distributed to the public.

Yingzao fashi is an accurate reflection of the scientific and technical levels of building construction during the Northern Song dynasty. Moreover, it is a book about the art of architecture in late-eleventh- and early-twelfth-century China. This remarkable work blends information from historical documents with detailed descriptions of the architecture of Song China. For example, Li Jie examined 283 items for the historical aspect of *Yingzao fashi.* The other 92 percent of the material discussed in the book, some 3,272 items, came from observation of the era's extant architecture and a review of the oral history of building construction as communicated to him by palace craftsmen. The book is also a uniquely complete historical document on the modular system that is the backbone of Chinese construction. The *cai-fen* system of standardization for size and grade of building components is explained not only for wooden building parts such as doors and windows, but also for brick and tile pieces, carving, and decoration. Furthermore, the text specifies popular styles of the time and explains rules for variation from the established norms.

Finally, *Yingzao fashi* has more illustrations than any other construction manual of its day. Most important among the drawings are the plans, elevations, and sections — *dipantu, zhengyangtu,* and *ceyangtu,* respectively. This is the first time that Chinese buildings are known to have been viewed in these three different ways, and this is the earliest known usage of names for those views in Chinese history. Other drawings are significant as well. The book includes detailed drawings of timber-frame joinery, including bracket sets; individual structural components including beams, columns, bracket arms, and bracket blocks; doors, windows, and balustrades; niches for Buddhist images and sutra cabinets; decorative painting and carving designs for buildings and building parts; and surveying instruments. Among the drawings are orthographic projections and close likenesses of axonometric drawings, both of which document lost or little-known techniques. Through them it has been possible to explicate an architectural tradition whose buildings have largely vanished. Indeed, *Yingzao fashi* is beyond doubt the most authoritative book on the traditional imperial practice of Chinese architecture. Reissued in the Southern Song and Yuan dynasties, it was still in use during the Ming dynasty.

Art and Techniques in Song, Liao, and Jin Architecture

The tenth through the thirteenth centuries are often considered the high point of the Chinese architectural tradition. Much that was accomplished in earlier architecture, especially during the Tang dynasty, but does not survive, can be seen in buildings from these centuries. Liao architecture added novel implementations of the timber frame and retained the strong focus on tall buildings along the main axis of Buddhist temple complexes. Song architecture offered increased decoration and detail to the Chinese tradition. All these innovations came together in Jin architecture.

During these dynasties, structures became works of art. Without question, the major innovations of the Song, Liao, and Jin periods occurred in wooden construction, and in particular the timber frame. Timber frames of these centuries can be categorized into three groups. First is the *tailiang* (column, beam, and strut) style, a system of framing used in eminent halls, or diantang, and halls of lesser rank, called tingtang (figs. 5.57 and 5.58, respectively). Diantang are composed of three layers of wooden frames — the roof frame, bracket-set frame, and column frame — as well as a foundation level. In structures in which the interior and exterior columns are the same height, such as at Moni Hall of Longxing Monastery, Zhengding, the columns project a checkerboard pattern at the base and at their tops.

Then there are the less significant tailiang-style halls in which the pillars across the front facade are shortest on either side of the central bay and increase in height symmetrically toward the front hall ends. This increase in pillar height is called *shengqi* or *shenggao,* "rise," and appears in such buildings as the main hall of Baoguosi in Yuyao county, Zhejiang. "Rise" makes the bracket-set layer of the structure appear curved. Short beams join the interior and exterior columns.

Timber-frame halls that use interior and exterior columns of unequal height are called composite halls. The bracket sets atop exterior columns form upper and lower ringlike frames. Daxiongbao Hall of Fengguo Monastery in Yi county, Liaoning, is an example of this type of structure. By contrast, the frames of timber pagodas and other multistory structures are tube-shaped with many layers of framing. Diagonal braces are added to enhance the structure's stability. The result — as seen at Guanyin Pavilion of Dule Monastery and the Timber Pagoda of Fogong Monastery — is a large empty space within the ring of each frame.

Another area of architectural technical achievement involves modules. As mentioned earlier, the sizing of wooden components of a Chinese structure according to modules was implemented at least as early as the Tang dynasty and is explained in *Yingzao fashi*. The measurement that generated the module in a wooden building was the cai, and it was based on the length:height ratio of the section of a bracket arm. Besides cai, there was a submodule, *qi,* which is sometimes thought of as a "filler" since it could be added to the measurement of cai to generate a measure known as *zucai.*

The two-dimensional cai was a module for which fifteen different portions in height and ten portions in width were possible. The qi was divided into six lengthwise portions and four in depth. In addition, both cai and qi had qualitative grades. The module thus determined not only the size of bracket-set components but also the lengths of columns and beams and the grade of material used in them. Someone aware of the distinctions of the modular system could recognize a structure's eminence or lack of it based on the size of its timbers and the quality of its wood.

Bracketing — the interface between columns and beams in a wooden structure — also developed considerably during this period. The sizes and positions of bracket sets were determined by a building's rank and

Figure 5.57. Drawing of the timber framing in a
diantang structure

1. Flying rafter or cantilever eave rafter
2. Eave rafter
3. Eave purlin
4. Bracket block
5. Bracket arm
6. Transversal bracket arm
7. Down-pointing cantilever
8. Capital block
9. Luohan tiebeam
10. Axial tiebeam
11. Board to conceal rafters
12. Board onto which bracket sets adhere
13. Architrave or connecting beam, lintel, girder
14. Lower architrave or lower lintel
15. Eave column
16. Interior or hypostyle column
17. Column footing
18. Plinth

19. Ox-spine purlin
20. Wooden member on which the main beam rests
21. Roof purlin
22. Ridge purlin
23. Wooden support between longitudinal bracket arm and eave purlin
24. Tiebeam under a purlin, resting on a bracket or tiebeam above a strut in roof frame
25. Camel's-hump-shaped support
26. King post
27. Crossbeam
28. Four-rafter tiebeam
29. Six-rafter tiebeam
30. Eight-rafter tiebeam
31. Ten-rafter tiebeam
32. Side brace connecting crossbeam with purlin

33. Main aisle exposed tiebeam
34. Four-rafter exposed tiebeam
35. Paneled ceiling tiebeam
36. Ceiling panel
37. Wall panel of one-story or multistory hall
38. Sun-screening panel
39. Door lintel
40. Cross-hatch overlapping-circle lattice decorated door
41. Floor tiebeam
42. Porch eave column
43. Porch exposed tiebeam
44. Porch slanting rough tiebeam
45. Lower roof rafter
46. Roof board
47. "Sumeru" (worship) platform
48. Inverted V-shaped brace

Source: Liu Dunzhen, *Zhongguo gudai jianzhu shi* (Beijing, 1980)

purpose. All bracket sets are composed of *dou* (blocks) and *gong* (arms). Sometimes they are the only members, but in every case an arm should join a block. In some bracket sets, one or more slanting arms known as *ang* (cantilever or level-arm) are present. In this case, the blocks and arms can join either the descending or ascending cantilever. Bracket sets of the Song, Liao, and Jin periods usually had two ang, except for bracketing under a pingzuo, which usually had only one ang.

Another distinction in bracket sets is whether they are *touxin* (stolen heart) or *jixin* (added [accounted] heart). The "heart" or lack of it refers to a lateral bracket arm that passes through arms that are perpendicular to the building plane. The use of the "added heart" led to more and more tiers of bracket arms that projected perpendicular to the building plane. Bracket sets with and without ang can be of the added or stolen heart variety.

Brackets in tenth- through thirteenth-century Chinese buildings were most commonly placed either on top of or between columns. The between-column type is known as an intercolumnar bracket set, and after the Tang dynasty their use became more common. Such additional bracket sets across the facade of a building helped reduce stress on the roof frame.

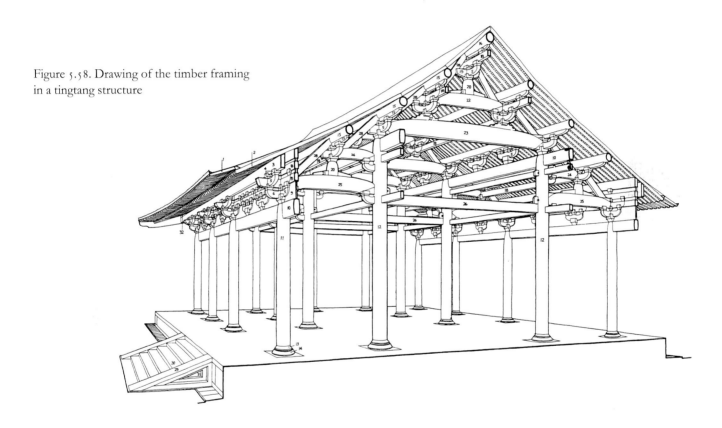

Figure 5.58. Drawing of the timber framing in a tingtang structure

1. Flying rafter or cantilever eave rafter
2. Eave rafter
3. Eave purlin
4. Bracket block
5. Bracket arm
6. Transversal bracket arm
7. Capital block
8. Axial tiebeam
9. Board onto which bracket sets adhere
10. Architrave
11. Eave column
12. Interior or hypostyle column
13. Column footing
14. Plinth

15. Roof purlin
16. Ridge purlin
17. Wooden support between longitudinal bracket arm and eave purlin
18. Tiebeam under a purlin, resting on a bracket or tiebeam above a strut in roof frame
19. Transversal bracket arm supporting side brace for ridge
20. King post
21. Joining bracket at junction of king post and beam or lintel
22. Crossbeam
23. Four-rafter tiebeam

24. Short beam connecting the bracket atop the porch king post and the interior column
25. Main aisle exposed tiebeam
26. Additional transversal tiebeam
27. Camel's-hump-shaped support
28. Inverted V-shaped brace
29. Side coping
30. Step
31. Triangular side framing of stairway

Source: Liu Dunzhen, *Zhongguo gudai jianzhu shi* (Beijing, 1980)

The great majority of Song, Liao, and Jin wooden architecture was squarish or rectangular in plan. Occasionally building plans were octagonal, T-shaped, or cruciform. More complicated and diverse plans than those that survive in actual buildings — with the exception of Moni Hall of Longxing Monastery, which is marvelously ornate — are found in Song paintings such as *Pavilion of Prince Teng* and *Yueyang Pavilion*.

The elevation of a structure was made up of the four building layers: base, columns, bracket sets, and roof. A standard platform rose five cai, about 0.8 to about 1.5 meters. The ratio of the height of a column to the total height of a structure from the column base (excluding the building platform) to the roof varied from 1:2 to 1:2.7. Bracketing and the roof took up a large proportion of the total building height. The roof occupied about one-third the total height of a diantang structure. In tingtang structures, the roof was about one-fourth the total height.

The most common roof forms were the simple hipped roof, known in Chinese as *wuding* or *si'ading*, which had a main roof ridge and four ridges of equal length projecting two each at the ends of the principal ridge; the nine-ridge roof *(jiuji)*, which combined the hip and gable forms; and the roof with just two slopes *(liangpoding)*, one at the front of the building and one at the back. The most complicated structures, such as the Pavilion of Prince Teng, now known only through paintings, featured combinations of these forms. The profile of the Song roof was an exquisite arch shape, a form that was repeated in both crescent-shaped beams and shuttle-shaped columns.

Most columns in a structure of this period exhibited batter *(cejiao)*—that is, they inclined slightly toward the building plane. They also displayed "rise" toward the corners of the front and back facades. Not only did these effects further respond to the curved outline of the roof, but they also allowed for the expansion and contraction of mortise and tenon joinery through humid and cold weather.

The positions of pillars defined the bays of a Chinese building. Bays could be of equal length across the front facade or unequal in length, but they were always symmetrically proportioned. Where the bays where unequal in size, those at the center were the widest (the center bay in a structure with an odd number of bays, and the center two in a structure with an even number), and the bays became progressively narrower toward the ends. In addition, no matter the width of a bay, the height of a column never surpassed that measurement.

Wooden Decoration

During the Song, Liao, and Jin dynasties, more and more wooden surfaces received decoration and the range and quality of designs increased significantly. The most important decorated wooden parts of the building were doors, windows, and ceilings.

Doors of the period can be divided into three types: panel doors, "crow's-head" doors, and lattice doors. All are described in *Yingzao fashi*. Panel doors were composed of two panels made of wooden planks. They were widely used in pairs at city entrances, in the wall of a garrison town, or in the center front of a single building. Crow's-head doors were installed only in city walls, not

Figure 5.59. Latticework, front facade of the main hall of Geyuan Monastery, Laiyuan, Hebei province, 966

single buildings; two large posts, different in shape from those of panel doors, were planted deep in the ground for joining the door to the wall. The upper portions of crow's-head doors had open latticework, and the lower portions were made of wooden planks. Crow's-head doors can be seen in many Song paintings, and both panel and crow's-head doors are illustrated as well as described in *Yingzao fashi*.

Lattice doors were the most elegant of the door styles and came in the greatest variety, many of which are illustrated in *Yingzao fashi*. Used in diantang, lattice patterns included squares, diamonds, and other parallelograms. Doors in the main hall of Geyuan Monastery in Laiyuan, Hebei province, dated 966, and Amitabha Hall of Chongfu Monastery in Shuo county, Shanxi province, dated 1143, retain excellent examples of tenth- and twelfth-century latticework (figs. 5.59 and 5.60, respectively). The most complicated latticing of the time, however, appears not in extant doors but in carvings of doors etched into the brick interior of the Dong family tomb in Houma, Shanxi, during the Jin period. There decorations are carved into the lower, as well as the upper, sections of the doors.

In the Tang period, the most common form of window was one made of simple slats. These provided a source of both light and air for a building's interior. By the Song period, windows with more decorative apertures, known as "lightning" windows and "wave-pattern" windows, are described and illustrated in *Yingzao fashi*. All these windows were stationary. An innovation of Song architecture was the window that could open. Seen in the painting *Traveling Along the Ji River in Snow* by Guo Shuxian (d. 977), the invention, called the balustrade-hook window, was both beautiful and functional.

Three types of ceilings dominated during this period: exposed, simple lattice, and cupola. All three varieties are present in Daxiongbao Hall of Baoguo Monastery near Ningbo, dated 1013, and the lattice and cupola are used in the main hall of Jingtu Monastery in Ying county, Shanxi, which was completed in 1124. In keeping with the differences between Northern Song construction of the eleventh century and Jin construction a century later, the ceiling of the Baoguosi hall is bold and simple, characterized by exposure of some of the ceilingless parts of the roof frame, whereas decoration of the Jin ceiling, much like that seen in Jin tomb interiors, is elaborated to the point of extravagance (figs. 5.61, 5.62, and 5.63).

Religious architecture was decorated in ways unique to its function. Cabinets and niches for the storage of

Figure 5.61. Ceiling of the main hall of Jingtu Monastery, Ying county, Shanxi province, 1124

Decorative Painting and Carving

Buddhist texts and niches for images provide some of the best examples of wooden decoration. Indeed, these cabinets and niches are the main focus of architectural rendering in small-scale wood construction *(xiaomuzuo)* of the period. Famous examples include the cabinets of the Sutra Repository of Huayan Monastery in Datong (1038), the statuary niche in the main hall of Erxian Daoist Monastery in Jincheng, Shanxi, of 1107, the Pavilion of the Revolving Sutra Repository at Longxing Monastery, Zhengding, Hebei (Northern Song), and the Feitian Repository at Yunyan Monastery, Jiangyou, Sichuan.

During the Liao, Jin, and Song periods, architectural components were often highly decorated. Portions of wooden buildings were painted, and stone and brick building parts were carved. Designs and rules for these kinds of decoration are prescribed in *Yingzao fashi*.

Whereas in Tang times architecture was painted primarily red and white, during the dynasties that followed blue and green pigments appeared, and shades of these colors embellished bracket sets and other wooden architectural parts. Blue and green shades ranged from jade to azure to colors imitating those of flowers and other plants. Among

Figure 5.62. Detail of ceiling, Jingtu
Monastery

Figure 5.63. Ceiling, Jingtu Monastery

Figure 5.64. Demon face,
Daxiongbao Hall, Guangji
Monastery, Mount Wutai, Shanxi
province

the few extant examples of painted architecture, some of the best are preserved in underground tombs, including the three excavated at Baisha, near Luoyang, one in Luoyang itself, and some from Liao cemeteries in Xiabali village and Kulun Banner. Aboveground, examples of painted wooden building parts survive at the Manjusri Hall of Geyuan Monastery in Laiyuan and the Bhagavat Sutra Repository of Huayan Monastery in Datong. Wooden decoration in the form of animal faces also appears atop columns and against architraves in buildings of Shanxi province from the Jin and Yuan dynasties (fig. 5.64).

Stone and brick pagodas of the era feature carvings on every part — base, shaft, and between the eave layers. Stone architectural members such as pillar bases and decorative pillars attached to pagodas are similarly ornamented. So are freestanding funerary, ceremonial pillars, and archways. Rules for decoration and specific patterns for stonework are prescribed in *Yingzao fashi*. The text specifies decoration for high relief, low relief, silhouettes, and even plain, smooth surfaces that may have little or no decoration. No matter what the design, carvers were charged with retaining the integrity of the outline of a form. Carving in the round was rare in Liao, Jin, or Song times; that technique was usually used only to create animals such as stone lions for the front of a palace or temple, or monumental stone figures that would line the pathway to a tomb.

On Sumeru altars (bases) of masonry pagodas, or altar bases inside Buddhist temples, decoration of each layer varied. The relief carving on the base was often most pronounced in the waist, or middle layer. But brick carving was advanced most dramatically in tomb interiors. Not only were brick architectural members carved to imitate timber ones; human events and long narratives were also carved on tomb walls. Some of the best examples survive in Jin tombs of the Dong family in Houma and other Jin tombs in Fenyang, Xiangfen, Wenshui, and Changzhi in Shanxi. Brick carving on shafts of Liao pagodas, such as the North Pagoda in Chaoyang or the Great Pagoda in Ningcheng, are aboveground examples of the tremendous skill of that era's craftsmen.

Like the period of the Northern and Southern dynasties, the three centuries following Tang featured rulers of more than one ethnic type and interactions among numerous cultural groups. Are there, then, features of the Liao, Northern Song, Jin, Southern Song, and border peoples such as the Xi Xia that can be said to define the architecture of this period?

Compared with materials used during the Tang period, building components such as bracket sets became smaller and more elaborate. The elaboration of detail also characterized other aspects of Liao, Song, and Jin buildings, in particular cupola ceilings. In addition, the Liao, Song, and Jin experimented with multistory construction, succeeding in developing taller and more structurally sound pavilions and pagodas. In wood or brick, it was common for a tall structure to have interior, mezzanine levels in addition to exterior ones, or interior stories that did not correspond to exterior stories. And beautiful decorations were added to almost every possible building surface, including doors, windows, and bracket sets — as well as corresponding surfaces in subterranean tombs — through the use of new pigments for painting and innovative carving techniques.

Perhaps most significant, there now existed a set of standards, the *Yingzao fashi*, by which construction could be regulated and the finished product could be assessed. Such a complete codification of architectural practice was not to recur for nearly five hundred years. As a result, the well-documented construction methods and styles of the Song became both the standard for measuring architectural success during that dynasty and a means for preserving the Chinese architectural tradition in the century to come, when all of China fell to foreign invaders.

CHAPTER 6

The Yuan and Ming Dynasties

PAN GUXI

The establishment of the Yuan dynasty by Mongol conquerors marked an end to years of confrontation among the Song, Jin, and Xi Xia dynasties in China. Under the Mongols, a vast area that included Tibet, Taiwan, and the Gobi Desert was unified, and for the next six hundred years, under the Ming and then the Qing dynasty, China was ruled by a single empire.

China had been governed by non-natives before, but rule by the Mongols was different. The leaders of the Yuan regime — Mongolian princes-of-the-blood, as well as hereditary nobles of ethnic peoples from the Western Regions and parts of Central Asia — imposed a policy that classified all subjects into four social strata. The highest level was reserved for Mongols, who enjoyed a multitude of privileges. The second level was for non-Mongol non-Chinese, including Tibetans, Nepalese, and others from Central Asia and farther west. The Han population (mainly northern Chinese) made up the next level, and the lowest level was for southern Chinese living in the area of the former Southern Song regime. Power over key central government departments and decision making was held by Mongolian nobles and a few ethnic nobles of non-Chinese heritage. This strict hierarchy was also in place in local governments, where the Mongolian *darughachi* (officers and overseers) acted as the highest officials, overseeing those of Han and southern China.

Details, figures 6.23 *(opposite)* and 6.1 *(above)*

Craftsmen were exempt from most restrictions. The Mongols believed that craftsmen possessed god-given talent, so since the days of Chinggis Khan Mongols had supported and protected them even when their kinsmen were slaughtered. The Mongols also kidnapped craftsmen from the farthest points of the Mongolian empire, including eastern Europe. Indeed only a few Chinese names can be found among the builders and craftsmen who created the architecture of the Mongolian empire. The majority of those craftsmen were neither Chinese nor Mongol, but peoples of North Asia, Central Asia, West Asia, and the region of Nepal-Tibet.

Despite the non-Chinese patrons and multinational population of artisans, Chinese-style architecture attained unprecedented grandeur in the thirteenth and fourteenth centuries. The Great Capital, Dadu, built by Khubilai Khan where Beijing now stands, followed Chinese patterns more closely than any Chinese imperial city before it. The imprint of *Yingzao fashi* can be seen in imperial construction, and residential and garden architecture maintained the standards of Southern Song China.

Only occasionally was the foreign presence revealed in architectural forms — for example, in the architecture of Lamaist Buddhism that was introduced from Nepal-Tibet during the Yuan dynasty, in a few structures of Khubilai's Great Capital, and in the tents in which he and the Mongolian princes-of-the-blood lived behind the Chinese-style city walls. When it came to burial, too, the descendants of Chinggis Khan, like their ancestors, were returned to the Mongolian steppe for interment in unmarked graves. In general, however, Chinese-style buildings and the walls that surrounded them provided a Chinese facade for Mongolian practice of private native rites. In this way, the Chinese architectural system was preserved for future generations of Chinese.

Yuan society did not abandon the commercialism that had characterized Song China. In fact, a result of the extent and power of the Mongolian empire was that European and Asian merchants and missionaries crossed the Asian continent in all directions, leaving detailed if sometimes exaggerated accounts of the Mongolian world. Famous among these travelers are Marco Polo, Friar William of Rubruck, John of Plano Carpini, John of Monte Corvino, Rabban Sauma, Ibn Battuta, and Qiu Chuji. Traveling by land and sea, they sojourned in the Mongolian capitals, the oases of Central Asia, and China's great coastal cities. Not only the voyagers themselves but also their religions were permitted to enter China between the mid thirteenth and mid fourteenth centuries, for the Mongols were as protective of men of the cloth as they were of artisans, believing them all to have god-endowed powers. One religion that received great attention from the Mongols was Lamaist Buddhism. Daoist architecture also reached unprecedented heights during this age.

Because the Mongol lords were never fully transformed into Chinese-style rulers, when native Chinese rule was restored by the Ming dynasty in 1368, a large percentage of Mongols returned north and were reintegrated into Mongolian society. Those left behind to continue the architectural tradition simply picked up where the Yuan had left off. So much Chinese-style architecture had flourished during the Mongolian century that native construction of palaces, temples, and imperial tombs resumed quickly.

As for urbanism, the Ming capitals followed Yuan-period innovations. Because so many of those advances followed the native Chinese system, city planning can also be traced without a marked break from pre-Yuan to post-Yuan centuries. In fact, the new Ming capital, established at Beijing in the first decade of the fifteenth century by the Yongle emperor (Zhu Di, 1360–1424), was built on top of the main building axis of Khubilai Khan's capital.

One construction project in which the Mongols did not participate was the Great Wall, probably because the wall as it stood impeded their aspirations to conquer the Asian continent. But the Ming government undertook construction of the wall with vigor, adding or repairing thousands of kilometers in order to separate themselves from the Mongols and their North Asian neighbors such as the Oirats (fig. 6.1). The Ming also expanded a previously built system of fortress towns that protected both the northern border and the Chinese eastern coast. In particular, some 156 defensive towns were established on the Chinese coast to prevent attacks from Japanese pirates.

Regional construction became more distinctive in the Ming period than ever before. The provinces south of the Yangzi River — Jiangsu, Zhejiang, Anhui, Jiangxi, and Fujian — are known for their innovative styles in residential architecture. Cities of the same provinces, notably Suzhou, experienced a rebirth in prosperity and garden construction similar to the flourishing of Song times.

Production techniques for brick and glazed ceramic tiles greatly improved during the Ming dynasty. The stronger brick became commonly used for walls both in cities and in the central towns of prefectures and districts. Enhanced molding and carving techniques led to more carvings on doors, window frames, and wall facings, for which the Ming are famous. Some of these improvements had their roots in Yuan carving at such structures as the archway at Juyongguan (Cloud Terrace Pass). And advancements in glazing led to the use of color

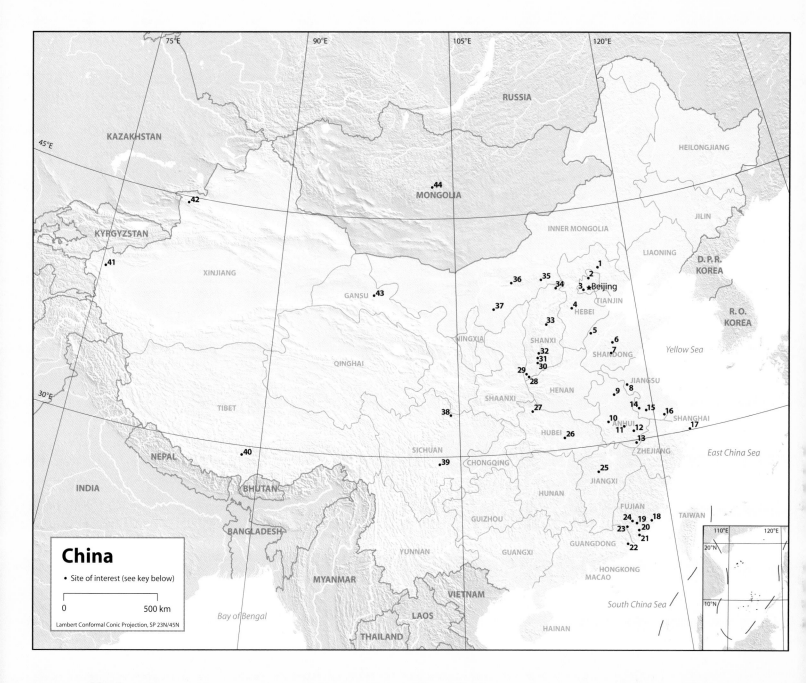

Map 6.
Yuan and Ming Sites

Baotou 36
Changping 1
Chaozhou 22
Dadu/Beijing 2
Dingcun 30
Dongyang/Linfen 31
Emeishan 39
Fengyang 9
Guotian/Xiamei 21
Guzhu/Yongding 23
Hohhot 35
Hongtong/Zhaocheng 32
Huizhou 13
Huocheng 42
Jiayu Pass 43
Jiuhuashan 12
Jurong 15

Kashgar 41
Karakorum 44
Lingqing 5
Longyan 24
Makeng/Sui'an 21
Nanjing 14
Pingwu 38
Putuoshan 17
Quanzhou 18
Qufu 7
Quyang 4
Ruicheng 28
Ruizhou 25
Shajian/Ting'an/Hua'an 19
Shangdu 37
Sihong 8
Suzhou 16

Taishan 6
Taiyuan 33
Tangyue 11
Tanzitou/Guizhen 21
Tongzhou 3
Wudangshan 27
Wutaishan 34
Xigaze 40
Xu 11
Yangwan/Dongshan 16
Yi 10
Yingtian 14
Yongji 29
Yuntou/Xiamei 21
Zhangpu 21
Zhangzhou 20
Zhongxiang 26

Figure 6.1. The Great Wall at Jinshanling in Hebei province

on previously white (or light stone) pagodas, gateways, archways, and screen-wall facades.

One of the main innovations in timber-frame construction was the transformation of the bracket set into a decorative element. This was made possible by new wooden components that helped do the bracket's job of supporting the roof. The decorative bracket sets were both smaller and more numerous than their pre-Ming counterparts.

Some view the Ming dynasty as the last to achieve greatness in native Chinese architectural styles. By the end of the Ming period, the exterior and interior of Chinese structures looked markedly different from their fourteenth-century counterparts, and many were magnificent. Were these innovations a result of a reawakened Song tradition, or were they inspired by a Mongolian influence? In many ways, the answer is both. The techniques and styles developed during the Song period were an obvious inspiration. But enough of the germination for Ming innovation can be traced to the period of Mongolian rule that the Yuan is seen as a transitional period in the remarkable architectural advances of the Ming.

Great Capital Cities of the Yuan and Ming

The three greatest cities constructed in China in the thirteenth, fourteenth, and fifteenth centuries are Dadu, built for Khubilai Khan; the first Ming capital at Nanjing; and the second Ming capital, Beijing. Built on the ruins of Dadu, Beijing has served continuously as a capital of China since its inception.

Located beneath the city of Beijing today, Dadu was neither the first capital used by the Mongols on their path of conquest toward China nor the first capital constructed on that site. Both the Liao southern capital, Nanjing (or Yanjing), and the Jin central capital, Zhongdu, served as focal points for the construction of Khubilai's great capital. Indeed, one of the most important factors in siting the new capital of the Mongols was the artificial body of water that had been created as a pleasure spot northeast of the Jin central capital. The small lake, named Taiye Pond in Yuan times, was fed by nearby lakes and rivers. The Mongols realized the value of this water source and constructed an imperial city with the unique arrangement of palaces on either side.

Looting and destruction of the Jin capital Zhongdu, which served as a basic starting point for the new capital, began in 1215 during the generation of Chinggis Khan. Yet the planning principles that led to the unique design of Yuan Dadu, as we shall see, are far more ancient than the twelfth century.

Construction of Yuan Dadu began in 1267 and lasted for two decades. Indeed, the magnificent triple-walled capital gave birth to a new generation of Chinese imperial city (fig. 6.2). About 50 kilometers square and 28.6 kilometers in perimeter, Dadu was about three-fifths the area of Chang'an in the Tang dynasty and approximately the same size as the Northern Song capital Bianjing. Inside the outer wall, the streets followed the orthogonal arrangement of earlier Chinese capitals, with widths between twenty-five meters for major streets and twenty-eight meters (twenty-four strides) for the main north–south road through the capital. Minor streets were about half as wide and lanes only a quarter as wide. The regularity of the arrangement and width of streets, as well as the systematic division of lanes between them, gave way to a city of exceptional majesty, thereby no doubt conveying the image sought by the Mongolian rulers but bespeaking little of their steppe origins.

The water supply that had been channeled into the Jin city was maintained, for both transportation and defensive purposes. Therefore the urban center of Dadu, namely its palace and imperial cities, was pushed southward from the city center. The residential portion occupied about two-thirds of its northern half. A decree of 1285 restricted occupancy within the Dadu outer wall to officials and the wealthy; the rest of the inhabitants were forced to live within the old walls of Jin Zhongdu. The two areas came to be known by Yuan inhabitants as the northern and southern cities, with sixty-two and seventy-five residential wards, respectively. Because of this, Yuan Dadu was a city more strictly bounded by wards than were its Song predecessors.

Government offices as well as residences of the nobility occupied the eastern half of the outer walled city. This area also contained the east market, and markets that catered to the needs of upper-class and wealthy customers by offering products like boots, wine vessels, books, and stationery and other writing materials. It was precisely here that engineer Guo Shoujing (1230–1310) had opened up Tonghui River and rerouted Haizi (Jishui Pool), termination of the Grand Canal, thereby creating a flourishing commercial district. In addition to the markets, this area of Dadu offered theaters and wine shops, as well as stores selling rice, noodles, satin, leather goods, fur hats, jewelry, ironware, and fowl.

In contrast to the upscale shopping area was the equally bustling district just north of the drum tower in the western part of the city. Known as Market of the

Figure 6.2. Map of Dadu, capital of the Yuan dynasty

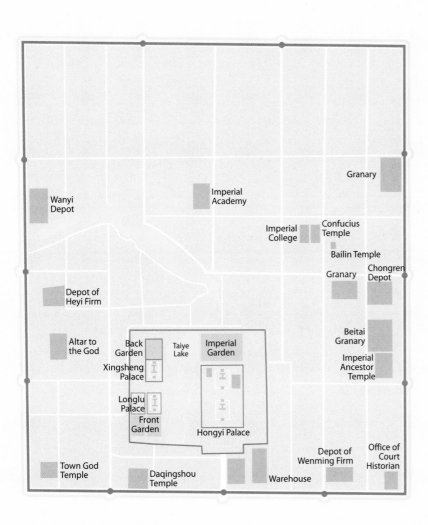

Poor Men, it had places for selling domestic animals including camels, sheep, cattle, horses, and mules. Even more gritty was the market in the southern city, the former Zhongdu. Catering to the shopping needs of the poorest residents of the capital, the southern city also had a shopping district for steamed cakes. When the impoverished Han Chinese needed carts, fruits, vegetables, or straw, they shopped in the new (northern) city, specifically in Guanxiang neighborhood, beyond Qian, Heping, and Xuanwu gates. It made sense that so much commerce was clustered at this meeting point of the old and new cities as well as on land and water routes. Although Dadu was a city of rigidly laid-out streets, human and geographic features dictated the final plan.

In one important way, the plan of Dadu was distinct from all earlier and later Chinese capitals: it was designed based on a midpoint. Even before the outer walls were completed, a stone marking the center spot of the city was laid, an act following the prescription for city planning in the classical text "Record of Trades" in the *Rituals of Zhou*.

Continuing the principle of a strong central focus, both the bell and drum towers — timekeeping devices since earliest imperial times — were positioned along the central north–south line of the city. Besides these, Dadu also had a copper water clock. The central focus, three walls, and numerous palatial halls concealed the Mongolian heritage of the rulers. Behind the facades and beneath the ceramic tile roofs, however, imperial Mongols lived in tents, and in the halls themselves animal skins decorated the walls in places where, in former Chinese imperial ages, paintings had hung.

When it came to the water supply, the Mongolian rulers took full advantage of the technological advancements available to them. They and the rest of the population depended on wells for drinking water. They also built gardens in the palace city for which water was directed from mountain springs in the west to the Taiye Pond dug by the Jin dynasty. Water for the moats that surrounded their city walls was channeled from the same western mountain springs. Dadu had sluice gates installed to compensate for the varying amounts of water in sections of the river; as a result, it was possible to transport grain from Tongzhou, in Guangzhou province, to Dadu via waterways year round.

The Jin had struggled unsuccessfully with many of the same issues. They had never been able to draw water from Lugou River (today's Yongding River), for instance. Guo Shoujing is credited with being the first to accomplish this task. He devised a way to draw water from all of the springs north and west of the capital to Gaoliang River, and from there to the Grand Canal by way of Jinshui Pool. Thus the Grand Canal, which in former Chinese dynasties had connected capitals at Chang'an and Bianjing with cities south of the Yangzi River, was now linked all the way to Dadu in Hebei province. Guo received a special commendation from Khubilai for this feat. Unfortunately, his accomplishment was short-lived. The officials, influential Buddhists, and Daoists of the capital drained off the newly available water to irrigate their own gardens and fields, crippling the water supply that was intended to serve national interests. In spite of the best efforts of the Yuan and the Jin, who had begun the process by digging Taiye Pond, a satisfactory way of connecting water between Dadu and Tongzhou in the far southeast was never achieved.

Nanjing, Ming Capital of Hills and Water

In 1368 the Mongolian government fell to the forces of Zhu Yuanzhang (1328–1398), who thereupon became the first emperor of the Ming dynasty (1368–1644), Taizu, also known as the Hongwu emperor. Knowing that his strongest support was in the south, Taizu returned there and built the first Ming capital at Yingtian. The city came to be known as Nanjing, southern capital. Upon the ascendancy later of China's greatest capital, Beijing, Nanjing became the secondary capital.

Geographically, Nanjing was a superior site. Located on the southern bank of the Yangzi River with the Qinhuai River flowing around it, this southern capital had an abundant water supply and thus convenient transport compared with Yuan Dadu. Moreover, a huge lake, Lake Xuanwu, was inside its boundaries. Combined with the Zhong Mountain Range in the east and Shicheng (stone city) in the west, its geomancy, or siting in nature, was outstanding. It was said, with allusion to the age-old directional animals associated with the Chinese space-time continuum, that Zhongshan coiled like a dragon in the east and Shicheng crouched like a tiger in the west. In addition to these auspicious signs, Zhu Yuanzhang's cap-

ital was near the sites of the third- to sixth-century capitals of the Six Dynasties. Already in 1366 Zhu had begun expanding and constructing palatial halls on the site of a Yuan-period commandery named Jiqinglu. Upon his accession to the throne in 1368, Nanjing was elevated to capital status. And twenty years later, it was an imperial capital in every sense of the word: it included an old city, a new imperial city, and a garrison; it had a masonry wall 33.7 kilometers in perimeter that surrounded all three parts; and its population exceeded one million.

The old city, located at the confluence of the Qinhuai and Yangzi rivers in the southwest of the capital, was the hub of business and communication and the most densely populated area of the capital. Handicraft workshops that served the court and mansions of high officials were there as well. The residence of perhaps Zhu Yuanzhang's greatest general, Xu Da (1329–1383), was in Dagong ward; state counselor Chang Yuchun (1330–1369) lived on Changfu Street; and sea navigator Zheng He (d. 1431?) resided on Mafu Street. Finally, Emperor Taizu ordered the construction of sixteen great restaurants in the southwestern part of the old city. The painting *Thriving Southern Capital* vividly depicts almost a thousand people of all occupations and more than a hundred shops with their colorful signboards along crisscrossed streets thronged with carriages.

The imperial city, with a palace city inside, was located east of the old city, with Fugui Mountain, a branch of the Zhongshan range, to its north and Qinhuqi River to its south. Like the capital itself, the imperial sectors were in excellent alignment with geomantic forces. The only drawback in this sense was the city's lowland position.

Barracks, a granary, storehouses, and weapons factories formed a special military area that supplied the 200,000 troops quartered inside and outside the city walls, mostly in the northwest. Ming Nanjing also contained tall bell and drum towers to announce the time of day, features inherited from Yuan Dadu.

Unlike Dadu, the streets of Nanjing were not laid out orthogonally. Nor were the outer walls straight; rather, they wound around the periphery of all three city parts, mountains, and water. In addition, there was no central axis along which major urban architecture was arranged.

The foundation of the outer wall of Nanjing was made of stone slabs. Much of its exterior, however, was covered in bricks, with the spaces between them filled in with earth. (The eastern and northern walls were made entirely of brick.) The bricks, ten by twenty by forty centimeters in size, were made in each of the 125 counties of the prefectures and subprefectures along the Yangzi River. On each brick was stamped the names of the craftsmen and laborers who had made it and the names of their supervisors. Each of the thirteen gates of the Nanjing outer wall had a gate tower. Such important ones as Jubao, Tongji, and Sanshan, all on vital transportation lines, were fortified by an additional wall in front known as a *wengcheng*. Originally 13,616 crenellations and two hundred guard stations were positioned on the wall. Now only a few of the battlements survive on the remaining 21.35 kilometers.

Because of the seriousness with which the new Ming government viewed defense, yet another wall, fifteen kilometers long with sixteen gates, was constructed beyond the northern outer wall boundary. Thus a fourth defensive line had to be broken in order to penetrate the Ming palace city.

Beijing in the Ming Dynasty

Khubilai's capital Dadu was renamed Beiping, "northern peace," shortly after the establishment of the Ming dynasty. In 1398, most of the structures that survived from the Mongolian capital were torn down. At the time of destruction, however, records were made of those buildings and their positions. As a result, reconstruction drawings and plans (such as fig. 6.2) can be made even though the entire city has not been excavated.

In 1370, Zhu Yuanzhang had made his fourth son, Zhu Di, the prince of Yan. In 1380, Zhu Di moved to the northern city, occupying imperial architecture that had been built by the Mongolian government. When the Ming founder's eldest son died in 1392, succession fell to that eldest son's oldest surviving son, Zhu Yunwen (1377–1402?). This grandson of Zhu Yuanzhang became the second Ming emperor, Huidi, in 1398, and ruled from the capital built by his grandfather at Nanjing. Meanwhile, a threat was brewing in the north; Zhu Yunwen's uncle, Zhu Di, was increasing his power base. The Ming emperor therefore launched attacks on provinces that bordered Zhu Di's territory of Yan (Beiping and its environs). The emperor was not successful, however, and by 1402, Zhu Di controlled most of China. In 1403, he was named the Yongle emperor. He renamed his northern city Beijing (literally, northern capital), and it remained the capital of Ming China until it was captured by the rebel forces of Li Zicheng, marking the fall of the Ming dynasty.

Already in 1370 work had begun on the outer wall of the northern city, Beijing. The Ming, fearing for their ability to defend themselves from reprisals of Mongolian loyalists that had fled north when Dadu fell, moved the northern

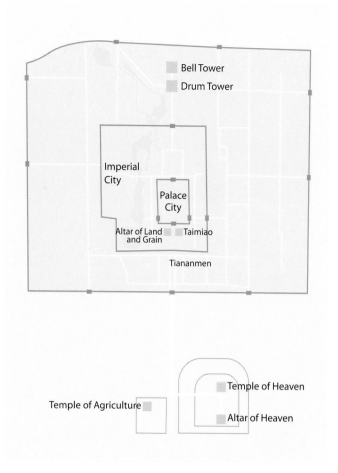

Figure 6.3. Plan of Beijing during the Ming dynasty

border of the old city 2.8 kilometers to the south, thereby reducing by 40 percent the enclosed area of the former capital. After 1416, when construction of palaces and government offices of Beijing began in earnest, the southern boundary was extended eight hundred meters southward to make room for offices of the five ministries and six districts. The outer boundary of Ming Beijing, which enclosed a space smaller than that occupied by Dadu, was extended again in 1553 during the Jiajing reign. The plan during both expansions was to follow the pattern of Ming Nanjing, with a concentric palace city, imperial city, and outer city. A shortage of funds in the mid sixteenth century, however, necessitated a change in the plan. The result was a city whose shape resembled an inverted T with four walled areas. Innermost was the palace city, better known as the Forbidden City. Surrounding it was the imperial city, which included the Jin-constructed areas east of the lake that had separated palaces in Khubilai's city. After 1553, the original Ming outer wall came to be known as the inner city, and the southern extension was the outer city. Because the water supply that had served the Mongols had become polluted even by early Ming times, the northern boundary

Figure 6.4. *The Splendor of an Imperial Capital,* Ming dynasty,
Museum of Chinese History

would never again be extended as far as it had been under Khubilai Khan. Rather, the area south of the palace and imperial sectors became more and more densely populated, with people as well as restaurants and shops — even though the most important ritual structure of the capital, the Temple of Heaven complex, was there too.

In size as well as beauty, Ming Beijing surpassed Yuan Dadu. The perimeters of the inner and outer cities were 23.5 and 22.5 kilometers, respectively, of which 6.7 kilo- meters were shared. After 1553, the area of Ming Beijing was 62 square kilometers (fig. 6.3). The earthen wall of Dadu, susceptible to erosion and natural deterioration, was now brick. The moats, too, were laid with brick and stone, and *yuecheng,* semicircular enclosures named after the shape of the crescent moon, were erected outside the city gates. Gate towers and embrasure towers called *jian- lou* (from which arrows could be shot) were built atop the nine gates of the original outer city (inner city after 1553),

and towers were built at the four corners of the city wall. Wooden bridges that spanned the moat around Beijing at each gate were replaced between 1436 and 1445 by stone bridges with a memorial archway in front of each.

The central axis of Ming Beijing extended eight kilometers, beginning at Yongding Gate on the outer city south wall and passing through Zhengyang and Daming gates, the main palatial halls of the Forbidden City, Jingshan (Coal Hill), the drum and the bell towers (which had been moved there), and finally to the center of the northernmost city wall. Imperial altars and temples, as well as government offices, were arranged symmetrically on either side of this main corridor. The one negative aspect of this splendid and majestic plan was that in order to get from south to north or east to west, one often had to travel completely around the Forbidden City, for it could be entered only by the imperial family, high-ranking government officials, or others who had specific business there (fig. 6.4).

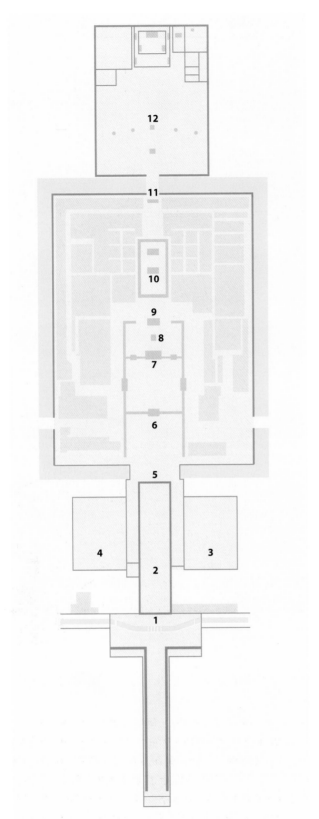

Figure 6.5. Plan of the Forbidden City, Beijing, during the Qing dynasty

1. Tiananmen
2. Uprightedness Gate
3. Imperial Ancestral Temple
4. Altar of Soil and Grain
5. Meridian Gate
6. Gate of Supreme Harmony
7. Hall of Supreme Harmony
8. Hall of Central Harmony
9. Hall of Preserving Harmony
10. Palace of Heavenly Purity
11. Gate of Military Prowess
12. Jingshan Park

The Forbidden City

The structures of Beijing's palace city, or Forbidden City, built in Ming times and rebuilt under the next dynasty, Qing, make up the largest surviving group of palatial architecture from premodern China. Occupied continuously by twenty-four emperors for five centuries, the Forbidden City consisted of 8,350 bays of buildings, most of them originally built between 1417 and 1420. Still today much of the Ming scale and layout can be seen. The plan combines aspects of Ming Nanjing and Yuan Dadu.

The Forbidden City measures 960 meters north–south by 760 meters east–west, with a gate at the center of each wall and a tower at each wall corner (fig. 6.5). It can be thought of as having two halves: to the south is the imperial court, also known as the Three Great Halls, where the emperor conducted state affairs, held grand ceremonies, entertained officials, and received guests; to the north are the inner quarters, the Three Back Halls, where the imperial family resided.

The Three Great Halls, Fengtian, Huagai, and Jinshen — better known by their Qing-period names of Taihe, Zhonghe, and Baohe — are elevated on a triple-layer marble platform shaped like a capital I. The center hall is the pinnacle of the north–south line of imperial architecture in Beijing (fig. 6.6). East and in front of the Three Great Halls (to their left) was Wenhua Hall, and to their right, Wuying Hall. Detached in their own courtyards, these were where the emperor entertained lower-ranking officials and where an emperor could reside upon retirement from court life. Wenhua Hall, which contained a portrait of Confucius, was also a place for study and lectures. Wuying Hall was where officials and ladies of rank came to offer congratulations to the empress on her birthday.

The Three Back Halls, also elevated on an I-shaped marble platform (but only a single-layer one), were named Qianqing, Jiaotai, and Kunning. East and west of this imperial residential sector were sets of six residences and five dwellings for concubines and palace maids. The highest-ranking concubine lived in the middle of the three eastern halls, closer to the Three Back Halls. Ruiben Palace, residence of the heir apparent and other princes, was also in this part of the palace city, as was Fengxian Hall, the "inner ancestral temple," which was built for the veneration of dynastic ancestors. Beyond the eastern group of six residences and five dwellings were Renshou Hall, where concubines and palace ladies of former emperors lived out their years, as well as offices for handling numerous routine affairs of the palace. To the west beyond the six residences and five dwellings were

Figure 6.6. Axial line of imperial Beijing, showing the Three
Great Halls rebuilt during the Qing dynasty

Cining and Xian'an palace complexes, residences of the
empress dowager, and Buddhist and Daoist monasteries.
At the very back of the Forbidden City was a small garden, the imperial garden, in which pavilions, trees, and
artificial hills were arranged. The scale and size made for
a space lacking the charm, mood, or artistic interest of a
traditional Chinese garden. Along the northern and western walls of the Forbidden City were rooms in which
necessities of the imperial household were stored.

The entry to the Forbidden City, Fengtian Gate (Taihe
Gate in the Qing dynasty), was the first in a line of gates
that ended at the center of the imperial city south wall. It
was here that the emperor met daily with officials and
made decisions about state affairs. In the corridor on either

side of the courtyard in front of Fengtian Gate were offices
where two records were compiled: the daily court record
(Qizhu zhu), which was composed of notes about the
emperor's daily activities, and the veritable record *(Shilu),*
which documented more major affairs such as imperial
decrees *(huidian)* and rules and regulations of the court.

South of Fengtian Gate was Wumen, Meridian Gate,
the main entrance to the Forbidden City, where high-
ranking civil and military officials gathered to wait for imperial audiences, where prisoners of war were presented,
and where other triumphal ceremonies were conducted
(fig. 6.7). The single, U-shaped form with five entries
evolved from the pair of *que* that marked the entry to
palatial architecture of Song, Tang, and even Han times.

With five marble bridges between it and Fengtianmen, the scene was one of unparalleled drama in the history of Chinese imperial planning.

The next major gate leading southward from the Forbidden City was Duanmen, Gate of Uprightedness. It took the form of a city gate but was never actually used. Chengtian Gate, the main south gate of the imperial city and the location of Tiananmen Square today, was next in line. Its form was the same as that of Duanmen. The emperor issued imperial edicts in front of Chengtianmen, and every autumn the supreme judiciary of the Chinese government pronounced sentences there on persons convicted of serious crimes. Last of the gates was Great Ming Gate (Da Mingmen), the central entry to the imperial city.

In accordance with Confucian etiquette traceable to the Zhou dynasty, the imperial city had not only those five gates, but also three courtyards. The three courts, or *sanchao,* were divided into the "outer court," or *dachao* (great court), and two "inner courts," *changchao* (frequent court) and *richao* (daily court). In Ming Beijing, the outer court was the three-hall complex in the front part of the Forbidden City. Although the emperor held court daily at Fengtian Gate, Fengtian Hall (later Taihedian, the Hall of Supreme Harmony) was used only for grand ceremonies such as those of New Year's Day, the winter solstice, the emperor's birthday, and state banquets. Huagai and Jinshen halls (later the Hall of Central Harmony and the Hall of Preserving Harmony) were utilized only for audiences with officials and banquets for the princes, and as places for changing imperial robes.

Southeast and southwest of the Three Great Halls, outside the Forbidden City but inside the imperial city, were the ancestral temple *(taimiao)* and the twin altars of soil and grain. Two of the rites that took place in these areas had roots in the inviolability of the sacred hereditary imperial authority: the recognition of imperial heredity by worship of the dynastic founder and his own ancestors at the temple, and the placement at the altars of five colors of earth — azure in the east, vermilion in the south, white in the west, black in the north, and yellow in the center (each sent from a different prefecture to symbolize the unity of the empire). Even though the Temple of Heaven complex became increasingly important in Ming China, supplanting the worship of the imperial ancestors, the original ancestral rites and their architecture were preserved in accordance with age-old specifications.

At the back of the Forbidden City was the man-made Longevity Hill (Wansuishan). Originally erected for defense, it eventually had palatial halls and pavilions built on it and fruit trees planted around it. Once a place for practicing archery was opened there, it was transformed into a gardenlike detached palace.

Most of the halls and gates of Ming Beijing not only were modeled after those of the first Ming capital but also had the same names as their Nanjing counterparts. This was true of the two sets of three halls that comprised the nucleus of the palace city, the six palaces east and west of the Back Halls, the three courts and five gates, the symmetrically positioned Wenhua and Wuying halls, the ancestral temple and soil and grain altars, and Rengong Hall. Still, four changes are apparent. First, the size and scale of buildings was greater at Beijing. Nanjing's palace city was two hundred meters shorter from north to south than Beijing's, and Meridian Gate at Nanjing was three-fourths as wide as the Beijing Wumen. Second, there was some improvement in imperial garden architecture. At Beijing, Taiye Pond, which had been built in Jin times, was dredged during the mid-Ming and expanded into the imperial gardens that encircled the area of Beijing known as the Lake District. Similarly, and third, the east garden that had been used initially for archery practice was transformed into a detached palace known as the "south inner" with hills, water, trees, flowers, halls, and pavilions. Finally, Wansuishan was also transformed into a detached palace.

It took only four years to complete the palatial halls of Ming Beijing — in part because of the superb adaptability and potential of the Chinese timber frame, for which materials could be prepared well in advance of actual construction. Beginning in 1407, the Yongle emperor sent officials to gather timber from Sichuan, Hunan, Hubei, Jiangxi, Zhejiang, and Shanxi. Bricks for the palaces were produced mainly in Linqing, Shandong province, and Suzhou in Jiangsu province. The square brick tiles produced in Suzhou, known as "gold bricks" *(jinzhuan),* were fine in texture, solid, durable, and as large as eighty by eighty by ten centimeters. Due to the complicated process by which they were manufactured, jinzhuan took twelve months to produce. The stone, meanwhile, came from Fangshan county, south of Beijing. It was a kind of marble, white and of even texture. The yellow, green, blue, and black glazed ceramic roof tiles were baked in kilns in the Beijing suburbs.

Fire, the fatal enemy of the Chinese timber frame, was still a very real threat. In 1421, just a year after the Forbidden City was completed, the Three Great Halls were struck by lightning and burned to the ground. In 1422, Qianqing Hall was also destroyed by fire. The structures were rebuilt, but fire destroyed them again in 1557 and

Figure 6.7. Wumen (Meridian Gate), entry to the Forbidden City, showing marble bridges between it and Fengtian (Taihe) Gate

yet again in 1597. The same covered arcades, verandas, and causeways that were the trademarks of Chinese architecture made entire building complexes easy targets for destruction by fire. Even though a few fire prevention methods were adopted by the Ming court — including firewalls, an additional fire-preventing tin sheet at the base of roof eaves, and high walls that separated each of the courtyards of the Three Back Halls — none could protect the wooden halls from lightning and the general deterioration of wooden members.

Despite the ravages of periodic fires, the imperial city was, and is, alive with color. Glazed ceramic roof tiles, white marble platforms and balustrades, red walls, and blue and green decorative paint characterize the unique architecture of Chinese imperial palaces and government offices. Together with black, the colors represent the five fundamental elements of the Chinese universe (yellow is the preeminent one) associated with the emperor and the roofs of his imperial halls. Beneath a blue sky or on a dark winter morning, the Forbidden City is brilliant, dignified, and luxurious.

Tomb Architecture

Unlike any rulers of any part of China before them, the imperial Mongols did not build great death monuments. Instead, the corpses of Mongolian rulers were returned to Mongolia near the Orkhon and Kerulen rivers and Lake Baikal for burial in unmarked graves at locations that elude archaeologists to this day. More than ten Yuan-period tombs believed to belong to Mongols, probably men and women of wealth but not necessarily imperial relatives, have been excavated in Chifeng county of Inner Mongolia, however. Buried in simple, single-chamber tombs, the occupants have been tentatively identified by clothing and headgear worn in portraits on tomb walls and by datable objects excavated from inside the burial area.

Imperial funerary architecture changed dramatically under the Ming. Most significant was the elimination of what had been known in Tang and Song times as upper and lower "palaces" (*shanggong* and *xiagong*, respectively). This meant that there were no longer "sleeping palaces" (xiagong) where female attendants who had served the emperor in life could reside while guarding the shang-gong. In other words, when some of the funerary cere-monies and sacrifices of earlier times were no longer enacted, the structures in which they took place disap-peared with them. In addition, the four-sided enclosures that had surrounded Tang and Song tombs — which had a gate in each wall, a pair of que in front of each gate, and towers at the wall corners — vanished. In their place the Ming emperors built a circular tumulus with a single gate in front. The que as well as a certain amount of grandeur disappeared from this architectural setting.

Such change was gradual. When Zhu Yuanzhang built tombs for his parents in Fengyang, Anhui province, between 1367 and 1375, the influence of imperial Song funerary architecture was still apparent in the truncated pyramidal mound and the gates that opened on each side of a wall enclosing it. The xiagong, however, the "bed chambers" for attendants to the tomb, were eliminated, and according to a map of these tombs drawn in the late Ming period, a new architectural form, *minglou* (spirit tower), was introduced. In 1384, Zhu Yuanzhang had a mausoleum built for his grandfather in Sihong county, Jiangsu province. Its plan and the structure and style of buildings were similar to those of his parents' tombs in Fengyang. It, too, had an entry gate on all four sides but no xiagong. It is thus fairly clear that by the beginning of the Ming dynasty the rest houses for tomb guards had disappeared from Chinese imperial burial sites.

Besides the tombs in Fengyang and Sihong, the Ming emperors had tombs in Nanjing, the Changping district of Beijing, and Zhongxiang, Hubei province. Only the most famous or representative imperial Ming tombs are discussed here.

Xiaoling is the tomb of Zhu Yuanzhang and his wife. Located in the eastern suburbs of Nanjing, only three to four kilometers from Chaoyang Gate, it is the center of a cluster of imperial tombs. East is the tomb of crown prince Zhu Biao; west, the tombs of imperial concubines. Zhu Yuanzhang's wife, Empress Ma, predeceased him and was laid to rest in Xiaoling in 1382. The sacrificial hall for the tomb was completed the following year, but the entire proj-ect took thirty years to complete. The stela pavilion was finished in 1405, and Great Gold Gate, the outermost gate of the funerary complex, was not completed until 1411.

Xiaoling is situated on Solitary Dragon Hill, south of the Zhongshan range. The highest peak of the mountain is at its back. Facing south, with a small mound in front that serves as a "table" for the tomb, two streams mean-der from the east through the mausoleum complex, and the foliage on the mountains is dense. There is no doubt that the tomb was sited with geomancy in mind (fig. 6.8).

Xiaoling is composed of three parts: the tumulus, the sacrificial area, and the spirit path. Northernmost is the tumulus, consisting of the natural mound and the burial chambers, or "underground palace" *(digong)* below it. Originally the mound was protected by a "precious fence" around it. In front of the mound was a spirit tower with a timber-frame superstructure and arched stone entry. In front of the tower, a stone bridge crossed a small stream that functioned like a "moat" outside the gate of a Chinese imperial city. A residence of the imperial dead, the tomb was planned with the architecture of a Ming imperial city in mind. The spirit tower here was the equiv-alent of the gate tower at a city entrance.

The sacrificial area extended southward from the spirit tower. When passing along a causeway, one came to the inner gate and, beyond it, Xiaoling Hall, where sacrificial rites to the emperor and empress were performed. (This building is comparable to the place where the emperor held audience in his palace, and the tumulus was like the sleeping chambers behind it.) Elevated on a triple-layer marble platform, the nine-bay hall followed the plan of Fengtian Hall (the same name as the above-described main hall of the Beijing Forbidden City) of the Nanjing palace city. Originally there were thirty bays of rooms attached to the east and west sides of Xiaoling Hall; Xiaoling Gate stood directly in front of it. East and west in front of Xiaoling Gate were kitchens for prepar-ing sacrificial foods, storage spaces, a well pavilion, and a pavilion for the slaughter of sacrificial animals, all needed to conduct the rituals. Farther to the south were an outer gate and gates named after the civil and military officials, all of which were made of brick with archways.

The spirit path that led to the sacrificial area of Xiao-ling followed a circuitous route of more than 1.6 kilo-meters. It began at Great Golden Gate (also known as Great Red Gate), led to a stela pavilion that housed a tablet inscribed by the Yongle emperor for his father, passed over a stream, and then passed between twelve pairs of monumental stone sculptures of animals. Behind the animals were a pair of stone pillars, two pairs of civil officials and two pairs of military officials, Lingxing Gate, and another bridge over water. The processional along the path would have resembled a parade approaching the Forbidden City.

Xiaoling occupied the area between the Nanjing outer wall on its west and Linggu Monastery on its east. A wall more than twenty kilometers in perimeter surrounded it. The area was covered with pine and cypress trees, and

Figure 6.8. Xiaoling, tomb of Zhu Yuanzhang, Ming Tombs, Nanjing

more than a thousand deer roamed there. Inside the walls, funerary administrators looked after Xiaoling; outside, more than one thousand troops stood guard.

The Yongle emperor and his twelve successors, all of the Ming emperors who came after him except the last, were laid to rest at the foot of the Tianshou Mountains in Changping county, Hebei province, about fifty kilometers northwest of the center of Beijing. Commonly known as the Ming Tombs, the site occupies slightly more than eighty square kilometers.

Builders began their work at the site for the first tomb, that of the Yongle emperor, between 1409 and 1413. The place had been chosen by the emperor himself during the same inspection tour when he gave the Tianshou (Heavenly Longevity) range its name. When the emperor died in 1424 during a military expedition in the north,

he was returned to the capital for burial at his mausoleum, named Changling, imperial mausoleum of long-lastingness. Building continued until 1427 under the direction of his son, Emperor Renzong (Hongxi, r. 1425), and grandson Emperor Xuanzong (Xuande, r. 1426–1435). It would be more than another hundred years before the last of the monuments planned for the approach to Changling were completed. Unlike imperial funerary architecture of the Song, a single approach and spirit path were shared by all thirteen emperors of the dynasty.

Since the first millennium C.E., the approach to imperial tombs had been known as *shendao* (spirit path). This one, completed in 1435, began at a quintuple-entry *pailou* (freestanding ceremonial gate) that was not erected until 1540 (fig. 6.9). Behind it were the Great Red Gate, stela pavilion, and 1.1-kilometer spirit path lined with twenty-

Figure 6.9. Five-entry archway at the approach to the Ming
Tombs, erected in 1540

four pairs of stone animals and twelve pairs of stone men
(fig. 6.10). Combining real and fantastic beasts, there were
two pairs of each creature, one standing and one kneeling,
signifying the twelve hours each of alertness and rest for
an imperial guard. The men all stood, however, for it was
forbidden to rest in the presence of an emperor.

The approach was largely the same as at Xiaoling, but
five times longer. Among the few differences was the
first appearance in imperial funerary architecture of a
pailou with five entries. It would remain a feature of Chinese imperial tombs through the Qing dynasty. The
Great Red Gate did exist at Nanjing; it marked the beginning of the approach to the tumulus of Zhu Yuanzhang.
But the Great Red Gate at the Beijing Ming tombs was
the largest in China, twenty meters wide and fourteen
meters high. The stela pavilion also existed at Xiaoling,
but whereas there it was only about one hundred meters
behind the Great Red Gate, in Beijing the gate and pavilion were separated by six hundred meters. The freestanding, ornamental white marble commemorative pillars
(huabiao) that marked the four corners of the spirit tower
also made their first appearance at the Beijing tombs.
Two stone columns marked the beginning of the Beijing
spirit path, whereas at Xiaoling the sculpture began with

a pair of animals. The sculptures of the Nanjing path
were also slightly fewer. Both Ming tomb sites had a
dozen pairs of animals, two each in the same order: lions, *xiezhai* (white mythological animals with horns that
symbolized justice), camels, elephants, the auspicious
mythological creatures known as *qilin* (which had stood
at Six Dynasties tombs in the vicinity of Nanjing), and
horses, with the first pair of each type kneeling and the
second erect. At Nanjing, the twenty-four beasts were
followed by octagonal pillars; at Beijing they were followed immediately by sculptures of humans. There were
only sixteen sculptures of men at Xiaoling, four pairs of
military officials followed by four pairs of civilian officials. In Beijing, the four pairs of each kind of official
were followed by four pairs of meritorious officials for a
total of twenty-four human sculptures. Next was the
five-entry Lingxing Gate, alternately known as Dragon
and Phoenix Gate, with Beijing's being more massive
than its counterpart at Nanjing. Five kilometers north of
Dragon and Phoenix Gate at the tombs in Changping
county were three bridges, two with five arches and one
with seven arches. Only then did one arrive at the triple-
entry gate to Changling. Not only was Changling the termination of the spirit path, but it was also the largest of

Figure 6.10. The spirit path of the Ming Tombs

Figure 6.11. The spirit tower of Changling, Ming Tombs

the thirteen tombs, both in the size of its mound and in total area (fig. 6.11).

After Changling, the most magnificent tombs were Yongling, tomb of Emperor Shizong (Jiajing, r. 1522–1567), under whose direction the outer wall of Beijing had been built, and Dingling, tomb of Emperor Shenzong (Wanli, r. 1573–1620; fig. 6.12). Both of these were also built during the lifetimes of the men interred in them. The other tombs — Xianling of Emperor Renzong (d. 1425), Jingling of Emperor Xuanzong (d. 1435), Yuling of Emperor Yingzong (d. 1465), Maoling of Emperor Xianzong (d. 1487), Tailing of Emperor Xiaozong (d. 1505), Kangling of Emperor Wuzong (d. 1521), Zhaoling of Emperor Muzong (d. 1572), Qingling of Emperor Guangzhong (d. 1620), and Deling of Emperor Xizong (d. 1627)—were all built posthumously. None took more than six months to complete, and the haste is evident in the workmanship of the wood and stone. Nevertheless, millions of taels of silver and tens of thousands of days of labor were spent on each one.

Figure 6.12. Underground chamber of Dingling, tomb of Shenzong, the Wanli emperor (d. 1620), and his two empresses

The last Ming emperor, however, Chongzhen, hanged himself when Beijing was overtaken by rebel forces under Li Zicheng and thus had no successor to tend to the construction of his tomb. He received a humble burial in Siling, in the tomb of one of his concubines that was opened and remodeled for him.

The plan of each of the thirteen Ming tombs, excluding the spirit path they shared, followed that of Xiaoling. Each had its own sacrificial area in front and tumulus behind. We can take Changling as exemplary. The sacrificial area of the tomb of the Yongle emperor consisted of a triple-entry gate, a stela pavilion to the side of the main line toward the funerary mound, a main gate named Ling'en (Heavenly Favors) Gate, a main hall (Hall of Heavenly Favors), a triple-entry back gate, a screen wall, a sacrificial altar, and a spirit tower. Three of its parts best represent imperial Ming funerary architecture: the Hall of Heavenly Favors, the spirit tower, and the tumulus with burial chambers underneath it.

The Hall of Heavenly Favors was one of the grandest structures built in Ming times (fig. 6.13). Named Ling'endian by Emperor Shizong in 1538, more than a hundred years after its construction, it is the largest memorial hall at an imperial tomb, comparable only to the Hall of Supreme Harmony (Taihedian, or Fengtian Hall) of the Forbidden City. Indeed in actual base dimen-

sions the Hall of Heavenly Favors is larger than Fengtian Hall. Its columns were made of machilus or phoebe nanmu (similar to cedar) and remain in good condition to this day. Like the palace hall, the Hall of Heavenly Favors is a nine-bay, double-eaved hall elevated on a three-layer marble platform. Side halls, ovens, and storage halls for animal sacrifices and other offerings stood on either side in front. The two side halls occupied fifteen bays each.

Among sacrificial halls, the next largest after Ling'endian was at Yongling, tomb of Emperor Shizong. Also a double-eaved hall, it measured seven bays across the front and had side halls of nine bays each. The sacrificial halls at the other Ming tombs in Beijing were five bays across the front with halls of five bays on each side.

The second characteristic feature of a Ming tomb complex is the spirit tower on a square base, *fangcheng minglou*. One of the most recognizable and important markers of an imperial tomb, it has its origins in towers on the inner wall that enclosed the imperial tomb of the Hongwu emperor's father at Fengyang. By the time the Hongwu emperor's tomb, Xiaoling, was built at Nanjing, there was only one spirit tower in front of the tomb and the wall had been renamed *baoshancheng* (precious mountain wall). At that time, the tower was wooden, rectangular in plan, with just one entry gate at the base. In the Ming tombs at Beijing, the spirit tower became a square masonry structure whose bracket sets and beams were also made of stone. Inside the tower was the stela on which was inscribed the emperor's title. (In other words, the spirit tower had become a stela pavilion.) The structure, which lacks a passageway at the bottom, cannot be thought of as a gate tower. Its proximity to the tumulus behind it and the name of its one entry, spirit resting gate, combined with the presence of a "silent courtyard" behind it in which stood a glazed screen wall with images carved on it, made it the obvious entryway to the subterranean chambers.

The third component of an imperial Ming tomb was the funerary mound. At Changling it stood directly behind Great Red Gate and was circular at the base. Among the thirteen tombs, oval-shaped and four-sided mounds also were found. A baoshancheng, or precious mountain wall, the same name as the wall that enclosed the spirit tower, surrounded the mound. At Changling, the space between baoshancheng and the mound was sufficiently large to be called a courtyard. Several of the larger tombs had this "courtyard of soundlessness and speechlessness." Unlike Xiaoling, Changling also had a glazed screen wall in the "courtyard" as well as five sacrificial stone altars, stone tables, and octagonal columns.

Figure 6.13. Hall of Heavenly Favors, Changling, tomb of the Yongle emperor (d. 1424)

The stela pavilion was erected in front of the entry to every tomb. Its stela was to contain an inscription by the deceased emperor's successor lauding his ancestor's achievements. But the successor of the Yongle emperor wrote an inscription of more than thirty-five hundred characters. After that ambitious precedent, no other Ming emperors inscribed such a stela.

Besides the main buildings for stelae and sacrifices, and the tumulus and structures of the courtyard between, the imperial tombs contained subsidiary structures such as housing for those who came to offer sacrifices at the tomb and for eunuchs in charge of guarding the tomb, storage for sacrificial tools and instruments, stables for the horses of those stationed at the tomb, barracks for guards stationed at the tomb, and residences for villagers who worked there. The villagers had been relocated to Changping to take care of the gardens and trees in the tomb area and do more menial jobs. Originally, too, a wall of more than forty kilometers had surrounded the tomb complex along the foot of the mountains. In addition to the Great Red Gate, its main gate, it had ten passes where troops were stationed at guard towers to protect the tombs from enemy attack.

Only one of the thirteen Ming tombs at Changping has been excavated: that of Emperor Shenzong, which was unearthed in 1956. The underground palace consisted of a main room as well as east and west side chambers arranged around two courtyards. Made entirely of stone with vaulted ceilings, the underground rooms extended ninety meters from the "entryway" to the back coffin chamber.

Finally, a Ming tomb survives in Zhongxiang county of Hubei. Named Xianling and built by Emperor Shizong for his father, Zhu Youguan (who never acceded to the throne), it was expanded and embellished from its original structure befitting the tomb of a prince.

Altars and Temples

Altars and temples are loci for the worship of deities and spirits. As we saw in Chapter 1, both were constructed in China five to six thousand years ago, long before monasteries or other kinds of religious structures were built. With time, the primitive structures for the worship of pantheistic spirits evolved into distinctly political structures. Indeed, they came to play such an important role in

Figure 6.14. Temple to the Northern Peak, Quyang, Hebei province, 1270

state ideology that the Chinese capital and even prefectural and district capitals could not be without them.

Altars and temples of the Yuan and Ming periods can be divided into three categories: those for the worship of deities of natural phenomena; those for the reverence of deities of terrestrial phenomena; and those for the veneration of men. Examples of the first type are altars and temples for worship of deities of the heavens, sun, moon, stars, planets, wind, clouds, thunder, and rain. In the second type, deities associated with imperial fields, soil, grain, crops, peaks, bodies of water, the city, earth, and the twelfth moon of the year are venerated. Finally, there are the temples for mortals: ancestors, past sages, historical worthies, and heroes.

In its original form, an altar was simply a platform without a superstructure, whereas a temple had walls and a roof. Both were built for the enactment of rituals, including sacrifices. Under Mongolian rule, such rituals of the steppe as sacrifices to spirits of the heavens and earth coexisted with native Chinese rites. On the day that corresponded to May 2, 1263, even before the construction of the outer walls of his great capital, Khubilai ordered the erection of an ancestral temple, which according to traditional Chinese custom was built on the east side of the capital. Ten years later, a new one was begun and was completed about three and a half years after that. The reenactment of traditional Chinese yearly sacrifices at altars of soil and grain, located on the west side of the city, were ordered by Khubilai in 1270. Other altars were also constructed. Altars for imperial sacrifices to agriculture and heaven were located south of Dadu, beyond its outer wall. The Altar of Agriculture was a twin with the Altar of Silkworms, and the Altar to the Earth was located northeast of Anding Gate, inside the imperial city.

The Mongolian government also continued the former Chinese imperial practices of building temples for the worship of sacred peaks. The extant building that most closely replicates a hall of the Dadu palace city is the Temple to the Northern Peak, built in Quyang, Hebei province, in 1270 (fig. 6.14). The two sets of roof eaves, two sets of intercolumnar bracket sets, and white marble balustrade whose posts support lions are all features described in texts about the Yuan imperial halls, which were destroyed in the late fourteenth century by order of the Yongle emperor.

Restoration of Chinese rule brought about a full-scale revival of rites and sacrifices that had flourished in pre-Yuan China. In the Ming central capital at Fengyang, where Zhu Yuanzhang built tombs for his parents and where imperial construction occurred at a rapid rate between 1369 and 1375, as well as in Nanjing and Beijing, heaven and earth were worshiped at suburban altars during the winter and summer solstices. Agriculture (the first crops), mountains, rivers, the planet Jupiter, silkworms, and the sun and the moon were also worshiped. Sometimes people worshiped more than one phenomenon at the same altar. As time passed, the ancestral temple and altars of soil and grain continued to exist, but their importance was eclipsed by the increased significance of the worship of heaven. All of the altars and their rites are detailed in the section on rituals *(lizhi)* in the *Standard History of the Ming*.

Prefectural and city governments were also ordered to erect altars. Most prefectures and many cities and towns had a temple to the city god *(chenghuangmiao)*, a temple to Confucius (and civil officials), and sometimes one to Guanyu or Guandi (god of war) and military officials. Confucius and Guandi were honored in national temples as well. In addition, certain gods or heroes were associated with specific places. The Temple of Taibo, the man who first developed the region around the city of Suzhou, which became the capital of the Kingdom of Wu (220–280), was located only in Suzhou. A temple dedicated to Wu Zixu, who had helped the king of Wu found a kingdom in the same area during the Spring and Autumn period (770–476 B.C.E.), also stood in Suzhou. Temples to the goddess Mazu were common only along the southeastern coast — in Fujian, for example — and are found today in Taiwan. Temples to all five sacred Daoist peaks, to Ba La (to whom sacrifices were enacted during the twelfth moon of the year), to Wenchang, god of literature, and to the Dragon King, who had the power to bestow rain, were constructed if they did not undermine or threaten the power of the local, regional, or central government. Temples and shrines where people could pray for soldiers and safety were popular during wartime and in border regions. And officials built temples throughout China to their families and descendants.

The Temple of Heaven Complex in Beijing

Of all the dynastic altars and shrines built anywhere and at any time in China, the Temple (or Altar) of Heaven complex in Beijing is the most significant. Indeed, the Temple of Heaven was entered only for the most important sacrifices of the year and only by the emperor himself. Since the Han dynasty, when the earliest discussions of the relation between nature, earth, and the cosmos were codified in written theories, such as that of yin-yang and the Five Elements, heaven was associated with yang and earth with yin. The altar for sacrifices to heaven was placed in the southern suburbs, because heaven was associated with the south, whereas the altar to earth was located in the north.

The first Temple of Heaven in Beijing was built by the Yongle emperor in 1420. It followed the model of Dasi (Great Sacrifice) Hall, built by the Hongwu emperor in Nanjing, in which sacrifices to heaven and earth were

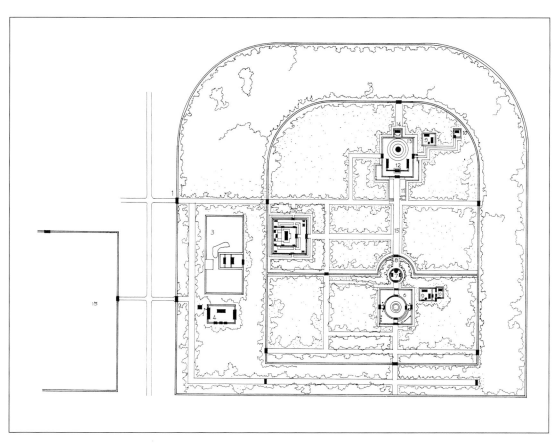

Figure 6.15. Plan of the Temple of Heaven complex

1. Western gate to the altars
2. Western Heavenly Gate
3. Ritual Instruments Office
4. Sacrificial Animals Stable
5. Abstinence Palace
6. Circular Mound
7. Imperial Vault of Heaven

8. Complete Virtue Gate
9. Imperial kitchen and storage
10. Slaughter Pavilion
11. Precious Clothing Platform
12. Gate of Prayer for a Prosperous Year

13. Hall for Prayer for a Prosperous Year
14. Hall of the Imperial Heavens
15. Yuelu Bridge

performed under the same roof. Dasi Hall was an eleven-bay structure with two sets of roof eaves. It had a gate in front and was enclosed by two walls.

In the year 1530, Emperor Shizong, the Jiajing emperor, decreed that the worship of heaven and earth in the same place violated the *Rituals of Zhou*. Thereupon, a circular mound was constructed south of Dasi Hall for sacrifices to heaven, and Dasi Hall became a place for *qigu*, prayers of the first moon of the spring season for a good harvest. At the same time, a square marsh altar *(dizetan)*, for sacrifices to earth, was created in the northern suburbs, an altar for sacrifices to the sun *(ritan)* was built in the eastern suburbs, and an altar for sacrifices to the moon *(yuetan)* was constructed in the western suburbs. These four suburban altars in a way framed the capital.

Only two of the structures built during the reign of Emperor Shizong survive at the Temple of Heaven complex today: the Gate of Prayer for a Prosperous Year (Qinianmen), and an abstinence palace *(zhaigong)*, where the emperor fasted in preparation for performing the rites. But even though most of the structures were repaired or rebuilt during the Ming and Qing eras, the general features of the Ming plan and the arrangement of buildings remain largely as they were in the middle of the sixteenth century (fig. 6.15).

Since the reign of Emperor Shizong, the Temple of Heaven complex has consisted of three main structures on an axial line enclosed by two concentric, horseshoe-shaped walls (fig. 6.16). The outer wall during Shizong's reign was just under 1.7 kilometers east to west and just under 1.6 kilometers north to south, enclosing an area of 270 hectares. Cypress trees grew everywhere. The main structures, the Circular Mound, Imperial Vault of Heaven, and Great Sacrifice Hall (later known as Hall for Prayer for a Prosperous Year), were positioned along a north–south paved-brick path 360 meters long and 28 meters wide. To the west were the Abstinence Palace as well as auxiliary facilities such as the Spirit Music Tower (Shenleguan), where musicians and dancers who performed in the ceremonies readied themselves, and an area where sacrificial sheep and cattle were raised.

The Circular Mound is a triple-terrace, open-air altar. During the Ming dynasty, the floor was paved with bluish glazed-brick tiles. In the eighteenth century, however, the tile was replaced by marble, which was also used for the white balustrade surrounding each terrace and the steps that led up to them. The circumference and height of each layer, the number of flagstones that formed each circle of each layer, and the number of steps were all multiples of nine, the number that symbolized the Chinese emperor. The entire altar was surrounded by two low walls known as *yi,* a feature of altars and temples.

The Imperial Vault of Heaven was a round structure north of the Circular Mound in which the tablet of the heavenly deity, Haotian Shangdi, was enshrined (fig. 6.17). On either side were smaller halls that housed tablets to lesser deities associated with Haotian Shangdi. Outside the east wall of the Imperial Vault were facilities where meat for sacrifices was prepared, statues were kept, and sacrificial animals were slaughtered.

First named Dasi Hall, and later in the Ming dynasty Daxiang Hall, the structure best known as the Hall for Prayer for a Prosperous Year is said to have been designed personally by Emperor Shizong. Its original form is thought to have followed that of the Mingtang. Elevated on three circular terraces of white marble, the layout illustrated the adage "Heaven is round, earth is square." The three sets of conical roof eaves are unique in Chinese construction (fig. 6.18).

Dasi Hall of the early Ming dynasty had azure tiles on the top set of eaves, golden tiles on the second set, and green on the lowest roof, representing heaven, earth, and the myriad of things (nature), respectively. After it was repaired in 1751 in the Qing dynasty and renamed Qiniandian (Hall for Prayer for a Prosperous Year), all three sets of eaves were azure. A ceremony for an auspicious harvest was performed there every first moon of spring. Behind this hall is Huangqian Hall, in which tablets of heavenly spirits are kept.

Because the altar complex was so far from the Forbidden City, it had to be heavily guarded. A defensive trench and two high walls surrounded it, and beyond those walls were another 160 bays of rooms where guard troops were stationed. The main hall where the emperor stayed was made of fire-resistant brick, not timber. Two pavilions stood on the platform in front of the hall: one had a bronze statue of a man holding a tablet on which the day of the fast was recorded, and the other featured a clock.

The emperor sacrificed to heaven during the winter solstice. Before the ceremony, he fasted for three days, and during the eve of the ceremony he stayed in the Abstinence Palace. At dawn the next morning, the tablet with the name of the heavenly deity was moved from the Imperial Vault of Heaven to the Circular Mound. The emperor proceeded south from the Abstinence Palace, stopping at a platform where he changed his garments before going on to the Circular Mound. At the mound, the emperor made burnt offerings to heaven and welcomed the heavenly deities with musical accompaniment. Next he burned incense, made supplications, made

Figure 6.16. Aerial view of the Temple of Heaven complex

Figure 6.17. Imperial Vault of Heaven, Temple of Heaven.

Figure 6.18. Hall for Prayer for a Prosperous Year (Daxiang Hall, later Qiniandian), Temple of Heaven complex, Ming-Qing dynasty

offerings of jade and silk, bowed three times, and watched the offerings burn as a way of seeing off the deities. At that point the ceremony was complete.

The Circular Mound and the Hall for Prayer for a Prosperous Year were the major structures of the Temple of Heaven complex from Ming times onward. When they were first built, construction lasted fifteen years. The dominant shapes of circle and square symbolized heaven above and earth below; further, the lower mound and the high hall, with its conical dome, symbolized the harmony of two very different structures. The path that connected the two halls with the Imperial Vault of Heaven between them sloped gradually upward, so that the ground beneath the Hall for Prayer for a Prosperous Year was a few meters higher than the area in front of it. From any side of that hall, then, one overlooked a sea of cypress trees. Similarly, from any point on the Circular Mound one looked up to the cypress forest. Thus the emperor, upon climbing to the Hall for Prayer for a Prosperous Year, might have felt like he was floating above the kingdom, a fitting spiritual perspective as he enacted the most solemn ceremonies of the Chinese calendar.

The Confucian Temple in Qufu

In 478 B.C.E., Duke Ai of the state of Lu had a temple built at the residence of Confucius to pay homage to the sage of his state. From these beginnings, the Temple to Confucius was born. In the second century B.C.E., the Han emperor offered animal sacrifices at this temple when he was passing through the Lu state's capital (today Qufu), and during the following century titles were conferred on the sage by the emperor. By the Tang dynasty, rites previously reserved for the emperor himself were conducted at a memorial service to Confucius, who in 739 had been elevated to the title of Prince Wenxuan. Beginning in the early Ming dynasty, memorial services to Confucius were held every two years at the temple. Through the Ming period, a temple to Confucius could be erected only by explicit imperial decree. Thereafter, in the Qing period, temples to the sage came to be built in most major cities of China.

Throughout the centuries since Han times, the temple at Qufu was repaired, rebuilt, or enlarged according to the desires of specific emperors or as a result of damage. In 1499 the temple was struck by lightning and burned to the ground, and it was rebuilt by imperial decree shortly afterward. Master craftsmen were sent from the capital and princely residences to work in Qufu, and high-ranking officials came to supervise the construction.

The general layout of the temple as it was rebuilt in about 1500 is preserved today (fig. 6.19), and it bears a remarkable resemblance to that of the Forbidden City. Timeliness of the Sage Gate (Shengshimen, fig. 6.20), Developing the Way Gate (Hongdaomen), and Star of Literature Pavilion (Kuiwenge, fig. 6.21) survive from this rebuilding. The Apricot Altar (Xingtang, fig. 6.22) and Memories of the Sage (Shengji) Hall survive from the end of the Ming dynasty. Several stela pavilions behind the Star of Literature Pavilion remain from the Jin and Yuan periods.

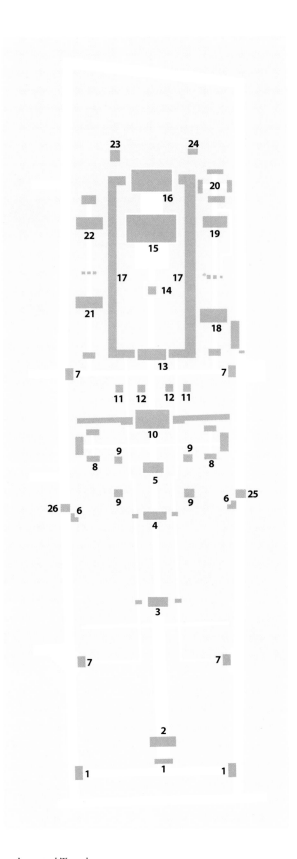

Figure 6.19. Plan of the Temple to Confucius, Qufu, Shandong province, rebuilt circa 1500

1. Memorial Archway	10. Star of Literature Pavilion	19. Ancestral Temple
2. Timeliness of the Sage Gate	11. Jin Stela Pavilion	20. Sacrificial Kitchen
3. Developing the Way Gate	12. Yuan Stela Pavilion	21. Music Hall
4. Gate of the Great Mean	13. Great Achievement Gate	22. Enlightenment by
5. Assimilating Culture Gate	14. Family School	Sage Hall
6. Corner Tower	15. Great Achievement Hall	23. Burning Silks Site
7. East and West Lateral Gate	16. Sleeping Quarters	24. Shrine for Earth God
8. Abstinence Palace	17. East and West Covered Corridor	25. Bell Tower
9. Ming Stela Pavilion	18. Poetry and Ritual Hall	26. Drum Tower

Figure 6.20. Lingxing Gate, framing Timeliness of the Sage
Gate on the approach to the Confucian temple

Figure 6.21. Star of Literature Pavilion (Kuiwenge), Temple
to Confucius in Qufu, rebuilt 1499

Figure 6.22. Apricot Altar, Temple to Confucius in Qufu, late Ming dynasty

Occupying an area of 4.6 hectares, the Temple to Confucius ranges from 141 to 153 meters wide and 637 to 651 meters long. It consists of seven courtyards, five in the front part of the complex and two in the back. The Hall of Great Achievement (Dachengdian), the main hall of the complex, stands in the sixth courtyard.

The axial approach to the temple begins even before Timeliness of the Sage Gate. Four archways — the Arch of the Sound of Metal and the Vibration of Jade, Gate of the Spiritual Star, Arch of the Original Ether of Supreme Harmony, and Arch of Virtue Equal to Heaven and Earth (all references to writings by Confucius) — form a direct line to Timeliness of the Sage Gate, Star of Literature Pavilion, and the Hall of Great Achievement. The courtyard of the four gateways is empty except for cypress trees. Behind it, in the courtyard in back of Timeliness of the Sage Gate, second in the complex, is a pavilion with two tenth-century statues that at one time stood in front of the tomb of the duke of Lu in Qufu. The second courtyard continues to the bridge over the River of the Wall. The third courtyard is in front of the Gate of Aug-

menting the Truth and the fourth courtyard is in front of the Gate of the Great Mean, an allusion to one of the most famous writings of Confucius, the *Doctrine of the Mean*. North of these buildings stands the Assimilating Culture Gate, and only then does one arrive at the Star of Literature Pavilion. Seven bays across the front and 27.95 meters high, the two-story structure was first built in 1018. In 1191, it was reconstructed and named Star of Literature Pavilion. Its lower story served both as a place where preparations could be made before proceeding to the hall for sacrifices to the sage and as a passageway to the monuments of the temple complex. As was often the case in two-story Chinese architecture, the upper story housed a vast library. The buildings on either side of the Star of Literature Pavilion — like the Abstinence Palace in the Temple of Heaven complex — provided residential space for the master of ceremonies and his assistants while they fasted in preparation for ceremonies.

Passing through the Star of Literature Pavilion, one comes to the main gate and hall of the complex, Dachengmen and Dachengdian, the Gate and the Hall of Great Achievement (fig. 6.23). This is the only structure outside the Forbidden City that has five gates along its approach. The four corner towers in the outer wall of the Confucian temple similarly are a sign of the rank of the structure. The towers serve no architectural purpose and were added in the early years of the Yuan dynasty only because ancient ritual prescribed that a ruler have a tower at each corner of the wall surrounding his residence. From the symbolism of the architecture, it is clear that Confucius was revered as highly as any person in Chinese history.

Indeed, structurally and in terms of its placement in the building complex, the Hall of Great Achievement was the equivalent of the Hall of Supreme Harmony in the Forbidden City or the Hall of Heavenly Favors at the imperial Ming tombs. The Hall of Great Achievement soared 24.6 meters above the 90-by-63-meter courtyard in front of it. The ratio of the distance between Great Achievement Gate and Great Achievement Hall and the height of the hall was 3.5:1, a grand scale that unfortunately has lost some of its drama because of the density of cypress trees. Elevated on a double-tier marble platform, ascending and descending dragons were carved on the ten pillars across its front facade. During the Ming period, the roof tiles were glazed in green, but they were replaced with imperial yellow tiles in the Qing period. Inside the 45.6-meter-wide hall were enshrined the tablet of Confucius and the tablets of fourteen other Confucian sages. The tablets of more than one hundred Confucian sages filled the forty bays of corridor on either side of the hall.

Figure 6.23. Hall of Great Achievement (Dacheng Hall), Temple
to Confucius in Qufu, 1483, repaired 1725

Figure 6.24. Cloud Terrace of Juyong Pass, Beijing, 1345

the residence of the Kong family, descendants of Confucius, discussed in more detail later. Its beginnings are traced to the eleventh century, when Song emperor Renzong enfeoffed the forty-sixth-generation descendant of Confucius as the duke of Yansheng.

Besides the Confucian temple and the Kong family mansion, the birthplaces and residences of Confucius and other scholars who lived and taught in Qufu are today cultural relics. So are their tombs. Approached by a spirit path modeled after that of a Chinese ruler, the tomb of Confucius is part of a two-hundred-hectare forest of stelae and tombs commemorating the great minds of sages who lived and preached morality in this unique Chinese town.

Religious Architecture

Although Khubilai Khan himself is said to have followed Lamaist Buddhism, the branch introduced to China from Tibet, he and his wife Chabi are famous for their interest in other forms of Buddhism, as well as Daoism. Khubilai's protection of religions native to China set the standard for the Yuan dynasty. Thus even though there were occasional persecutions of Daoists and strife between Buddhists and Daoists during Mongolian rule, in general religions present in China before the time of the Mongols flourished and Yuan emperors who succeeded Khubilai continued to patronize Buddhist and Daoist monasteries. Indeed, the multicultural population of the Mongol world was evident in many great monuments of the age, such as the archway at Juyongguan (Cloud Terrace Pass), the underside of which was decorated with Lamaist deities and an inscription translated into six languages of the empire: Sanskrit, Tibetan, Mongolian, Uyghur, Chinese, and Tangut (fig. 6.24).

Gold, silver, land, and households were awarded to temples and monasteries — indeed, it is estimated that a staggering two-thirds of state revenue was spent on Buddhism. By the year 1291, there were more than forty-two thousand Buddhist establishments in China and more than two hundred thousand monks and nuns. As the state religion, Lamaist Buddhism received the strongest government support, much more than Chan (Zen), which had been a favorite form of the Southern Song court, or Lüzong (Vinaya), introduced to China during the Tang dynasty. In the Yuan period, Lamaist architecture, sculpture, and decorative arts spread to the farthest reaches of the Mongolian empire in China.

Even though native rule returned to China in 1368,

In the courtyard west of Great Achievement Hall were a hall in memory of Confucius's parents and a hall for temple musicians to practice in, for music was an integral part of the ceremonies at the Confucian temple. To the east were the Hall of Poetry and Rituals (Shilitang) and a temple for the descendants of Confucius. Directly behind Great Achievement Hall, also following the precedent of imperial planning in a palace city, was the "sleeping chamber," built in honor of Qiguan, the wife of Confucius. In the back of the complex, on either side of Dacheng Hall and the private hall behind it, were halls with 120 illustrations of Confucius's life carved in stone. There is also a marker at the spot in the wall where the ninth-generation descendant of Confucius built a double wall to hide books when the First Emperor, Qin Shi Huangdi, ordered the burning of all classical texts. Finally, there was a storage hall for Confucian tablets, a kitchen, and places for burying and burning sacrificial animals.

In imperial times, more than thirty routine ceremonies were conducted at the Confucian temple every year. A major ceremony was held every season and attended by nearly one thousand people, who crowded into the courtyard to see the offering of sacrifices in Great Achievement Hall and the performances of 110 musicians and dancers on the platform in front of the hall.

Perhaps most extraordinary is the complex of buildings behind the Confucian temple. Entered through a humble side gate and with roofs capped with gray tiles is

Figure 6.25. Meidaizhao Lamasery, Inner Mongolia, Ming dynasty and later

Figure 6.26. A shrine at the Meidaizhao Lamasery

Lamaist Buddhism was in China to stay. Lamaism was extremely popular during the Ming period, especially the mid-Ming when Altan Khan (1507?–1582?) was in power. This Mongolian chieftain plagued Ming China for more than three decades: he succeeded in uniting Mongolian tribes and wreaking havoc in northern Shanxi and Beijing, and he took a part of Qinghai and Tibet, as well as for a brief time northernmost Shanxi and Hebei. During his ascendancy, Lamaist Buddhism became increasingly popular in all those regions, as well as where it already had a presence — those provinces and regions with large Tibetan populations like Qinghai, Gansu, and Sichuan, or in provinces that bordered Tibet. Moreover, during the fifteenth century there was a tremendous rise in Buddhist monastery construction in Tibet itself. The Four Great Monasteries of the Gelu sect — Gandansi, Zhebengsi, Selasi, and Zashilunbusi — were all built at this time. Vast in size, all four combined tall Buddha halls and sutra libraries with low buildings for monks' residences. In Inner Mongolia, there are said to have been seven great, eight smaller, and seventy-two "nameless" monasteries in Hohhot (Huhehaote) alone. Among them the most famous are Dazhao, Xilituzhao, and Meidaizhao, the last situated in Tumd Right Banner on the Hohhot–Baotou Highway. The lamaseries of Qinghai,

Gansu, and Sichuan exhibit strong Tibetan influences, whereas those of Inner Mongolia are a mixture of northern Chinese and Tibetan styles with regional features (figs. 6.25 and 6.26).

Chan Buddhism flourished in central and south China. Monasteries of the Four Great Peaks dominated Buddhism during the Ming period, supplanting the influence of the Five Mountains and Ten Monasteries that had prevailed in the Song and continued to prevail in the Yuan period. Each of the Four Great Peaks was associated with a bodhisattva — Manjusri on Mount Wutai, Avalokitesvara on Mount Putuo, Samantabhadra on Mount Emei, and Kshitigarbha on Mount Jiuhua. Grand in scale, the temples rose like forests in these mountains, demonstrating the great numbers of Buddhist structures in the Ming dynasty (fig. 6.27).

Ming monasteries were spread out, but in general those on flatter land lay along strict axial lines. Whereas in early monasteries there had been a Shanmen in front, for example, during the Ming period there were two more structures, a Diamond Hall (Jinggangdian) in front and a Hall of Divine Kings (Tianwangdian) behind it. The main Buddha hall also came to be two or three structures. Tianjie Monastery in Nanjing exemplified the Ming plan, with the main Buddha Hall, Hall of the Three Sages, and

Figure 6.27. Great Hall at Xiantong Monastery, Mount Wutai, Shanxi province, Ming dynasty

Hall of Vairocana arranged one behind the other. There also was an entry gate with a bell tower and drum tower placed symmetrically behind it to the right and left, respectively. On either side in front of the Buddha Hall were the Guanyin (Avalokitesvara) Hall and Revolving Sutra Cabinet Hall. All were standard halls in Ming monasteries.

During this period, a new type of Ming monastery building was introduced called a "beamless hall" *(wuliang-dian)*. Made of brick and characterized by the widespread use of the arch, such construction had previously been used only underground in tomb architecture. Beamless halls provided much safer storage than wooden buildings for Buddhist scriptures, which during the Ming period were sometimes conferred to monasteries by the imperial household. About a dozen beamless halls remain in China today. Good examples are at Linggu Monastery in Nanjing, Yongzuo Monastery in Taiyuan, Wannian Monastery on Mount Emei, Xiantong Monastery on Mount Wutai, Kaiyuan Monastery in Suzhou, and on Mount Baohua in Jurong (fig. 6.28).

As much Daoist architecture as Buddhist architecture survives on sacred peaks from the Ming dynasty. The most magnificent Daoist temple complexes were built on Mount Wudang in Hubei by order of the Yongle emperor. Important Daoist buildings also survive on Mount Tai, the eastern peak in Shandong province associated with death where the emperor went to perform sacrifices to the god of the mountain.

Finally, Islamic architecture became increasingly important in Yuan China, in part because of the number of Muslims in the service of the Mongolian khans. Both mosques and shrine-mausoleums of holy men were constructed under Ming rule. Islamic architecture in China during these periods often made extensive use of vaulting and intricate designs on surfaces of glazed tiles. Both of these features are present in the most famous extant shrine-mausoleum of the Yuan period — the tomb of Tughluq Temür, built in Huocheng, Xinjiang, in 1363–1364 for the descendant of Chinggis Khan who was the first to embrace Islam in the province. Idkah Mosque in Kashgar, built in 1422 but heavily restored since then, was similar in style. In other cases, however, mosque architecture took on the characteristics of Chinese architecture. The most famous example of this phenomenon is the

Figure 6.28. Interior of the Beamless Hall at Linggu Monastery, Nanjing, Jiangsu province, built during the reign of the Hongwu emperor (1368–1398)

Figure 6.29. Great Mosque, Xi'an, fourteenth century

Figure 6.30. Detail of murals inside Yongle Daoist Monastery, now at Ruicheng, Shanxi province

Great Mosque in Xi'an, built in the late fourteenth century at the end of the Hongwu reign (fig. 6.29).

Superior examples of Buddhist and Daoist monastery architecture of the Yuan period can be seen at two monasteries, both in southern Shanxi province. A pagoda in Beijing and a monastery in Tibet, by contrast, represent the best of Lamaist construction during the reign of Khubilai Khan.

Four Yuan buildings, one gate and three halls, survive from the Yongle Daoist Monastery *(gong)* in the town of Yongji at the southern tip of Shanxi province. Rediscovered in 1954, these buildings were recognized as so important that when a waterworks project threatened their fate in 1957, the entire monastery, including nearly five hundred scenes of in-situ wall painting and scores of stelae, was moved approximately twenty-five kilometers south to Ruicheng, where it stands today (fig. 6.30).

When active, Yonglegong was a major center of Quanzhen-sect Daoism in China. Known for its syncretism of the three major faiths, Buddhism, Confucianism, and Daoism, the sect became popular in northern China during the Jin dynasty. The hagiography of the sect's most famous transcendant, Lü Dongbin, is painted on the middle of three Yuan-period halls, and on the back hall more fragmentary murals illustrate the life of the sect's official founder, Wang Zhe. Some of the most vivid paintings of Chinese architecture preserved from any time period are used to divide the scenes of both men's lives. Some of the buildings in these paintings are consistent with architectural details of the time, such as bracket sets with three cantilevers and two sets of brackets between those on top of columns (fig. 6.31).

The front hall, Sanqingdian (Hall of the Three Purities), on whose interior are painted hundreds of deities from the Daoist pantheon, is one of the most splendid buildings that stands today from the Yuan period, comparable to Dening Hall of the Temple to the Northern Peak. Seven by four bays (28.4 by 15.3 meters) with a simple hipped roof, Sanqing Hall is elevated on an enormous platform (15.6 by 12.2 meters) with side projections in front of it (fig. 6.32). The bracket sets atop pillars across the front facade are six *puzuo,* or composed of six fundamental parts. Two clusters of bracket sets are positioned between those on top of the columns. The corner sets have three cantilevers, like those found in murals inside the hall dedicated to Lü Dongbin. The bracketing, roof type, and platform, all features of high structural eminence, also are found at the Temple to the Northern Peak.

Sanqing Hall, moreover, is the only Yuan-period structure with three cupolas in its ceiling, another declaration of its architectural rank. The only extant Song building with this feature is Daxiongbao Hall of Baoguosi.

The main hall in a Chinese temple complex need not be the first hall along the main building line, but at Yonglegong it is. The halls dedicated to Lü Dongbin and Wang Zhe, Chunyang and Zhongyang halls, respectively, exhibit features of lesser architectural rank in comparison to Sanqingdian (fig. 6.33). The second and third halls are five bays by four, each with a combination hip-gable roof, and each with bracketing of the five-puzuo type. Chunyang Hall, second in rank of the three, has one cupola at the center of its ceiling. Typical of the period style (rather than a sign of its rank), Chunyang and Zhongyang halls, like Sanqing and Dening halls, have two bracket sets across the front and back lintels between columns. One unusual feature of the three Yonglegong halls is the absence of windows or back doors. This is due to the desire to cover all interior wall space with paintings. To let as much light as possible into these structures, in all three buildings four-panel doors with extensive latticework filled every bay across the front arcades except the end ones.

The second best place to see multiple examples of Yuan-period halls in China is also in Shanxi province, just under two hundred kilometers northeast of Ruicheng at Guangsheng Monastery (figs. 6.34 and 6.35). Both a Buddhist and a Daoist hall from the Yuan dynasty are preserved here. Another distinctive feature of the site is its elevation: a hill divides Guangshengsi into an upper and lower monastery. The Yuan buildings stand east and west of each other in the lower monastery, and the upper monastery has one of the most beautiful examples of a glazed pagoda of the Ming period, the thirteen-story Flying Rainbow Pagoda (figs. 6.36 and 6.37).

The Yuan-period structures at Guangshengsi stand in sharp contrast to the architecture of Yonglegong. The Buddha hall, one of the humble examples of Yuan construction that survives, provides an excellent comparison with Sanqing Hall of Yonglegong. Three small stairs lead to the front of the Guangshengsi Buddha hall, in contrast to the elaborate platform in front of Sanqingdian. The bracketing at the Guangshengsi hall is only five puzuo, and there are no intercolumnar bracket sets across the building facades. The roof is a hip-gable combination. One distinctive feature of the Guangshengsi hall, however, is the alignment of its pillars. A total of eight columns stand across the front and back of the hall,

Figure 6.32. Sanqing Hall, Yongle Daoist Monastery,
thirteenth–fourteenth century

Figure 6.33. Chunyang Hall, Yongle Daoist Monastery,
thirteenth–fourteenth century

Figure 6.34. Beams inside main gate, Guangsheng Monastery, Hongtong county, Shanxi province, Yuan period

Figure 6.35. Inverted V-shaped beam of front hall, Guangsheng Monastery

defining seven bays. Inside, then, only two transversal rows of pillars, four in each, support the roof frame. The elimination of pillars from the inside of a structure and the movement of pillars off lines anticipated by pillar placement on the exterior of a structure are both features that emerge in Chinese construction during the Liao period and persist in Jin and Yuan architecture. In Ming times, however, one finds a return to more complete column grids. At times not even one pillar is removed from a complete grid of columns inside a Ming building.

The elimination of pillars and repositioning of interior pillars are both features of the Daoist hall at Guangshengsi, Shuishenmiao. Dedicated to the Dragon King, an inscription inside the hall is presumed to provide dates for both Yuan structures. According to the inscription, a fire destroyed the monastery in 1303, with rebuilding commencing in 1305. Construction of the Dragon King Temple and the painting of its murals were definitely completed by 1324, in time for the performance of a play whose actors are painted on one of the walls (fig. 6.38). During the Jin and Yuan periods, drama was a popular activity in towns of the Fen River valley in Shanxi. A stage dated 1345 at the Temple of the Eastern Peak in Dongyang village (in Linfen, Shanxi) is one of more than ten that remain from the thirteenth and fourteenth centuries.

The White Pagoda of Miaoying Monastery is another major Yuan accomplishment. Located on the west side of Beijing, the White Pagoda was originally part of Shengshou Wan'an Monastery in the Yuan capital, Dadu. Con-

struction of the present pagoda took place between 1272 and 1288 (fig. 6.39). A Buddha image housed inside, as well as the doors and windows, were originally entirely gilded. Veneration images of Khubilai and the crown prince, Temür Oljeitü (1265–1307), were in Shenyu Hall. In 1368, a fire destroyed all of the buildings except the White Pagoda. The monastery was rebuilt in Ming times and renamed Miaoyingsi.

Khubilai's close Nepalese adviser Anige is credited with the design of the White Pagoda. Known for his skill at making bronze images of the Buddha, Anige had been sent to Tibet with other craftsmen to help build a golden pagoda. They returned to Dadu with Khubilai's master craftsman, Phags-pa lama, who worked on the White Pagoda Monastery on Mount Wutai as well as the White Pagoda in the capital.

Rising fifty-one meters, the White Pagoda of Miaoying Monastery has a brick core and is covered with white plaster. Five fundamental parts are visible on the exterior from bottom to top: base, shaft, "wheel," harmika, and crowning jewel. The plan of its base was a twenty-sided stepped cross, faced by two layers of decorated moldings known as a Sumeru altar (after the sacred Mount Sumeru in India). Above the two tiers was an inverted lotus petal that supported the shaft. Next up, above the shaft, was the "wheel," which was composed of thirteen circular plates symbolizing the thirteen Buddhist paradises. Above these were plates that resembled an umbrella, from which hung tassels and wind chimes. At the very top was the jewel.

Figure 6.36 (left). Flying Rainbow Pagoda, Guangsheng Monastery

Figure 6.37 (above). Detail from the Flying Rainbow Pagoda

Figure 6.38. Detail from murals in the God of Water Temple, Guangsheng Monastery, early fourteenth century

The form of the White Pagoda was imported from Tibet and characterized Buddhist architecture of Nepal and Tibet at the time of Mongolian rule in China. It had a far-reaching effect on all later pagoda construction in China. Examples of pagodas of this bell-shaped form, sometimes called *dagoba,* were constructed in Ming and especially in Qing times.

Xialu Lamasery is located southeast of Xigaze in Tibet. First built in 1040, during the Yuan period Xialu was one of the thirteen "great households" of Tibet, a division of the area similar to a prefecture with a population of as many as ten thousand households. In 1320, when the chief of the prefecture invited the Budun Renqinzhu lama (1290–1364) to take charge of the lamasery, it was greatly expanded. The Yuan emperor appropriated a great deal of money for Xialu Lamasery and sent three gold and silver statues of the Buddha there. Timber for the expansion was transported from southern Tibet and craftsmen were brought in from China. The resulting structure had a timber frame and sloping roof with ceramic tile eaves. It combined the best of the Chinese and Tibetan traditions of the time (figs. 6.40 and 6.41).

Entered at the east, the main section of the Xialu

Figure 6.39. White Pagoda of Miaoying Monastery, Beijing, built
in 1272–1288

Figure 6.40. Xialu Lamasery, near Xigaze, Tibet, Yuan dynasty

Lamasery consisted of four parts from east to west: a courtyard, front hall, hall for reciting scriptures, and chapels on the west, north, and south of the scripture hall. A walkway surrounded the entire western section. The structures behind the front courtyard had two stories.

The arrangement of architectural elements was in accordance with a Tibetan monastery, although other elements of the architecture were Han Chinese. The first two-story hall, for example, had two sets of hipped roof eaves, and those behind had a single hip-gable combination roof. All of the roofs were glazed with green ceramic tiles. Bracket sets were of the five-puzuo type with two cantilevers, similar to those at Chunyang and Zhongyang halls of Yonglegong. Finally, the timber frame of one of the Xialu Lamasery halls had tiebeams that spanned four rafter lengths, above which a king post and inverted V-shaped truss supported the roof purlins. These details can be found in provincial Yuan-period architecture as well. The wall paintings, however, which covered the arcade around the courtyard and the second floor of the front hall, displayed purely Lamaist imagery of Nepalese-Tibetan style.

Major Achievements in Ming Religious Architecture

Mount Wudang is the home of a major Daoist architectural achievement, one of the seventy-two Blessed Plots designated by Daoists in China. Daoists believe that this spot, located in Danjiangkou in Hubei province, is where Zhenwu, the Perfected Warrior, attained immortality and became a transcendant. The Yongle emperor believed Zhenwu had come north to help his victorious ascent to the Chinese throne, and showed his appreciation through patronage of large-scale construction of temples and monasteries to the Daoist lord on the mountain. In 1412, the minister of the Board of Works and some two hundred thousand military and civilian laborers were sent from Nanjing to help with building projects on the sacred Daoist mountain. Over a period of eleven years, eight of the most eminent Daoist temple complexes (named *gong*, the Chinese word for palace complex); two monasteries *(guan)*, temple complexes of the next rank equivalent to Buddhist monasteries *(si)*; and thirty-six hermitages *(an)*, lower still in the Daoist architectural scheme, were constructed along the rivers and valleys from the prefectural city to Tianzhu Peak, the highest point on the mountain. Thus was created a sixty-kilometer pilgrimage road, the culmination of which was the worship of Zhenwu in a golden-roofed "forbidden city." Upon completion of the construction, the Yongle emperor bestowed the name Great Peak of the Great Harmony Mountain on the site, selected two hundred Daoists to take charge of purification and caretaking, and put nine Daoist masters in charge of supervising and administering sacrificial affairs. In addition, he presented the Daoists with 277 hectares of land of their own.

Yuxugong was the largest of the Daoist palaces (gong) on Mount Wudang. Covering three courtyards of buildings and an area of six hectares (370 by 170 meters), a bridge, four gates, a stela pavilion, and two halls stood along its main axis. Yuxugong burned in 1745; today only two gates, hall foundations, and part of the stela pavilion remain. Other Ming structures that survive at Wudangshan are a stone memorial archway (the Archway of Governing the World from the Black Peak, fig. 6.42), Yuzhengong, Tianjin Bridge, Purple Empyrean Daoist Palace (Zixiaogong), Gate of the Three Heavens, Palace of Great Harmony, the "forbidden city," and the Golden Hall.

Figure 6.41. Two-story hall from Xialu Lamasery, Yuan dynasty

Figure 6.42. Stone archway at Mount Wudang, Hubei province, fifteenth century

Purple Empyrean Palace was one of Wudangshan's largest monasteries. The building group was elevated structure by structure along the ascent to the top of the peak. First came the gatehouse, known as the Hall of the Dragon and Tiger, which housed statues of the White Tiger and Azure Dragon lords. Behind it were a pair of stela pavilions, one on either side; a square hall; Purple Empyrean Hall; and Hall of the Father and Mother. Purple Empyrean Hall, the main hall of the complex, was elevated high on a two-tier platform (fig. 6.43). Five bays across the front with a double-layer hip-gable combination roof, the hall had lower eaves supported by bracket sets made of five fundamental components with two cantilevers, and upper eaves made of seven constituent parts with two cantilevers and a single wing. A statue of the Jade Emperor was the focus of the interior of the hall.

The tallest peak of Wudangshan, Tianzhufeng, was enclosed by a four-sided stone wall 1.5 kilometers in perimeter with an entry at each side. It was here, in 1416, that the Yongle emperor built the Daoist forbidden city with its Golden Hall (fig. 6.44). The hall was made of gilt bronze, with each architectural component made in imitation of a wooden building part. Three bays (5.8 meters) wide and 4.2 meters deep, the double-eaved structure had lower eaves supported by bracketing of seven fundamental parts with two cantilevers and a single wing; the upper

eaves had nine main parts, two wings, and two cantilevers, which were more complex than any described in the Song building manual *Yingzao fashi*. The bracket sets were densely spaced, with nine sets crowding the lintel across the center bay of the front facade. Although small, the hall was highly elaborated. Pillars, bracket sets, painting on architectural members, doors, windows, and animals that decorated the roof ridge are all believed to have followed the official style of the early Ming court. Inside, Zhenwu stood barefooted with long hair; in front of him were the Dark Warrior, the tortoise with a two-headed serpent entwined around him, a golden youth, a jade maiden, guardians, and spirits of water and fire. All the statues were cast in bronze. Rising in the clouds and mists, this mountain fortress of the Lord Zhenwu was mysterious as well as elegant.

Zhihua Monastery, located in the eastern district of Beijing, is another significant religious building complex. Built by the eunuch Wang Zhen in 1443 as a private monastery, it has a plan typical of a small monastery of its day. Entered via a gate, the monastery had symmetrically placed bell and drum towers just inside the entrance. Next were a Hall of the Heavenly Kings and the main hall with images of the Buddha Sakyamuni and twenty arhats *(luohan)*. The two halls on either side in front of the main hall were Dazhi (Great Wisdom) on the east and the Hall of the Cakra Pravartana (Turning of the Wheel of the Law) Sutra on the west. Great Wisdom Hall housed images of the Four Wisdom Bodhisattvas: Avalokitesvara, Manjusri, Samantabhadra, and Kshitigarbha (known in China as Guanyin, Wenshu, Puxian, and Dizang). The sutra hall housed a fine copy of the sutra itself. Behind the main hall was a two-story structure, the lower story of which was called Rulaidian, Hall of the Tathagata (Buddha in his transformation body on earth). Above it, more than nine thousand images of the Buddha were stored in niches. Thus it also went by the name Ten Thousand Buddha Hall (figs. 6.45 and 6.46). Although never one of the grandest halls of the Ming dynasty, the Zhihua Monastery's Rulai Hall had exquisite woodwork and murals. Its ceiling, now in the Nelson-Atkins Museum in Kansas City, Missouri, is an outstanding example from the fifteenth century.

Kaiyuan Monastery, founded in 686, on the west side of Quanzhou in Fujian province, has four Ming-period buildings standing in a line. This is the same monastery where two stone pagodas survive from the Southern Song period. The Ming structures are a screen wall, gate (Shanmen), main hall, and initiation altar. At the end of the Yuan period, Kaiyuansi was destroyed by fire. In

Figure 6.43. Purple Empyrean Hall, Mount Wudang, Hubei province, fifteenth century

Figure 6.44. Golden Hall, Mount Wudang, Hubei province, 1416

Figure 6.45. Interior of Rulai Hall (Hall of the Tathagata), Zhihua Monastery, Beijing, 1443

Figure 6.46. Zhihua Monastery, with Rulai Hall just beyond the covered walkway

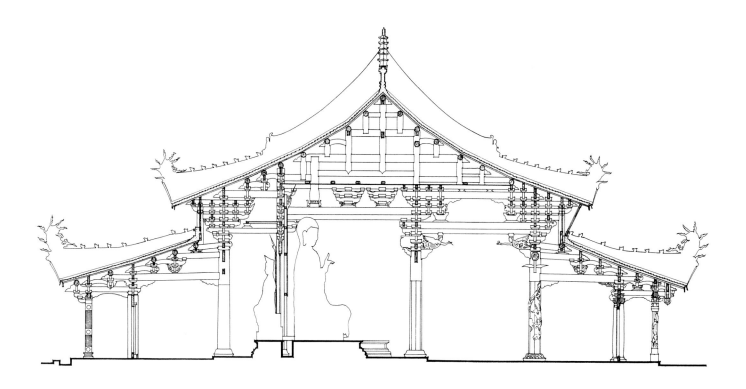

Figure 6.47. Sectional view of Hundred Column Hall, showing especially its intricate bracketing; Kaiyuan Monastery, Fujian province, 1390s

the last years of the Hongwu reign period, in the 1390s, the Shanmen (front gate), main hall, and initiation altar were rebuilt; the screen wall was rebuilt in 1576. The Shanmen actually survives from two rebuilding periods. Its central three bays are from the Hongwu era, but the end bays of the front and its "worship pavilion" *(baiting)* are very recent. The main hall is nine bays square. A huge and extraordinary structure with two sets of hip-gable roof eaves, its nine bays in each direction suggest a hundred-column structure and led to the nickname Hundred Column Hall (fig. 6.47). In fact, there are only eighty-six pillars, fourteen having been eliminated from two rows of the interior. Carried over from Liao, Jin, and Yuan times, this practice identifies the hall as early Ming. The ceiling of the main hall is an example of *chuandou,* or column-and-tiebeam structure, characteristic of south China. The bracket sets are massive and set far apart from one another, characteristic of southern Song architecture. Other outstanding features are the *apsaras* (flying heavenly musicians) that are carved into the bracket arms inside the hall (fig. 6.48). They are evidence of influences from India that continued to enter Quanzhou during the Ming period. Finally, the structure of the initiation altar was unique. With a veranda and enclosing corridor on

each side and double-layer octagonal roof on top, it was the jewel of a resplendent architectural group.

Yet another monastery of note is the extremely well preserved fifteenth-century Bao'en Monastery. Situated in Pingwu county in northwestern Sichuan province, an outlying mountainous region, Bao'ensi was built by a local chieftain, Wang Xi, between 1440 and 1446 to show his gratitude to the Ming emperor. The sculpture, wall paintings, and plaster decorations were completed by 1460.

Occupying 2.5 hectares, the front of Bao'ensi is an open square courtyard. Along an axial line behind it are the gate, Hall of Heavenly Kings, main hall, and Ten Thousand Buddha Pavilion. Just inside the gate on the east is a bell tower, but breaking Ming customs of architectural symmetry, no drum tower was built on the opposite side. In front of the main hall are, on the east, Dabei Hall (fig. 6.49), which enshrines a thousand-armed image of the bodhisattva Guanyin (or Avalokitesvara), and on the west, Huayan (Avatamsaka) Hall, which enshrines a revolving sutra repository. Stela pavilions stand in front of the pavilion to Guanyin on the east and west. Descendants of the founder Wang Xi built a residence for the chief abbot, a meditational hall, a hall for fasting, or austerities hall, and storage halls.

Figure 6.48 *(top)*. Interior of Hundred Column Hall at Kaiyuan Monastery, showing particularly its apsaras, or flying heavenly musicians, at the top of each column

Figure 6.49. Dabei Hall, Bao'en Monastery, Pingwu county, Sichuan province, built in 1440–1446

Figure 6.50. Gold leaf in a house in Suzhou

The main hall of Bao'ensi, characteristic for its time but rarely found today, is five bays across the front with a double-eave hip-gable roof. Slanting covered arcades *(xielang)* join it on the east and west sides. As in every hall at the monastery, part of its ceiling was exposed, characteristic of official Ming style. Above the exposed ceiling, however, the roof frame was of the chuandou style, not so different from the roof frame of the main hall of Kaiyuan Monastery, in Quanzhou.

The decorative details of the Bao'en Monastery structures are period-style masterpieces. The most outstanding examples of Ming decorative sculpture and painting are the wooden Avalokitesvara in Dabei Hall, the sutra cabinet in the pavilion opposite Dabei Hall, the sculpture in the main hall, and the murals in Ten Thousand Buddha Pavilion.

Residential Architecture

We have already seen that, since earliest times in China, a house was far more than a place to live — it was a symbol of its inhabitants' social status. In Tang and Song times, the government ensured that such social distinctions were maintained by issuing specific regulations about dwellings for officials and commoners. During the Song dynasty, for instance, officials of the sixth rank or below were not allowed to erect crow's-head doors *(wutoumen)* in walls in front of their residences, and those without official status were limited to building houses that were no larger than five purlins in depth, had a doorway no wider than one bay, had eaves that did not curve upward at the ends, had no more than two bracket arms and bracketing

no greater than the four-puzuo variety, did not have a lattice pattern in the center of a cupola ceiling, and were decorated with five or fewer colors. As a result, it was often evident from the outside if a house belonged to someone with an official title.

By the early Ming period, the sumptuary laws governing residential architecture were more stringent. Officials were not allowed to have houses with hip-gable roofs, two sets of roof eaves, two arms in the bracket sets, or a complicated pattern at the center of a cupola ceiling. In other words, many of the restrictions for commoner dwellings in Song times were applied to official residences in the Ming dynasty. Only members of the imperial family could build houses with hip-gable roofs. Others, even high-ranking officials, were restricted to overhanging eaves and "camel-back" roofs (flat side facades with a "hump" at the top). In addition, the residential architecture of dukes, marquises, and other officials was assigned four grades, with restrictions on the number of bays of a gate or hall and the colors of paint that could be used. Commoners were permitted residences of not more than three bays, with no bracket sets and no color.

The regulations can be seen as an example of the generally restrictive nature of early Ming society. Yet the laws were not perfectly enforced: they were violated throughout China, for example in the residential architecture of Suzhou, where gold leaf was used in painted decoration and brick and stone were elaborately carved in the ceiling rafters of residences (fig. 6.50).

Our information about residential architecture of the Yuan period is spotty. Most of our insights about Yuan dwellings, for example, come from paintings, such as the rendering of a residence in south China by the Yuan

Figure 6.51. Courtyard-style house in Ding village, Xiangfen county, Shanxi province, built in 1593

painter Sun Junze entitled *Villa by the River*. But some extant buildings do exist, and they suggest that under the more limited bureaucratic system of the Yuan, residential restrictions were not enforced. The brick foundation of a courtyard-style residence known as Houying Mansion excavated inside the outer wall of Yuan Dadu, for instance, includes carved stone lions of the kind that may have been restricted during the Ming period. Also uncovered is a rare impression of a door panel with a lattice window. Houying Mansion is believed to have belonged to an official who served the Mongolian government. His nationality is unknown.

From Ming times, numerous residences remain. About one hundred are found in Jiangsu, Zhejiang, Anhui, Shandong, Shanxi, Shaanxi, Fujian, Guangdong, and Sichuan. Geography, climate, customs, cultural heritage, and earlier architecture in the vicinity led to distinct features in the housing of each of China's geographic regions. The six types of Ming house discussed here each represent a distinctive regional and cultural style.

Dingcun (Ding village) is south of Xiangfen county in Shanxi province. Thirty-one traditional-style residences survive there, two from the Ming dynasty. One, a courtyard-style house built in 1593, stands in the northeast corner of the village. With a central courtyard enclosed on four sides, the home had an entry gate in the southeast, beyond which were the main building of three bays as well as east and west side rooms of two bays each.

It was more common for rooms to consist of three bays, but if this had been the case for the side rooms, the bays would have been too narrow to contain the traditional heated beds *(huokang)*. The rooms on the sides of the courtyard were not joined to the main one by arcades. Rather, at the Dingcun house the individual structures alone (the main hall, side halls, and gate) provided the four sides of enclosure. The two-bay room dimension was within the three-bay restriction for commoner dwellings, but the single color in which the brocade-like floral patterns were painted on the beams broke with regulations stipulating that no color could be used (fig. 6.51).

In 1612, the second surviving Ming residence in Dingcun was built east of the first. Originally a two-courtyard complex, the second home now consists of only a front gate and an inner courtyard. The structures opposite the main one and connected to either side of an outer courtyard have disappeared. So has the highly decorative "suspended flower" gate that originally joined the two courtyards. Based on current remains, each courtyard probably resembled the single four-sided enclosure arrangement of the other Ming house in the village.

Certain aspects of both residences reflect the cold winters of Shanxi province. In order to get maximum sunlight, the north–south dimension was longer than the east–west, which resulted in a long and narrow inner courtyard. All of the walls were thick. Because there was little rainfall, too, these second-rank residences were able

Figure 6.52. Main gate of the Kong family mansion, Qufu,
Shandong province, circa 1503

Figure 6.53. A hall of the Kong family mansion

to abandon convex roof tiles and use only concave ones. Both Dingcun residences had their principal rooms facing south and the main gate facing southeast, a popular arrangement in mid-Ming times because it was believed to be geomantically auspicious.

As mentioned earlier, beginning with the forty-sixth-generation descendant in the eleventh century, the eldest male descendant of Confucius in every generation was enfeoffed with the title duke of Yansheng. In 1104, dukes with this title were put in charge of sacrifices to Confucius at his temple in Qufu as well as the affairs of the Kong family.

The residence of the duke of Yansheng was located adjacent to the Confucian temple in Qufu, to the east. Known as the Kong family mansion, it is the best preserved residential complex of this scale from Ming times. Most of it, including the main (front) gate, second gate, main hall, second and third halls, side rooms, principal rooms of the front courtyard, gate to the inner (or women's) quarters, and Baoben Hall of the eastern courtyard, stand as they did in 1503 (fig. 6.52). Some structures were built or rebuilt in the Qing dynasty, however, and in 1886 the women's quarters were destroyed by fire.

The Confucian mansion occupies a total of 4.6 hectares and consists of five parts: the *yamen,* or the offices from which the duke of Yansheng administered the affairs of the town, inner quarters where women associated with the Kong household resided, an eastern study, a western study, and back gardens. No other yamen in China were built so close to a residence and temple complex. Indeed, the Kong family had a unique role in Chinese history because its members were leaders in both local and national government. In plan, the office complex was standard: a central main hall was preceded by three gates in a row and had rooms adjoining it as east and west wings. Behind the main hall cluster was the second hall, where officials were received and family affairs were handled; again, an example of public and private business being incorporated into one space. This second hall was joined to the first by a corridor so that the two buildings, with the corridor, formed a gong plan, the shape symbolic of Chinese imperial construction (in contrast to the *siheyuan,* or four-sided enclosure, which is more common in Chinese residential space). Also following a pattern of imperial planning, offices of six departments were in rooms of the east and west side wings.

The inner quarters and back gardens of the Confucian mansion were purely residential and private. The east study was where the duke of Yansheng met his official guests and worshiped the Kong ancestors. The west study was where the Kong family studied, ate, and entertained friends. Bamboo, trees, flowering plants, unusual rocks, and potted miniature landscapes were planted throughout the courtyards. The back garden had even more trees and shrubs, but they were spread throughout the area rather than arranged like the greenery in more traditional gardens of the period.

The north–south length of the Kong family mansion was 250 meters along nine courtyards, the same number as the Confucian temple adjacent to it and a number associated with the Chinese emperor. Following Confucian custom, a gate clearly marked the separation between the men's area and the women's quarters behind it. The demarcation was so strict that even water could not be brought in by men: it was drawn from a well outside the inner quarters and carried over a wall into the women's area. When fire broke out in the inner quarters in 1886, the women's part of the residential complex was allowed to burn because even in such an extreme situation men normally forbidden entry dared not pass through the gate to extinguish the blaze. The rigidity of constructed space and Confucian ritual was in accord with the saying, "The gate of the nobility is as inaccessible as the ocean."

In spite of the unique privileges awarded the descendants of Confucius in Qufu, the duke of Yansheng was an official of the second rank. Thus even though he lived like a first-rank official and wore first-rank robes, every building of his residence was a *tingtang*. No hall was wider than five bays across the front and nine purlin-lengths in depth; roof tiles had zoomorphic decorations on the ends; and beams, bracket sets, and eaves were painted an azure color (fig. 6.53). Every detail of every structure was built and maintained in accordance with Confucian doctrine. No gate was wider than three bays or deeper than five-purlin lengths; gates were painted dark green; and their knockers, shaped like animal faces with rings in their mouth, were made of tin. Gate roofs had two sets of overhanging eaves (fig. 6.54). Although some of the painting on Ming buildings was substituted with gold and other elements of the official Qing style, the traditional Ming color of azure remains in the hallway, third hall, and gate in front of the inner quarters.

Propriety Gate (Yimen), located third on the main building line of the mansion, right in front of the main hall, had one of the most distinctive structural features in Ming architecture. Also known as Multiple Brightness Gate because an inscription on a placard across the top reads "The Heavens bestow multiple brightness," it is the earliest extant example of a "suspended flower" gate. When constructed in 1503 it was a three-bay, three-story freestanding gate whose wooden columns were held tight in drum-shaped stone bases. On top of the columns were heavy eaves from which were suspended lotus pendants to provide more support. Propriety Gate was opened only for grand ceremonies such as the receipt of imperial edicts or when sacrifices were offered.

The town Suzhou was at the forefront of economic and cultural development in Ming China, and as a result retired officials, literati, and wealthy merchants settled there. Many of their residences remain in the town of Dongshan, a suburb of greater Suzhou in Ming times. Located on the main street of Yangwan village in Dongshan, the Zhao family residence represented vernacular architecture of the lower stratum of Chinese society (fig. 6.55). It is an example of a *sanheyuan,* or three-sided enclosure, in this case with a main structure of five bays on one side and two one-bay wing structures at either side. Its plan is somewhat irregular because it was altered: originally the main gate was on the east, facing the street, but

Figure 6.54. Chongguang (Rekindled Glory) Gate, Kong family mansion

it has since been moved to the south wall. The timber frame of the principal structure is simple — it employs logs for beams and its joining points between beams and columns are cut into crescent shapes. These features were common in Ming residential architecture of the time. The veranda in front of the hall was supported by a single crescent-shaped beam, noticeable because it is the only one of its kind in the entire structure.

Another residence in Yangwan, that of the humble Wang family, had a central gate that opened directly onto the main road of the village. It had only two courtyards, front and back. There were two small rooms on either side of the front courtyard, and a multistory structure in the back was used for sleeping and for entertaining guests. Between the two courtyards was a tall, thick wall that had been erected for security. The Wang family house in Yangwan is an example of a small residence whose space was used for maximum efficiency. Small courtyard-style residences of this plan were common in the Yangzi River region during the Ming dynasty.

The Lu residence in Dongyang stood outside the east gate of the walled town of Dongyang county in Zhejiang province. It was built between 1456 and 1462, and it was

ridor, forming the gong plan associated with the most eminent Chinese architectural spaces. Originally Suyong Hall had a hip-gable roof, but it was later changed to two sets of roofs with overhanging eaves. The change may have been made to avoid trouble with the authorities, because the Ming building code did not allow official residences to have hip-gable roofs. The techniques of joining the corners of the timber skeleton inside remain unchanged, as do the highly elaborated bracket sets. In all, the Lu family mansion is rare among Ming structures.

Among all of the regional residential architecture of Ming China, that of Huizhou in Anhui province is the most famous and in many ways the most distinctive (fig. 6.57). Huizhou residences are an example of a style that developed in response to its natural surroundings. Located in a mountainous yet densely populated region, the principal rooms and wing rooms of Huizhou residences were two-storied, built around a central skywell, and constructed of large logs (timber was cheap). When land was particularly scarce, three-story residences were erected. Because it was not possible to expand horizontally or beyond three stories, families exhibited their wealth in exquisitely carved wood and brick decorations (fig. 6.58). But because these decorations were not permitted under

Figure 6.55. Zhao family residence, Yangwan village, Dongshan, Jiangsu province, Ming dynasty

Figure 6.56. Part of the Lu family residence in Dongyang, Zhejiang province

then continually rebuilt until it became one of the largest residential complexes in the area, consisting of more than ten courtyards along a north–south line and occupying more than five hectares. Beginning with a screen wall, the axial line passed through three stone memorial archways and then Suyong, Leshou, and Shiyong halls. A stream meandered through the complex, and nine rainbow-arched bridges crossed it to connect the residence with the outside world. The road in front of the residence led westward to the east gate of Dongyang county's city wall. The presence of memorial archways suggests that it was at one time the home of officials (fig. 6.56).

Suyong Hall is the main hall of the Lu family residence, and it is in many ways similar to the main hall in the Kong family mansion. In both of these large-scale residential complexes, the main hall has extensions on either side wing and is joined to a hall behind it by a cor-

Figure 6.57. A village in Huizhou, Anhui province

local regulations, homeowners usually concealed these elaborations in rooms that faced the inner courtyard. From the exterior, Anhui residences seemed to be made of just white walls and gray tiles. Only tiny windows opened onto the street side of a house.

One residence of an unknown family stands in Xixinan village, a distant suburb of She county, Huizhou (fig. 6.59). Next to the residence was a pond, and near it, a pavilion. An inscription on a purlin of the pavilion gives the date 1456; the residence seems to have been built at about the same time. At one time a group of residences was clustered here, but now only one courtyard-style house remains. Oriented southwest, the two-story house was built around a small courtyard and its main entry opened on a narrow lane. Rooms of the first story were low, but those of the second floor were higher and larger with more wood decoration. The layout suggests that residents spent most of their time on the second floor. A small pond in the courtyard collected rainwater, the most common method of getting water in this part of Anhui province.

Other fascinating architectural features can be seen in numerous surviving earthen multistory residences in Longyan and Zhangzhou districts of Fujian and Chaozhou county, Guangdong. These homes were constructed by people who had fled south from the Central Plain in times of internal strife. During Ming times, amid continued fighting among clans and attacks by mountain bandits and Japanese pirates, fortresslike buildings were constructed in which many members of a clan lived together. According to a recent survey in Zhangpu county, Fujian province, approximately two hundred multistory earthen structures remain there, four of which survive from the Ming dynasty: Yidelou in Makeng village, Sui'an, built in 1558; Yiyanlou in Guotian village, Xiamei, constructed in 1560; Qingyunlou in Yuntou, also Xiamei, erected in 1569; and Yanhailou in Tanzitou village, Guizhen, built in 1585. Important examples of post-Ming multistory construction during this period include Wuyunlou and Zhengulou in Guzhu village, Yongding; Shenpinglou in Shajian, Hua'an county; and Rixinlou in Ting'an village, Hua'an.

In general, these earthen structures are three or four stories. They go by the generic name *tulou,* which means multistoried structures with earthen outer walls. Tulou can be divided into three types. First is the line style, found in such places as Rixinlou in Hua'an, where

Figure 6.58. Carved decorations on a building facing an inner
courtyard, Huizhou

Figure 6.59. Xixinan village residence, built in 1456

three earthen buildings are arranged along a line, according to the lay of a sloping landscape. The main gate of Rixinlou is in the lowest building. A stone placard with the inscription "Built by the Zou clan in the second moon of the thirty-first year of the Wanli reign [1603]" still hangs above the gate today. Second is the circular style, of which the Shengping House in Shajian, Hua'an, is a good example (fig. 6.60). A granite outer wall is the most solid part of that structure. Qiyunlou, also in Shajian, is the same shape; it was rebuilt sometime after 1911. And third is the square style. The three-story Yiyanlou in Zhangpu and the fourstory Zhengulou in Yongding are good examples of this type of multistory clan residence. So is the smaller three-story Wanbilou in Zhangpu.

Outer walls of all these residences were made thick for defense. Often they were 1.5 meters at the bottom and thinner above. Windows on the first floor opened only into the central courtyard. Windows of the upper stories did open onto the outside, but they were small and usually trapezoidal-shaped like the windows of guard stations that were opened only for defensive purposes. The inner walls of multilevel structures were usually laid with mud brick. Floors were made of wooden planks, and roofs were supported by timber frames covered by concave and convex ceramic tiles.

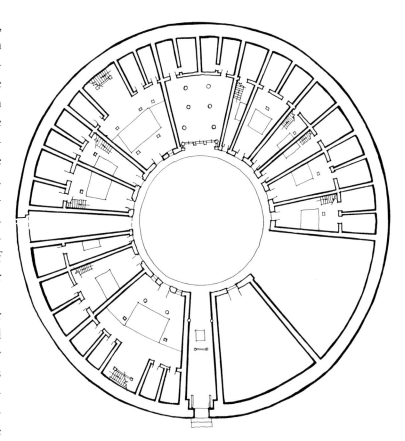

Figure 6.60. Plan view drawing of Shengping House in Shajian, Hua'an county, Fujian province, Ming dynasty

The Flowering of Chinese Geomancy in the Ming Dynasty

The origins of what is often called Chinese geomancy, *fengshui* (literally, wind, water), lie in Chinese folk beliefs of ancient times. The purpose of the practice was to choose the most auspicious environment possible, one sited in harmony with natural phenomena and the physical and psychological needs of man. Geomancy influenced the site selection of residences, tombs, religious structures, and even entire towns and cities. For purposes of siting, structures were designated in one of two categories: a yin location, the designation of most funerary architecture, or a yang location, the designation for residential and religious spaces.

Some believe that Chinese geomancy has rudimentary elements of engineering as its basis. Others trace the origins of Chinese siting back three thousand years to the Western Zhou practice known as *buzhai,* or "divining for one's house," which led to the practice of site selection of everything from cities to tombs to individual dwellings based on the configuration of land and the "taste" of water. The concept and most theories of Chinese geomancy were in place by Han times. The compass, which helped with geomantic orientation, was invented in the Tang dynasty. And during the Song dynasty, two sects of fengshui existed, the Jiangxi and the Fujian.

Fengshui flourished in China in Ming times, so much that it might be argued that the practice was the basis for almost all construction. Important Ming geomantic treatises included Liu Ji's *Kanyu manxing* (The spread and flourishing of geomancy), Jiang Pingjie's *Shuilongjing* (Classic of water and dragon) and *Yangzhai zhinan* (Compass for the positive siting of residences), Gao Lian's *Xiangzhai yaoshuo* (Essential notes on residential layouts), Zhang Daozong's *Dili quanshu* (Complete writings on geomancy), Zhou Jingyi's *Shanxiang zhimi* (Mysteries on the direction of mountains), and *Dili zhenzhi yuanzhen* (Geomancy points to the original truth) by the monk Mu Jiang.

Jiangxi and Fujian remained the most influential sects of fengshui in Ming times. The Jiangxi sect was considered the more practical. Its theories emphasized connections between the forms of mountains, streams, and houses. The Fujian sect was considered the more theoret-

Figure 6.61. South Lake (formerly Moon Pond), Hong village, Yi prefecture, Anhui province, built in the early fifteenth century

ical and focused on astrology and directional orientation. In fact, the writings of both emphasize the relationship between topography and outcome, and even though the two sects criticized each other in writing, in practice each borrowed from the other and both employed the compass as the primary device for the initial siting. One might characterize the writings of both sects as "classics of the compass."

Fengshui pervaded every aspect of construction in Ming China. In selecting the site of a village, geomancers were called in. Ideally, they sought to create a dragon in the configuration of the land: mountains at the back and a river, symbolizing the azure tail, flowing from the mountain and running along the front of the entire village. The mountain at the back of a village was seen as a pillow or screen to shield and protect it. In regions without mountains, the flow of water was used for this important role of the dragon. In those cases, the village was oriented with water at the back and a road in front.

One of the most important aspects of Ming fengshui was *shuikou,* "mouth of the water." A reference to where a waterway entered or flowed out of a village or town, it was the subject of numerous geomantic treatises. With time, shuikou referred only to the exit of water from a village. But it also was a reference to a town or village's water source as the hub of its activity: roads led to it, and the ancestral tem-

ple, pavilions, and bridges were built there. The shuikou concept was implemented in villages of Huizhou, Anhui province, whose houses were described earlier.

Sometimes the placement of a pavilion or other tall structure such as a pagoda could compensate for natural defects. Such a structure might even turn a potentially ominous outcome into a propitious one. This belief is one reason that such structures might have become the central locus of a town. During the Zhengde reign (1506–1521), for instance, Kuang Pan, magistrate of Ruizhou in Jiangxi province, noticed how few of the many talented people in his prefecture had succeeded in passing the national examinations. After surveying the topography of the prefecture, he discovered a problem in the location of the prefectural school: east and west were not in harmony. On the west side in front of the school was the west wall of the prefecture, but on the right side there was nothing to balance it. In addition, the back of the school pressed right up against the granary, leaving no space at all. Kuang solved the problem by having the granary moved and by building on the east side of the school a towering structure that he named Tower of Approaching Sages (Jinxianlou). After further discussions with his colleagues, Kuang decided as well that the lack of structure on the south of the school made it impossible for students to achieve academic suc-

cess. He also concluded that the area south of the school, Stone Drum Mountain (Shiguling), was flat and barren, so inauspicious for a scholar that it was virtually impossible for someone to attain the imperial colors. So he built Scholar's Peak Pagoda (Wenfengta), a structure of more than ten stories, so high that it reached the clouds. Afterward, when it was rumored that three men from Ruizhou might attain the positions of *taifu, taishi,* and *taibao,* the highest scholarly positions in Ming officialdom, he had the Shi and Jin rivers dredged and linked. This example of how fengshui was thought to change the fate of a village is typical of the Ming period. It was standard to build pagodas and pavilions named for scholarly virtues in order to alter the fate of a city or town. For example, a Scholar's Peak Pagoda also was erected on the wall in front of the prefectural school in Datong, Shanxi.

Although in theory every structure that marked the Chinese landscape was subject to geomantic forces, houses received the most attention from geomancers. And although each sect of fengshui had some specific ideas, the goal of auspicious siting was shared and so were certain most fundamental principles. Before any design or construction took place, almost every geomancer used some kind of compass and assessed every aspect of a site, down to the specific measurements of individual structures, for the maximum production of *qi* (inherent positive energy) or maximum potential for qi. Most important was the location of the main entry gate, the place through which qi could pass out from or into a residential compound. The goal was for a main gate to face a natural source of qi such as a mountain or waterway. Mountain passes could not be too close, however, lest qi escape through them. It was also not desirable for a main gate to face a neighbor's main gate or lane, because then the positive qi might have to be shared with another or might be drawn away by an ill-wisher. If there was no alternative to placing a main gate toward a neighbor's gate or lane, a geomancer would recommend the erection of a stone tablet or talisman opposite his client's entry. Through the inherent powers of that blocking force, auspicious qi might be preserved. It was thought that even the smallest component of a residence such as a toilet or well, when correctly or poorly positioned, could influence a family's fortune for generations.

The one situation where fengshui was always used on the national level was for siting an imperial tomb. But finding an auspicious location for the emperor's tomb was also a matter of rational engineering. Construction of the Ming tombs began by order of the Yongle emperor in 1409, the seventh year of his reign. After a geomancer from Jiangxi

Figure 6.62. Ceremonial archway in Xu village, Anhui province

found a desirable stretch of land in a mountainous area of Changping county, it was personally approved by the emperor and named Tianshou (Heavenly Longevity) Range. A geomancer helped each of the next twelve Ming emperors build his tomb in the same region.

The auspicious topography of the Ming tomb site is formed by mountains that shield it on the east, west, and north and the open land each tomb faces to the south. Several streams wind through the mountains, all converging in the open land and then flowing southeast. Two small mountains guard the six-kilometer spirit path, the one on the east a "dragon mountain" and the one on the west a "tiger mountain." The names refer to two of the four directional animals, the green dragon and the white tiger, which had been associated with planned Chinese space since the Han dynasty. In geomantic terms, Heavenly Longevity Range represents the strong pulse of the dragon, or the emperor himself. The other mountains are the emperors' bodyguards and the open land represents positive, prospective qi. The broad expanse of land, luxuriant grasses and trees that grow on the mountains, and bright sacrificial funerary halls should yield inex-

haustible "vitality." Geomancers concurred that this was a site of heavenly manifested qi.

As mentioned earlier, the towns and villages of Huizhou are hilly. In geomantic terms, these hills yield prospects for auspicious qi: the background mountains are pillows, the winding rivers move qi through them, and the lower hills screen in the qi in front. In villages for which no mountains could provide a pillow, the waterways were considered "pulses of dragons." Or, upon finding defects, as noted in the story of Kuang Pan, geomantic precautions could remedy topography through such measures as digging a pond, building a dam, bridge, or pavilion, or planting trees.

At Hong village in Yi prefecture, Anhui province, during the reign of the Yongle emperor (1403–1424), for example, a geomancer from the neighboring county of Xiuning prescribed that a pond be dug at the end of a stream to ensure the success of future generations in the national examinations. The pond was named Moon Pond (Yuetang). Even today, the beautiful pool is treasured by the local population and used to wash and to quench fires. During the Wanli reign (1573–1620), locals suggested building a dam and another pond to store more water. Their hope was to turn inauspicious luck into auspicious fortune. The enlarged pond was known as South Lake (Nanhu, fig. 6.61).

Indeed, water is as important to a geomancer's design as are mountains. Water is a sign of wealth and the source of energy. All qi depends on transport by water. Thus the ability to seal in water, whether by mountains, water, or a gate, is crucial to successful siting. In the towns and villages of Huizhou, for example, "wind and rain bridges" were often built to help contain qi where it might escape. Such bridges became focal points for town activity. In Xu village, Anhui province, for instance, a pailou (ceremonial archway), pavilion, and garden were built near High Bright Bridge (Gaoyangqiao, fig. 6.62). Tangyue village, too, has a similar bridge and corresponding town structures. In Tangyue, seven small hills named the Seven Star Mounds (Qixingdun) were added along a stream to help seal in the qi.

Although the superstition-laden practices associated with Chinese geomancy were to influence Chinese construction until the end of premodern times, the four centuries of Yuan and Ming rule of China marked the last expression of much that is considered traditional about Chinese architecture. During China's last dynasty, the Qing, so many local architectural styles flowered that at the beginning of the twentieth century it would be hard to find anything but the Forbidden City that clearly linked China with its architectural past.

CHAPTER 7

The Qing Dynasty

SUN DAZHANG

In 1644 the Manchus established China's last dynasty, the Qing. But even as the Manchus rose to political dominance, they welcomed other influences and indeed sought to adopt the sophisticated style of previous Chinese rulers. Han Chinese were appointed to official posts, and the Manchus quickly set about learning the Chinese language and the details of its literary, artistic, and architectural forms.

After some tumultuous early years under Qing rule, the Chinese enjoyed a period of considerable prosperity. During the reigns of the Kangxi and Qianlong emperors, many magnificent imperial palaces, temples, and lamaseries were built that contribute significantly to China's architectural heritage. In addition, the Qing government allowed the practice of all religions and especially supported Lamaism. Under the direction of Qing builders, both the structure and the decorative style of lamaseries developed and inspired new elements in other religious buildings.

Prosperity meant that the Chinese could decorate their architecture more elaborately. Imperial gardens became more numerous and beautiful than ever before, and it became the vogue for wealthier classes to incorporate the art of the imperial garden into their homes. In the buildings themselves, too, many different varieties of decorative materials came to be used.

Full view, figure 7.61 *(opposite)*, and Chengde Lake Center Pavilions *(above)*

Hardwoods, bronze, gold, paper, silk, jade, shells, lacquers, colored glaze, and porcelain — as well as glass, which was imported from abroad in the mid-Qing period — added artistic touches to both public and private structures.

During this time, too, an unprecedented building boom increasingly stretched timber resources to the limit. As a result, traditional wood buildings were increasingly replaced by those built with bricks and stones. Other materials such as bamboo, reed, and lime were also used in some locations. The wide range of building materials not only advanced the technology of building but also greatly changed the appearance of the many structures built during this time.

One significant change occurred in wooden-framed architecture. To make the interior frame more compact and thus stronger, sometimes tendons were used to join the beams and pillars directly, instead of using bracket systems. To substitute for the pillars and beams used in large buildings, smaller poles were bound together by iron bands and wrapped with hemp-fibered plaster to look like whole trunks. This method not only helped save large timbers but also made it easier to construct multi-storied buildings one level at a time.

The look of buildings changed greatly during the Qing dynasty. The styles of the Song and Yuan dynasties faded, and the traditional outlines, characterized by huge protruded eaves, soft roof outlines, large brackets, thick pillars, raised eave columns, and columns with batter, became less prevalent. Structural elegance was no longer considered the main objective in architecture. Instead, the appearance of a group of architectural elements — their variable shapes and the decoration of the minute parts — was stressed. When building single structures, architects were no longer satisfied with square types based on the division of bays, but sought to change the shapes of the eaves, roofs, corridors, doors, and walls so as to give the entire building greater artistic appeal.

Particularly outstanding achievements were made in the decoration of buildings. Decorative painting, minor carpentry, balustrades, the finishing of interior eaves, carving, and molded walls became widespread. In a departure from established Ming patterns, decorative painting was combined with lead powder and gold foils to add magnificence to many buildings. Windows, too, were much more varied than they had been during Ming times; some lattice windows were even carved with overlapping patterns. In areas south of the Yangzi River, where decorating bronze wares with ancient patterns became common and woodcarving was well developed, pieced screens with vivid carvings of birds, flowers, and landscapes became widespread as ornaments for houses. Other interior ornaments included decorated partitions, awnings, and shelves, all of which were used to make spaces that were partially divided. Such widespread decorative art expressed the imaginative powers of China's builders and further developed the traditional conception of aesthetics in China.

Qing Forbidden Cities and Royal Tombs

The emperor's city had been one of China's most profound symbols since earliest imperial times, and the founders of the Manchu government, who sought to rule as Chinese emperors, had no reason to change existing palace structures. Wu Sangui (1612–1678), a Chinese military leader working for the Manchus, entered the walls of the former Ming imperial city on June 6, 1644, just six weeks after the last Ming emperor had committed suicide there. (Li Zicheng [1606?–1645], leader of a rebellion against the Ming, had briefly controlled the capital in the aftermath of the suicide but soon fled, burning as much of the city as he could en route.) The Manchus had been poised for this moment for several decades, having ruled from Shenyang, Liaoning province, since about 1624, and several other nearby towns since 1616. By October 1644 the Manchu headquarters had been relocated to Beijing, and the Shunzhi emperor (r. 1644–1662), the first ruler of the Qing dynasty, had taken power.

The outline of Beijing under Manchu rule was much the same as it had been in Ming times, but the new government transformed the oldest part of the city and further developed the suburbs. The most important change in the old Ming city was the replacement of much of *huangcheng* (the imperial and administrative sectors) with additional dwelling space. This included the destruction of the northern part of the administrative city that had contained the twenty-four *yamen,* the local government offices in charge of internal affairs. A sector of intersecting lanes and alleys known as *hutong,* a residential system that became a trademark of Qing Beijing, was installed in their place. The so-called *nannei,* an area of imperial offices in the southeastern part of the Ming imperial city, was torn down, too, to be replaced by a Lamaist temple called Tangzi. The area in the western part of the imperial city known as Xishiku (Western Miscellany) was remade as a residential quarter, as was the Supreme Military Office of the Ming government, west of Tiananmen Square. Granaries in the eastern part of the Ming city were made into

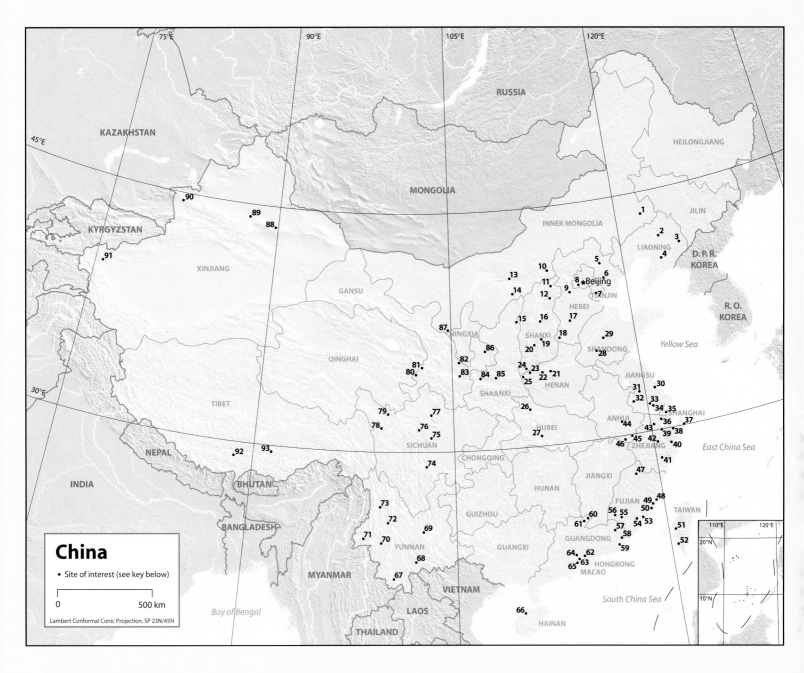

Map 7.
Qing Sites

Aba 79	Hezhou 81	Luoyang 22	Shantou 59	Wuxi 33
Baoji 84	Honghe 68	Maowen 77	Shaoxing 39	Xiahe 80
Baotou 13	Hui'an 48	Meizhou/Meixian 57	Shenyang 2	Xigaze 92
Beijing 8	Huizhou 45	Nanjing 32	Shexian 18	Xinbin 3
Chaozhou 58	Hunyuan 11	Nanjing (Fujian) 54	Shixing 61	Xishuangbanna 67
Chengde 5	Ikezhaomeng 14	Nanxiong 60	Shunde 65	Yangzhou 31
Chengdu 75	Jia 15	Ningbo 38	Songjiang 35	Yili 90
Dali 72	Jianchuan 73	Panyu 63	Suzhou 34	Yixian 9
Dehong 71	Jiangling 27	Pinglu 24	Taigu 19	Yongding 55
Dongguan 62	Jiaxing 36	Pingyao 20	Taihecheng 70	Zhangzhou 53
Dongyang 42	Jinghong 67	Putian 47	Tainan 51	Zhelimumeng 1
Emeishan 74	Jining 10	Putuoshan 37	Taishan 29	Zhenjiang 30
Fengping/Luxi 71	Jining 28	Qianxian 85	Taiyuan 16	Zhenning/Anshun/
Foshan 64	Jinjiang 50	Qingtian 41	Tianjin 7	Liupanshui 82
Ganzi 78	Jiuhuashan 44	Qingyang 86	Tianshui 83	Zhongwei 87
Gaoxiong 52	Kashgar 91	Qiyunshan 46	Tiantai 40	Zunhua 6
Gongxian 21	Kunming 69	Quanzhou 49	Turpan 88	
Guanxian 76	Lhasa 93	Quyang 17	Urumqi 89	
Hainan 66	Liaoyang 4	Sanmenxia 23	Wudangshan 26	
Hangzhou 43	Lingbao 25	Shanghang 56	Wutaishan 12	

Figure 7.1. Detail of a
painting of Qianmen,
Beijing, showing commercial
activity, by Xu Yang, 1776

housing, and new grain storage was constructed in the
Tongzhou and Zhangjiawan areas.

The Manchu princes chose not to live in the old Ten
Princes' Residence of the Ming located in the Wangfujing
district; it subsequently became the Xianliang Monastery.
Instead, Taiji Mill became the home of Prince Yu, and
Taiping Granary and Cao Granary, both in the western
part of the city, became the residences of Prince Zhuang
and Princes Guo and Shenjun, respectively. The imperial
princes Yong, Jian, He, and Kang used other former Ming
buildings as their new homes. Indeed, by the time of the
Qianlong emperor (r. 1736–1796), there were more than
forty princely residences inside the capital. At the same
time, the old inner city (the residential area of the northern
part of Beijing beyond the Forbidden City and administrative sectors) turned into an area only for Manchu residents,
either officers of the Qing government or men of the
Eight Manchu Banners and their families. The non-
Manchu peoples, such as the Han Chinese or ethnic
groups such as the Hui, were moved to homes in the outer
city (the southern walled area). The result was an immediate development of this outer area, which had been walled

in the mid sixteenth century. The commercial centers of
the inner city were now Dongdan, Xisi, and the main street
in front of the drum tower; in the outer city, the new commercial districts were near Qianmen, Caishikou, and
Huashi, the flower market (fig. 7.1).

New temples and monasteries were built in both the inner and outer cities. Theaters, teahouses, shops of all kinds,
guild halls, academies of classical learning, and public buildings also appeared throughout the Manchu capital. Finally,
although the Altar of Heaven complex remained where it
had stood in Ming times, its ceremonies were altered.

The other major change initiated by the Qing occurred
outside the walls of the former Ming city. Residential
estates and neighborhoods developed not only beyond
the city gates but also far beyond the western and southern walls. The Southern Garden and Tuanhe Detached
Palace were built on the foundation of Feifang Lake of
the Yuan dynasty in the southern suburbs, to give the emperor a place to practice military skills, hunt, and review
his troops. Imperial garden construction in the western
suburbs began during the Kangxi reign period, first with
Changchunyuan, followed by Qingyiyuan, Jingmingyuan,

Figure 7.2. View of the Forbidden City in Beijing

Figure 7.3. Hall of Supreme Harmony (Taihedian, or Fengtian Hall), Forbidden City, Beijing, after seventeenth-century rebuilding

Jingyiyuan, and Yuanmingyuan during the Qianlong reign. The emperors spent increasing amounts of time in these gardens, and always brought large entourages of officials and guards, so that these scenic areas came to be political centers outside of the city walls.

Changes at the Forbidden City

In the aftermath of destruction wrought by military leader Li Zicheng, the first emperor of the Qing dynasty (Shunzhi) repaired, restored, and rebuilt the Forbidden City according to the layout of the Ming dynasty. The Three Great Halls, Three Back Halls, Six Eastern and Western Palaces, and five main gates along the north–south axial line remained, so that the Forbidden Cities of Ming and Qing Beijing were nearly the same (fig. 7.2). Many halls and gates were renamed by the Manchu dynasty, however: from south to north the main gates were now called Zhengyang (or Qianmen, "front gate"), Da Qing, Tianan, Duan, and Wu. (Their Ming names had been Zhengyang, Da Ming, Chengtian, Duan, and Wu, respectively.) The ancestral temples, twin altars of soil and grain, Back Imperial Garden, Cining palace complex,

Wenhua Hall, and Wuying Hall all remained as well (and kept their previous names). Changes in buildings or layout were architecturally slight but functionally significant. The covered arcades on either side of the Hall of Supreme Harmony (fig. 7.3) became walls with flues for heating, the position of the Hall of the Preservation of Harmony was slightly altered, the interior of the Kunning Palace (which had formerly been the residence of the empress) was given an altar for Manchu sacrifices to the spirits, and Qianqing Palace became the place where the emperor summoned ministers and conducted court affairs, business that had been conducted in Yangxin Hall

during Ming times. Under the Qing, a throne was placed in the central bay of five-bayed Yangxin Hall and the building was equipped with everything the emperor needed to perform court formalities. Left and right of the throne bay, the east and west side rooms were heated. In the eastern wing the emperor slept and summoned court officials, and the western wing was reserved for the emperor's confidential affairs.

During the reign of the Qianlong emperor, the five rooms in which imperial princes had resided on the western side of Qianxi Palace were turned into Chonghua palace complex and the West Garden. On the western

Figure 7.4. Corner watchtower in the Forbidden City

side of Cining palace complex, the Shoukang palace complex was added as a place where the imperial concubines could spend the last years of their lives. In 1775, the fortieth year of the Qianlong reign, Wenyuan Pavilion was built to the north of Wenhua Hall to house a set of the greatest bibliographic compilations of the Qing court, the forty-four fascicle *Siku quanshu* (Complete writings in the four imperial treasuries).

The most significant change inside the Forbidden City was the construction of Ningshougong, a palace complex that occupied 4.74 hectares on the Outer East Road where Renshougong, Huailuangong, and Xiefenggong had stood in the Ming dynasty. Construction of Ningshougong began in 1698, the thirty-seventh year of the Kangxi reign. The palace complex was expanded in 1772 during the Qianlong reign, and when the Qianlong emperor reached his sixtieth year of rule and stepped down as emperor in 1796 (out of respect for his grandfather Kangxi, who had reigned sixty years), he retired there. The arrangement of inner and outer courts and side palaces at Ningshougong was modeled after the Three Great Halls, Three Back Halls, and Eastern and Western Palaces of the Forbidden City. In this case the halls that flanked the line of main buildings on the east were an opera pavilion, an imperial study, and a multistory structure for religious ceremonies; on the west were four building groups of kiosks, towers, pavilions, and halls of the Qianlong Garden (fig. 7.4).

By maintaining the axial building line and continuing to place structures symmetrically in relation to this line, the Qing Forbidden City maintained the image of imperial power suggested by that axis since China's earliest times. Yet it was still to add halls and building groups, and concealed within the multiple walls, gates, and building axes, individual architectural complexes such as Ningshougong and Yangxingong became more autonomous and better suited to private living (figs. 7.5 and 7.6).

The Forbidden City in Shenyang

Shenyang, also known as Fengtian, was the site of the Manchus' first capital, the one established by Manchu rulers before the founding of the Qing dynasty and its capital in Beijing. The capital had its origins in smaller outposts of Manchu governance that had been established starting in 1616 by Nurhaci, the man who would come to be known as the dynastic founder Taizu. Finally in 1625 Shengjing (today Shenyang) was established as the capital by Nurhaci for his dynasty, which named itself Latter Jin, a reference to the non-Chinese dynasty of 1115–1234, which had emerged from the same part of northeast Asia (fig. 7.7). Shenyang would remain the capital through the reign of Nurhaci's successor, Huang Taiji (r. 1626–1643).

The imperial city of Shenyang occupied an area of sixty square kilometers and was divided into three parts. The central part, the palace city, had four main structures along its central axis: Great Qing Gate, the Hall of State Affairs, Phoenix Tower, and Pure Tranquillity Palace (Qingninggong). The last structure was the residence of the emperor and empress. Manchu rites were conducted in the western part of Qingninggong. Along the southern, western, and northern walls of the imperial city were arranged swastika-shaped *kang* (heated platforms used as beds) that had been used to warm floors for ceremonies in northeast Asia since the time of the Jin, Bohai, and Koguryo kingdoms of Korea. In addition, a *sulun* (sacred pole) was erected in the southeastern corner. Thus even though the axial arrangement of buildings in the central section of the Shenyang palace city suggested Chinese architectural precedents, the insides of these halls, especially the fourth one, were equipped to reflect the native heritage of the builders.

East of the palace city was the octagonal Great Hall of Administration where the Grand Rites of the Manchu court were conducted. To its south was a 140-meter-long open area, on either side of which were five halls (known as the Ten Princely Pavilions). The four pairs closest to Dazheng Hall were offices of the ministers of the Eight Banners under which the Manchu tribesmen were divided, and the two halls farthest south were for Princes of the Right and Left. The trapezoidal shape of the space between the administrative hall and the pair of structures farthest from it made it seem more expansive than it actually was (fig. 7.8).

The western precinct of the Manchu imperial city was built later than the other two. A multistory structure linked to several other courtyards of buildings, it corresponded to Wenyuan Pavilion of the Forbidden City and housed another copy of the literary compilation *Siku quanshu*.

Shengjing was not as grand or expansive as the Forbidden City of Beijing in Qing or Ming times. Instead it should be viewed as the initial Manchu attempt at imperial architecture that retained elements of the Manchus' native past — elements that were abandoned by 1644, when they moved south to Beijing. Shengjing had an axial line of main halls, but it was not nearly as long or complex as the one in Beijing. The layout of Shengjing's eastern sector, however, reflected military barracks more than anything built by

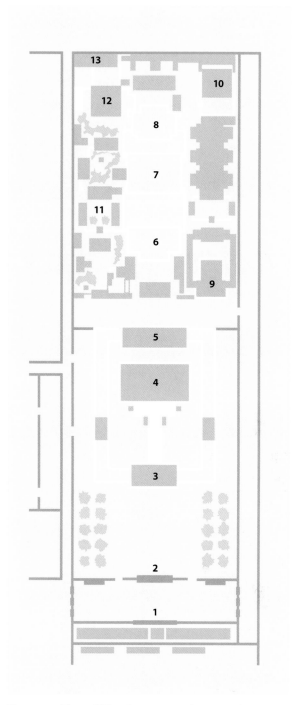

Figure 7.5. Plan of Ningshougong, palace complex in the Forbidden City, during the reign of the Qianlong emperor

1. Nine Dragon Wall
2. Imperial Norm Gate
3. Tranquillity and Longevity Gate
4. Imperial Norm Hall
5. Tranquillity and Longevity Palace
6. Nurturing Nature Hall
7. Bliss and Longevity Hall
8. Nurturing Harmony Pavilion
9. Pleasure Music Pavilion
10. Great Bliss Palace
11. Tranquillity and Longevity Palace Garden
12. Auspicious View Pavilion
13. Weary of Laborious Duties Studio

Figure 7.6. Interior of
Dongnuan Pavilion,
Yangxingong

Figure 7.7. Shengjing, imperial capital of the predynastic Manchus, today in Shenyang, Liaoning province

Figure 7.8. Great Hall of Administration, Offices of Eight Banners, and Halls of Princes of Right and Left, Shenyang, 1625–1643

Chinese emperors in the past. The heated platforms inside Pure Tranquillity Palace along with the hall's golden ceramic tile roof reflect a similar combination of Manchu and imperial Chinese taste.

The Manchus were far from the only non-Chinese ethnic group whose presence was proclaimed in architecture of the empire, even in its capitals. Elements of Mongolian and Tibetan architecture also were found in Shengjing's imperial city. They included square pillars that supported the "sparrow-beak" braces, beam ends in the shape of dragon heads, Sanskrit on ceiling lattices, animal-faced decoration carved into pillar tops, and Tibetan designs such as the "golden net" carved as eave decoration on Chongzheng and Dazheng halls. In addition, the roofs of palace buildings had gold or green border patterns, the tops of stairs leading to halls and the bases of walls were made entirely of glazed brick, and flying blue dragons decorated glazed brick on purlins and eave-end boards.

Qing Imperial Tombs

The mausoleums of Manchu rulers are located at six sites, four of which were constructed before the founding of the Qing dynasty. Known as the "outer tombs" and all located in Liaoning province, the early group is composed of Dongjingling (the eastern capital mausoleum) in Liaoyang, Yongling in Xinbin, and Fuling and Zhaoling in Shenyang. The Eastern and Western Qing Tombs of northern Hebei, located in Malan Valley, Zunhua, and at the foot of Mount Yongning in Yi county, respectively, were constructed after 1644.

Dongjingling was a tomb site for Nurhaci's uncles, sons, and nephews. Yongling was his ancestral mausoleum, the resting place of his father, grandfather, and great-grandfather. Neither of these sites had a spirit path or a stela pavilion enclosed by a wall. Yongling consisted of an entry gate called Da Hongmen (Great Red Gate) and four equal-sized memorial towers *(minglou)* on square bases in a side-by-side row. Nurhaci himself and his wife were buried at Fuling, also known as Dongjingling because it is east of their capital. Beiling, or Zhaoling, north of the capital, was the burial site of Huang Taiji and his empress. Similar and in some respects almost identical, Fuling and Zhaoling had a pair of stone lions at the front gates, ceremonial columns *(huabiao),* and stone memorial archways *(pailou)* all in front of the Da Hongmen; behind it was a spirit path consisting of pairs of lions, horses, camels, and tigers followed by a stela pavilion and fortress-like wall surrounding the back region. The southern entry to the wall is called Long'en (Flourishing Favor) Gate, and at the north stands a memorial tower with a double-eave hip-gable roof (fig. 7.9). It also has corner towers with double-eave hip-gable roofs. Although not huge (not even large compared with tombs of the imperial Ming), like the palaces in Shenyang, the wall, towers, and symmetry suggest an imposing grandeur befitting a much larger building complex (fig. 7.10).

The five emperors Shunzhi, Kangxi, Qianlong, Xianfeng, and Tongzhi, as well as their empresses and concubines, are buried at the Eastern Qing Tombs ([Qing] Dongling), east of Beijing in Zunhua, Hebei province. Shielded by the Changrui Mountains of the Yanshan (mountain range) from the north, and with water of the Sida and Laishui rivers running through it, all of which contributed to positive geomancy for the site, Dongling was also a place of exquisite scenery.

The principal tomb of Dongling, Xiaoling, belongs to the Shunzhi emperor. The mausoleum is at the terminus

Figure 7.9. Stone archway and main access to Zhaoling, tomb site of the Manchu ruler Huang Taiji, in Shenyang

Figure 7.10. Hall facing the "square city" (fangcheng) in front of it, at Fuling, where the Manchu ruler Nurhaci was buried in 1626, Shenyang

Figure 7.11. Spirit path at the approach to the Eastern Qing
Tombs, Zunhua county, Hebei province

of an approach nearly ten kilometers long that originates roughly from the southeast and consists of a stone archway, Great Red Gate, Stela Pavilion with a tablet that eulogized the meritorious and supernatural achievements of the Shunzhi emperor, eighteen pairs of stone men and animals along a spirit path, Gate of the Dragon and Phoenix, Spirit Path Bridge, another stela pavilion, Gate of Flourishing Favor, Hall of Flourishing Favor, three more gates, two Lingxing Gates, five stone altars, a memorial tower enclosed by a square wall, and, last, an underground palace, or burial chambers (fig. 7.11).

The Yongzheng, Jiaqing, Daoguang, and Guangxu emperors, as well as their empresses and concubines, were laid to rest at the Western Qing Tombs ([Qing] Xiling) in Yixian (Yi county), Hebei province, on the western side of Beijing. As at the Eastern Tombs, the focus was the tomb of the first emperor buried there, in this case Yongzheng. About one-third the size of the Eastern Tombs, however (about 800 as opposed to about 2,500 square kilometers), the Western Tombs are scattered along the southern slope of Mount Yongning, whose topography was not as choice as that in Zunhua. In spite

of their smaller size, the Western Tombs do not form a coherent group like the eastern ones. The stone archways in front of Da Hongmen, the entry gate, are unique features. Three five-entry archways stand at the east, west, and south of a square at the entrance to the tomb. Each archway has eleven roofs supported by bracket sets, one above each of the six columns and a longer one over each of five arches (fig. 7.12).

To a certain extent the layouts of the imperial Qing tombs on both sides of Beijing were passed down from Ming imperial funerary architecture and rituals. Each has a single spirit path and memorial tower enclosed by a four-sided wall (fig. 7.13). Along the spirit paths are four of each animal, two standing and two kneeling. Mountains form a kind of screen wall behind and on either side, offering a natural "mouth of the dragon," and water runs through the Ming and Qing tomb sites near Beijing. In spite of topography, each individual tomb faces roughly south. The approach to the principal burial site and the individual structures of each tomb are roughly, but not perfectly, axial in arrangement. The four majestically carved pillars that stand at the corners of the Qing

Figure 7.12. Archway at the entrance to the Western Qing Tombs, Yi county, Hebei province

Figure 7.13. Eastern Qing Tombs; the emperor's memorial tower is the large rectangular building at right

stela pavilions, which emphasize their grandeur and thereby the heroic deeds of the emperors eulogized on the stelae, also surround the stelae pavilion at the Ming tombs.

One change between the Ming and Qing tombs occurred in the individual burials of emperors, empresses, and concubines. This shift from group burial cannot be attributed to Manchu custom. Throughout history dynasties chose joint or separate burial, and some dynasties constructed imperial tombs of both types. Another change, the development of more elaborate aboveground funerary architecture, may have been the result of either a willingness and ability to spend more on tomb construction, or perhaps a desire to focus more attention on a postmortem imperial presence aboveground. At the Eastern and Western Qing Tombs, aboveground buildings are more numerous and often more decorated than their Ming counterparts. The Dragon and Phoenix Gate is an example of the additional elaboration (fig. 7.14). Besides the gate, the Qing tombs had more archways, both stone and wooden, more bridges, and long lines along which buildings were constructed. The line of buildings was so long that stops for resting were created for those

paying homage at the tomb. In contrast to Ming tombs, the underground chambers were fewer, dug less deeply into the ground, and generally restricted to a single row of rooms, as opposed to the several rows of main and subsidiary chambers. But the Qing underground chambers that did exist were, like the architecture aboveground, more elaborately decorated than their Ming counterparts. The underground palace of the Qianlong emperor, for instance, occupied only 372 square meters,

Figure 7.14. Dragon and Phoenix Gate at the Eastern Qing Tombs

Figure 7.15. Interior of the tomb of the Qianlong emperor (d. 1799), Eastern Qing Tombs

but every centimeter of it was faced with light green marble (fig. 7.15). Further, every wall, ceiling, door panel, and window had carvings of Buddhist imagery or of passages from sutras. So extensive was this carving that it has been estimated it took more than fifty thousand work days to complete. The latest Qing tomb, that of Empress Dowager Cixi, is more extravagant still. Made of decorated fragrant woods ormosia and phoebe, every centimeter of the brick wall between the wood was also carved. Gold leaf was then pasted on the brick to give the effect of unbridled extravagance (fig. 7.16).

Garden Design

Under Qing rule, imperial garden design in China reached unprecedented heights. The gardens created and improved through court sponsorship during this period, especially in Beijing, were so extraordinary that we think of them as extensions of the Forbidden City and its architecture — more like detached palaces or residences outside the Forbidden City designed for imperial delight than parklike settings for the appreciation of nature.

The evolution of the imperial garden system in Qing times can be viewed as a three-stage process. It began

Figure 7.16. Interior of the tomb of Empress Dowager Cixi (d. 1908), Eastern Qing Tombs

with the revival of older gardens in the first Qing reign periods. The second stage, the great age of garden building, occurred under the Qianlong and the Jiajing emperors from 1736 to 1820. And the last phase, one of comparative decline, began with the Daoguang reign (1821–1850). The phases were directly linked to the economy. Wealth was accumulated during the first three Qing reigns, Shunzhi, Kangxi, and Yongzheng, and spent during the long, prosperous, and relatively stable Qianlong and Jiaqing reigns. After the 1820s, when the nation began to collapse economically, significantly less attention was paid to such details as imperial gardens.

Initially, imperial attention to gardens in Qing China was focused on the repair of the Nanyuan (south gardens) and Xiyuan (west gardens) areas of the capital. The next priority was construction of two gardens in Beijing, Changchunyuan and Yuanmingyuan, and a summer resort "for avoiding the heat" (Bishushanzhuang) in Chengde, northeast of the capital in Rehe (Jehol), today in Hebei province. The architecture of all these gardens was simple and plain; their structures had gray tile roofs and walls made of rubble, and they were undecorated, even unpainted.

The prosperity of the Qianlong-Jiajing period was reflected in continued construction in the area known as Xiyuan, as well as garden building in the western sub-

urbs of Beijing and at the summer palaces at Chengde. Forty-eight scenic spots were added to Yuanmingyuan. Changchunyuan and Yichunyuan were built anew, with Baroque-style buildings for the northwestern area of Changchun Garden designed by Jesuit priests living in Beijing. The waterways in Beijing's western suburbs were redirected as part of the garden-construction program, giving way to Qingyiyuan, the huge detached palace that was the predecessor to Beijing's most famous imperial garden, Yiheyuan. And Jingmingyuan in the Yuquan Hills, along with Jingyiyuan in the Fragrant Hills, were expanded to form the palace-garden section west of Beijing known as Three Hills and Five Gardens (fig. 7.17).

The summer mountain resort in Chengde was also further enlarged during the Qianlong reign. Thirty-six scenic spots and the surrounding temples were added. Although designated a resort, Chengde functioned as the political center outside of the capital.

At the same time, private garden construction was on the rise. Private gardens were built primarily in three regions of China during the Qing period: the capital, Jiangnan (southeastern China south of the Yangzi River), and the Pearl River delta. The most famous private garden of the mid-Qing period was Lean West Lake Garden in Yangzhou.

With the waning of imperial authority and economic

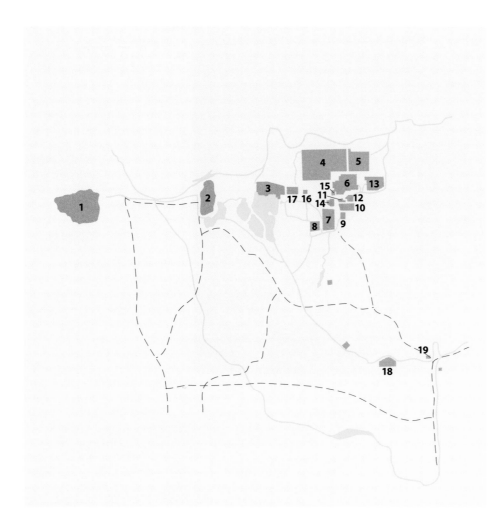

Figure 7.17. Plan of Qing gardens in Beijing. *Source:* Liu Junwen, *Beijing: China's Ancient and Modern Capital* (Beijing: Foreign Languages Press, 1982)

1. Calm and Delightful Garden at the Fragrant Hill
2. Tranquil and Bright Park at Jade Fountain Hill
3. Clear Ripples Park at Longevity Hall
4. The Round and Brilliant Garden
5. Eternal Spring Park
6. Gorgeous Spring Park
7. Joyous Spring Park
8. Western Flower Garden
9. Magnificent Elegance Park
10. Lovely Spring Park
11. Calling Crane Park
12. Bright and Moist Park
13. Congenial Spring Park
14. Luxuriant Beauty Park
15. Hanlin Literary Grove Park
16. Park of One *Mu*
17. Self-Contentment Park
18. Benevolent Goodness Park
19. Leaning on the Rainbow Park

decline during the Daoguang reign, there were no longer resources for large-scale garden construction. The only project carried out under the Guangxu emperor was renovation at Qingyiyuan, by that time known as Yiheyuan. Coincident with the scaling down of construction was a change from gardens designed for the purpose of creating a scenic view to more practically designed gardens suited to meet basic artistic needs. Thus although many gardens were constructed in China during the nineteenth century, few were noteworthy.

One garden area of particular note encompassed the Xiyuan part of Beijing, which is often referred to as the Lake District, Three Lakes, or Beihai (fig. 7.18). This last name, "north lake," describes the presence in Xiyuan of one of three lakes (north, middle, and south) into which waterways were pooled in the Ming dynasty. Previously, in the Yuan dynasty, the area had included Qionghua Island, an artificial ritual-pleasure island with Guanghan Hall at the center of Khubilai Khan's two-part palace city. The Yuan had themselves reused and made additions to the island on which the Jin had built an artificial hill and pleasure palace, and the Jin

had built on a water source used by the Liao. Beihai, in other words, has been the focal point of waterways through a millennium of history at Beijing. The Ming name Xiyuan meant, simply, a garden west of the palace city.

When the Qing came to build at Beihai, they inherited from the Ming three islets (again, north, middle, and south). Avid garden builders, the Qing added many new scenic views to the west garden area. Most important, however, was the erection of a white pagoda of lamaist style, a dagoba, on the former site of Guanghan Hall. It became not only the focal point of this garden complex but also a beacon whose Lamaist form symbolized both Manchu appropriation of Beijing and, because it rose higher than the White Pagoda of Miaoying Monastery, a new standard to surpass that of the last non-Chinese dynasty to rule Beijing, the Mongols. The White Pagoda of Beihai also established an axis on the Qing island for construction of Yong'an Monastery to the south and Yi-lan Hall and Daoning Studio behind it (fig. 7.19).

Construction continued at this exquisite beauty spot under the Qianlong emperor, always with the awareness that any structures would add to a view that already included the White Pagoda. The Qianlong emperor added some small gardens and Buddhist architecture in the vicinity of Beihai, including Haobu Torrent, Painted Boat Studio, Mirror of Purity Studio, Xitianfanjing, Kaixue Hall, Chanfu Monastery, and Xiaoxitian. Thus was a natural, open garden of the Ming transformed into a garden focused on structures, landscape, and views created by the merging of these artificial and natural elements. Particularly noteworthy Qing building groups were centered around Qinzheng Hall, Fengze Garden, and Ying Platform. A famous garden designer named Zhang Ran was brought north from the Jiangnan region to oversee the construction of artificial hills.

Three Hills and Five Gardens became a popular nickname for the imperial pleasure palaces and their scenery west of Beijing after the massive building projects of the Kangxi and Qianlong emperors. Specifically, these hills and gardens were Jinyi Garden on Fragrance Hill, Jingming Garden on Jade Spring Hill, Qingyi Garden on Longevity Hill, Yuanming Garden, and Changchun Garden. The western side of the capital had been famous for its natural scenery since the Liao dynasty. It was considered so picturesque that it has been compared to China's greatest natural beauty spots south of the Yangzi River.

Emperors created gardens to be both beautiful and functional: they helped to increase the water supply for the capital and to prevent floods. Under the Qianlong

Figure 7.18. Plan of Beihai, the north lake in the Lake District of Beijing. *Source:* Liu Junwen, *Beijing: China's Ancient and Modern Capital* (Beijing: Foreign Languages Press, 1982)

 1. Hall of Received Light
 2. Everlasting Peace Monastery
 3. White Dagoba
 4. Celebrating the Evening Tower
 5. Beautiful Jade Luster Hall
 6. Reading Classics Tower
 7. Hall of Ripples
 8. Pearls of Wisdom Hall
 9. Entering the Mountain Gate
10. Hao and Pu brooks
11. Boat dock
12. Studio of Painted Pleasure Boat
13. Altar to the Goddess of Silkworms
14. Mirrorlike Clarity Studio
15. Western Buddhist Paradise
16. Nine-Dragon Wall
17. Hall for Gazing at the Water
18. Temple of Revealing Happiness
19. Pavilion of Ten Thousand Buddhas
20. The World of Ultimate Bliss — Afterlife World
21. Five-Dragon Pavilion

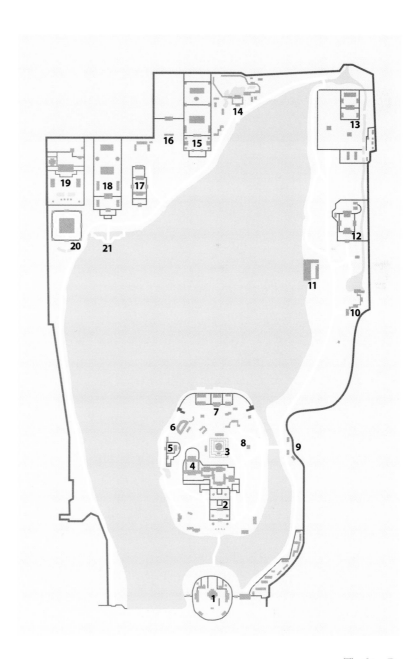

Figure 7.19. The White Pagoda of Beihai, built in 1651, Beijing.
Construction at the lake continued through the Qianlong reign
(1736–1796).

emperor, the waterways of the Western Hills had been
dredged extensively. The water level of Yu River was increased, reservoirs and water gates were built, the Yu and
the Chang rivers were linked, West Lake (later known as
Kunming Lake) was enlarged, and the stream that ran
through Yuanming Garden was joined to other bodies of
water. All this attention to water laid a good foundation
for any future garden construction projects west of the
capital, so that once water flowed adequately in and
around this part of the city, Jinyi, Yuanming, Jingming,
Changchun, and Qingyi gardens — and Yichun, an
appendage of Changchunyuan — were either built anew
or expanded between 1738 and 1775. Through the flow
of water, not only were the five gardens and three hills
considered a unit, but also farmland and cottages in
nearby villages were integrated into the landscape. During this period, more than twenty gardens were bestowed
on royal families and ministers by the emperor. Because
the topography varied, each garden was a unique architectural entity. Some were largely artificial, others mostly

natural. As a group, every aspect of the best of traditional
Chinese garden design was represented.

Changchun Garden, built in 1684 on sixty hectares of
land from the abandoned site of Qinghua Garden, is an
area of particular beauty and importance. It was formerly
the villa of a wealthy relative of the Ming royal household
named Li Wei. Dikes and hills divide the garden into
front and back lake areas. West Lake, the center of the
garden, includes the scenic structures Ruijin Kiosk, Lin-
xiangshan Cottage, and Yanshuang Tower. Lilacs are
planted on a long embankment on the east side of the
lake, and peach trees and orchids grow on the west.
Lotus flowers grew in the lake itself. In Qing times,
Changchunyuan was a veritable botanical garden.

Yuanming is another noted garden, given to the Yongzheng emperor when he was still a prince. When he
ascended the throne, he expanded it into a detached
palace. In 1737, his successor, the Qianlong emperor,
enlarged it again. Subsequently, Changchunyuan and
Yichunyuan were appended to it and together the three

were known as the Three Yuanming Gardens (fig. 7.20). Located north of Haidian in the western suburbs of the capital, Yuanming Garden is covered with greenery and rich in foliage. It occupies more than 350 hectares, contains 123 building complexes, and is often referred to as the "garden among a myriad of gardens." From the Yongzheng through the Xianfeng reigns, Qing emperors spent much of their time here, holding audience and conducting other affairs of the court. For this purpose, administrative offices and offices for government ministers and military advisers were built there as well. All of this ended in 1860 when, while the imperial family was at the summer resort in Chengde, much of Yuanmingyuan was looted and destroyed by British and French troops attacking Beijing.

Yuanming Garden is relatively flat and one of its major attractions is water. Front and back lakes form the central part of the garden, which features the palace area and nine islands along the shores of the lakes. Each island has its own scenic spots (figs. 7.21 and 7.22). The largest is named the Nine Continents of Pure Entertainment, in reference to the belief that everything under heaven belongs to the emperor. East, west, and north of the back lake are outer scenic spots, some of them small gardens, so that the formation of this back area of Yuanmingyuan might be compared to stars that shine around the moon.

The outer scenic spots included Anyou Palace, where the Qing emperors offered sacrifices to their ancestors; a fortresslike Buddhist monastery named Sheweicheng; an area with streets built to imitate the hustle and bustle of a commercial district; Wenyuange, which housed a library; Tongle Park for dramatic performances; Wulingchunse, built in imitation of the Peach Blossom Spring; Windy Lotuses of Quyuan, created to be reminiscent of West Lake in Hangzhou; Zuoshilinliu, modeled after the Orchid Pavilion in Shaoxing; and West Peak of Exquisite Color, built to imitate Mount Lu. The three main scenic areas used Happiness Lake (Fuhai) in the east as their central focus. Inside this body of water were three islets, arranged like the three legs of a tripod in an allusion to the Three Isles of the Immortals in the Eastern Sea. Twenty scenic spots, all with water as a theme, were arranged around the lake. Finally, water villages were located on a long narrow strip beyond the north wall of Yuanmingyuan, creating yet another effect, rusticity.

Changchunyuan, which joined Yuanmingyuan, was itself divided into northern and southern scenic areas. Chunhua Kiosk was the central structure of the southern area. It had ten scenic spots on its island and surrounding lake, each arranged according to topography. They included Ru Park, Jian Park, Lion Forest (Shizilin),

Haiyuekaijin, and Hall of Exquisitely Carved Jade. The northern area was a long horizontal strip on which stood the six Baroque-style palaces. Construction began in 1745, following the presentation of drawings by Giuseppe Castiglione, Michel Benoît, and Jean Denis Attiret, all Jesuits at the Qianlong court. Known as the Western-style Multistory Halls, they were named Xieqiquan, Xushuilou, Yangqiaolong, Fangwaiguan, Hai'antang, and Yuanyingguan. The columns, eave corners, doors, and windows of these buildings were European in style, as were their general appearances, but the carving and other details were Chinese. Water in front of these halls was provided by fountains rather than natural waterways. Although this is considered the first completely European building project in China, it also should be thought of as a Sino-European attempt at garden architecture.

The garden Yichunyuan joins the other side of Yuanmingyuan. It was created by combining and expanding private gardens that together had about thirty scenic views. Following no set rules for its layout, the scenic spots are integrated by streams that crisscross through them, forming a small and delicate, but unified, network.

Like most Chinese gardens, Yuanmingyuan harmonized the use of land and water. But rather than striving to accomplish a preconceived plan for the whole, construction of Yichun Garden unfolded piece by piece and section by section. As a result, the three-garden complex with Yuanmingyuan at its heart can be thought of as a pastiche of artificially interconnected land, water, views, and scenic spots — in other words, nearly one hundred elements of mountains, layers of land, and structures interspersed, each subunit itself a miniature garden. This principle applied to the buildings as well. At Yuanmingyuan, systems of traditional groupings of buildings and individual units were broken down to accommodate new design ideas. Styles of residential architecture from all over China were used, depending on what was aesthetically pleasing, what worked best with other design elements, and what blended in with the natural environment. Whatever was necessary to make the most effective garden was undertaken — even removing trees and plants from south China, where they could bloom for four seasons, and acclimatizing them to Beijing winters. If a new building or layout promised to enhance a specific view or the overall effect, it was attempted.

The Jingyi Garden, situated at the eastern end of the Western Hills, is another magnificent garden of the era. Begun at the foot of a hill and continued up its slope, it consisted of three parts: an inner garden, an outer garden, and detached precincts. The inner garden was located in

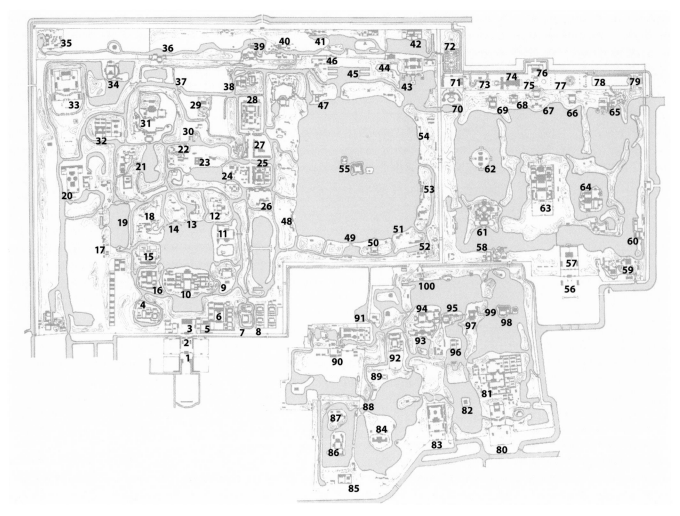

Figure 7.20. Plan of the Three Yuanming Gardens, Beijing

Sights of Yuanmingyuan — Perfection
and Brightness Garden

1. Main Palace Gate
2. Gate Where the Worthy and Good Go In
   and Out
3. Just and Honorable
4. Eternal Spring Fairy Lodge
5. Being Diligent in Administering State
   Affairs and Keeping
   Near the Worthy
6. Preserving Harmony and Supreme
   Harmony
7. Previously Bestowed Heavenly Blessings
8. In the Depths of a Cave
9. Carving the Moon, Unfolding the Clouds
10. Peace for All-China
11. Natural scenery
12. Bidong (Azure Grotto) Academy
13. Cloud of Compassion Protects All
14. Oneness of Sky and Water
15. Be Frank and Open
16. Enfolding Both the Past and Present

17. High Mountain and Long River
18. Wine Shop in an Apricot Flower Village
19. Universal Peace
20. Living in Clouds Under the Moon
21. The Spring Beauty of Wuling
22. Orchid Fragrance over the Water
23. Simple Life and Peaceful Surroundings
24. Sitting On Rocks and Looking Down
    over the Winding Stream
25. Sharing Pleasure Park
26. Winery and Lotus Pool
27. Business street
28. Shewei City
29. Literary Origin Pavilion
30. Clear Water and Rustling Trees
31. Zhou Lianxi's Wonderful Place for Study
32. A Jade Temple Under Bright Sky
33. Great Kindness and Eternal Blessing
34. An Academy for Great Talents
35. Purple and Green Cottage
36. Abundant Crops like Clouds
37. Hearing Orioles Among Willow Waves

38. The Magnificent View of West Mountain
    Peaks
39. Fish Leaping and Kite-Bird Flying
40. The Far-Northern Mountain Village
41. Open-Minded and Eminently Fair
42. The Universe Is Clear and Bright
43. A Wonderland on Fanghu Island
44. Three Lakes Reflecting the Moon
45. The Big Boat Dock
46. Two Peaks Penetrate into the Clouds
47. A Smooth Lake Under Autumn Moon
48. Taking a Bath, for Body and Mind
49. Reflection of Two Streams and Zither-
    Sound Waterfalls
50. Palace of Universal Nurture
51. The Evening Bell at the Southern Screen
52. A Place of Unique Beauty
53. Cottage with Beautiful View
54. Containing the Void in a Bright Mirror
55. Immortal Abode Jade Terrace on Penglai
    Island

the southeastern part of Jingyiyuan, about halfway up the slope. Its main scenic areas were a palace area and two large temple complexes, Xiangshan and Hongguang, with Yingluo Peak and other natural spots scattered among them. The outer garden, still in existence, is situated high in the Fragrant Hills (Xiangshan). It sprawls over a huge area with fifteen scenic spots, each a small park with excellent views of its own. The detached garden is in the north of Jingyiyuan and includes Zhao Temple and Zhenning Hall. In the northwestern part of this area are large sectors of deciduous huanglu trees. Large crowds of visitors come to see the forest in the fall, when the leaves turn a glorious red and gold.

Jingming Garden was built on a small mountain in the Yuquan (Jade Spring) Hills, west of Qingyi Garden, in the eastern section of the Western Hills. The mountain itself is captivating in its beauty; it is covered with trees, unique rockeries, deep caverns, and undulating streams. Built in 1753 on the foundation of a traveling palace, it was enlarged into a detached palace named Jingmingyuan. With mountains as its principal scenery, Jingmingyuan was kept primarily a natural garden, formed from bodies of water and other natural surroundings.

Like other Qing imperial gardens, Jingmingyuan was divided into three parts. The largest section was south of the mountain and the other two were east and west of it.

The southern area also had the best scenery and encompassed palace architecture, Jade Spring Lake, and a series of small scenic spots. The northwestern side was shielded by the mountain, which was decorated with the Huazang and Yufeng pagodas, causing the area to resemble a peak encircled by a moat. The area offers a picturesque disorder — open and closed, high and low spaces. The eastern mountain region included the eastern slope of Jade Spring Mountain and many small lakes at its base. Due to the small size of the buildings, this part of the garden appears larger than it is. The focus of the northern part of the garden was Miaogao Pagoda on the northern peak. The western part of the mountain, in contrast, was a broad open stretch of land that was the location of the most extensive architectural groups, including the Temple to the Eastern Peak, Shenyuan Monastery, and Qingyuan Meditation Cave. In other words, the scenic highlights of the western section were the religious architecture.

Qingyi Garden occupied 290 hectares of land west of Yuanmingyuan in the northwestern suburbs of Beijing. Urn Hill, or Wengshan (later known as Longevity Hill, or Wanshoushan), accounted for about one-third of the area. The rest of the natural garden was primarily water. Construction occurred between 1750 and 1764, during the middle period of the Qianlong reign. Wanshoushan alone dominated the northern part of the garden, and

Sights of Changchunyuan — Everlasting Spring Garden

56. Palace Gate of Park of Everlasting Spring
57. Tranquil Heart Hall
58. Madder Garden
59. Ru Garden
60. Mirror Garden
61. Far-Reaching Thoughts
62. The Sea and the Mountain Open One's Mind
63. Pure Transformation Kiosk
64. Jade Exquisiteness Lodge
65. Lion's Grove
66. Turning-Fragrance Sail
67. Thoroughwort Hall
68. Precious Likeness Monastery
69. Fahui Monastery
70. Harmonious Intriguing Interests
71. Cage for Raising Birds
72. Myriad-Flower Labyrinth
73. Residence of Buddhist Monks
74. Hall of Seafood Feast
75. Observing the Waterway

76. View of Distant Yingzhou — An Island of Immortals in the Eastern Sea
77. Xianfa Hill
78. Fang River
79. Xianfa Wall

Sights of Qichunyuan — Gorgeous Spring Garden

80. Palace Gate of Gorgeous Spring Park
81. Hall of Spreading Spring
82. Azure-Reflecting Pavilion
83. Buddha Awareness Monastery
84. Purifying Heart Hall
85. River-God Temple
86. Joyous Harmony Hall
87. Green-filled Pavilion
88. Scenery of Unique and Enchanting Beauty
89. Lovely Clouds Lodge
90. Sunshine-filled Tower
91. Prolonging Life Monastery
92. Study Suitable for Four Seasons
93. Hall Where Plants Grow in Winter

94. Spring-Luster Studio
95. Composing Poetry and Matching the Rhymes
96. Buddha Realm of Adornment
97. Autumn-filled Lodge
98. Phoenix and Qilin Isle
99. Terrace for Receiving Dew
100. Dreaming of the Moon Under Wind-Blown Pines

Figure 7.21. A view of Yuanming Garden, painting by Tang Dai and Shen Yuan, 1744

Figure 7.22. Bitong Garden, as seen in a painting by Tang Dai and Shen Yuan, 1744

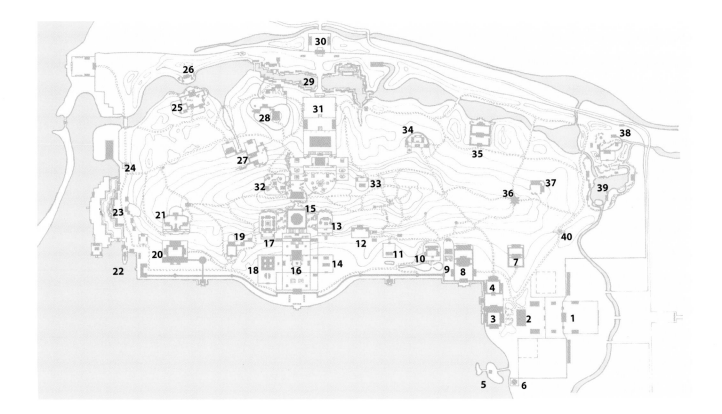

Figure 7.23. Plan of Qingyi Garden, after 1888 known as Yiheyuan (the Summer Palace), northern suburbs of Beijing, built in 1750–1764

1. Eastern Palace Gate
2. Diligence in Government Hall
3. Jade Ripples Hall
4. Propriety of Weeding Lodge
5. Heralding Spring Pavilion
6. Literary Prosperity Pavilion
7. Pleasant Spring Hall
8. Bliss and Longevity Hall
9. Free Flow of Benevolent Wind
10. Nurturing Cloud Pavilion
11. Unlimited Benefits Pavilion
12. Writing or Painting About Autumn Pavilion
13. Revolving Archive

14. Compassion and Happiness Tower
15. Buddhist Fragrance Pavilion
16. Prolonging Life Monastery
17. Precious Cloud Pavilion
18. Buddhist Arhat Hall
19. Cloud and Pine Tree Nest
20. Listening to Orioles Lodge
21. Strolling Through a Picture-Scroll
22. Boat of Purity and Ease — Marble Boat
23. Business Street in the West Place
24. Evening Clouds Eaves
25. Gazing at Beautiful Scenery Pavilion
26. Time of Watching the Rising Clouds
27. Embracing Spring Park

28. Reaching into Void Studio
29. Suzhou Street
30. Northern Palace Gate
31. Sumeru Mountain Spiritual Realm Temple
32. Rue and Aloe Monastery
33. Goodness Observing Monastery
34. Flower Bearing Pavilion
35. Tranquil and Calm Hall
36. Night-Blooming Cereus Pavilion
37. Increasing Longevity Hall
38. Snow Clearing Pavilion
39. Huishan (Kindness Hill) Park
40. Scarlet Wall, Rising Like Rosy Clouds

some architecture was placed on it for the purpose of creating scenic overlooks. Kunming Lake is south of the mountain, presenting a wide, expansive view. Destroyed in 1860 during the attack on Beijing by the English and French, Qingyi Garden was rebuilt by the empress dowager Cixi during the middle period of the Guangxu reign. The restoration cost 20 million taels of silver, money that had been set aside for the navy, and when it was completed in 1888, the garden was renamed Yiheyuan. It generally goes by the name Summer Palace.

Yiheyuan is divided into four parts, each with a different function. First is the Renshou Hall building group, east of Wanshoushan, where court was held and where the emperor lived and received officials (fig. 7.23, #1–10). In this part of Yiheyuan, each building is carefully placed, with particular attention to the reverence and authority befitting the Son of Heaven. The second part of Yiheyuan lies in front of Wanshoushan (#13–18). Facing Kunming Lake, the most important structures of the garden stand in this wide, expansive space: two tall buildings, Paiyun Kiosk (#17) and Foxiang (Buddha Fragrance) Pavilion (#15), as well as more than ten smaller building groups.

Figure 7.25. Covered arcade at the Summer Palace, 1880s

Opposite
Figure 7.24. Buddha Fragrance Pavilion (Foxiangge) in the
Summer Palace, or Yiheyuan, built in the 1880s

Foxiangge, octagonal in plan, elevated on a high stone platform and four stories high, dominates the landscape (fig. 7.24). With the Paiyun Kiosk, it establishes an axial line for the entire garden. On either side of this line are two secondary axes on which stand Zhuanlun Sutra Repository, Cifu Tower, Baoyun Pavilion, and Luohan Hall. Below Wanshoushan, a seven-hundred-meter covered arcade follows the lake to join the east and west axial lines (fig. 7.25).

The back area of Wanshoushan and the lake behind it make up the third part of the Summer Palace. Of uneven topography, but with steep slopes and a narrow lake, the space is closed and intimate. Although there are religious buildings in the central regions and a commercial district on either side behind the lake, a lush growth of trees cov-

ers the mountain slope and small-scale architecture stands in parkland on either bank of the lake. The scene is one of peace and tranquillity, quietude and somberness, in poetic contrast to the more active scenes in front of the mountain (fig. 7.26).

The west and south lakes of Kunming Lake form the fourth part of the Summer Palace. Architecture and bridges of different shapes and styles stand on islands in the lake. Most famous are the Seventeen-Arch Bridge, the Six-Arch Bridge and Dike, and the Jade Belt Bridge (fig. 7.27). Spanning a lake of weeping willows, the scene looks as if it were transposed from marshland south of the Yangzi River.

Qingyiyuan is a summation of many of the principles of imperial landscape architecture and garden design of

Figure 7.26. Back Lake at the Summer Palace

the mid-Qing. The buildings of the garden are enormous, with glazed ceramic roof tiles, bold pigments, and extensive and expensive decorative painting arranged along an axial line. All of this reinforces the singular power of the Chinese emperor and marks a sharp contrast to the design principles and message of a literati garden of the Qing or earlier. The landscape elements borrow from views and embody the best of south China's gardens: the overall design imitates that of West Lake in Hangzhou; the West Dike was fashioned after Su Dike of West Lake; Jingming Tower was built to replicate Yueyang Tower in Hunan province; Phoenix Platform was modeled after Huangbu Platform in Wuxi, Jiangsu province; and Huishan Garden was inspired by Jichang Garden, also in Wuxi.

Qingyiyuan also has some of the most stunning examples of *jiejing,* "borrowing a scene," a practice made famous by Qing emperors. It was accomplished by using islands and shores to separate South Lake into disjointed sections, thereby allowing for an increased number of scenes; by using West Dike and West Lake as focal points so that Jade Spring Hills, the Western Hills, and pagodas, temples, and trees could be incorporated into the scenery of the garden; and most important, by positioning the garden so that Yuanmingyuan and Changchunyuan appeared to be eastern extensions of Wanshoushan. Wanshoushan, "Longevity Hill," was the hub of Qingyiyuan, itself the supreme achievement in Qing garden design. Because Wanshoushan incorporated

the best of design and beauty from both within and beyond the borders of China, it became an ultimate symbol of imperial display that began in Beijing but spread as far as Qing visions of imperialism could take it.

Mountain Resort for Escaping the Summer Heat

Bishushanzhuang, the Mountain Resort (literally, station) for Escaping the Summer Heat, was begun in 1730 under the sponsorship of the Kangxi emperor. One of his main purposes was political: consolidation of the northeastern frontier, which separated China from the Mongols. Besides placing a palace here to emphasize their tie to the Mongols and the area, the Qing emperors chose this location for Mulanqiuxian, their autumn hunt in the Mulan, a yearly large-scale event that offered not only sport for the troops but also a chance for the imperial family to observe their soldiers.

The Summer Resort was located about 250 kilometers northeast of Beijing, near the Wulie River (fig. 7.28). Known for its sweet springs and dense forests, the area was considered one of the most beautiful in China and it offered everything necessary for garden construction. The basic framework of the resort, thirty-six scenic spots, was completed under the Kangxi emperor. Under the Qianlong emperor, thirty-six new scenic spots were added between 1751 and 1790. A wall surrounded the 5,600-square-kilometer area, which begins on the west bank of Wulie River. It is divided into four sections, each with different topography. The palace complex at the south is flat; beyond it are the lake and marsh area, the large plain, and the hills. Both emperors spent long periods of time at the Summer Resort every year, so that it became a political center of the empire, second only to Beijing. Today its location is called Chengde. Formerly it was known as Rehe, with the Anglicized name Jehol.

The palace area of the Summer Resort consists of four main building complexes, all enclosed by a wall: the main palace (fig. 7.29, #1), Songhe Studio attached to it on the east (#2), Wanhesongfeng to their north (#4), and the eastern palace (#3). The main palace area was where the Qing emperor held court and entertained (fig. 7.30). Arranged in traditional Chinese fashion, with the hall of audience in front and private residences behind, the palace area featured eight buildings on its main axis. From south to north they were Meridian Gate, itself located directly behind the entry into the resort from the outer wall gate named Lizhengmen; the main gate of the palace on which the Kangxi emperor himself wrote the name Bishushanzhuang; Danbojingchengdian (Hall of Simplicity and Sincerity), which was made of unpainted *nanmu* (wood) to reflect the rustic beauty of this area where the emperor celebrated his birthday and received foreign visitors; Sizhishu (Four Wisdoms Chamber), created for receptions and banquets; Wansuizhaofang (Chamber for Illumination for Ten Thousand Years); Yanbozhishuangdian (Hall of Refreshing Mists and Waves), which served as the emperor's own bedchamber and where in 1860 both the Treaty of Peking with France and Germany and the Sino-Russian Treaty were signed; Yunshanshengdilou (Tower for Looking Up

Figure 7.27. Jade Belt Bridge over Kunming Lake, built in the 1880s

Figure 7.28. Aerial view of the Mountain Resort for Escaping the
Summer Heat (Bishushanzhuang), or the Summer Resort,
Chengde, Hebei province, built 1730–1790

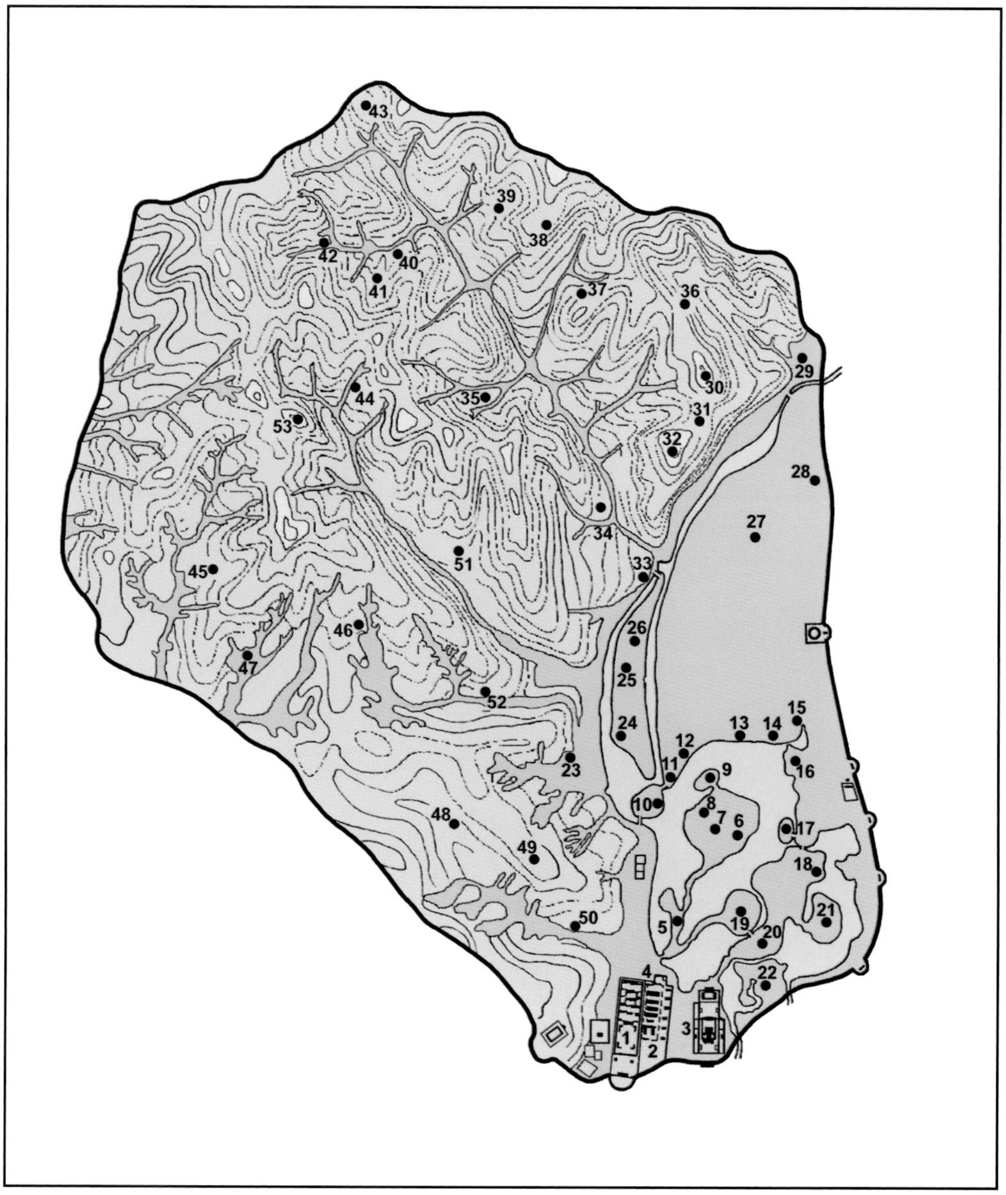

Figure 7.29. Plan of the Summer Resort at Chengde. *Source:* Zhou Shachen, *Beijing Old and New* (Beijing: New World Press, 1984)

1. Main palace
2. Pine Tree and Crane Studio
3. East Palace
4. Myriad Ravines, Wind-Blown Pines
5. Magic Mushroom Path and Cloud Dike
6. A Single Cloud
7. No Summer Heat but Cool and Refreshing Air
8. Azure Wave Isle
9. Misty Rain Tower
10. Facing Fragrant-Plant Villa
11. The Water Is Flowing and the Cloud Lingers
12. Leisure Thoughts at Hao and Pu Brooks
13. Orioles Twittering in Tall Trees
14. The Shade of Shrubs in Pu Field
15. Duckweed Fragrance in the Pond
16. Fragrance Coming from Afar Is More Delicate
17. Hall of Heavenly Bestowal of Universal Joy
18. Flower-Spirit Temple

19. Color-of-the-Moon and Sound-of-the-Water Islands
20. Clear and Comfortable Mountain Lodge
21. Avoiding Avarice Hall
22. Lion's Grove in the Literary Garden
23. Zhuyuan Monastery
24. The Sound of Spring Could Be Heard Far and Near
25. One Thousand Feet of Snow Pavilion
26. Ford of Literature Pavilion
27. Yurt
28. Eternal Blessings Monastery
29. Clear View Studio
30. Northward Resting on Twin Peaks
31. Green Maples and Azure Isle
32. Piled Snow on Southern Mountains
33. The Appearance of Clouds and the Aspect of Water
34. Clear Brook Flowing Afar
35. The Reflection of Moon in the Water Nunnery

36. Goddess of the North Star Pavilion
37. Near the Mountain Pavilion
38. Vast Origin Palace
39. Open Clarity Studio
40. Enfolding Green Studio
41. Azure Tranquillity Hall
42. Jade Peak Vihara
43. Pleasant Reflection Studio
44. Creating Attainment Studio
45. Elegantly Rising Hall
46. Eating Sugarcane Abode
47. Fundamental Truth Pavilion
48. Azure Peak Monastery
49. Sun Setting on Hammer Peak
50. Pine Tree and Crane in the Cool Shade
51. Pear Blossoms Accompanying the Moon
52. Viewing the Waterfall Pavilion
53. Cloud Covered Mountains All Around

at Clouds and Mountains), the highest point in the palace complex; and Xiuyun (Cave and Clouds) Gate. The entrance to Songhe Studio was a door in the Hall of Refreshing Mists and Waves.

Songhezhai, the Studio of Pines and Cranes complex, built in 1749, was alongside the main palace. It was the residence of the empress dowager, Qianlong's mother, and his concubines. The tree and the bird referred to in its name are both signs of longevity. Beginning in 1790 it was used by the Jiaqing emperor for his residence.

Wanhesongfeng (Myriad Ravines, Wind-Blown Pines) is directly behind Songhezhai and in front of Xia Lake. Without an enclosing arcade or wall, or a straight building line, its architecture can be considered transitional, buffering and merging the formal palatial complexes and the beginning of the natural area of the lake and marsh. It is said that the Kangxi emperor spent many hours here with his grandson, who later became the Qianlong emperor.

The East Palace is where imperial ceremonies and banquets were held. Entered directly from the outer wall like the main palace complex, it also was backed by the lake. Its main buildings were Pure Sound (Qingyin) Pavilion, Garden of Prosperity and Longevity (Fushouyuan), Diligent

Administration (Qinzheng) Hall, and Zhuan'ashengjing (Inspecting the Surrounding Borders) Hall. In keeping with the overall tenor of the mountain resort, all of its buildings followed the humble style of residences of the peoples of north China. Roof tiles were unglazed, and the exterior wood did not have decorative painting.

The lake and marshland area makes up fifty-five hectares north of the palaces. It consists of seven lakes and numerous islands, some of them large, linked by long dikes and bridges that create an image of floating clouds over shimmering water (figs. 7.31, 7.32, 7.33, and 7.34). Attractions include Scepter Islet, Azure Lotus Island, Golden Hill, and Color-of-the-Moon and Sound-of-the-Water islands. The names and natural features are a combination of activity and passivity. Many of the scenes are based on beauty spots south of the Yangzi that the Kangxi and Qianlong emperors admired. Lion's Grove in the Literary Garden, for example, was built as a copy of a garden in Suzhou with the same name. Tianyuxiang-changdian, the Hall of Heavenly Bestowal of Universal Joy, was modeled after the main hall of Jinshan Monastery in Zhenjiang, Jiangsu province. The Tower of Smoke and Rain on Azure Lotus Island was a copy of the tower of

Figure 7. 31. Lake area, Chengde, with Jinshan in the background

Figure 7.32. Chengde Lake Center Pavilions

the same name in Jiaxing, Zhejiang province, and Isle of the Surging Waves, similarly, was built and named after the Canglang (Surging Waves) Pavilion in Suzhou. Every scenic spot in the area of lakes and marshes was inspired by water. Although the space is free-flowing and flexible, the disparate scenes are linked by pedestrian routes.

The plain lying to the north of the lake and marsh area consists of Wanshuyuan (Ten Thousand Trees Garden) and Yongyousi (Eternal Blessings Monastery), and at the foothills of the mountains in the west, Ningjing (Tranquillity and Quietude) Pavilion, Qianchixue (One Thousand Feet of Snow) Pavilion, Yuqin Hall, and Wenjinge (Ford of Literature Pavilion). Ten Thousand Trees Garden stands on a large stretch of grassland with patches of verdant pine and cypress trees, typical of the wild scene of north China. The Qianlong emperor often gave banquets here, in the open country, for leaders of other tribes, accompanied with displays of fireworks and river lanterns as well as circus and acrobatic performances. Other structures on the plain included Ningjingzhai (Studio of Tranquillity and Quietude) and Yupigan (Kiosk of the Jade Lute). The multistory Ford of Literature Pavilion, built in 1774, like its counterparts in the Forbidden Cities in Beijing and Shenyang housed a complete set of *Siku quanshu*, the famous literary compilation of the Qianlong court.

The rest of the Summer Resort, 80 percent of the whole, is taken up by the area known as the hills. Included in the 430 hectares are the five gullies Pine Cloud, Pear Tree, Pine Forest, Hazelnut, and West. The area of continuous hills provides excellent protection for the other areas of the Summer Resort from the fierce winter winds that come from the northwest. The natural features have been preserved to the greatest possible extent, and the few small residential-style buildings, not adorned with decoration, are somewhat elegant but simple and small-scale. In the eighteenth century, at the peak of imperial activity at the Summer Resort, there were forty-four gardens or structures in the hills. One of the most famous sites was Zhuyuan Monastery in Pear Tree Gully. It contained Zongjingge (Ancestral Mirror Pavilion), made of 205 tons of bronze. In addition, for a brief period, the mother of the Kangxi emperor lived in a two-courtyard residence in Hazelnut Gully. Today many visitors consider Pine Cloud Gully, a forest of pines and cypresses, the most seductive spot. Walking along the

Figure 7.33. Architectural decoration from a Chengde lake-area pavilion

Figure 7.34. Simple Living but Sincere and Respectful Hall, Summer Resort, Chengde

Figure 7.35. Courtyard of the Cranes, Lingering Garden, Suzhou, built 1573–1620

Figure 7.36. Covered archway, Garden of the Unsuccessful Politician

paths of the valley, listening to the singing of birds and the soughing pines and looking at the distant towering peaks enshrouded in mist, one can still lose oneself in the secluded environment.

Private Gardens

Under Qing rule, most of the nobility, officials, landowners, and wealthy merchants lived in cities or nearby suburbs. With abundant material for creating gardens and a culture that encouraged garden building, members of all these groups constructed private urban pleasure spots. Such individual gardens surpassed Ming gardens not only in number but also in design. Qing private gardens can be divided into three groups: those of the north Chinese, those of the south Chinese (of the Jiangnan region, or south of the Yangzi and Lingnan regions, or south of the Five Peaks), and those of peoples living in the regions of Guangdong and Guangxi.

Private gardens in north China were concentrated in the vicinity of Beijing, and at one time numbered more than 150. The most famous were Cuijin Garden and Bangu Garden on the palatial estate of Prince Gong. Fit into a walled compound in the city, much of the scenery of Cuijin Garden was located in the south and west, but the focus of the garden was the central building axis along which buildings rose higher and higher, culminating in the Platform Where One Seeks the Moon (Yaoyuetai). Both the main building line and the elevated and dominant structure recall the plan of Qingyiyuan.

Most private gardens in the Beijing suburbs were in the Haidian district, in the western suburbs. Most famous were Yimu (One Hectare), Weixiu, Shuchun, Xichun, and Hanlin gardens. These were primarily built around water rather than land scenery. Due to the cold climate and limited building materials, these gardens were self-contained, not lavish, and solidly built. The axial building line employed in Cuijin Garden was typical of private gardens in suburban Beijing as well. Often local stone was used, in particular azure stones and stones from northern Lake Tai, which created strong and bold forms. With evergreens and deciduous trees, scenery changed from winter to summer. The boldly polychromed buildings made up for the drab color of the earth and some of the local plants.

Garden design in Jiangnan, the area south of the

Figure 7.37. Waterfront hall, Lion's Grove in the Literary Garden, Suzhou

Yangzi, was concentrated in the vicinity of Yangzhou (just north of the river), where transportation was well developed and the economy flourished during the early Qing period — although many of the gardens there and elsewhere had pre-Qing histories. After the Qianlong emperor's reign, private garden architecture also flourished in Wuxi, Songjiang, Nanjing, Hangzhou, and Suzhou. In Yangzhou, Lesser West Lake had twenty-four scenes, each a garden in its own right. Xiaopan Gully, Pianshishan Residence, He Garden, and Ge Garden were there as well. The Unsuccessful Politician (Humble Administrator) Garden, Lingering Garden, and Garden of the Master of the Fishnets were in Suzhou. Wuxi had Jichang Garden. The temperate climate and humidity, network of waterways, and luxuriant growth of flowers and trees all influenced garden architecture (figs. 7.35, 7.36, 7.37, and 7.38).

In contrast to private gardens in north China, those in the south can be described as more graceful, light, and open. These effects were achieved by more windows, roofs whose eaves sloped at the corners more than their northern counterparts, and so-called moon gates (*yuedong*), large circular openings in walls that usually were made of stucco. Trees in the south are primarily deciduous, and plantings include annuals and perennials. Among these plantings are not only evergreens but also green ratters, bamboo groves, banana plants, and grapes that provide color throughout the year. Most of the rocks come from the region of Lake Tai or are golden in color. Rocks can be piled or scattered, but their purpose is to simulate an effect ranging from mountain to grotto, cave to cliff, jagged bank to projection over water. Slim, lean, porous rocks from Lake Tai, for example, are used to create the effect of a solitary peak. Light-colored architecture such as faded red walls blends with dark-green roof tiles and brown pillars to produce a refreshing elegance.

Only a few private gardens from Qing times survive in the Lingnan region of south China. Qinghui Garden in Shunde, Keyuan Garden in Dongguan, and Yuyin Mountain Villa in Panyu, all in Guangdong, are representative.

Figure 7.38. Wangshiyuan (Garden of the Master of the Fishnets)
in Suzhou

Figure 7.39. Corner of the Shuiquan courtyard of Biyun
monastery, Beijing

Several others remain in Fujian and Taiwan. A prime concern in garden design in this region is the hot, humid climate; ventilation is of utmost importance. Gardens of Lingnan are the most open and airy in all of China. Some of these gardens reflect the influence of Western geometry in their plans, and buildings tend to be closer together than in other gardens of China. Stone in Lingnan gardens is often molded like sculpture, according to a technique known as *sushi* that makes it possible for single rocks to take on a great variety of shapes.

Private gardens of the Qing dynasty benefited from design breakthroughs of the past great ages of Song and Ming garden building. One of the differences between Qing gardens and those of earlier times, however, is the merging of residence and garden, a process that had occurred gradually since pre-Qing days. By combining the architecture of two different purposes, practical and pleasurable, residences were built so that the views and scenic spots of gardens could be appreciated in them and so that new functions, such as walking for pleasure and swimming, could be a part of the space. Because of this combination of residence and garden, new types of architecture entered garden spaces; and because private gardens were generally located in cities, which in Qing China were even more crowded than they had been in Ming times, garden builders worked even harder than

before to create the most diverse and interesting views possible in very limited spaces. In the Lingering Garden in Suzhou, for example, architecture stands even at the entry. The Garden of the Master of the Fishnets has a similar entry. The key to success was a quick change of view — for example, from open to closed, bright to dark, or large to small. The result was a wealth of views. Rocks were used to full advantage; for instance, to create majestic mountains rather than flat hills. Indeed, every garden designer had a theory about the use and placement of rocks. One of the most famous was Ge Yuliang, who built Huanxiu Mountain Villa in Suzhou during the reign of the Qianlong emperor.

Some of the features introduced to garden design in Suzhou at this time were the paving of floors with ornamental slabs, the setting of inlay into walls, the carving of doors and windows, greatly sloping roof corners, more interior furnishings, both horizontal and vertical placards for inscriptions, calligraphy and paintings, covered arcades with tiny openings, containers for flowers, and marble benches. It is fair to say that some private garden designs at this time became overdone, so that spaces were overcrowded, decoration excessive, and rockeries placed without enough regard for natural plantings. All this could only have a negative effect on the future of traditional-style gardens in China.

Other kinds of private gardens are found in the landscapes of Buddhist and Daoist monasteries. Among them are three subcategories: gardens attached to monasteries, gardens that include monasteries, and gardens and monasteries that are one entity. Examples of gardens adjacent to monasteries are Water Spring Garden of Biyun Monastery and the Courtyard of the Buddha's Relics at Dazhengjue Monastery, both in Beijing, and, in Chengde, the garden that symbolizes the Buddhist world in the back part of Puning Monastery and the artificial mountain that symbolizes Mount Wutai in the back area of Shuxiang Monastery. Not only are the Chengde sites attached to monasteries, they are also of a type known as symbolic gardens (fig. 7.39).

In Beijing the best examples of gardens with monasteries in them are the West Garden of the Monastery of the Reclining Buddha, the Jietan Precinct of Tanzhe Monastery, and Yunjishan at the White Cloud Daoist Monastery (Baiyunguan), headquarters of the Quanzhen sect.

The last type, sites where it is hard to tell where the monastery stops and the garden begins, include Guchang Daoist Monastery on Mount Qingcheng in Guanxian and Fuhu Monastery on Mount Emei, both in Sichuan; Yuquan Daoist Monastery in Tianshui, Gansu, and Taihe Daoist Monastery in Kunming, Yunnan.

Figure 7.40. Interior of palace-style building, Norbu Linka, the
Treasure Garden, near Lhasa, Tibet

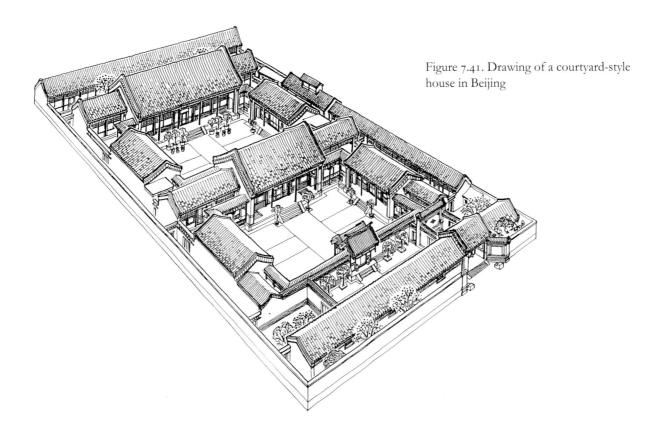

Figure 7.41. Drawing of a courtyard-style house in Beijing

Finally, some developments in garden architecture occurred in the traditional residential architecture of the various nationalities of the Qing empire. The Hui often built garden-style courtyards adjacent to their houses simply to improve their living environment. In Tibet during the Qianlong period, the local government built a garden called Norbu Linka (Treasure Garden) in the western suburbs of Lhasa for the Dalai Lama to enjoy during his summer residence there. Unlike Chinese gardens, Norbu Linka does not have artificial mountains and lakes or winding arcades. Instead, in a wooded forest with a square pond it has Tibetan-style palace architecture (fig. 7.40) as well as clear, solemn, open spaces that reflect the lifestyle of people who graze sheep and watch cattle on the vast grasslands of Tibet.

Residential Architecture

The multiplicity of ethnic groups that populated the Qing empire along China's borders is nowhere more evident than in residential architecture of the period. No fewer than forty residential architectural styles are identifiable from this 250-year period. Most prominent of these styles are the courtyard, subterranean, elevated on stilts, tent, Tibetan, and Uyghur. Courtyard-style dwellings have the longest history in China and are the most popular, even among the so-called minority peoples. Built in Qing China by north Chinese peoples, the courtyard-style house was defined by the courtyard itself, the center of activity enclosed by buildings on at least three sides to create both interior and exterior spaces. In general, each structure around the courtyard has at least three bays, but because native traditions of the house builders as well as building materials and climate differ, courtyard-style houses are distinct in the various regions in which they are constructed. The three principal types of courtyard-style residences are *heyuan,* or straightforward enclosure; *ting jing* or *tianjing,* enclosure around a skywell; and *zuqun,* grouped courtyards.

In standard courtyard enclosures, each main building unit has its own courtyard in front of it. The building often is attached on both sides to the covered arcade or wall that defines the courtyard. In some cases covered arcades join a series of buildings and courtyards, but each main building and its courtyard might also be an independent pair. Courtyard-style structures tend to be of tailiang (column, beam, and strut) construction, with sturdy eaves, thick outer walls, and doors and windows that open on the courtyard side — all features that in the summer allow maximum ventilation and in the winter keep out cold winds while allowing sun to enter from the south, the side toward which the majority of courtyards are oriented. Thus this style was especially popular in the cold climates of northern China.

The lanes and alleys *(hutong)* of Qing Beijing were famous for their courtyard-style houses (fig. 7.41). A typical courtyard-style house there had three court-

Figure 7.42. Courtyard-style house in Jinyu Hutong, Beijing

Figure 7.43. House number 7 in Qiangulou precinct, Beijing

Figure 7.44. Courtyard of the Qiao family mansion, Qi county, Shanxi province

Figure 7.45. Brick relief with motif "Announcing Good News," Qiao family mansion

yards. The main entertainment and residential structures were flanked by east and west wings. *Chuanshan* (penetrating mountain) and *chaoshou* (hand-folding) corridors join the rooms for easy passage from one to the next with the main entrance to these buildings on their southeast. Large courtyard-style houses may have an additional axial line of buildings, a garden, and a study (figs. 7.42 and 7.43).

Large or small, each room of a courtyard-style dwelling has its own function. The first building *(daozuo)*, for example, has a room for receiving guests, a room for the man in charge of the family's finances, and a room for the doorman. The functions of the main entertainment hall and main residential hall are clear from their names. They might be the same or nearly the same in outward appearance, but the first was formal and for visitors and the second was for the family alone. Within the main residential building, the oldest generation residing in the compound used the central room, and those on the sides were ranked according to family seniority, with the older children and their families closer to the center than the younger siblings. The back buildings were for servants, cooking, and storage. Space was determined according to

Figure 7.46. Ding village house, Xiangfen, Shanxi province

Figure 7.47. Wood carving and brick engraving, Ding village

the patriarchal system, which was so strong that a plan alone can tell us who lived in, used, and could enter each of the main buildings and its interior compartments.

Courtyard-style houses of central Shanxi were largely the same, except that courtyards tended to be narrower — in other words, rectangular rather than square-shaped. In southeastern Shanxi, the courtyard system was followed, but residences had two or three stories (figs. 7.44, 7.45, 7.46, and 7.47). In central Shaanxi, where courtyards were also long and narrow, roofs of the wing rooms were sloped only on one side. In Ningxia, courtyard-style houses of the Hui had more flexible plans that were not necessarily oriented to the south and might include gardens. The courtyard-style houses of the Manchu in Jilin province, by contrast, were extremely large, usually oriented to the west, and had along the three other sides the swastika-shaped *kang* (heatable brick platforms) used in the Forbidden City in Shenyang. In Qinghai the courtyards were enclosed by mud walls and the structures had flat roofs. Residences of the Bai in the vicinity of Dali, Yunnan, had screen walls, a central courtyard with four smaller ones, and skywells in the center of each (fig. 7.48). Finally, courtyard-style houses of the Naxi were similar to

Figure 7.48. Courtyard-style houses of the Bai nationality in Dali, Yunnan province

those of the Bai, except that there was a Tibetan feature, a covered arcade in front on both stories (fig. 7.49).

By contrast, houses with skywells have roofed structures on four sides and an open square interior to allow light to enter. In Chinese, the interior spaces are called either tingjing (residence well) or tianjing (skywell). The central courtyard is most often paved and enclosed by drainage ditches, which catch the water that falls into the courtyard from eaves of the side roofs. In front there is generally a wide porch or deep eaves, also to keep rain from entering the courtyard. Sometimes rooms of the house are open to the courtyard, sometimes even without doors, to allow for free passage without concern for rain.

Most houses with skywells are of the *chuandou* (column and tiebeam) style, suitable for climates with very hot summers. This construction allows for the maximum flow of air into the house. The open central space is the focus of daily life, which takes place equally indoors and outside. This type of house is popular in the Yangzi valley and to the south, especially in Jiangsu, Zhejiang, Anhui, Jiangxi, Hubei, Hunan, Fujian, and Guangdong.

Many examples of this residential style have been found in the vicinity of Lake Tai. There, each residential compound consists of several courtyards of houses in a long, narrow space. The structures of a residential compound are, from front to back, a screen wall, gatehouse, sedan hall, hallway, main room where guests are received, and women's rooms (where the women reside, also known as the "upper house"), which are often U-shaped. Few of the Suzhou residences have rooms on the sides of the main rooms. The front and back rooms are connected by covered ways and enclosed on both sides by "gabled walls." A two-story, elaborately carved brick gate is usually built on one side of the skywell as a sign of the owner's wealth. Residences with skywells owned by well-off Suzhou merchants also often had attached gardens, many of which survive.

Houses with skywells also remain in Huizhou, Anhui province. These have structures on three or four sides and are multistoried. Skywell houses in Dongyang, Zhejiang province, are famous throughout China for their wood carvings and for their H-shaped plans, which often featured thirteen rooms. In Western Hunan the Miao, Tujia, and Han all built two-story skywell houses with firewalls that rose higher than the roofs of the houses themselves. From a distance, the houses were thought to resemble official seals, and so were nicknamed seal houses. In Sichuan, skywell houses had large doors that opened onto the skywell from the central bay, called Dragon Gates, whose interiors were elaborately decorated. *Yikeyin*, "one seal," is the name of a style of small, delicate house found near Kunming, Yunnan, that encloses a skywell on four sides. In Quanzhou, Fujian, the residences follow the tradition of *hucu*, or protection style. Large, with three main central rooms aligned north–south, each is flanked by side wings. The hucu style was also very influential in Chaozhou and Shantou, both in Guangdong province, in Guangxi, and in Taiwan. In Guangdong and Jiangxi, however, even though there are many varieties of skywell houses, people of the middle and lower classes preferred living in three-bay houses with two side wings so that they could use the rest of their land more efficiently (fig. 7.50).

Another prominent type of courtyard-style residence, called grouped courtyards, joins together courtyards to serve more than one family. Sometimes entire clans live in this kind of dwelling. From the outside these appear to be huge, fortified compounds. They are common among people known as the Kejia, or Hakka, in western Fujian, in particular Yongding and Nanjing counties; in eastern

Figure 7.49. Courtyard-style houses of the Naxi people in Tibet

Figure 7.50. Skywell house, Wuzhen, Tongxiang, Zhejiang province

Guangdong, especially Meizhou, Chaozhou, and Shantou; and in southern Jiangxi. The compound might be circular or four-sided, but it always has a courtyard in the center (figs. 7.51 and 7.52).

Chengqilou in Yongding county, Fujian, is an example of a Qing-period structure inhabited by a Kejia (Hakka) clan. A full 62.6 meters in diameter, its four stories are

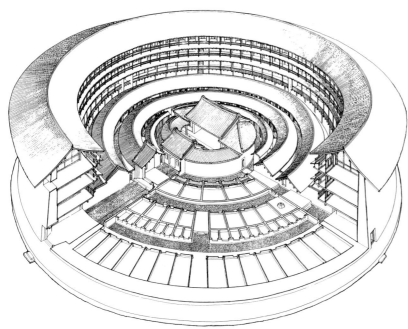

Figure 7.51. A house of the Kejia, or Hakka, people in Yongding county, Fujian province

Figure 7.52. Drawing of a Kejia house in Yongding county

supported by a timber frame of the chuandou type. The building material above the frame is pounded earth. Only a few doors and fewer windows provide exterior access. When these are all closed, the structure is like a fortress. All activity is focused on what happens inside the walls. Chengqilou has a clan shrine in the central courtyard, as well as wells and granaries (fig. 7.53).

Another type of residence grouped around a courtyard is found in Hulei, Kanshi, and Gaopo townships of Yongding county. These residences are four-sided in plan, have a mixture of gabled and hipped roofs, and feature multiple stories — with each building from north to south shorter than the one before. Locals call the highest building Five Phoenixes Hall (fig. 7.54).

In Meixian, Guangdong, a Kejia clan built a style of residence known as "three halls, two side rooms, all enclosed." Like its descriptive name, the group residence has three front-to-back rows of rooms with additional

Figure 7.53. Interior courtyard of a Kejia house, Yongding county

Figure 7.54. Courtyard-style house with Five Phoenixes Hall at rear, Yongding county

Figure 7.55. Xinglie-style house of the Kejia, Fujian province

residential rooms on either side. The semicircular enclosure joins the side rooms at the north end and then continues around.

In Nanxiong and Shixing of northern Guangdong a type of Kejia residence known as *xinglie* (ranked) style is found. Used for both clans and large families, living space is divided by status in the group. In Zhangzhou, one finds individual-style group residences. Large multistory earthen dwellings with three-bay units for individual families are grouped in the compound (fig. 7.55). In Chaozhou and Shantou, one also finds small units grouped together into huge U-shaped compounds.

Subterranean dwellings, sometimes known simply as cave houses and other times as earth-sheltered residences, are one of the most ancient Chinese architectural forms. Popular in China's loess regions like central Shaanxi, where precipitation is infrequent, these easy-to-build residences are cool in summer and warm in winter. Positive features are their separation from many environmental hazards and their use of only nonarable space, but lighting is a problem, as is ventilation.

Cave dwellings are found in five regions of China: central Shanxi, western Henan, eastern Gansu, northern Shaanxi, and southern Inner Mongolia. Chinese earthen dwellings can be divided into three stylistic categories: cliff, sunken courtyard, and aboveground but still cavelike. Cliff dwellings are carved directly into natural earth. They can have only one room or as many rooms as a large courtyard-style compound, and each room has a vaulted ceiling. Sunken courtyard-style dwellings are sometimes called earthen courtyards, basement courtyards, or concealed villages. They are made by first carving out a vertical shaft and then digging horizontally

Figure 7.56. Cave dwellings in Mizhi, Shaanxi province

Figure 7.57. Exterior courtyard of a cave dwelling in Yanchuan, Shaanxi province

under the ground. This type of cave dwelling is found in Gongxian, Sanmenxia, and Lingbao, Henan province; Qianxian, Shaanxi province; Qingyang, Gansu province; and Pinglu, Shanxi province (figs. 7.56 and 7.57). Found on plains, aboveground cave-style dwellings are individual structures with rectangular plans that resemble excavated caves with vaulted ceilings, on top of which are supported flat-roofed structures of brick, stone, or earth on which to dry food and grain. Most of them are found in western Shanxi and northern Shaanxi.

Houses raised on stilts are most popular in the

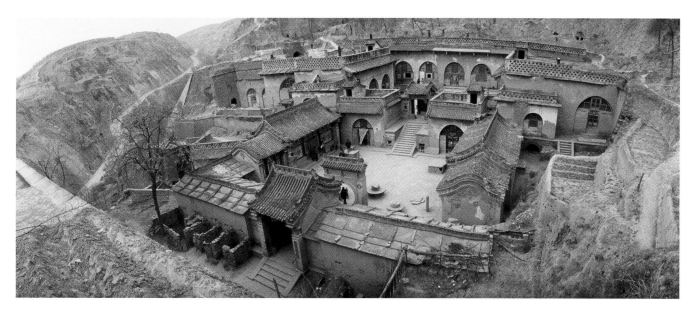

Figure 7.58. Drawing of a stilted dwelling of the Dai nationality, Jinghong county, Xishuangbanna, Yunnan province

Figure 7.59. Stilted houses, Yunnan province

subtropical regions of southeastern and southwestern China — Guangxi, Guizhou, Yunnan, Hainan, and Taiwan — areas with complex topography and few stretches of flat land. Dry and safe from the wet earth as well as less vulnerable to theft or animal attacks, stilted homes also offer better ventilation than a house built on the ground. Courtyards are rare in stilted houses, and the structures themselves tend to be small, just three to five rooms. All aspects of daily life and activity are carried out inside the house. Houses raised on stilts are a frequent choice of dwelling for the Dai, Zhuang, Dong, Miao, Li, Jingpo, De'ang, and Buyi peoples.

Stilted houses of the Dai people are built with combination bamboo and wooden frames; steep, thatched roofs with broadly sloping eaves; bamboo mats for floors and sitting areas; and wide, open corridors in which to dry clothes (figs. 7.58 and 7.59).

Stilted houses of the Zhuang, built in column-and-tiebeam style, are known as *malan* and usually have five bays. A fence around the lower level of the house keeps in the animals, and the family resides in the upper part. There, the central bay is the formal room for family events such as weddings and for receiving guests; the outer rooms are used as bedrooms (fig. 7.60).

For homes located in Guangxi, Guizhou, and southern Hunan, the Dong also built houses on stilts. Compared to homes of the Zhuang, Dong residences are more open to the outside. Stilted houses of the Dong tend to have open corridors and towers with overhanging eaves. A special feature of Dong architecture is a tall, multistory drum tower that stands in every village as the focal point of public activity (fig. 7.61). Over time, villages have competed to create the most interesting one.

Stilted houses of the Miao are only partly raised. That is, they are partially supported by stilts and partially built directly on or into the ground. The Li, who live in the Wuzhi Mountains of Hainan where strong winds and typhoons are frequent and the climate is humid, have lived in small houses raised on low stilts since ancient times. The thatched roofs are vaulted, so that the residences resemble boats. Li houses have no windows but do have front and back doors. Outside the front door is a small porchlike structure that makes the house look long and narrow like a boat. For this reason, Li houses are sometimes called boat-style houses. Finally, the Buyi of the Zhenning-Anshun-Liupanshui region of Guizhou build a variant of stilted houses — a raised home made of stone — because wood is scarce there.

Another major type of housing is the yurt, or *zhanfang*, which is a portable, circular tent with a willow-bark frame suitable for folding and carrying and an outside made of felt (fig. 7.62). This type of residence has been used since earliest times by seminomadic peoples of the steppe and grasslands. Today yurts are still popular in Inner Mongolia, northern Xinjiang, and parts of Qinghai, especially among the Mongols, Khazaks, and Tajiks.

The type of felt used in yurts varies from region to region. In the milder regions of Xinjiang, Qinghai, and Gansu, sheepherders live in tents covered with canvas or fine wool, sometimes even cashmere. In the colder regions of Qinghai and Tibet, the tents are black, covered with felt made from yak skin.

Figure 7.61. Tower and stilted houses in Dong village, Guizhou province

Figure 7.62. Yurts, northern Xinjiang Uyghur autonomous region

Figure 7.63. Tibetan block house in Xiahe, Gansu province

Another common dwelling type in Tibet is made of blocks of stone. Sometimes called fortified or block houses, most of these homes are three stories or more (fig. 7.63). The lowest level is used for animal pens, the second story is for entertaining and sleeping, and on the third floor are the family's Buddhist altar and exposed platforms for drying food. The walls are made of stone rubble, piled in layers. With few openings to the exterior and the stairway inside, block houses are like fortresses — easy to defend and hard to penetrate. Windows are trapezoid-shaped and painted black, and have eaves on top.

Block houses also exist outside of Tibet. In Aba and Ganzi counties of Sichuan, more wooden decorative parts are used. In southern Gansu, Tibetan-style block houses are shaped like nests, a form also used in Qinghai. In the tall block houses of the Qiang in Maowen district of Sichuan, walls are made of stone slabs and are clustered together with towers on either side of a street, creating heavily fortified towns. Block houses of the Hani in Honghe prefecture of Yunnan are called earth-rubbed houses *(tuchang fang)*. Two stories, with flat roofs and no windows to the outside, these earthen dwellings are among those most like the block houses of Tibet. Clearly, regional factors and local materials have a greater effect on the details of residential architecture than do stylistic considerations.

Found in Kashgar in southern Xinjiang, the Uyghur house, earthen with a flat earthen roof, is well suited to a hot and dry climate with little rain and lots of wind and sand. Residences are divided into rooms for winter and for summer. Summer rooms are built in the front part of the house and are nothing more than wide covered porches in which the family works, eats, and receives guests from May through November. Rooms inside the houses, used for winter, have rugs on the floors and heavily decorated plaster walls with lots of small niches.

Although there are too many examples to name them all here, various other areas also had their own style of residential architecture, suited to their climate and available construction materials.

Social Issues of Qing Residential Architecture

By the end of the seventeenth century, nomads and semi-nomads who had lived at China's borders for centuries before 1644 had become more sedentary, perhaps in part because of the sinification of the Manchu population. Moreover, new peoples of North and Southeast Asia, in particular, were increasingly part of or at odds with the empire of the Manchus. Management of the numerous ethnicities, the potential military threat of these populations (especially those who practiced the same Lamaist Buddhism as the Qing household), and the extent to which the Qing should interact with them were ongoing concerns of the imperial court. One way in which the various minorities could express their ethnicity, and thereby separate themselves from the Qing government, the Chinese people, and one another, was by constructing their own native-style residential architecture. In seventeenth-, eighteenth-, and nineteenth-century China, houses were as much a sign of ethnic identity as a place to live.

Other factors also affected residential architecture in Qing China. A decline in timber supply was matched by an increase in the amount of available brick. In addition, increased consumption of all kinds of goods occurred in decades of economic growth, Western-style architecture was introduced, and populations moved from one area of China to another.

In spite of the multiplicity of ethnic groups and corresponding styles of residential architecture, the most common residential style in Qing China was *siheyuan,* a four-sided enclosure around courtyards. This residential style inherited from Ming China became popular from the farthest northeastern reaches of the empire, the birthplace of the Manchu ruling family in Jilin province, to Yunnan. Manchu princes and Bannermen in Beijing built standard courtyard-style houses, and the Bai and Yi in Yunnan built modified versions of courtyard residences with local materials. The accommodation of the Zhuang to the Han Chinese system was their abandonment of houses raised on stilts for houses on the ground. Although called seal-shaped houses, the Han and Yi in Kunming actually lived in courtyard-style dwellings. The Li on Hainan Island, for their part, gave up boat-shaped houses with thatched roofs in favor of ceramic tiles and pyramidal roof lines. And some peoples of southern Gansu left block-style dwellings for houses of wood or rammed earth. None of these looked exactly like a courtyard-style residence of a Ming official, but all exhibited signs of Chinese influence in their native forms.

Population was also a factor in residential architecture. The population of Ming China remained between 50 and 60 million through the nearly three hundred years of rule. The population of China at the beginning of the Qianlong reign, however, exceeded 100 million and continued to grow so that by the mid-Qianlong period it was 200 million and by the end of the dynasty, 400 million. Given that the amount of land deemed suitable for housing had not increased, farmers built their houses on less land than in the past and, for the first time, economy in use of land was a factor in house building. In Beijing this meant getting rid of sidewalks in front of houses. In central Shanxi, dwellings rose to two or three stories. In southeastern China it became common for closely placed houses to line lanes and alleys as well as the coast. In Fujian and Guangdong, long thin houses, four or five bays deep and nicknamed bamboo tube houses, appeared. Minority peoples of Guizhou, Guangxi, Sichuan, and Hunan moved their houses into the mountains to make more cultivable land available. Houses raised on stilts became more popular in this part of China because they could be built on sloped river banks that were unsuitable for farming. Built as close to one another as were the houses of the southeastern Chinese coast, dwellings of minority populations of southwestern China had fire gables to help protect them from widespread destruction in the event of a fire.

Commerce and handicrafts also had an effect on residential construction in Qing China. The most significant change was the inclusion of both shops and dwellings in the same structure: in this new form, usually the store opened to the street and the living quarters were behind it. In towns south of the Yangzi, and in southern Shaanxi, Sichuan, Hunan, and Guangdong, houses became two-storied, with shops on the first floor and residential space above. In Pingyao and Taigu, Shanxi province, lending houses had residential space behind. In Zhejiang province and in Beijing, rental property appeared in the form of blocks of homes within one unit.

Handicrafts also influenced the decoration of residential architecture. Carving became detailed and elaborate on banisters, screen walls, gates, including *chuihua* (suspended-flower) gates, bracket sets, corridors, window frames, interiors, and furnishings. Brick carving was popular in Huizhou and Hezhou, Anhui province; Foshan, Chaozhou, and Shantou, Guangdong province; and Beijing and Suzhou. Wood carving was especially prevalent in Jianchuan, Yunnan province, Dongyang, Zhejiang province, Suzhou, and Heizhou; and stone carving flourished in Quyang, Hebei province, Qingtian and Shaoxing, Zhejiang province, Hui'an and Jinjiang, Fujian province, and Chaozhou and Shantou, Guangdong province. Particularly complicated examples of stone-carved decoration are doors and windows found at Dongyang in Zhejiang and Dali in Yunnan. In Dali, marble was sometimes inlaid into the walls; in Sichuan, pieces of porcelain decorated roof tiles; and in Fujian, gold leaf ornamented houses.

Another factor that led to the appearance of minority architecture outside its places of origin and to the adoption of mainstream Chinese styles such as siheyuan by minority peoples is what might be termed internal relocation. In an attempt to feed the increasing population, the Manchu government instituted a policy known as *jiedi yangmin,* or "reclaiming land to feed the people." In particular, people were relocated to Inner Mongolia — from Hebei to Zhelimumeng (Jerim League) and from northern Shanxi and Shaanxi to Jining and Ikezhaomeng (Ikju League)—and encouraged to turn the grassland of southern Inner Mongolia into farmland. Houses in the newly opened areas were built in the style of Shanxi and Shaanxi, with long, narrow courtyards, wing chambers, and short but deep eaves. There were even some subterranean dwellings that reflected the rare vernacular form of Shaanxi. Similarly, at the end of the Ming dynasty, when Sichuan was in turmoil and its population greatly reduced, people from Hunan, Hubei, and Guangxi were relocated to Sichuan. Some towns were made up completely of immigrants. Thus it is not surprising how widespread the residential styles of Hunan and Hubei were in Sichuan, with large door and window frames and brick ceremonial pillars on the tops of windows. In 1762, after fighting with the Xinjiang Uyghurs, troops of Manchu Bannermen, Mongol troops, and soldiers from the Green Brigade and their families were resettled in more than 120 cities from Urumqi to Yili. The new population of Xinjiang took on aspects of local residential architecture and introduced some styles from their places of origin.

Then there was the policy of *gaitu guiliu,* "changing the land for a return of fertility." This was a reference to the return of people of Han origin, which influenced the lifestyles of local minority peoples. Finally, in the late Ming and early Qing, residents were resettled from Putian and Chaozhou in Fujian and Toushan in Guangdong to Tainan and Gaoxiong in Taiwan. Even today the traditional residential style of Taiwan is very much a reflection of residential architecture of Fujian; it is rare to see homes built in the style of the Taiwanese aborigines.

More important than any of these shifts in population or the merging of home and business into one building was the decrease in available timber. This shortage was the primary reason for the popularity during the mid-Qing of the saddleback roof, which created a curved side facade in stucco or brick without timber framing. Limited supplies of wood also encouraged maintaining ancient forms of subterranean housing and stone houses. Even when wood was used, pillars, purlins, and beams were smaller and narrower than their Ming counterparts. Unnecessary pieces of bracket sets were given up, and rainbow-shaped beams were substituted with straight ones. In cities of the Jiangnan region (south of the Yangzi) such as Suzhou, logs, circular in section but uncut, were used to support beams, as another means of preserving the precious resource. All of these measures, including some simplification and in particular a greater amount of brick and stone construction, changed the appearance of Chinese residential architecture.

Nevertheless, there were merchants and officials with great wealth who aspired to build magnificent, courtyard-style residential compounds with grand entertainment rooms and adjacent gardens. This kind of timber-frame construction continued in every part of China that had a wealthy population.

Religious Architecture

Lamaseries were the most important religious building complexes in Qing China. They added a new visual experience to Chinese cityscapes and the countryside. Other religions that built architecture in China during the Qing period were Islam, Daoism, and Buddhism (both the Northern and Southern schools).

During the early Qing period, Tibetan Buddhism, most commonly referred to as Lamaism, particularly the Yellow sect of it, flourished in Tibet, all parts of Mongolia, and Qinghai. Tibet, where the entire region practiced this form of Buddhism, was a theocracy, and the lamasery was a religious, cultural, and educational center. Although at certain times in certain parts of China, monasteries of some Buddhist sects such as the Chan had served the same multiple roles, the Tibetan Buddhist monastery was unique in appearance compared to all previous Chinese architecture.

A lamasery included, first of all, a religious center — worship halls with images and pagodas. It also encompassed the *zhacang,* or academy of learning; the administrative center, which was also the residence of the living Buddha; and the scripture debating ground, dormitories for monks, storage halls, kitchens, and administration buildings. The most magnificent lamaseries were those with palatial architecture, such as Potala Palace, where the Dalai Lama and Panchen Lama stayed. Besides pagodas and Buddha halls, the Potala Palace, the largest Lamaist monastery in Tibet, contains stupas beneath which are the remains of Dalai Lamas of the past. It and other large monasteries also have multiple halls of learning and a greater number of image halls than do the smaller ones.

Architecturally, monastery architecture of Lamaist Buddhism traces its origins to the block-style houses of Tibet, those structures with brick and stone walls, flat

Figure 7.64. Potala Palace, Lhasa, Tibet, second half of the seventeenth century

roofs, and small windows that appear so heavily fortified from the outside. In fact, the lamasery represents a combination of native Tibetan residential architecture and buildings erected to fulfill the needs of worship, religious education, and administration of such a large and multi-purpose compound.

Although all lamaseries trace their origins to Tibet, they differ region by region. In general, the architecture of Lamaist Buddhism can be divided into three types: the purest Tibetan style, found in Tibet as well as in parts of Qinghai and Sichuan inhabited by Tibetans; the mixed Han (Sino)-Tibetan style seen primarily in parts of Inner Mongolia, the Ningxia Hui autonomous region, and Gansu with Tibetan and Mongolian populations; and the most Chinese (or Han) styles, found in Hebei and Shanxi.

One of the features that has distinguished Lamaist Buddhist architecture of Tibet is topography: most of it

has had to be built in some of the most mountainous regions of the globe. Thus freedom and flexibility of layout have overcome the conformity to spatial principles such as axiality and symmetry that characterizes so much other Buddhist architecture in Asia. Within the monastery, almost every building is made of stone with a flat roof and small windows. Often the walls are painted white; roofs are dark red with parapets at the corners. Portions of the roofs are sloped in the manner of Chinese rooflines and supported by bracket sets, but building parts are smaller than their Chinese counterparts and the framing is simpler. Bells hang from various places on the exterior, including roofs. Streamers and wheels representing the Wheel of the Law also hang from roofs, and paintings sometimes hang on exterior walls. Inside, these castle-style religious structures are supported by huge square pillars that are often intricately carved and painted

in bold, contrasting colors. Walls are covered with religious murals, banners, and streamers.

The most important Tibetan lamasery is the Potala Palace (fig. 7.64). It is also one of the most architecturally extraordinary structures in the world. Located on Mar-po-ri (Red Mountain), north of Lhasa, it dominates the city. Although its history can be traced to the Tang dynasty, the structure seen today is a result of a rebuilding and enlargement project that started in 1645 and ended fifty years later, when palatial living quarters for the fifth Dalai Lama were complete. Some parts of the original structure are said to remain beneath the lowest story of the palace.

Potala Palace is a complex of palaces, temples, mausoleums, and administrative buildings stretching 370 meters east to west and rising 115.7 meters in height. In addition to the palaces on the hill, parts of the square-shaped city at the foot of the hill and gardens behind it are considered integral to the overall layout. The "city" contains offices of the local government, printing houses for religious texts, and residences of officials.

The Red Palace, the center of Tibetan religious life, stands in the middle of a nine-story complex enclosed by a red wall that gives it its name. The four lower stories provide only a structural foundation, but the upper five are actively used. The fifth story from the bottom contains the Great West Hall, where religious ceremonies are

Figure 7.65. Zhashenlunbu Monastery, Xigaze, Tibet, founded in 1447, with later additions

Figure 7.66. Buddha Hall of Shouxi Temple in Labuleng Monastery, Xiahe, Gansu province, 1710 and later

performed, and the four top stories house funerary pagodas with the remains of the first four Dalai Lamas as well as more than twenty additional Buddhist halls. The whole area is enclosed by a corridor with a skywell in the middle. The roof of the Red Palace is flat with the exception of a few small hip-gable roofs covered with gilt-bronze tiles, which glitter in sunlight and add color to the structure.

The White Palace is east of the Red Palace and takes its name from the white paint that covers its walls. Seven stories high, it was the Dalai Lama's residence and administrative center. The lowest story is a structural foundation. The second contains an entrance on its eastern end. The third story is narrow, essentially a sandwich layer between the bottom and upper levels. Great East Hall, main residence of the Dalai Lama, occupies the fourth story. And the top three levels, like the top four of the Red Palace, are surrounded by a corridor with a skywell in the center. They contain offices for the regent and other high officials, kitchens, and storage areas. The very top level is

known as the Hall Where the Sun Radiates from East to West. The Dalai Lama lived there until 1959.

In front of the Red and White Palaces is a large, square courtyard divided into eastern and western parts. The Buddha Sunning Platform is situated inside a high wall along the steep hillside below the western courtyard. During festivals, huge woven images of the Buddha are hung on this wall.

The architecture of the two palace complexes was constructed so as to merge as seamlessly as possible with the hill on which it stands and the mountains behind it. The protective wall with four defensive battlements that encloses the two palace complexes also follows the natural topography. So do the long, winding stepped ramps that provide access to the Potala at the foot of the mountain. The bright colors, flat roofs, abundance of windows — and most important, natural features — create a romance and aesthetic unique to Tibet.

Three other lamaseries represent the purest forms of Tibetan Lamaist architecture, and all underwent large-scale renovations during the Qing dynasty. Zhashen-lunbu (Tashilhunpo) Monastery in Xigaze (Shigatse), about 150 kilometers southwest of Lhasa, was founded in 1447. It was the residence of the Panchen Lama. The fourth Panchen Lama and later successors expanded it into a huge complex of palaces, offices, worship halls, and funerary monuments (fig. 7.65). Like the Potala Palace, it does not have a clear axial arrangement. Rather, it consists of rows upon rows of structures, the sort of organic and flexible plan that follows natural topography and defines the Tibetan monastic aesthetic.

Labuleng Monastery in Xiahe, Gansu, is also an example of a Tibetan-style lamasery as well as one of the six great monasteries of Tibetan Buddhism (fig. 7.66). (The other five are Zashenlunbusi, Gandansi, Balasi, Zhe-bangsi, and Ta'ersi.) Begun in 1710, Labulengsi consists of six halls for study of the scriptures, eighteen Buddha temples, eighteen offices for the Living Buddha, and tens of thousands of residential rooms for the monks. It is so large that it can be thought of as a small town. With Dragon Mountain at its back and the Daxia River in front, its tall structures are all situated in the northern foothills of the mountain. Rows of buildings and corridors spread southward in an orderly array.

In Inner Mongolia, Tibetan lamasery architecture is represented by Wudangzhao in Baotou. With a majority of construction from the Kangxi through the Qianlong reign periods, the Wudangzhao dips and rises, sometimes with large spaces between its parts, from the top to the bottom of a steep slope. Its bright colors, so fundamental a characteristic of Tibetan lamasery architecture, are provided by the green pine trees and blue sky against which the whitewashed monastery walls stand.

Most Lamaist monasteries that reflect the merging of Tibetan architecture and native traditions of north China are found along the northern stretches of the Central Plain. Adhering to axial arrangements that characterize traditional Chinese religious and palatial architecture, two buildings seen in most of these lamaseries are a great sutra hall with simplified rather than complicated ornamental design and one or more funerary pagodas.

Xilituzhao in Hohhot (Huhehaote) can be considered a typical example (fig. 7.67). Its main structures stand along a firm axis, but the dominant structure is the Great Sutra Hall at the end of the building line. Rebuilt in 1696, the Great Sutra Hall is a tripartite structure. First is the front porch, next the hall that contains the scriptures, and last

Figure 7.67. Xilituzhao, Hohhot, Inner Mongolia, founded during the Ming dynasty, with significant rebuilding and expansion in the Qing dynasty

Figure 7.68. Putuozongchengmiao ("Potala Palace"), Chengde,
Hebei province, 1771

the Buddha hall. All three rise on a single building platform. The roofs of all three parts are formed by a Chinese-style timber frame, but the layout of three halls merged into one structure is characteristically Tibetan. Outside, the walls are covered with glazed blue ceramic bricks, and red lattice windows are set into the entry at the front porch. Gilded ornaments are pasted on the walls. The decorative features add to the magnificence of the structure, but the imposing aspect of a Tibetan block-style lamasery is lost.

The lamaseries and other Buddhist architecture of the Qing summer retreat at Chengde are primarily Sino-Tibetan in style. Their number and splendor add to the distinctive flavor of this city that perhaps more than any other reflects the merging of Manchu, Chinese, and other imported styles sought by and characteristic of Qing rule.

By the seventeenth century, the Qing leaders had decided that the peoples of the territory formerly known as Outer Mongolia and the adjacent regions, and by extension Russia, were among the greatest threats to their empire. Thus they rallied around the people of Inner Mongolia and Tibet, with whom they also shared their primary religion. While construction of the Summer Resort was under way, twelve Lamaist Buddhist building complexes were built to the east and north. Parts of eight of them stand today. Originally administered by eight different offices, they are often referred to as the Eight Outer Temples.

Two of the temple complexes, Purensi and Pushansi, were built during the Kangxi reign. Only Purensi, begun in 1713, survives. The others with extant architecture, and their dates of completion, are Puningsi, 1755; Puyousi, 1760; Anyuanmiao, 1764; Pulesi, 1767; Putuozongcheng-miao, 1771; Shuxiangsi, 1776; and Xumifushoumiao, 1780. These rich sites illustrate the architectural developments of the era in China, Tibet, Xinjiang, and Mongolia.

One feature that most Chengde monasteries share is structures of northern Chinese style in the front and non-Chinese, primarily Tibetan, style in the back. Buildings in the front part of the monastery include front gates, stelae pavilions, halls of the Divine Kings, and the main Buddha hall (Daxiongbaodian) along a single line. Back areas tend to be dominated by Great Sutra Halls in a mountainous Tibetan setting that offers a kind of overlay to the Chinese buildings. At Putuozongchengmiao, for instance, a replica of the Potala Palace (with red and white structures of the kind described earlier) creates a picturesque disorder behind the buildings at the front of the monastery (fig. 7.68). Xumifushoumiao was built to imitate Zhashenlunbusi and thus has in the back a tall red platform on which stood the circular Great Sutra Hall. The square platform and circular hall, surrounded by

Figure 7.69. Hall of the Great Vehicle, Puning Monastery, Chengde

pagodas, symbolize a mandala. The same forms stand at the back of Pulesi. Most impressive are the buildings in the back part of Puningsi. At the center is the Hall of the Great Vehicle (fig. 7.69). Behind it are pavilions raised on platforms and Lamaist-style pagodas symbolizing the eight great continents and four lesser ones, respectively (fig. 7.70). The jagged wall at the very back symbolizes the Buddhist world described in sutras.

Figure 7.70. Lamaist pavilion of Puningsi, 1755

Figure 7.71. Pavilion of the Light of Dawn (Xuguangge), Pule Monastery, Chengde, 1767

Figure 7.72. Interior of the Pavilion of the Light of Dawn at Pulesi, showing the circular ceiling above a four-sided altar

All principal structures of the Eight Outer Temples are impressive, whether inspired by Chinese architecture or by non-Chinese traditions. They are of huge proportions and often located on the highest spot in the complex; their purpose was to bring worshipers to a state of ecstasy. The Hall of the Great Vehicle of Puningsi, for example, is a three-story structure with six tiers of roof eaves. Each set of eaves is smaller in circumference than the one below it, and the whole is topped by five separate roofs. The Pavilion of the Light of Dawn (Xuguangge) of Pulesi is circular in plan with a double-eave, pointed conical roof (figs. 7.71 and 7.72). Eight glazed brick pagodas stand at its sides. At Putuozongchengmiao, the Great Red Platform follows the intricate shape of the topography, with a jagged plan and unevenly sized rooms. Thus Tibetan art forms entered the world of Han architecture and craftsmanship to create buildings of unique magnificence.

Ta'ersi, in Qinghai province, is also an example of Sino-Tibetan Lamaist architecture (fig. 7.73). Its earlier buildings, Dazhao Hall and Xijingang Hall, for example, are essentially Chinese. Yet its later structures, in particular the Great Sutra Hall, are largely Tibetan in style. Its Hall for Expounding the Sutras exhibits elements of both styles.

Figure 7.73. Ta'ersi (Kumbum Monastery), Qinghai province

Temple complexes of Lamaist Buddhism constructed according to traditional Chinese building standards are also quite important. One of the best examples is Yonghegong, the palace of the Yongzheng emperor, which was turned into the largest lamasery in Beijing. Its halls are singular not only because of the Chinese style of Lamaist Buddhism practiced there but because of the Qing palatial forms seen in the structures themselves (fig. 7.74). Falundian, the Hall of the Wheel of the Law, has five small pavilions symbolizing the peaks of Mount Sumeru rising from its roof, the central one larger than the other four. Wanfu Pavilion consists of three pavilions in a row joined by "flying" (elevated) bridges *(feiqiao)*, which symbolize heavenly pavilions (fig. 7.75).

From the outside, although Lamaist Buddhist architecture appears more fortified than Chinese Buddhist architecture (a consequence of the influence of block-style dwellings native to Tibet), it also appears more mystical and perhaps awe-inspiring. Six features lead to these aesthetic assessments. First are the actual structures. The Great Scripture Hall tends to be huge and elevated, so that it dominates even in a mountainous setting. Just one part of a complex that also contains corridors with revolving sutra cabinets, dormitories, storage spaces, and in Tibet administrative buildings and residences for important lamas, the hall, like all of Lamaist architecture, inevitably seems exotic wherever it is located in China. Second, Lamaist architecture spans mountainous terrain more flexibly and less systematically than any other building complexes known to China, including Daoist monasteries located in mountains. Third, not only are Lamaist principal structures imposing because of their huge size, but they also are of varied form, with circular as well as four-sided features. Often, too, an enormous structure is encircled by smaller ones, creating three-dimensional spaces symbolic of the Buddhist world — sometimes an entire mandala, other times smaller areas such as Mount Sumeru or heavenly palaces. An example is the back area of Pulesi, in Chengde, where eight Tibetan-style pagodas surround the circular hall.

Fourth, the huge structures and new forms, down to the details of pillars — which were pasted or inlaid with gold — and framed roofs without bracket sets to support them, challenged the traditional Chinese building system so fundamentally that anyone who saw, for example, the Great Vehicle Pavilion of Puningsi or the triple-pavilion complex with five roof pavilions at Wanfu Pavilion at Yonghegong, could not help but be inspired. Fifth, even compared with Lamaist architecture such as the White Pagoda of Miaoying Monastery in Beijing, Qing-period Lamaist architecture was more creative. Whereas the thirteenth-century pagoda was a single mass, Qing-period Lamaist architecture stressed the combination of structures, their variable shapes and the decoration of the minute parts — indeed the beauty of the individual structure was no longer considered the main objective.

Finally, the interiors of Lamaist halls were highly elaborate and awe-inspiring, with gilded and robed images, pillars embellished with cloth as well as carvings, and walls fully painted as well as adorned with tankas and streamers. The pervasive mystique of Tibetan architecture in China reinforces the drama of ceremonies performed in the buildings and on altars set against mountainous backdrops.

The popularity of Lamaist Buddhism in China led to a corresponding decline in traditional Han Chinese Buddhist sects. Support for non-Lamaist Buddhism came only from the population, whereas the Qing emperors patronized Lamaism almost exclusively. In spite of these hard times for Han Buddhism, construction of some large-scale monasteries continued. Artistically, the new buildings were comparable to some of the finest structures that had come before. Jietai Monastery in Beijing, for instance, had the largest altar in China. The Hall of the Five Hundred Arhats (Luohan) at Biyun Monastery, also in Beijing, resolved the problem of fitting in the many images while getting enough light into the hall by erecting a four-sided structure with windows and aisles that crossed in the center so that worshipers could walk up to the image groups. When Jiangtiansi, formerly known as Jinshansi and located on the bank of the Yangzi in Zhejiang, was rebuilt, it was transformed into a scenic spot in which the harmonious placement of pavilions, kiosks, and platforms was a priority. Tiantong Monastery in Ningbo, which had been a famous Chan monastery since the Tang and Song dynasties, came to have a Great Buddha Hall whose upper roof eaves spanned twelve purlin lengths and whose lower eaves extended three purlin lengths in

Figure 7.74. Yonghe Palace, Beijing

front and three behind for a total span of eighteen purlins, one of the most magnificent roofs ever constructed.

Some of the most major contributions to non-Lamaist Buddhist architecture of the Qing period occurred on the four sacred Buddhist peaks — Wutaishan in Shanxi, Emeishan in Sichuan, Jiuhuashan in Anhui, and Putuoshan in Zhejiang — and other important or scenic mountains and pilgrimage sites. The most famous of the Buddhist peaks throughout Chinese history has been Mount Wutai,

Figure 7.75. Wanfu Pavilion at Yonghegong

Figure 7.76. Baoguo Monastery, Mount Emei, Sichuan province, Qing period

dedicated to the bodhisattva Manjusri. Its two Tang-period halls, at Nanchan Monastery and Foguang Monastery, were discussed in Chapter 4. Of the more than one hundred active monasteries on the mountain, most have a Ming-period history and at least one structure that dates to the Ming dynasty. Many of the Ming monasteries, however, were originally built in the official style of the Ming with regular layouts, that is, with buildings constructed around courtyards and courtyards arranged one behind another on axial lines. Only later were some of these monasteries converted to lamaseries, with their mountainous setting enhancing the newly created elements of Tibetan-style or Chinese-Tibetan architecture. Among today's most popular monasteries on Wutaishan that feature later Chinese architecture are Pusa Ding and Longquansi, both famous for elaborate archways, the one wooden and the other in stone, at the end of a 108-step approach; Xiantong Monastery, known for its bronze hall and beamless hall, both from the Ming period; and Tayuan Monastery, with a fifty-meter white stone Lamaist pagoda that also dates to the Ming period.

Emeishan, whose main peak towers 3,099 meters above sea level, is approached via a fifty-kilometer wind-

Figure 7.77. Fayu Monastery, Mount Putuo, Zhejiang province

ing stepped path that requires several days of walking to complete. It is a repository of non-Lamaist monasteries whose architecture nevertheless follows flexible, free-flowing layouts dictated by topography. Most of the approximately seventy temple complexes are located near the top of the mountain. The halls of Baoguosi (fig. 7.76), for example, are built on terraces of different levels. The entry to Fuhusi is approached by a pavilionlike bridge. Some of the structures of Leiyinsi are raised on stilts. And the buildings of Qingyinge follow a rectangular but irregular layout in which the narrow stretch of land between the Black Dragon and White Dragon rivers offers changing scenic views. Thus the static plans of earlier Buddhist monasteries, including the seven-structure plans of Chan, are broken down or even ignored in the quest to take full advantage of the magnificent natural scenery. In this way, the Buddhist architecture of the Qing period might be said to follow the priorities of both Lamaist architecture and garden construction of the Qing court.

Most of the monasteries of Mount Jiuhua are small, some of them merely hermitages with small halls and others temple complexes with thatched huts. Still others are composed of only a few small meditation halls for monks. Because of this small scale, many of the buildings on Jiuhuashan resemble local residential architecture more than Buddhist monasteries of the past: they have walls made of rubble and painted occasionally in white but not other colors, small azure roof tiles, few paintings or other decoration on the walls, and only simple architectural decoration. Some of the temple complexes are built right up to roads or with roads cutting through them, a plan that was convenient for pilgrims but lacked the dramatic approach afforded most Buddhist monasteries. With architecture that might be called fresh, simple, natural, or airy, the monasteries of Jiuhuashan have none of the mystery of Tibetan Buddhist architecture or the solemnity of traditional Chinese Buddhist forms.

Putuoshan is a small island on the Zhoushan archipelago on the eastern coast of Zhejiang province. Three major monasteries — Pujisi, Fayusi, and Huijici — as well as numerous small nunneries, convents, and monasteries composed largely of huts, were sites of pilgrimage for Buddhists from all parts of East Asia since the ninth

Figure 7.78. Suspended in the Air Monastery, Hunyuan county,
Shanxi province

century. Putuoshan is unique in that it is a locus of religious activity as well as a sea environment, with the spiritual mood enhanced by natural rock outcroppings that provide a backdrop for Buddhist imagery and worship cells for monks (fig. 7.77).

The syncretism of Buddhist, Daoist, and Confucian worship in one monastery, which, as discussed in Chapter 6, was characteristic of certain Yuan-period Daoist sects, occurred at Buddhist temple complexes during the Qing period. One of the monasteries known for blending these traditions is the famous Suspended in the Air Monastery (Xuankongsi), located in Hunyuan county, Shanxi, approximately halfway between Datong and Mount Wutai (figs. 7.78 and 7.79). Built right on a cliff, the buildings are attached to the mountain by plank roads and suspended bridges. Structurally, the monastery is a feat of engineering unparalleled in Chinese history. Gao Temple in Zhongwei, Ningxia, is also a syncretic worship site. With the buildings of its back part located right on the city wall, it uses the architecture as its mountain.

The Dai of Xishuangbanna autonomous region and Dehong prefecture of Yunnan, whose residential architecture was discussed earlier in this chapter, traditionally

Figure 7.79. Vertical posts and horizontal beams supporting Suspended in the Air Monastery

Figure 7.80. Dai monastery, Jinghong, Xishuangbanna autonomous region, Yunnan province

Figure 7.81. Buddha Hall at Dai monastery in Xishuangbanna

Figure 7.82. White Pagoda of Manfeilong Monastery, Jinghong,
Xishuangbanna, Yunnan province

Figure 7.83. Octagonal pagoda at Jingzhen Monastery, Menghai
county, Yunnan province, 1701

followed the Southern sect of Theravada Buddhism, which was still popular in the bordering countries of Myanmar (formerly Burma) and other parts of Southeast Asia. Its architecture reflects local and regional styles as well as those of Burma and Thailand, sometimes so much so that Dai temple complexes are called Mansi, or Burmese monasteries.

Dai monasteries are most often built either on high ground or in the center of a village. Their plans are free-flowing, without enclosing corridors or courtyards. Major structures are the Buddha hall, sutra library, main gate, monks' quarters, and one or more pagodas (fig. 7.80).

The principal structure of a Dai monastery is the Buddha hall. Tall, with hip-gable roofs that slope sharply with layers of eaves arranged like steps, the Xishuangbanna Buddhist halls have many carved decorations, and ceramic tiles or other ceramic decoration attached to each layer (fig. 7.81). Buddha halls in the Dehong region tend to have roof eaves less steep than those elsewhere, more similar to those of monastery architecture in western Yunnan than of Myanmar or Thailand. The underside of roof eaves is painted red, with gold decoration attached. An identifying feature of the Dai Buddha hall is that it is entered on the east, with the main image oriented toward the entryway. As a Theravada structure of this Southern sect, the only image present is that of the historical Buddha Sakyamuni.

Pagodas of Xishuangbanna and Dehong are shaped like cylinders and have solid (as opposed to hollow) interiors. Existing both individually and as groups in monasteries, the most famous single pagodas are the front and back pagodas at Great Buddha Monastery in Fengping, Luxi, and the best-known pagoda group is the Manfeilong White Pagoda in Jinghong, Yunnan, where eight small Buddha shrines rise in an octagonal shape on a circular dais (fig. 7.82). Each pagoda-shrine is capped by a conical pagoda, and a large cone-shaped pagoda stands in the center of the group. The group is commonly called the Bamboo Shoot Pagodas because the structures remind the locals of bamboo shoots that grow after a spring rain.

Sutra halls of the Dai are generally smaller versions of Buddha halls. The sutra hall of Jingzhen Monastery is an exception. Octagonal in plan, its roof is an eleven-layer cone with exquisite decoration (fig. 7.83).

Islamic Architecture

No Muslim community can exist without a mosque. This is true in China as well as in those parts of the world with significantly larger or predominantly Muslim populations. Mosques outside of West Asia and North Africa reflect a unique blending of traditional Islamic elements

Figure 7.84. Roofs of Houyao Hall, Dahuoxiang Mosque, Tianjin, 1703

and building traditions of the local population. Chinese mosques are no exception, although those of Xinjiang, in the past as well as today, more closely resemble mosques of the Arabian Peninsula or Iran than architecture of the Central Plain or southeastern China.

Certain features must exist in any mosque. First, worship must be directed toward Makka (Mecca), meaning that, in East Asia, a mosque is generally oriented east–west with its *qiblah* (wall that includes the *mihrab,* or prayer niche, directing worship toward Makka) on the west. Inside the main worship hall in which the qiblah is located, one finds no images and thus no altar, a sharp contrast to the great majority of Chinese religious halls. In fact, one rarely finds human figures or animals among the decoration, which most often includes plant or floral motifs, purely ornamental patterns, and inscriptions (frequently Quranic verses in decorative calligraphy). Inside the main hall, one may also find a pulpit or enclosed space for worship by the community leader or a prince. Outside the main hall, sometimes freestanding and sometimes part of it, is the minaret, the tower from which worshipers are called to prayer. Among all the buildings of a mosque, the minaret has been most easily adapted to Chinese architecture, in the form of a pagoda or gate tower. One also finds a pond or fountain in a central courtyard for preworship ablutions.

Chinese mosques have been constructed by local craftsmen in almost every major city and most provinces with a variety of local materials and in many styles. Still, mosques in China lend themselves to division into two main groups, those of the Hui and those of the Uyghurs.

Hui refers to a large nationality among the population of greater China who live for the most part in Ningxia, Gansu, Qinghai, Hebei, Henan, Shandong, Yunnan, Anhui, Xinjiang, Liaoning, and the cities of Beijing and Tianjin. Both the layout of Hui mosques and individual features of the buildings tend to follow patterns of traditional Chinese architecture. That is, buildings are arranged along strict axial lines and positioned around courtyards; halls and groups of halls are often symmetrical; archways resembling pailou (Chinese ceremonial archways), screen walls, brick multistory gates, and residential-style gateways are often included; and structures tend to be as colorful as those of Han Chinese temple complexes. Those unaware that they were standing in a mosque would assume that its minaret was a pagoda or pavilion. In general, the overall impression of a Hui mosque can be called orientalizing as opposed to Islamic.

Great East Mosque in Jining, Shandong province, is a good example of a Hui mosque. Oriented east–west, all the roofs are hipped or hip-gable and decorated with glazed ceramic tiles. They cover the components of the main compound in a progression from low to high, sheltering worshipers from rain and allowing light to enter the inner courtyard. Because these two features, lighting and protection from rain, are a concern of all mosque builders, a series of five interrelated or interconnected structures of graduated height is fairly common in mosque design. It is found, for example, at Ox Street Mosque in Beijing, the Great Weizhou Mosque and Shizuishan Mosque in Ningxia, and the Great West Mosque in Jining, Shandong province.

Another feature of the roofs of Hui mosques that reminds us that they have a place in the Chinese architectural tradition is tall pavilions placed on top of roofs. Dahuoxiang Mosque in Tianjin, for example, has five double-eaved square pavilions and six double-eaved hexagonal pavilions arranged in rows on top of Houyao Hall (fig. 7.84). The undersides of eaves at Hui mosques, however — including the corners of eaves on the main worship hall of Ox Street Mosque — tend to have decorative patterns common to traditional Chinese architecture. When pointed arches typical of Islamic architecture are found, the Arabic letters may be carved along the lines of the arch, but other spaces are filled in with Chinese floral and leaf patterns, and the common Chinese decorative colors, red and gold, may be painted or inlaid to enhance the patterns. This appealing mix of Chinese and Islamic styles can be seen in both stone and wood carvings.

Most Uyghur mosques are in southern Xinjiang, known for its arid climate. Historically, this has been the part of Asia connected by land and history to both East and West Asia. Often one story with wooden pillars and mud facades, they feature archways and domed ceilings, all constructed of mud-earth.

Although the layouts of Uyghur mosques tend not to be symmetrical, the main worship halls most often are rectangular in plan, sometimes built around or facing courtyards. Carved on the courtyard side may be an *iwan,* a three-dimensional pointed-arch niche closed on all but the courtyard or exterior side. An iwan similarly may mark the entrance to a Uyghur mosque, a minaret may stand at its side, and, typical of construction in the Islamic world farther west in Asia, this facade may also face the town square. Like houses of the Uyghurs, the mosque is often divided into inner halls for winter use and outer halls for use in warmer months. The inner hall is smaller and closed, whereas the outer hall, the one used for

Figure 7.85. Emin Mosque, Turpan, Xinjiang Uyghur autonomous region, 1778

more of the year, is more spacious and open, even to the sky (fig. 7.85). The tall, thin pillars and other supports for its timber frame are exposed in this outer hall. Such outer pillars of a Uyghur mosque are painted in bright colors, often green, brown, and blue, and ceiling areas are white. Simple and open, these outer areas offer little mystique.

Decoration is concentrated on the interior of the worship hall. Niches including the mihrab, the coffered ceiling, lattices of windows in the wall that divides inner and outer halls, and pillars are the focal points of decorative attention, with geometric and floral patterns pressed into stucco parts. Pillars often consist of three parts — base,

body, and capital — each with its own decoration. Capitals may have small pointed-arch indentations resembling flowers in full bloom (figs. 7.86 and 7.87).

Another material found on Uyghur mosques that is directly derivative of Islamic architecture is brick mosaic. The Emin Minaret in Turpan is at least forty meters tall and has unique brick geometric mosaic patterns: the sizes of the tiles change according to the decreasing diameter of the tower from bottom to top. The seemingly limitless changes in pattern are characteristic of Islamic architecture and have no Chinese counterparts; the only places such decoration exists in China is on the structures of Muslims.

Figure 7.86. Interior of Idkah Mosque in Kashgar, Xinjiang Uyghur autonomous region, begun in 1426, with many later repairs

Figure 7.87. Column decorations of Apakh Hoja Mosque in Kashgar, begun in 1640

Daoist Architecture

Of all the religions in China during the Qing period, Daoism had the least presence. New construction involved primarily rebuilding small temples or temple groups, sometimes together with Buddhist structures. Nothing of the scale or magnificence of White Cloud Monastery, Yonglegong, or the monasteries of Wudang-shan was initiated, and the powerful sects of former times such as Quanzhen (centered in Shanxi, north China) were on the decline. Architecture did survive at those sites and similar ones, and at some sites interest in the structures revived in the twentieth century. New building, however, was initiated primarily along the densely populated coastal regions of southeastern China.

In order to increase its influence in China, Daoism incorporated local and popular deities, often heroes and demigods who at one time had been mortals. Those worshiped included Wenchang (god of literature and especially popular in Sichuan), the Eight Immortals, Lü Dongbin (one of the Eight Immortals and the most influential transcendent of the Quanzhen sect), and Guandi (associated with war and patron of military officials). The Chinese built temples, shrines, and veneration temples to them to encourage religious participation by the local populace.

The transformation of a former Daoist monastery into a more popular religious temple complex can be observed at Temples to the Eastern Peak (Dongyuemiao). Dongyue Dadi, the Lord of the Eastern Peak, originally was a natural spirit who resided at Taishan, one of the sacred Daoist peaks. He was said to have power over life, death, and the spirits who controlled human affairs. Because of these awesome and tremendous powers, temples to the Lord of the Eastern Peak were built in almost every city and town in China. Beginning in the Song dynasty, dramatic performances were enacted at temple festivals as a way of encouraging the locals to become more involved with the life of these and other temples. Eventually, temples and monasteries came to be the locations of fairs and other activities that brought large groups of people inside their walls.

A feature that distinguished Daoist architecture of the Qing period was that it tended to be located in towns. This had not been the case historically. The earliest Daoist architecture is believed to have been in secluded locations — among mountains, grottoes, and forests, for example — whose natural settings enhanced meditation, austerities, alchemical experiments, and trances. Not one of the Thirty-Six Heavenly Grottoes and Seventy-Two Blessed Plots designated as sacred to

Figure 7.88. Qingyang Daoist Monastery, Chengdu, Sichuan province

Daoists was located in a city or town. But as Daoism became a more urbane religion, reaching out to citizens of Qing China, monasteries by necessity came to be built in densely populated areas. Numerous large Daoist monasteries were built or rebuilt in cities or towns during the Qing dynasty, including Qingyanggong in Chengdu (fig. 7.88); Fulongguan in Guan county, Sichuan; Sanqingge in Kunming, Yunnan; Jintaiguan in Baoji, Shaanxi; Yuquanguan in Tianshui, Gansu; and Gaomiao in Zhongwei, Ningxia. Even monasteries of Mount Qingcheng in Guan county, historically a thriving center for Daoist practice in a mountainous setting, were moved dozens of kilometers down the mountain to make access more convenient for worshipers.

In spite of the accommodations to city life, as Daoist monasteries these complexes maintained the traditional flexibility and freer flow of layouts that differentiate them from many Buddhist temple compounds. Some, such as Chunyanggong in Taiyuan, Shanxi, and Qingyanggong, had symmetrical plans, but others, such as Yuquanguan, adhered to no formal arrangement. Making full use of Qing architectural and engineering capabilities, Daoist architecture often had buildings of many stories, symbolizing the belief that immortals could transcend this world to live in lofty towers. Wohuanggong in Shexian, Hebei, had a main hall of four stories, and Wenchang Pavilion in Shanghang, Fujian, was six stories on the exterior with a differently styled roof for each level, creating a uniquely exquisite silhouette. The back structure of Gaomiao in Zhongwei, which, as mentioned

earlier, was constructed on a tall dais on the city wall, is one of the many buildings of that complex that used the natural environment to best advantage. Other buildings at Gaomiao were heavenly gates, heavenly bridges, heavenly pools, and heavenly palaces, all three-story structures whose names and forms symbolized otherworldliness. The most common technique used to express the ethereal aspect of Daoism in architecture, however, was the construction of three *tianmen* (heavenly gates), placed according to the natural terrain. Examples of such gates are found at Taihecheng in Kunming, Yuquanguan in Tianshui, Yuanmiaoguan in Jiangling, Hebei, and Qiyunshan in Anhui.

Syncretism, however, was the main attraction of Daoism for Qing China. In some instances, Buddhist rites were adopted by Daoist monasteries. In other cases, Buddhist monasteries merged with Daoist ones. Such blending could result in primarily Buddhist temple complexes where certain elements of Daoist worship were retained, as was the case at Baiyunshan in Jia county, Shaanxi; half-Buddhist, half-Daoist settings such as Gaomiao in Zhongwei; or fully syncretic monasteries in which Buddhas, Laozi, and Confucius were all worshiped, such as the Xuankongsi in Hunyuan, Shanxi.

The increased decoration of Daoist buildings of the Qing period was probably also due to this syncretism. Relief sculpture and carved decoration were more common than in the past. In south China, Daoist architecture was noticeably more decorative on the exterior, with roof corners that turned up higher, more layers of roof eaves, and

Figure 7.89. Dragon head and colored paintings

more elaborately decorated roof ridges. Sometimes the decoration was highly detailed to the point of being dainty. In fact, Daoist architecture of south China is more decorative than any other group of religious buildings of Qing China.

Technical Aspects of Qing Architecture

More buildings were constructed during the Qing dynasty than in any previous period of Chinese history. With dwindling timber resources, builders trained in the age-old wooden tradition had to turn to new materials to keep up with the building boom. Brick and tile came to be widely used, with brick in particular overcoming its humble past and becoming a material used in upscale homes. Houses were also made of combinations of brick

and stone or brick and wood. In addition, bamboo, thatch, and white lime became commonly used.

The variety of decorative materials also increased. Among the materials that opened up new possibilities for ornamentation were hardwoods, carved woods, bronze, gold paper, silk, jade, shell, lacquer, glazed tiles, and porcelain. From the mid-Qing on, imported glass was also used, for windows. The wide variety of materials not only led to technological advances; it also greatly changed the outward appearance of architecture in China (figs. 7.89 and 7.90).

Meanwhile, techniques used in wood joinery changed and in some cases were eliminated. Standard Yuan-Ming features whose origins lie in much earlier Chinese construction — such as entasis, rise, and large bracket-set components — gradually disappeared or at least fell out of use; the *cai-fen* system of proportions all but disappeared.

Instead, building components became smaller and sturdier, as well as more decorative. One place where the decorative quality of Qing architecture can be observed is in the beaklike component tucked under the lintel alongside a pillar. Another place in which the new decorative aspect is seen is in the joining of one piece of wood to another. Regardless of whether the structure was a pavilion, large building, building with more than one beam, or building with a complicated roof, the pieces that held bracket sets in place were removed from the undersides of eaves and instead were tenoned to one another, forming a stronger, more compact frame. Multistory buildings in which this technique was employed include Great Vehicle Pavilion of Puningsi in Chengde, Foxiang Pavilion at the Summer Palace in Beijing, and Wanfu Pavilion at Yonghegong. In addition to bracket sets, pillars and beams were removed from these buildings and replaced by smaller wooden

poles bound together by iron bands and wrapped with hemp-fiber plaster. The end result, as described earlier, resembled pillars made from whole tree trunks and was called the "saving by binding" method. Not only did this method succeed in economizing wood, it made story-by-story construction easier.

The China that approached the modern era shone with examples of expert construction and decoration with all sorts of materials, as well as evidence of increased regionalism (figs. 7.91 and 7.92). Four-storied structures, for example, were as successfully made with rammed earth or cobblestone in Fujian and Guangzhou as with wood. In Tibet, builders constructed high walls of stone without using ropes, parapets, or levelers to keep them steady or to check their placement of materials. Such was the case also among builders of walls of stone slabs in Tiantai, Zhejiang province, stone walls and roofs in

Figure 7.90. Decorative painting on architectural components

Figure 7.91. Window latticework of Manjusri Temple, Chengdu, Sichuan province

Figure 7.92. Charity Archway at Tangxue, Qing dynasty

Hui'an, Fujian province, and completely stone buildings in Zhenning, Guizhou province.

A comprehensive official architectural manual, the second in Chinese history, survives from the Qing period. Although other officially sponsored building manuals were also written during Qing times, and nonofficial manuals such as the fifteenth-century *Lu Ban jing* (named for a fifth-century B.C.E. craftsman who later attained demigod status) had been written as well, *Gongbu gongcheng zuofa zeli* (Engineering manual for the Board of Works) is considered the successor to the twelfth-century *Yingzao fashi*. The version of *Gongbu gongcheng zuofa zeli* generally considered most authoritative was issued in the twelfth year of the Yongzheng reign, or 1734.

Like *Yingzao fashi*, *Gongbu gongcheng zuofa zeli* was intended first of all to set the standards for laborers in the construction of official building projects. In it were regulated such aspects of building as costs of materials, antic-

ipated hours for construction, and wages. The first twenty-seven of its seventy-four *juan* (chapters) describe methods for the construction of twenty-seven different sizes of building frames; the next fourteen address bracket sets; the following six juan discuss stone and tile work; thirteen juan then comment on work quotas and amounts of materials to be used; and the last fourteen juan deal with issues of labor.

In several important ways this work differs from *Yingzao fashi*. First and most important, the original was not illustrated — even though the version most often used today is an illustrated book produced in the 1930s by Liang Sicheng and other members of the Society for Research on Chinese Architecture, who added illustrations to clarify the original text. Second, the Qing text exists in several different versions, all issued between 1727 and 1747. (*Yingzao fashi* was reissued forty-two years after its initial publication and later, but there is only one official version.) Third, specific buildings are mentioned. Most of them are structures of the Qing Summer Palaces or Yonghegong in Beijing and architecture in Chengde. It has been suggested that the treatise was written specifically to address issues relevant to imperial Qing construction at these locations.

Like *Yingzao fashi,* the book is a product of the Board of Works. The leaders of two of its offices, Lei Fada of the Office of Designs and Liu Tingzan of the Office of Final Accounting, were probably involved in the completion of *Gongbu gongcheng zuofa zeli* and other similar writings, perhaps to the extent of Li Jie in Northern Song times. The Qing work is also used today in ways similar to the use of *Yingzao fashi*. That is, the explanations of the module (known as *doukou* rather than cai-fen), descriptions of ratios of building parts such as diameter to height of a pillar, and detailed analyses of methods of roof construction both help current scholars understand eighteenth-century building practice and guide our as-sessment and dating of buildings found without accompanying inscriptions, stelae, or textual records. The document is also used with *Yingzao fashi* to confirm that those features that are perceived as defining Qing structures — significantly smaller but more numerous intercolumnar bracket sets, taller and more slender columns, and greater ratios of column height to size of bracket set, for example — were indeed standard elements of Qing building practice and not just a reflection of the more somber and detailed style of eighteenth-century official buildings in China.

It is always difficult to describe an architectural aesthetic. A summary of structural features that are believed to be unknown before a certain time, or at least do not survive in earlier examples, may aid in that definition. For the Qing period, certain buildings and forms not seen in China before the seventeenth century stand out, and thus help pinpoint what is Qing about the Chinese building tradition. Certainly the architecture of Lamaist Buddhism — in particular lamaseries and palace-lamaseries built in Tibet, the architecture of the Eight Outer Temples at Chengde, the Yonghegong, and perhaps the main halls of Sino-Tibetan monasteries — is more closely associated with China under Manchu rule than at any other time, even if the structural origins of each building predate the Qing. Houses that reflect regionalism first and principles of Chinese architecture second also are emblems of what we call Qing. So are the imperial gardens in Beijing and the Chengde Summer Palace. Perhaps the houses might have been constructed even if Qing rule had never occurred, but the many peoples whose union both defined Qing society and challenged its elasticity encouraged national and regional expression in vernacular construction. Ethnicity, and at the same time the management of ethnicity, were as integral to Qing construction as they were to Qing society. To the extent that the last Chinese empire can be called multicultural, so can its architecture.

SELECT BIBLIOGRAPHY

Research on Chinese architecture has taken place almost exclusively in China, not only because the buildings are there, but because so many of them have been difficult for outsiders to reach. Since the beginning of the modern study of Chinese architecture—that is, for most of the past century—access to Chinese buildings has been limited either by the government or by physical obstacles to getting to the sites. Often the only way to reach buildings outside China's metropolitan areas is on foot. Still today, even the most adventuresome readers of this book will find it extremely difficult and occasionally impossible to see some of the buildings discussed, or to enter them once there. Most of the literature about Chinese architecture, then, has been written in Chinese. And because it has been assumed that many readers of this book will not read Chinese, we decided to provide information about references and research tools at the end of the book rather than in notes consisting almost entirely of Chinese titles.

There are fewer books about Chinese architecture, even in Chinese, than about almost any other multi-millennial architectural tradition in the world. Perhaps this is because the search for China's old buildings and archaeological remains is very much ongoing. Since 1950, when widespread excavation in China was initiated, not a year has passed without the discovery of a building or site of profound importance for China's architectural history. Anyone engaged in primary research on Chinese architecture is aware that the opening of such new sites may significantly alter published assumptions. Thus the study of Chinese architecture relies heavily on periodical literature, most of which is sponsored by national or provincial research institutes whose affiliates are engaged in site work. Indeed buildings of fundamental importance continue to be uncovered so rapidly that only a small fraction of China's most significant buildings and sites have been studied beyond their initial publications or site reports.

Reference Works and Dictionaries

Although occasionally findings of architectural importance have been accidental, major progress in the identification and subsequent uncovering of China's old buildings began in the early twentieth century with a search through Chinese historical records and relevant sections in provincial, prefectural, or governmental agencies. Through the 1930s researchers combed the Chinese countryside in search of buildings mentioned in those records. Then as now no definitive dictionary, encyclopedia, or data base of Chinese buildings, sites, or architectural terms exists. The works listed here, however, should be helpful in reading the primary sources in Chinese, from which the field grew, as well as broader studies of Chinese architecture. Key examples of those works and several seminal English-language references listed below offer valuable background information for the study of Chinese history as well as Chinese architecture and technology.

Ershisi shi 二十四史 (History of twenty-four dynasties). Beijing: Zhonghua shuju, 1974 and later.

He Benfang 何本方and Yue Qingping 岳庆平. *Zhongguo gong-ting zhishi cidian* 中国宫廷知识词典 (Dictionary of Chinese palatial architecture). Beijing: Zhongguo Guoji Guangfan Press, 1990.

Hucker, Charles O. *A Dictionary of Official Titles in Imperial China*. Stanford: Stanford University Press, 1985.

Jianzhu dacidian 建筑大辞典 (Dictionary of architecture). Beijing: Seismology Publishing House, 1992.

Lü Songyun 吕松云and Liu Shizhong 刘诗中. *Zhongguo gudai jianzhu cidian* 中国建筑词典 (Dictionary of premodern Chinese architectural terminology). Beijing: Quanguo Xinhua Book Company, 1992.

Mote, Frederick. *Imperial China: 900–1800*. Cambridge: Harvard University Press, 1999.

Needham, Joseph. *Science and Civilization in China*. 7 vols. Cambridge: Cambridge University Press, 1956–present (ongoing); esp. vol. 4.

Tan Qixiang 谭其骧, chief ed. *Zhongguo lishi ditu ji* 中国历史地图集 (Historical atlas of China). 8 vols. Beijing: Cartographic Publishing House, 1982–1987.

Twitchett, Denis, and John K. Fairbank, eds. *The Cambridge History of China*. New York: Cambridge University Press, 1978–.

Wang Xiaoqing 王效青, chief ed. *Zhongguo gujianzhu shuyu cidian* 中国古建筑术语词典 (Dictionary of terminology of premodern Chinese architectural art). Taiyuan: Shanxi People's Press, 1996.

Wilkinson, Endymion. *Chinese History: A Manual*. Cambridge: Harvard University Press, 1998.

Zhongguo mingsheng cidian 中国名胜词典 (Dictionary of famous places in China). Shanghai: Shanghai Dictionary Press, 1981.

Zhongguo wenwu ditu ji 中国文物地图集 (Atlas of Chinese cultural relics). Ongoing project published by publishing house of each province, 1991–.

Zhonghua Renmin Gongheguo fensheng ditu ji 中华人民共和国分省地图集 (Atlas of each province of the People's Republic of China). Beijing: Cartographic Publishing House, 1977.

Illustrated Series

Multivolume works on Chinese architecture with numerous high-quality illustrations have been undertaken by some of China's major art and architecture publishing houses. The following are often used by researchers of Chinese architecture.

Zhongguo gujianzhu daji 中国古建筑大系 (Chinese premodern architecture series). 10 vols. Beijing and Taipei: China Building Industry Press and Kwangfu Book Enterprises, 1993.

Zhongguo kaogu jicheng 中国考古集成 (Compendium of Chinese archaeology). 22 vols. Published by provincial or city presses, 1994–1999.

Zhongguo meishu fenlei quanji 中国美术分类全集 (Compendium of categories of Chinese art). Zhongguo jianzhu yishu quanji 中国建筑艺术全集 (The art of Chinese architecture series). 24 vols. Beijing: China Building Industry Press, 1999–.

Zhongguo meishu quanji 中国美术全集 (Compendium of Chinese art). Jianzhu yishu bian 中国艺术编 (Architectural art series). 6 vols. Beijing: China Building Industry Press, 1991.

Chinese Periodical Literature

The most important information about Chinese architecture usually appears in the journals listed below. The one that introduced the historical and scholarly aspects of Chinese architecture, *Zhongguo yingzao xueshe huikan,* was printed in only seven volumes between 1929 and 1942. Many of the studies in it remain the sole report of research on a subject, and every serious student of Chinese architecture has read every article in every issue. Some are reprinted in collections of essays by their authors (listed in the next section). Among the other periodicals, *Wenwu* and *Kaogu* with their predecessors (with similar titles) have had the longest continuous histories. Other journals have been more intermittently published, but are also considered essential reading. In the following list, titles are given by standard abbreviation and then the full title; the translated title or the area of China covered by the periodical is given in parentheses.

BSRCA	*Zhongguo yingzao xueshe huikan* 中国营造学社汇刊 (Bulletin of the Society for Research in Chinese Architecture; 7 vols. only)
BFWW	*Beifang wenwu* 北方文物 (the three Northeastern provinces: Liaoning, Jilin, Heilongjiang)
BJWB	*Beijing wenbo* 北京文博 (Beijing)
DNWH	*Dongnan wenhua* 东南文化 (Nanjing and southeastern China)
GGBWYYK	*Gugong Bowuyuan yuankan* 故宫博物院院刊 (Palace Museum Bulletin)
HXKG	*Huaxia kaogu* 华夏考古 (primarily Henan)
JZSLWJ	*Jianzhushi lunwen ji* 建筑史论文集 (Architectural history and theory; most authors affiliated with Qinghua University)
JZLSYJ	*Jianzhu lishi yanjiu* 建筑历史研究 (Architectural history; 2 vols. only)
JZLSYLL	*Jianzhu lishi yu lilun* 建筑历史与理论 (Architectural history and theory)
KG	*Kaogu* 考古 (Archaeology)
KGXB	*Kaogu xuebao* 考古学报 (Studies in archaeology)
KGWW	*Kaogu yu wenwu* 考古与文物 (Archaeology and cultural relics)
KJSWJ	*Kejishi wenji* 科技史文集 (Essays on history of science and technology; vols. 7,3 [1981] and 11,4 [1984] devoted to Chinese architecture)
LHWW	*Liaohai wenwu* 辽海文物 (primarily Liaoning)
NFWW	*Nanfang wenwu* 南方文物 (Southeastern China)
NMGWWKG	*Nei Menggu wenwu kaogu* 内蒙古文物考古 (Inner Mongolia)
SCWW	*Sichuan wenwu* 四川文物 (devoted to Sichuan)
WB	*Wenbo* 文博 (primarily Shaanxi)
WW	*Wenwu* 文物 (Cultural relics)
WWCQ	*Wenwu chunqiu* 文物春秋 (primarily Hebei)
WWJK	*Wenwu jikan* 文物季刊 (primarily Shanxi)
WWTD	*Wenwu tiandi* 文物天地 (Cultural relics of heaven and earth)
ZGWWB	*Zhongguo wenwu bao* 中国文物报 (short notices of major discoveries)
ZJC	*Zijincheng* 紫禁城 (Forbidden City)
ZYWW	*Zhongyuan wenwu* 中原文物 (primarily Henan)

General Studies and Collections of Essays

The following recommended works are surveys of Chinese architecture; books about types of architecture, such as cities, religious buildings, tombs, houses, or gardens; books about architecture of one province that cover more than one time period; and collections of essays. The essay collections include seminal articles by China's most eminent architectural historians, some of which are hard to obtain in their original versions. They also include studies undertaken in the 1930s about buildings no longer extant, which authors were only recently able to publish.

An Jinhuai 安金槐, ed. *Zhongguo kaogu* 中国考古 (Chinese archaeology). Taipei: Nantian shuju, 1992.

Ancient Chinese Architecture. Beijing and Hong Kong: China Building Industry Press and Joint Publishing Company, 1982.

Blaser, Werner. *Chinesische Pavillion Architektur.* Stuttgart: G. Hatje, 1974.

Boerschmann, Ernst. *Die Baukunst und religiöse Kultur der Chinesen.* 2 vols. Berlin: G. Reimer, 1911–1914.

———. *Chinesische Architektur.* 2 vols. Berlin: E. Wasmuth, 1925.

Boyd, Andrew. *Chinese Architecture and Town Planning.* London: Alec Tiranti, Ltd., 1962.

Bulling, Annelise. *Die chinesische Architektur von der Han-Zeit bis zum Ende der Thang-Zeit.* Lyon: Imprimérie franco-suisse, 1936.

Chai Zejun gujianzhu wenji 柴泽俊古建筑文集 (Essays on premodern architecture by Chai Zejun). Beijing: Wenwu Press, 1999.

Chen Mingda gujianzhu yu diaosu shi lun 陈明达古建筑与雕塑史论 (Essays on the history of premodern Chinese architecture and sculpture by Chen Mingda). Beijing: Wenwu Press, 1998.

Dong Jianhong 董鉴泓 et al. *Zhongguo chengshi jianshe shi* 中国城市建设史 (History of Chinese cities). Beijing: China Building Industry Press, 1985.

Fairbank, Wilma. *Liang and Lin: Partners in Exploring China's Architectural Past.* Philadelphia: University of Pennsylvania Press, 1994.

Fu Xinian jianzhushi lunwen ji 傅熹年建筑史论文集 (Collected essays on the history of Chinese architecture by Fu Xinian). Beijing: Wenwu Press, 1998.

Han Baode 汉宝德. *Dougong de qiyuan yu fazhan* 斗拱的起源与发展 (Origin and development of the bracket system). Taizhong: Tung-hai (Donghai) University Press, 1973.

He Yeju 贺邺钜. *Zhongguo gudai chengshi guihua shi* 中国古代城市规划史 (History of premodern Chinese cities). Beijing: China Building Industry Press, 1996.

———, ed. *Jianzhu lishi yanjiu* 建筑历史研究 (Research on Chinese architectural history). Beijing: China Building Industry Press, 1992.

Itō Chuta 伊藤忠太. *Shina kenchiku shi* 支那建筑史 (History of Chinese architecture). Tokyo: Yuzankaku, 1931.

———. *Shina kenchiku sōshoku* 支那建筑装饰 (Architecture and decoration in China). 5 vols. Tokyo: Tōhō bunka gakuin, 1941–1944.

———. *Tōyō kenchiku no kenkyū* 东洋建筑の研究 (Research on East Asian architecture). Tokyo: Ryujinsha, 1936.

Jianzhu sheji cankao tuji 建筑设计参考图集 (Collected illustrations for research in architecture). 10 vols. Beijing: Society for Research in Chinese Architecture, 1930s.

Keswick, Maggie. *The Chinese Garden.* New York: Rizzoli International Publications, 1978.

Knapp, Ronald. *China's Traditional Rural Architecture*. Honolulu: University of Hawaii Press, 1986.

Li Yuming 李玉明, ed. *Shanxi gujianzhu tonglan* 山西古建筑通览 (Panorama of premodern architecture in Shanxi). Taiyuan: Shanxi People's Press, 1986.

Liang Congjie 梁从诫, ed. *Lin Huiyin wenji: Jianzhu juan* 林徽音文集: 建筑卷 (Collected essays of Lin Huiyin: Architecture volume). Beijing: Baihua wenyi Publishing House, 1999.

Liang Sicheng 梁思成. *Zhongguo jianzhu ziliao jicheng* 中国建筑资料集成 (Collected materials on Chinese architecture). Taipei reprint: no date.

————. *Liang Sicheng wenji* 梁思成文集 (Collected essays of Liang Sicheng). 4 vols. Beijing: China Building Industry Press, 1982–1986.

————, ed. *Zhongguo jianzhu yishu tuji* 中国建筑艺术图集 (Collected illustrations of the art of Chinese architecture). 2 vols. Beijing: Baihua wenyi Publishing House, 1999.

Liang Ssu-ch'eng (Sicheng). *A Pictorial History of Chinese Architecture*, ed. Wilma Fairbank. Cambridge: MIT Press, 1984.

Liu Dunzhen 刘敦桢. *Zhongguo gudai jianzhu shi* 中国古代建筑史 (History of premodern Chinese architecture). Beijing: China Building Industry Press, 2nd edition, 1984.

————. *Zhongguo zhuzhai gaishuo* 中国住宅概说 (Chinese residential architecture). Beijing: China Building Industry Press, 1957.

————. *Liu Dunzhen wenji* 刘敦桢文集 (Collected essays of Liu Dunzhen). 3 vols. Beijing: China Building Industry Press, 1982–1987.

Liu Qingzhu 刘庆柱. *Gudai ducheng yu diling kaoguxue yanjiu* 古代都城与帝陵考古研究 (Research on archaeology of Chinese capitals and imperial tombs). Beijing: Science Press, 2000.

Liu Zhiping 刘致平. *Zhongguo jianzhu leixing ji jiegou* 中国建筑类型及结构 (Typology and structure of Chinese architecture). Beijing: China Building Industry Press, 2nd edition, 1987.

Luo Zhewen 罗哲文. *Luo Zhewen gujianzhu wenji* 罗哲文古建筑文集 (Essays on premodern architecture by Luo Zhewen). Beijing: Wenwu Press, 1998.

————, ed. *Zhongguo gudai jianzhu* 中国古代建筑 (Premodern Chinese architecture). Shanghai: Guji Publishing House, 1990.

————. *Zhongguo lidai huangdi lingmu* 中国历代皇帝陵墓 (Chinese imperial tombs through the ages). Beijing: Foreign Language Press, 1993.

Pirazzoli-T'Serstevens, Michèle. *Living Architecture: Chinese*. New York: Grosset and Dunlap, 1971.

Prip-Møller, Johannes. *Chinese Buddhist Monasteries*. Hong Kong: Hong Kong University reprint of 1937 publication, 1967.

Qi Yingtao gujianzhu lunwen ji 祁英涛古建筑论文集 (Collected essays by Qi Yingtao on premodern architecture). Beijing: Huaxia Publishing House, 1992.

Qiao Yun. *Classical Chinese Gardens*. Hong Kong and Beijing: Joint Publishing Company and China Building Industry Press, 1982.

Sekino Tadashi 關野貞. *Chūgoku kōkogaku kenkyū* 中国考古学研究 (Research on Chinese archaeology). Tokyo: Tokyo University Press, 1963.

————. *Shina no kenchiku to geijutsu* 支那の建筑と芸術 (Chinese architecture and art). Tokyo: Iwanami shoten, 1938.

Sickman, Laurence, and Alexander Soper. *The Art and Architecture of China*. Harmondsworth: Penguin Books, revised edition, 1971.

Siren, Osvald. *A History of Chinese Art*, vol. 4: *Architecture*. London: 1930.

Steinhardt, Nancy S. *Chinese Imperial City Planning*. Honolulu: University of Hawaii Press, 1990.

————. *Chinese Traditional Architecture*. New York: China Institute, 1984.

Tanaka Tan 田中淡, ed. *Chūgoku geijutsushi no kenkyū* 中国技术史の研究 (Research on the history of Chinese building techniques). Kyoto: Kyoto University Press, 1998.

————. *Chūgoku kenchikushi no kenkyū* 中国建筑史の研究 (Research on the history of Chinese architecture). Kyoto: Kyoto University Press, 1998.

Thilo, Thomas. *Klassische chinesische Baukunst*. Leipzig: Koehler and Amelang, 1977.

Wenwu yu kaogu lunji 文物与考古论集 (Essays on cultural relics and archaeology). Beijing: Wenwu Press, 1986.

Xiao Mo 萧默, ed. *Zhongguo jianzhu yishu shi* 中国建筑艺术史 (History of the art of Chinese architecture). 2 vols. Beijing: Wenwu Press, 1999.

Xin Zhongguo de kaogu fazhan he yanjiu 新中国的考古发展和研究 (Research and developments in archaeology in New China). Beijing: Wenwu Press, 1984.

Yan Chongnian 阎崇年. *Zhongguo lidai ducheng gongyuan* 中国历代都城宫苑 (Cities and palaces of China through history). Beijing: Palace Museum Press, 1987.

Yang Hongxun 杨鸿勋, ed. *Jianzhu kaoguxue lunwen ji* 建筑考古学论文集 (Collected essays in architectural archaeology). Beijing: Wenwu Press, 1987.

Yang Kuan 杨宽. *Zhongguo gudai ducheng zhidushi yanjiu* 中国古代都城制度史研究 (Research on the history of the capital system in China). Shanghai: Shanghai guji Publishing House, 1993.

————. *Zhongguo gudai lingqin zhidushi yanjiu* 中国古代陵寝制度史研 (Research on the history of the imperial tomb system in China). Shanghai: Shanghai guji Publishing House, 1985.

Ye Dasong 叶大松. *Zhongguo jianzhu shi* 中国建筑史. Vol. 1, Taipei: Xinming Press, 1971. Vol. 2, Taipei: China Electric Company Press, 1976.

Ye Xiaojun 叶骁军, ed. *Zhongguo ducheng lishi tulu* 中国都城历史图录 (Historical atlas of Chinese capitals). 4 vols. Lanzhou: Lanzhou University Press, 1987.

Zhang Yuhuan 张驭寰 and Guo Husheng 郭湖生, eds. *Zhonghua gujianzhu* 中华古建筑 (Premodern Chinese architecture). Beijing: China Science and Technology Press, 1990.

Zhang Yuhuan and Luo Zhewen. *Zhongguo guta jingcui* 中国古塔精粹 (The cream of Chinese pagodas). Beijing: Science Press, 1988.

Zhao Liying 赵立瀛. *Shaanxi gujianzhu* 陕西古建筑 (Old architecture in Shaanxi). Xi'an: Shaanxi People's Press, 1992.

Zhongguo gudu yanjiu 中国古都研究 (Research in premodern Chinese cities). 8 vols. Beijing and elsewhere: Zhongguo shuju, 1985–1993.

Zhongguo gujianzhu xueshu jiangzuo wenji 中国古建筑学术讲座文集 (Collected lectures on premodern Chinese architecture). Beijing: China Future Publishing House, 1986.

Zhongguo jianzhushi lunwen xuanji 中国建筑史论文选集 (Selected and edited essays on the history of Chinese architecture). 2 vols. Taipei: Mingwen Book Company, 1983.

Zhongguo kaoguxue yanjiu 中国考古学研究 (Essays in Chinese archaeology). Beijing: Wenwu Press, 1986.

Zhongguo simiao daguan 中国寺庙大观 (Panorama of Chinese monasteries and temples). Beijing: Yanshan Press, 1990.

Recommended Specialized Studies

CHINESE ARCHITECTURE OF THE THREE DYNASTIES

More is being written today about this subtopic of Chinese architecture than about any other. The rapid rate of publication is related to the intensity of excavation in the People's Republic. Additional information may be found in *The Formation of Chinese Civilization: An Archaeological Perspective* (New Haven: Yale University Press, in press) and the bibliography in that book.

Chang Kwang-chih. *Shang Civilization*. New Haven: Yale University Press, 1980.

Hsu Cho-yun and Kathryn Linduff. *Western Chou Civilization*. New Haven: Yale University Press, 1988.

Li Xueqin. *Eastern Zhou and Qin Civilizations*, trans. K. C. Chang. New Haven: Yale University Press, 1985.

Loewe, Michael, and Edward L. Shaughnessy. *The Cambridge History of Ancient China*. Cambridge: Cambridge University Press, 1999.

Rawson, Jessica, ed. *Mysteries of Ancient China*. London: British Museum, 1996.

QIN AND HAN DYNASTIES

Cheng Te-k'un. "Ch'in-Han Architectural Remains," *Zhongguo wenhua yanjiusuo xuebao* (Journal of the Institute of Chinese Studies of the Chinese University of Hong Kong) 9 (1978), 503–584.

———. "Ch'in-Han Mortuary Architecture," *Zhongguo wenhua yanjiusuo xuebao* 11 (1980), 193–270.

Han Chan'ancheng Weiyanggong 汉长安城未央宫 (Weiyang Palace of Han Chang'an). 2 vols. Beijing: Zhongguo Dabaike Universal Book Company, 1996.

Han Duling lingyuan yizhi 汉杜陵园遗址 (Remains of the royal tomb Duling [of Emperor Xuandi and his wife] of the Han dynasty). Beijing: Science Press, 1993.

Sichuan Handai shique 四川汉代石阙 (Stone towers of the Han in Sichuan). Beijing: Wenwu Press, 1992.

Wang Zhongshu, *Han Civilization*, trans. K. C. Chang et al. New Haven: Yale University Press, 1982.

THREE KINGDOMS, WESTERN AND EASTERN JIN DYNASTIES, AND NORTHERN AND SOUTHERN DYNASTIES

Bei Wei Luoyang Yong'ningsi 北魏洛阳永宁寺 (The Northern Wei Yong'ning Monastery in Luoyang). Beijing: Zhongguo Dabaike Universal Book Company.

Su Bai 宿白. *Zhongguo shikusi yanjiu* 中国石窟寺研究. (Research on Chinese rock-carved temples). Beijing: Wenwu Press, 1996.

SUI, TANG, AND FIVE DYNASTIES

Ma Dezhi 马德志. *Tang Chang'an Daminggong* 唐长安大明宫 (Daming palace complex at Tang Chang'an). Beijing: China Science Press, 1959.

Steinhardt, Nancy S. "The Mizong Hall of Qinglong Si: Space, Ritual, and Classicism in Chinese Architecture," *Archives of Asian Art* 44 (1991), 27–50.

Thilo, Thomas. *Chang'an: Metropole Ostasiaens und Weltstadt Des Mittelalters, 583–904*. Wiesbaden: Harrassowitz Verlag, 1997.

Xiong, Victor. *Sui-Tang Chang'an: A Study in the Urban History of Medieval China*. Ann Arbor: University of Michigan Center for Chinese Studies, 2000.

LIAO, SONG, XI XIA, AND JIN DYNASTIES

Chai Zejun 柴泽俊, ed. *Shuozhou Chongfusi* 朔州崇福寺 (Chongfu Monastery in Shuo county). Beijing: Wenwu Press, 1996.

Chai Zejun et al. *Taiyuan Jinci Shengmudian xiushan gongcheng baogao* 太原晋祠圣母殿修缮工程报告 (Report on the repairs of the Sage Mother Hall at the Jin Shrines in Taiyuan). Beijing: Wenwu Press, 2000.

Chai Zejun and Li Zhengyun 李正云. *Shuozhou Chongfusi Mituodian xiushan gongcheng baogao* 朔州崇福寺弥陀殿修缮工程报告 (Report on the repairs of Amitabha Hall at Chongfu Monastery in Shuo county). Beijing: Wenwu Press, 1993.

Chen Mingda 陈明达. *Yingxian muta* 应县木塔 (The Timber Pagoda in Yingxian). Beijing: Wenwu Press, 1980.

———. *Yingzao fashi damuzuo yanjiu* 营造法式大木作研究. (Research on greater carpentry in the *Yingzao fashi* [Building standards]). 2 vols. Beijing: Wenwu Press, 1981.

Ecke, Gustav, and Paul Demiéville. *The Twin Pagodas of Zayton*. Cambridge: Harvard University Press, 1935.

Kuhn, Dieter. *A Place for the Dead: An Archaeological Documentary on Graves and Tombs of the Song Dynasty, 960–1279*. Heidelberg: edition forum, 1996.

Sekino Tadashi and Takeshima Takuichi 竹岛卓一. *Ryō-Kin jidai no kenchiku to sono Butsuzo* 辽金时代の建筑と其佛像 (Liao-Jin architecture and its Buddhist sculpture). 2 vols. Tokyo: Tōhō bunka gakuin Tokyo Kenkyūjo, 1925.

Steinhardt, Nancy S. *Liao Architecture*. Honolulu: University of Hawaii Press, 1997.

Takeshima Takuichi. *Ryō-Kin Jidai no kenchiku to sono Butsuzō*. Tokyo: *Ryūbun shokyoku, 1944.*

Tamura Jitsuzo 田村实造 and Kobayashi Yukio 小林行雄. *Ch'ing-ling* (Keiryō) [Qingling] 庆陵. 2 vols. Kyoto: Kyoto Daigaku bungakubu, 1953.

Xu Cheng 许成 and Du Yubing 杜玉冰. *Xi Xia ling* 西夏陵 (Tombs of the Xi Xia). Beijing: Far Eastern Press, 1995.

YUAN AND MING DYNASTIES

Many of the building complexes dated to the Ming period are better dated Ming-Qing because construction occurred over several centuries. Thus several titles listed here also are references for chapter 7.

Cameron, Nigel, and Brian Brake. *Peking: A Tale of Three Cities*. New York: Harper and Row, 1965.

Jiang Huaiying 姜怀英 and Liu Zhanjun 刘占俊. *Qinghai Ta'ersi xiushan gongcheng baogao* 青海塔尔寺修缮工程报告 (Report on the repairs of Ta'er Monastery in Qinghai). Beijing: Wenwu Press, 1996.

Qufu Kongmiao jianzhu 曲阜孔庙建筑 (Architecture in the Confucian temple in Qufu). Beijing: China Building Industry Press, 1987.

Su Bai. *Zangchuan Fojiao siyuan kaogu* 藏传佛教寺院考古 (Archaeological studies of Tibetan monastery architecture). Beijing: Wenwu Press, 1996.

Yang Jiaming 杨嘉铭 et al. *Zhongguo Zangshi jianzhu yishu* 中国藏式建筑艺术 (The art of Tibetan architecture in China). Chengdu: Sichuan People's Press, 1998.

Zhang Zhongyi 张仲一 et al. *Huizhou Mingdai zhuzhai* 徽州明代住宅 (Ming-period residences in Huizhou). Beijing: China Building Industry Press, 1957.

QING DYNASTY

Beijing gujianzhu 北京古建筑 (Premodern architecture in Beijing). Beijing: Wenwu Press, 1986.

Chayet, Anne. *Les temples de Jehol et leurs modèles tibétains*. Paris: Editions Recherche sur les Civilizations, 1985.

Chengde gujianzhu: Bishushanzhuang he Waibamiao de jianzhu yishu 承德古建筑: 避暑山庄和外八庙的建筑艺术 (Ancient architecture in Chengde: The Summer Palace for Escaping the Heat and the Eight Outer Temples). Beijing and Hong Kong: China Building Industry Press and Joint Publishing Company, 1982.

Shan Shiyuan 单士元 and Yu Zhuoyun 于倬云, eds. *Zhongguo Zijincheng xuehui lunwen ji* 中国紫禁城学会论文集 (Essays from the conference on the Forbidden City). Beijing: Forbidden City Press, 1997.

CONTRIBUTORS

Nancy S. Steinhardt is a professor in the department of Asian and Middle Eastern studies at the University of Pennsylvania and curator of Chinese art at the University of Pennsylvania Museum of Archaeology and Anthropology.

Fu Xinian, professor of architecture at the Institute of Architectural History and the China Building Technology Development Center, is also a practicing architect and a member of the State Council's planning group for editing and publication of ancient books.

Guo Daiheng is a professor in the School of Architecture at Qinghua University, Beijing, and deputy director of the Ancient Building Research Society of China.

Liu Xujie is professor of architecture at Southeast University in Nanjing and senior fellow at the Research Institute for Architectural Studies, Southeast University.

Pan Guxi is professor of architecture and director of the Research Institute for Architectural Studies at Southeast University, Nanjing.

Qiao Yun, formerly associate editor-in-chief of the China Architectural Industry Publishing House, is the author of books on Daoist architecture, the history of architecture in ancient China, Yuban Ming and Qing cities, and Chinese landscape art.

Sun Dazhang is a senior architect at the Institute of Architectural History and senior research fellow at the China Building Technology Development Center, both in Beijing.

ACKNOWLEDGMENTS

A great many individuals and institutions participated in the making of this book. Special thanks and deep gratitude are given to those institutions that provided some of the photographs for the book: the Cultural Relics Press, the Museum of Chinese History, and China Pictorial.

Those who translated the Chinese texts into English, and in some cases offered advice on how to deal with complex and thorny issues, are Jin Shaoqing and Ni Jimiao. We thank them for their painstaking work, which was often performed under very tight deadlines. Professor Lü Zhou of Qinghua University School of Architecture carefully read the English manuscript and gave helpful comments and criticisms.

Over the course of some eight years several editors at New World Press successfully coped with the plethora of details associated with planning and editing the manuscripts. Chen Xiuzheng, former editor-in-chief of New World Press, offered excellent advice and counsel on preparing the manuscript. Zheng Mouda, also a former editor-in-chief of New World Press, ably and enthusiastically handled the initial planning and arrangements for the book and organized the meetings with the various scholars involved. Liu Shigeng, the deputy editor-in-chief of New World Press, worked with great commitment and dedication to coordinate the final years of work on the manuscript. Li Shujuan assisted with checking the English manuscript and coordinating the translation work.

Toward the end of editing this book, we were very fortunate to have the former senior vice president of the China International Book Trading Corporation and senior editor Xiao Shiling join the work at New World Press. His experience and knowledge were invaluable and irreplaceable. The head of the copyright division of New World Press, Jiang Hanzhong, also contributed a great deal toward the completion of this volume. He translated Nancy S. Steinhardt's introduction into Chinese, so that Chinese readers could understand an American scholar's views on Chinese architecture. The art editor He Yuting worked day and night designing the layout of the Chinese version of the book. Our special thanks go to the vice president of the China International Publishing Group, Huang Youyi, without whose careful guidance and wholehearted support it is hard to imagine that this book could have been published so smoothly.

This work would also not have been possible without the superb work of Lan Peijin, who advised and skillfully assisted in the collection of the needed photographs. Sun Shuming also greatly assisted in the collection of photographs. We are also indebted to the help given by Liao Pin. A special thanks is given to all those photographers who provided us with their photos.

At Yale University Press another team was involved in making the book. Jonathan Brent, editorial director of Yale University Press, offered invaluable assistance in the final stages of producing the book. Mary Pasti, managing editor of the Culture & Civilization of China series at Yale University Press, superbly and cheerfully coordinated the work among her editorial colleagues. Special thanks are given to two superb editors, Julie Carlson and Philip King, who skillfully shaped and polished the text.

Julianne Griffin, special projects manager for the Culture & Civilization of China at Yale University Press, worked with great ability, resourcefulness, and energy under extremely tight deadlines to bring this book to fruition. Jo Ellen Ackerman designed the English version with much grace and artfulness under pressure. Anandaroop Roy drew the maps and plans with great technical and artistic skill.

Chang Taiping, consulting editor for the Culture & Civilization of China, provided invaluable and efficient work on the translations for the maps and drawings in the book, checked parts of the English text for technical accuracy, and in a host of other ways expedited and assisted the work on the book. Her translation of terms in the drawings of gardens and palaces was designed to capture the evocative tenor and tone of the Chinese original. Chris Dakin ably worked on early drafts of the maps and drawings.

Peter Wang, president of Redstone, Inc., scanned and color-corrected the artwork and provided advice on collecting additional illustrations. We would like to thank several people and organizations for the use of their photographs: Nancy Steinhardt, Chiu Lem, Ru Suichu, Huang Taoming, Hua Zhongming, Luo Wenfa, Jiang Jingyu, Ren Shiyin, Zhang Zaoji, Du Zequan, Wang Deying, Song Shijing, Li Chunsheng, Liu Liqun, Lin Jinghua, Luo Zhewen, Wang Rending, Wang Dagang, Sun Zhongwei, Tang Jianwei, Zhang Zongkun, Daya Culture, and pic 21.

The editorial advisory boards for the Culture & Civilization of China series both in the People's Republic of China and in the United States have been an important and continuing source of support and excellent advice.

Finally, let us thank Cai Mingzhao, president of the China International Publishing Group, and his predecessor Yang Zhengquan, both ably assisted by vice president Huang Youyi, and John G. Ryden, director of Yale University Press, whose unstinting support and unswerving belief in the cooperative spirit of this project made all the difference.

Zhou Kuijie   James Peck
Editor-in-Chief   Executive Director
New World Press   Culture & Civilization of China

INDEX

References to illustrations are in **boldface**

mounds (*cont.*)
third- to sixth-century tombs, 73–74, 76
Three Dynasties period and, 27
Mount Jing Monastery 径山寺, 172
mu 目 (building form), 130
mud bricks
Ming dynasty, 255
Neolithic period and, 19
Northern Wei pagodas and, 84
Three Dynasties period and, 21
mudao 墓道 (ramp), 158. *See also* ramps
mud-straw mix, 14, 21–22
multichamber construction, 20, 22
multistory construction
Dong architecture and, 313, **314**
Han dynasty, 54–55, 58
Liao, Song, and Jin era, 170
louge pavilion form and, 122, 180–183
Ming houses and, 252–**253**, 255
Northern Wei dynasty, 72–73, 83–84
Qing dynasty and, 313, **314**, 341
Tang brick pagodas, 122–123
Three Dynasties period and, 20–21
murals
Han tombs, 37, **48, 54**
Jin dynasty, 150, **151**
Liao tombs, 160
Song tombs, 156
Tang dynasty, 108–109, **113, 114**
in third to sixth centuries, 71, **77, 83**
Yuan dynasty, **234, 235,** 237, 240
music, 230
Muzong, Emperor (Longqing emperor;
Ming dynasty), 217
Muzong, Emperor (Tongzhi emperor;
Qing dynasty). *See* Tongzhi emperor

Nanchan Monastery 南禅寺, **114–115,**
328
Nandu xinggong ji 南渡行宫记 (Record of
the detached palace of the southern
capital) 163
Nanjing. *See also* Jiankang; Zhongdu
as Liao capital, 138, **143**–145, **144**
as Ming capital, 206–209, **207, 211,** 212
Ming monasteries in, 231, **232**
Ming tombs in, 214–**215**
Southern dynasty tombs and, **75–76**
Nanyang 南阳 county, Han city in, 37
Nara, Japan, 98, 132–133
natural environment, 5–6, 206. *See also*
gardens; geomancy; topography
natural vision, and gardens, 9
Naxi 纳西 people, Tibet, 305–306, **307**
Neo-Confucianism, 136
Neolithic period, 12–19
burial practices in, 16
ritual architecture in, 16–18
social structure in, 12–15
technical achievements in, 18–19

Ningcheng 宁城, Inner Mongolia. *See*
Zhongjing
Ningshougong 宁寿宫 (palace complex),
268, **269,** 270–**271**
Niuheliang 牛河梁, Liaoning province,
17, 18
Niya 尼雅, Xinjiang, 46–47
Norbu Linka (Treasure Garden), Tibet,
301, 302
Northern dynasties, 64. *See also* Eastern
Wei dynasty; Northern Qi dynasty;
Northern Wei dynasty; Northern
Zhou dynasty; Western Wei dynasty
Buddhist architecture and, 62, 88–89
palaces and, 71–72
tombs and, 78
Northern Han kingdom, 117
Northern Qi dynasty, 64, 78. *See also*
Northern dynasties
Northern Song dynasty, 135, 136. *See also*
Liao, Song, and Jin era; Song dynasty
Northern Wei dynasty, 64, 65. *See also*
Northern dynasties
Buddhist architecture and, 80–85
palaces, 68, **69,** 71–72
tombs, **73,** 74–75, 76–78
Northern Zhou dynasty, 64. *See also*
Northern dynasties
Nurhaci (Taizu; Manchu ruler), 268–269,
273
tomb of, **273**

octagonal buildings. *See also* Timber
Pagoda
Liao, Song, and Jin pagodas, **141,**
180–183
Qing dynasty, 269
Sui-Tang period, 130
ornamentation. *See* decoration
Osaka, Japan, 98
outer walls
Ming Beijing, 207
Three Dynasties period and, 20
outside influences, 6–7, 44, 61, 85, 200,
231, 238, 240, 245, 281

pagoda courtyard *(tayuan)* plan, 44
pagodas. *See also* names of *specific pagodas*
architectural forms and, 85–86
brick (masonry), 122–123, 180–183,
197
centrality and, 80, 83, 112–113, 118,
166, 256
at Dai monasteries, 335
funerary, 118, 122–123, **124**
Liao, Song, and Jin era, 166, 170, 177,
180–183
Sui-Tang era, 112, 118–123
in third to sixth centuries, 61, 80, 83–84,
85–86

timber frame system and, 83–84, 118,
122, 170, 173–179
twelve-sided, 61, 86, **87**
pailou 牌楼 (ceremonial archway), 215,
216, 258, 259, 273, 336
palace-city plans, 68, **99, 101, 105**
palaces, 4. *See also* detached palaces
Han dynasty, 34–36
Liao, Song, and Jin era, 144, 145,
146–150
Ming Beijing, 210–213
for pleasure versus governance, 26
Qin dynasty, 34, 39–41, **40,** 58
Sui-Tang era, 98–106
in third to sixth centuries, 68–73
Three Dynasties period, 20–21, 25–26
Pan Geng 盘庚 (Shang ruler), 22
Pan Guxi, 199
panel doors, 192
Panlongcheng 盘龙城, Hubei province,
24
pantheism, 219–221
pavilions
Han dynasty, 55
Liao, Song, and Jin monasteries, 166,
167–168, 170, **171, 172, 174, 175**
Sui-Tang era, 101–**102,** 122, 127
twin pavilions, 166–168, 170
paving. *See also* floor tiles
Han tunnels, 42
Sui-Tang era, 104
Phags-pa lama (craftsman), 237
philosophical influences, 9
pillar network, 1
pillars. *See* columns
Pine Cloud Gully, Chengde, 294, 297
Ping 平, King (Eastern Zhou ruler), 24
Pingjiang 平江 (Song capital), **142**
Pingliangtai 平粮台, Huaiyang 淮阳
county, Henan province, 21–22
Pingshan 平山 county, Hebei province,
28, **29**
pingzuo 平座, 55
pit tombs, 53
plank roadways, 58
planning principles. *See also* city plans;
garden plans; *Yingzao fashi*
Liao, Song, and Jin era, 147–148, 150
Neolithic period and, 19, 20
Three Dynasties period and, 6, 20, 28,
29, 30–31
Yuan Dadu and, 204, 205
plans *(for specific places). See* city plans; garden plans
population, and residential architecture,
316–317
port cities, 146
Potala Palace, Tibet, 317, **318,** 319–320
"Potala Palace" (Putuozongchengmiao),
Chengde, **322,** 323